D1498099

Personality-Guided
Cognitive–Behavioral Therapy

Personality-Guided
Cognitive–Behavioral Therapy

Paul R. Rasmussen

Series Editor Theodore Millon

AMERICAN PSYCHOLOGICAL ASSOCIATION
WASHINGTON, DC

Published by
American Psychological Association
750 First Street, NE
Washington, DC 20002
www.apa.org

To order
APA Order Department
P.O. Box 92984
Washington, DC 20090-2984
Tel: (800) 374-2721
Direct: (202) 336-5510
Fax: (202) 336-5502
TDD/TTY: (202) 336-6123
Online: www.apa.org/books/
E-mail: order@apa.org

In the U.K., Europe, Africa, and the Middle East, copies may be ordered from
American Psychological Association
3 Henrietta Street
Covent Garden, London
WC2E 8LU England

Typeset in Goudy by World Composition Services, Inc., Sterling, VA

Printer: United Book Press, Inc., Baltimore, MD
Cover Designer: Berg Design, Albany, NY
Technical/Production Editor: Devon Bourexis

The opinions and statements published are the responsibility of the authors, and such opinions and statements do not necessarily represent the policies of the American Psychological Association.

Library of Congress Cataloging-in-Publication Data
Rasmussen, Paul R.
    Personality-guided cognitive-behavioral therapy / Paul R. Rasmussen.— 1st ed.
      p. cm.—(Personality-guided psychology)
    Includes bibliographical references and index.
    ISBN 1-59147-230-X
    1. Cognitive therapy.   2. Personality disorders.   3. Personality assessment.
    4. Personality—Classification.   5. Typology (Psychology) I. Title. II. Series.

    RC489.C63R375 2005
    616.89'142—dc22   2004025352

British Library Cataloguing-in-Publication Data
A CIP record is available from the British Library.

Printed in the United States of America
First Edition

To Vickie, Shayna, and Taylor

CONTENTS

Series Foreword ix

Acknowledgments xi

Chapter 1.   Introduction 3

Chapter 2.   An Integration of the Cognitive–Behavioral
Therapy and Personologic Models 11

Chapter 3.   The Paranoid Prototype 49

Chapter 4.   The Schizoid Prototype 73

Chapter 5.   The Schizotypal Prototype 89

Chapter 6.   The Antisocial Prototype 101

Chapter 7.   The Borderline Prototype 121

Chapter 8.   The Histrionic Prototype 147

Chapter 9.   The Narcissistic Prototype 167

Chapter 10.   The Avoidant Prototype 191

Chapter 11.   The Dependent Prototype 215

Chapter 12.   The Compulsive Prototype
(Obsessive–Compulsive) 235

Chapter 13.   The Depressive Prototype 259

Chapter 14.   The Negativistic Prototype 275

Chapter 15.   The Sadistic and Masochistic Prototypes 291

Appendix A: The Millon Clinical Multiaxial Inventory 311

Appendix B: Format for Case Conceptualization
    and Treatment Plan 313

Appendix C: Sample Client Case Conceptualization
    and Treatment Plan 317

References 323

Author Index 337

Subject Index 341

About the Author 355

SERIES FOREWORD

The turn of the 20th century saw the emergence of psychological interest in the concept of individual differences, the recognition that the many realms of scientific study then in vogue displayed considerable variability among "laboratory subjects." Sir Francis Galton in Great Britain and many of his disciples, notably Charles Spearman in England, Alfred Binet in France, and James McKeen Cattell in the United States, laid the groundwork for recognizing that intelligence was a major element of import in what came to be called *differential psychology*. Largely through the influence of psychoanalytic thought, and then only indirectly, did this new field expand the topic of individual differences in the direction of character and personality.

And so here we are at the dawn of the 21st century, ready to focus our attentions ever more seriously on the subject of personality trait differences and their impact on a wide variety of psychological subjects—how they impinge on behavioral medicine outcomes, alter gerontological and adolescent treatment, regulate residential care programs, affect the management of depressive and PTSD patients, transform the style of cognitive–behavioral and interpersonal therapies, guide sophisticated forensic and correctional assessments—a whole bevy of important themes that typify where psychologists center their scientific and applied efforts today.

It is toward the end of alerting psychologists who work in diverse areas of study and practice that the present series, entitled *Personality-Guided Psychology*, has been developed for publication by the American Psychological Association. The originating concept underlying the series may be traced to Henry Murray's seminal proposal in his 1938 volume, *Explorations in Personality*, in which he advanced a new field of study termed *personology*.

It took its contemporary form in a work of mine, published in 1999 under the title *Personality-Guided Therapy*.

The utility and relevance of personality as a variable is spreading in all directions, and the series sets out to illustrate where things stand today. As will be evident as the series' publication progresses, the most prominent work at present is found with creative thinkers whose efforts are directed toward enhancing a more efficacious treatment of patients. We hope to demonstrate, further, some of the newer realms of application and research that lie just at the edge of scientific advances in our field. Thus, we trust that the volumes included in this series will help us look beyond the threshold of the present and toward the vast horizon that represents all of psychology. Fortunately, there is a growing awareness that personality variables can be a guiding factor in all spheres of study. We trust the series will provide a map of an open country that encourages innovative ventures and provides a foundation for investigators who wish to locate directions in which they themselves can assume leading roles.

Theodore Millon, PhD, DSc
Series Editor

ACKNOWLEDGMENTS

Worthy of note are the efforts of several individuals without whose assistance I would have been unable to complete this volume. First, I must acknowledge the efforts of a series of undergraduate psychology students at Furman University who assisted in the research for the volume. Jason Pagan and Johanna Meyers were present at the start and helped to put together the conceptual scheme. Lesley Black was invaluable during the bulk of the writing, and Tia Stevens helped to wrap it up and bring it to completion. My thanks as well to the numerous students who educated me while giving me the opportunity to educate them; I learned a great deal by reading their papers and thinking about their questions.

In addition, I acknowledge the encouragement of my colleagues at Furman, including Professors Gil Einstein, Elaine Nocks, and Charles Brewer, who kept my confidence up throughout the writing. A special thanks to Professor Brewer, who possesses the expertise and willingness to point out a poorly constructed passage and a readiness to assist in its clarification. A special thanks also to Beth Pontari, a social psychologist at Furman, who allowed me the opportunity to occupy her time and intellect while working out several of the concepts presented in the volume. Her clarity of thought is reflected in this project. To my running partner, Professor Lloyd Benson, who heard every aspect of this volume before it was committed to paper, I offer special gratitude. Thanks also to Art Freeman, who invited me to participate in this series, and to Ted Millon for his formulation of an elegant conceptual model that availed itself so readily to integration. Finally, the patience, support, and encouragement of my wife Vickie are at the foundation of the volume.

Personality-Guided
Cognitive–Behavioral Therapy

1

INTRODUCTION

The cognitive model of psychotherapy has been established as a clinically useful and empirically valid conceptual theory and treatment approach. Initially developed by Aaron Beck as a means to understand and treat depression (Beck, 1963, 1967, 1973; Beck, Rush, Shaw, & Emery, 1979), it has been expanded to include approaches for treating anxiety conditions (Beck & Emery, 1985); personality disorders (Beck, Freeman, & Associates, 1990), including the challenging borderline personality (Linehan, 1993b); substance abuse (Beck, Newman, & Liese, 1993); trauma (Follette, Ruzek, & Abueg, 2001); and, very recently, schizophrenia (Kingden & Turkington, 2002). In many of these treatment models, the cognitive approach is combined with the more traditional behavioral models in such a way that behavior changes complement and solidify cognitive changes.

At its foundation, the cognitive–behavioral therapy (CBT) approach emphasizes the role of faulty information processing as the precursor to painful emotions and maladaptive behaviors (Beck & Weishaar, 2000). Therapeutically, through efforts to alter one's information processing strategy, or to change the way one thinks about a situation, changes will be observed in how one feels and how one behaves. Nonetheless, attention to specific feeling states and to behavior skills deficits and implementation problems can enhance the changes to one's cognitive orientation and information processing style. Figure 1.1 presents the CBT model at a simple level. In this model, an event activates a thought, which in turn activates

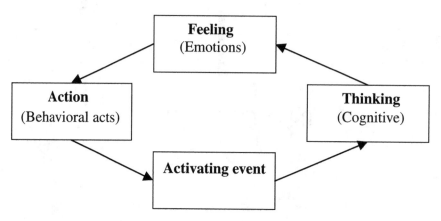

Figure 1.1. The simple cognitive–behavioral model.

a feeling, which then compels a behavioral response, which then modifies the situational event. At a more complicated level, it is understood that the relationship between thinking, feeling, and acting is far more complex and interactive. In Figure 1.2 the simple model is elaborated on in such a way that the greater complexity is revealed. In this more elaborate model, the pattern of effect is bidirectional; for example, one might alter one's thinking based on observations of one's own behavior, one's thinking can be affected by conditioned emotional patterns activated nonconsciously, what one does affects how one feels, and events can have an impact on behaviors independent of cognitive processes. Even in its complexity, however, the basic premise of the CBT model is that how one thinks about both internal and external events is critical to understanding how one reacts to and copes with those events. Thus, to alter one's pattern of feeling and

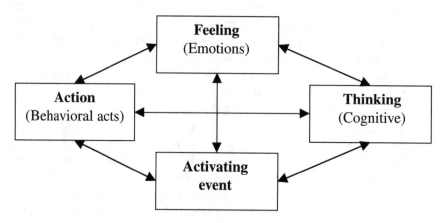

Figure 1.2. The complex cognitive–behavioral model.

acting, it is most important to change how one processes cognitively the inputs received from the internal and external environments.

In the current volume, the cognitive–behavioral model is integrated with the personologic model developed by Millon (1990, 1996, 1999; Millon & Davis, 1996b, 2000). The purpose and advantage of this integration lie primarily in the provision of an evolutionary underpinning for the cognitive–behavioral approach. Beck and others discussed the evolutionary foundations of cognitive and behavioral processes (Beck, 1996; Beck et al., 1990), yet integrating the personologic model yields an elaborated evolutionary model that is useful in guiding a cognitive–behavioral conceptualization and treatment approach. Through this integration, the clinician is able to understand the clinical condition not simply as the outcome of distorted and biased thinking or simply as the reflection of behavioral excesses and deficits, but rather as consisting of immediately adaptive reactions to existential challenges. Alfred Adler (1956), the Freud contemporary and antagonist, argued that in most clinical cases the problem that a client presents in therapy is not so much the problem per se as the client's ineffective solutions to life challenges. Thus, to Adler the problem was not the clinical condition as much as it was something about the person's ineffectual style of engagement with the world. By considering the evolutionary foundations of the cognitive–behavioral approach, Adler's early contention may reach the level of understanding he intended. Regarded by some as the original cognitive theorist, Adler's contentions are being increasingly discussed within the context of a cognitive–behavioral conceptualization (Freeman & Urschel, 1997; Shulman, 1985; Shulman & Watts, 1997; Sperry, 1997; Watkins, 1997; Watts & Critelli, 1997).

The current volume emphasizes the adaptive value or purpose of the emotional experiences defining the clinical conditions. Thus, the clinical condition, rather than being the problem, is the logical outcome of the individual's personality attributes given situational demands. Indeed, as Millon (1999) described it, personality, including the cognitive, behavioral, and affective processes making up the personality, defines the individual's unique orchestration of resources necessary to meet existential challenges. In some circumstances that orchestration leads to pleasant, harmonious outcomes, but in others the outcome is less pleasant and even painful.

The specific goal of this volume is to present the value of a theoretical model that emphasizes clinical conditions in relation to their evolutionary adaptiveness as reflected in clients' personalities. This model will be helpful for students learning to conceptualize clinical cases and to practitioners devising treatment strategies. The model should (a) enhance practitioners' understanding of clients and the contributions of clients to their own clinical conditions, (b) improve selection of appropriate interventions, and (c) optimize therapeutic benefit in minimal treatment time.

The current zeitgeist in psychiatry and psychology is, arguably, most dramatically defined by neuroscience and psychopharmacology. Researchers are looking diligently for the neurological foundations of clinical conditions, and new medicines are being introduced to treat psychiatric conditions at such a pace that it is difficult to keep up with the newest developments. These efforts, one might argue, have led the public to believe that clinical conditions are the result of rogue chemicals, reflecting bad genetics and not one's overall style of engagement with the world. Thus, if one is encountering unpleasant emotions, the problem is biochemical and the remedy pharmaceutical. Although one cannot argue against the efficacy of many of these medicines in altering mood states, and one must acknowledge the important role of biological processes in human experiences, it would not be wise to overgeneralize the conclusions and efficacy of a purely medical approach to treating human emotional miseries. It is humane and beneficial to help people manage their emotional pain, but altering what might prove to be adaptive processes in that pain may in the long run prove detrimental to the individual and to society. Treating only the pain associated with a broken ankle, for example, may provide some relief from the pain, but if the broken bone remains untreated, recurrent pain is quite likely.

To be sure, neuroscientists, psychologists, and others have gotten quite efficient at explaining the integrated biochemical processes underlying clinical conditions, but they have not yet been able to reliably and adequately distinguish between biological cause and simple covariation. Although no clinical condition can occur without biological processes, to assume *cause* when one is addressing only *covariates* of an adaptive condition not only is of limited therapeutic value but also may be ethically suspect. No doubt biological pathologies exist, and it is indeed fortunate that those processes are sufficiently understood that medical treatments can be provided, but this notion should not be overgeneralized.

Unfortunately, the advent of new medicines has been accompanied by an increase in the casual use of diagnostic criteria (Koerner, 2002; Kutchins & Kirk, 1997; Medewar, 1997). Indeed, to receive a medicine, one must have a disorder. Thus, if a psychiatrist is to prescribe a new medicine, the patient must have the condition for which that medicine has been approved. The relative subjectivity in the criteria found in the *Diagnostic and Statistical Manual of Mental Disorders* (4th ed., text revision [DSM–IV–TR]; American Psychiatric Association, 2000) results in an unintentional ambiguity; mood and anxiety conditions can be defined and described so broadly that a case can almost always be made for the medical treatment. If practitioners are to be more judicious in their diagnoses and treatment, they must derive a more precise and optimally useful understanding of psychopathology.

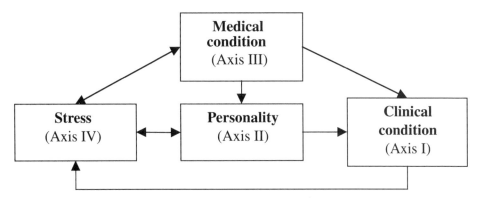

Figure 1.3. The integrated model.

The objective in using the integrated model presented in this volume is to understand the individual first and then to conceptualize the clinical condition relative to the understanding of the person. As suggested by Sir William Osler (1932), to understand the disease, one must understand the patient. In this context, the practitioner attempts to understand the individual in such a way that the clinical condition makes sense as something other than simply a random biochemical anomaly or simply a learned pattern of behavior. Clinical pathology in this model does not stand by itself but, rather, is part of the individual's overall style of evolutionary adaptation. Critical to this discussion is the immune system metaphor that Millon and Davis (2000) presented. They conceptualized clinical conditions as pathological outcomes mediated by personality variables, analogous to physical disease endpoints being mediated by the immune system.

To illustrate, Figure 1.3 presents stress, as registered on Axis IV of the *DSM–IV–TR*, as any event that requires an adaptive response by the individual. Stress is both an objective and a subjective phenomenon determined by the nature and intensity of the actual events and by the idiosyncratic meaning of these events to the individual. Important in determining the stress response are aspects of the individual's personality, represented in specific structural and functional attributes that combine to form personality style and that are registered on Axis II of the *DSM–IV–TR*. Stressful events act on the individual, necessitating an adaptive response, but whether something is judged as stressful or not is also a function of personality attributes contributing to the perception and interpretation of stress. The clinical condition, recorded on *DSM–IV–TR* Axis I, reflects an adaptive means of reacting to and dealing with that stressor.

To say that a clinical condition is adaptive is not to suggest that it is either optimally adaptive, or even functional. *Adaptive* in this context implies simply that the condition is a better means of coping with a situation than not responding. Subsequently, a displayed reaction may be immediately adaptive yet optimally quite maladaptive. As an example, although it is optimally maladaptive to be clinically depressed, periods of withdrawal from a hopeless situation may be quite adaptive in an immediate situation (Brown, 2000; Gilbert, 2000; Nesse & Williams, 1994; Price, 1972). Similarly, whereas sustained anxiety is ultimately exhausting and potentially harmful, in many circumstances anxiety is immediately quite adaptive (Öhman, 2000) because it prepares the individual for potential dangers. In the integrated model, the adaptive value of many clinical conditions is discussed relative to the personality attributes mediating between stressor and clinical outcomes.

In chapter 2 of the current volume, the basic premises of the personologic model are briefly described. There is no pretense of adequately covering this model; rather, the major concepts are highlighted, specifically as they relate to an integrated model. Similarly, in chapter 2 the basic premises of the cognitive–behavioral model are presented. The work of Aaron Beck and his colleagues is critical to this theoretical foundation, but the focus on a cognitive–behavioral approach involves concepts beyond those typically discussed by Beck and others. For instance, the role of emotional experiences is embellished in this book to complement and accommodate the theoretical integration. In this second chapter, the two approaches are integrated in such a way, I hope, that neither approach is seriously compromised and clinicians grounded in the cognitive–behavioral perspective will find useful. Because I make no pretense of adequately covering both theoretical perspectives within the limitations of the volume, the reader is referred to the publications cited for elaborations on these theories.

In chapters 3 through 15, each of the DSM–IV–TR personality disorders is presented relative to the integrative model. The chapters are organized according to DSM–IV–TR cluster categories. This organization is simply for the sake of convenience and is less a means of combining theoretically related conditions, although to the extent that the developers of the DSM–IV–TR organized the clusters into meaningful groupings, some benefit should be realized here. In addition to the cluster disorders, discussed in the final section are personality styles that Millon and his colleagues currently recognize and that either are included in the DSM–IV–TR as research criteria inviting further study (e.g., depressive, negativistic) or are currently overlooked by the DSM–IV–TR (i.e., sadistic and masochistic). Considering the dearth of information on the sadistic and masochistic styles, discussion of these prototypes is combined into one chapter and is briefer in detail and example.

The treatment chapters have a similar organization. Basic characteristics of the conditions are discussed, followed by a discussion of the evolutionary foundation (polarity balances) of the personality style and a personality-guided cognitive–behavior conceptualization. Following the integrated conceptual model, the pathologic process associated with each personality is described. Although embellished in the personality chapters, the model, depicted in Figure 1.3, highlights the relationship between personality, stress, and clinical condition.

Following presentation of the pathologic process, chapters 3 through 15 provide a brief description of clinical conditions and their relative adaptive value given the personality style. Also, subtle variations on the traditional or pure form of the personality style are presented, along with some comment on greater or lesser vulnerabilities. Finally, on the basis of the integrated conceptualization, these chapters introduce cognitive and behavioral treatment strategies, and most include a case example.

It is important to offer some preliminary qualifications on the treatments. An entire volume could be devoted to personality-guided treatment for each specific disorder; indeed, many of the volumes in this series do so. Page limits in the current volume, however, preclude an in-depth discussion of treatment for the different disorders and different personality subtypes, and consequently this book provides only an overview discussion of how the personality-guided approach might contribute to a cognitive–behavioral approach. The treatment sections cannot, therefore, be considered guidelines for any one client; they should prove useful, however, as an illustration of how treatment could be adapted to individuals presenting with specific personality attributes.

Important in each of these chapters is a focus on the personality attributes contributing to the clinical condition. The discussion certainly does not ignore the specific clinical condition (e.g., depression), but the focus is on the personality; which is not atypical. What is unique to the discussion in this volume is that regardless of the clinical condition, the treatment need not vary substantially. Considering that the model puts the clinical condition in the position of personality-based outcomes, the assumption is that if one alters the personality, the clinical condition too will change. Admittedly, this should not be blindly assumed, and it is the responsibility of the clinician to see that treatment objectives are being met. In this volume, the *DSM–IV–TR* is relied on primarily for its organizational structure, and throughout the distinction is made between individuals with a personality disorder and those with a prototypal personality style. Understanding that personality pathology exists on a continuum rather than as a binary phenomenon, the discussion is of the contribution of personality attributes to the experience of clinical conditions, rather than the role of personality disorders in the expression of clinical conditions. Thus, when the antisocial prototype is referred to, for instance, it does not imply an antisocial personality-disordered individual but, rather, one whose personality is most similar to the antisocial personality disorder. In most cases it is clear that the reference is to a personality prototype or style rather than to a personality disorder. References to a personality disorder are specifically acknowledged.

2

AN INTEGRATION OF THE COGNITIVE–BEHAVIORAL THERAPY AND PERSONOLOGIC MODELS

The integrative model combining cognitive–behavioral therapy and the personologic model maintains a cognitive emphasis on information processing and on internal and expressed reactions that follow interpretations of information from the environment. The personologic perspective provides a critical foundation, based on evolutionary principles and their defining impact on personality, guiding the nature of the information-processing and schema-based reactions (i.e., orienting memories, beliefs, and attitudes that are relevant to the situational event; discussed later in this chapter). Personality is presented in this model as the overarching organizational theme that describes schema-based mode reactions (e.g., cognitive, affective, motivational, and behavioral reactions; discussed later in this chapter) to situational demands organized in the service of the survival or existence imperative. The practical value of this model is that it provides guidelines for assessment, case conceptualization, and treatment goals and planning.

This chapter discusses an integrated model in which the critical components of a cognitive–behavioral model are interfaced with the personologic model. Although one could simply choose from the personologic model those components that complement a cognitive–behavioral perspective, I have chosen to provide discussion that interfaces the two perspectives in as much detail as possible and that neglects none of the critical components of either theory. The following sections are organized in a progressive fashion. I begin with a foundation defined by the evolutionary imperatives and their role in defining personality, including associated schemas and mode reactions. The chapter concludes with general comments concerning the implications of the model for therapeutic planning and practice.

AN EVOLUTIONARY-BASED FOUNDATION: THE IMPERATIVES

Millon described the *evolutionary imperatives* as the logical foundation for deriving a holistic and unified theory of personality and human functioning (Millon, 1990, 1992, 1999; Millon & Davis, 2000). Just as a species' survival is dependent on its ability to meet the changing constraints and challenges of the environment, so too does the functioning of the individual depend on his or her ability to meet existential challenges. Likewise, just as a species is characterized by inherited assets and liabilities, the individual is also endowed with basic advantages and disadvantages that influence his or her adaptive abilities. Within this model, normal, healthy personality is characterized by the ability to cope with the environment in a flexible manner and by perceptions and behaviors that foster increments in personal satisfaction (Millon & Davis, 2000). Failure to act flexibly in meeting circumstantial demands, combined with characteristic perceptions and behaviors that undermine one's sense of personal satisfaction, are fundamentally maladaptive and compromise the individual's ultimate level of health and ecological fitness.

The evolutionary imperatives provide a conceptual frame of reference for answering the classic question in psychology, "Why do people do what they do?" Reliance on the evolutionary model allows one to conclude that behaviors are enacted for the simple reason that they are perceived by the actor as the best immediate means for satisfying wants and perceived needs. In simple terms, the behaviors are enacted because they are perceived as effective, at least to some degree, in meeting critical evolutionary challenges. As the term *imperative* indicates, these are the rules or principles that compel behavior. Indeed, we can think of the imperatives as the foundation of what is referred to as *human nature*. No person can escape the imperatives, and every human undertaking can be explained relative to these imperatives. This very straightforward notion provides the foundation for the theoretical integration.

The Existence Imperative

The first imperative is *existence*. At the most basic level, the critical task is the preservation of life—survival. Our ancestors were those who were able to survive to sexual maturity, pass along their genes, and bring their offspring to sexual maturity. These were the individuals who were effective at avoiding immediate dangers and other threats to survival such as exposure and starvation. In addition to basic life preservation, survival involves efforts to enhance existence—that is, to bolster the viability of the organism and ultimately the species.

In sum, the existence imperative involves the avoidance of negative, survival-threatening stimuli and the pursuit of positive, life-enhancing outcomes. In ancestral times, negative events included physical injury, starvation, abandonment, exposure, domination, and attack, among other threats to survival. Pleasurable outcomes included food, shelter, security, and copulation. Our ancestors learned through experience what to avoid and what to pursue to enhance survivability. In modern times, humans have embellished both notions such that negative outcomes include those tasks and activities that are viewed as unpleasant or undesirable (often associated with threat to social status), although they may not be threatening to one's survival. Likewise, humans tend to seek out desirable outcomes that have little value beyond, perhaps, status enhancement, and they are inclined to pursue indulgences beyond basic life-sustaining needs. Nonetheless, the need to enhance and protect the self is the critical component in understanding this evolution-based model of client conceptualization and treatment. In all aspects of human functioning, the basic challenge of enhancing or protecting the self can be observed in the thoughts, feelings, and behaviors of every individual.

Although the primary motives are to avoid pain and discomfort and to seek positive outcomes, the specific focus for any one individual may be different than the specific focus for another. For instance, in a given situation, one may be willing to tolerate considerable negative experiences to derive maximal positive outcomes. Many young adults endure the challenges of college to derive the benefits of a well-paying and enjoyable job. Athletes are willing to go through the rigors of sustained practice and physical exertion to compete and experience victory. One may also be willing to sacrifice beneficial outcomes for greater safety; for instance, one may forgo the benefit of rapid air travel for the perceived safety of travel by train. Another person may avoid the potential joy of sport to avoid the risk of social ridicule and embarrassment. For one person, the threat of negative outcomes is not sufficient to prevent the pursuit of positive outcomes; for another, the threat of failure is too great a price to pay. According to the model, one person may be more oriented toward attaining pleasurable outcomes (a pattern most often seen in those with an antisocial personality), whereas another is more strongly oriented to the avoidance of negative outcomes (a pattern seen most typically in individuals with paranoid, avoidant, compulsive and depressive personalities).

This distinction between pleasure pursuit and pain avoidance does not, however, constitute a classic polarity in which one is high at one end and low at the other. Instead, the distinction marks a bipolarity in which one may be high on one or both ends of the continuum or low on one or both ends. Consequently, one could be pain avoidant while also pleasure seeking; such an individual must be very strategic in his or her efforts to avoid painful consequences while pursuing pleasurable outcomes. This existence orientation can be observed in those with a compulsive or sadistic style. Similarly, an individual low on both pleasurable pursuit and pain avoidance would make little effort to avoid painful consequences while also making little effort to pursue pleasurable outcomes. Such a pattern is observed in those with a negativistic or masochistic personality style. Consequently, this model describes a bipolarity in which, at both ends of the pleasure–pain (preserving–enhancing) polarity, the individual might display situational or dispositional (or both) high, medium, or low orientation.

Reliance on this model should be particularly appealing to cognitive–behavioral theorists because it implies a direct conditioning model of behavior mediated by levels of cognitive assumption and affective expression. Although it may be true that the behaviors of many people are inherently maladaptive, it is also most often true that those behaviors are "effective" means of deriving some degree of reinforcement, either through the acquisition of some desired, enhancing outcome (that may or may not be desired by others) or as relative relief from a more unpleasant state (that may or may not be perceived as unpleasant to others). Similarly, the conclusions drawn by the individual reflect an idiosyncratic system of understanding based on previous experiences and derived associations, which are held in consciousness in the form of memory and associated affect (i.e., via limbic activity). In this evolutionary model, thoughts, feelings, and behaviors are maintained through classical and operant principles oriented around principles of evolutionary challenge and fitness. Reinforcing outcomes occur as rewarding, self-enhancing experiences or as self-protected relief from threat or unpleasant experiences.

The Adaptation Imperative

The second component of the evolutionary model is *adaptation*, which refers to one's style of approaching and interacting with the environment with the intent of satisfying the first imperative (i.e., survival or existence). Without the ability to adapt, one would surely perish; one would be overwhelmed by the random and chaotic nature of survival demands. Thus, survival is dependent on the organism's ability to either *adapt to its environment*—a passive, accommodating approach—or *adapt the environment to its needs*—an active, modifying approach.

Passive adaptation implies "going with the flow" or helpless surrender, without asserting significant effort to alter the environment. Such an approach can be adaptive; however, it requires that the environment be conducive to meeting life-preserving needs. As an example, a passive organism such as a plant requires that the environment provide needed resources at critical times (see Millon, 1991a). During times of drought or excessive moisture, plants may not survive. In this situation, survival is dependent on the caprice of the environment—whether that includes climatic patterns or the whim and responsibility of a plant owner. Some humans (and other organisms) take a similar approach. As long as necessary resources are made available, passively oriented individuals are able to function more or less adequately. Such a circumstance might be observed in those who have grown up in an environment characterized by minimal demands and ample resources.

As long as the environment continues to provide support and resources, a passive orientation is adaptive. However, alterations in the environment brought about by financial crisis, parental loss, or other circumstances can lead to significant impairments in adaptive functioning and thus threaten one's survival. Also, for humans reaching maturity, the demands of the environment may change such that a passive orientation, which was effective for some period, is no longer sufficient. Young adults leaving home who have come to rely on parents for economic and other resources may find the active challenges of independence to be overwhelming. In fact, it is not uncommon to find parents pursuing counseling because of their frustration with an adolescent child who has developed a passive orientation; although the parents would prefer greater initiative and independence on the part of the adolescent, that adolescent has become quite content with things the way they are (e.g., Durbin, Darling, Steinberg, & Brown, 1993). Likewise, many adults present for therapy because the passive approach adopted in childhood and maintained during adolescence is not sufficient for meeting adult demands and responsibilities, and as adults they are faced with the consequences of those deficient skills.

A passive approach can also be effective when the demands made by the individual do not exceed the resources of the environment. Maslow's (1970) notion of the self-actualized individual characterizes a person who is able to accept the world as it is, without insisting that things be more personally accommodating. This passive–content approach is less common in Western culture, which is characterized by the accumulation of goods and resources. Many individuals presenting for treatment of depression find themselves unable to sustain the pace of life required to maintain a particular standard of living (Carpiniello, Lai, Pariante, Carta, & Rudas, 1997; Saugstad, 2000). It is also true that in a passive orientation, one would not take advantage of the opportunities to learn new, adaptive skills that may prove useful at a later time. Thus, the passive orientation entails both benefit and cost, depending on the accommodation of the environment.

In the active, modifying orientation, the person enacts behaviors to create an environment that is of his or her personal preference and design. The modifying organism does not wait for the environment to provide necessary supports and resources but acts to ensure that the environment is most conducive to meeting its wants and needs. This strategy is also marked by benefits and costs. Active adaptation provides the occasion for maximal gain; the individual is able to create and take advantage of more opportunities than does a person taking a passive approach. However, an active adaptation may place one at greater risk as a result of increased exposure to potentially dangerous situations. Thus, although passive adaptation offers low risk but low reward, active adaptation offers greater potential reward but at greater potential cost.

One might take an approach that is marked by active avoidance. In this approach, the individual is active in his or her efforts to avoid unpleasantness, which might include potential social embarrassment, unwanted responsibility, or the expectations of another, rather than being active in the pursuit of enhancing outcomes. The most direct example of such an approach is that taken by individuals with an avoidant personality, who commit a high percentage of their coping resources to avoiding potentially negative social encounters.

Unlike the poles of the survival tasks, in which the individual may be high or low at both ends of the polarity, the adaptation task reflects a true polarity, and the individual is characteristically more of one adaptive style than another. Although some individuals exist somewhere in the middle between an active and a passive orientation, most people can be described as either active or passive in their adaptive style, with some more active or passive than others.

The Reproduction–Replication Imperative

The third component of the imperative model concerns *reproduction–replication*. This imperative includes two means of species regeneration: self-orientation and other-orientation. The *self-orientation* is characteristically more male oriented; perpetuation is better guaranteed through maximal copulatory opportunities. The wider the seed is spread, the greater the likelihood of conception and of offspring being brought to maturity. Because there is no latency period in reproductive ability (i.e., pregnancy) for men, a self-focused approach is maximally beneficial. This approach is more descriptive of an individual who is egotistic, insensitive, inconsiderate of others, and less caring (Millon, 1990; Millon & Davis, 2000), qualities that would promote the objective of maximum copulation.

The second means of species regeneration, *other-orientation*, is characterized as more typically female and focuses less on copulatory opportunities and more on bringing conceived offspring to maturity. Considering the 9-month gestational period and lower benefit of maximal copulation for women, perpetuation is maximized through a greater focus on the welfare of those children conceived and born. Thus, this strategy is other focused and characterized by greater affiliative efforts, intimacy, communication, and protection (Gilligan, 1982a, 1982b; Rushton, 1985). It is not surprising that men who showed a greater initial investment in parenthood during their wives' pregnancy showed a greater long-term investment (Gurwitt, 1995; Parke, 1996). The concern within the current context is, How do these differences affect survivability?

Self- versus other-orientation influences several aspects of survivability through adaptation. To summarize, this influence concerns the focus of orientation relative to existential concerns. Does the individual attend to the reactions and responses of others to obtain existential feedback? Or does the individual attend only to personal ideas and feelings to assess and evaluate existential concerns? In the first circumstance, the orientation is toward the other, whereas in the second, the orientation is toward the self.

For example, a person with a passive–dependent orientation, such as observed in the dependent personality, predominantly attends to the actions of others to determine personal effectiveness in adaptation. For these individuals, as long as others are providing necessary survival resources, existence is secure, but when others fail to provide survival resources in the form of either enhancement opportunity or protection, attention and adaptive efforts are directed at reenlisting the investment of others. Alternatively, one with an active–independent orientation, such as observed in the antisocial personality, is far less concerned with the actions and reactions of others and focuses on his or her own personal feelings and opportunities, relatively independently of the behaviors, thoughts, or feelings of others.

Another way of conceptualizing the reproductive focus involves consideration of sources of reinforcement. For individuals with a greater focus on others, reinforcement, whether positive or negative, is derived through the actions of others. Thus, enhancement is contingent on the provision of reward by others. If rewards are thought to be controlled by others, a focus on others is most adaptive. Similarly, if one views the self as distinctly unable to provide protection from threat, one must turn to others for sources of relief from danger. Again, an external focus is most adaptive. For others, rewarding outcomes and protection are derived through personal efforts.

Thus, the focus is more on personal initiative than on the availability and actions of others. Rotter's (1966) description of an internal versus external locus of control echoes this distinction. Similar to the first imperative, the distinction between self-orientation and other-orientation reflects a bipolarity; although one may be more self-oriented than other-oriented, one could also show levels of focus at each of the self–other polarities. Thus, one might be high on both self- and other-orientation, low on both, or some combination.

In conceptualizing patterns of pathology, as well as of healthy functioning, consideration of these evolutionary imperatives provides an opportunity to understand the reinforcement-based motivations for an individual's behavior. A person is compelled by means of these imperatives to enhance the self, through positive or rewarding experiences, and in a related manner to protect the self against painful and unpleasant experiences. To these ends, one can take either an active, modifying approach to meeting survival and enhancement challenges or a more passive approach, accepting what the environment provides. Furthermore, one may show greater or lesser self- and other-orientation such that concern is with the self, with others, with self and others, or, potentially, with neither self nor others.

In the present discussion, the survival task is viewed as a superordinate challenge and relates to opportunities for enhancement or the need to protect self-integrity. How one adapts and where one focuses attention is relative to the survival task. In this regard, an individual is more or less oriented to maximizing opportunities for enhancement or protecting the self from experiences that threaten the integrity of the self. I use the term *integrity* to refer to one's sense of completeness or wholeness. This wholeness is experienced cognitively and affectively as an experience of safety, security, and well-being. When one has a sense of integrity, aspects of one's life are experienced as being as they should be, and needed survival resources are perceived as both available and obtainable. In this circumstance, negative emotions are not out of proportion to the situation and serve simply to compel adaptive behaviors to correct minor problems associated with resource availability. Likewise, positive experiences are not pursued without consideration of the risk or cost associated with such pursuits. As a survival imperative, *sense of integrity* refers to physical safety and wholeness as well as to a sense of psychological security and relative satisfaction.

The relative balance of the individual between the various poles of these imperatives creates a central orientation to situational demands that can be defined by common personality attributes. This basic orientation is refined by the specific experiences of the individual that have been more or less effective over the years relative to the existential challenge—that is, they have been effective in enhancing or protecting the integrity of the individual. A healthy, optimally adaptive balance is simply that—a

TABLE 2.1
Personality Prototypes and Evolutionary Imperatives

Prototype	Evolutionary Imperative					
	Enhancement	Preservation	Passive	Active	Self	Other
Schizoid	Weak	Weak	Strong	Weak	Average	Weak
Schizotypal	Weak[a]	Weak[a]	Weak[a]	Weak[a]	Weak[a]	Weak[a]
Paranoid	Weak[b]	Weak[b]	Weak[b]	Weak[b]	Weak[b]	Weak[b]
Histrionic	Average	Average	Weak	Strong	Weak	Strong
Narcissistic	Average	Average	Strong	Weak	Strong	Weak
Borderline	Average[c]	Average[c]	Average[c]	Average[c]	Average[c]	Average[c]
Dependent	Average	Average	Strong	Weak	Weak	Strong
Antisocial	Average	Weak	Weak	Strong	Strong	Weak
Avoidant	Weak	Strong	Weak	Strong	Average	Average
Compulsive	Weak	Average	Strong	Weak	Weak[c]	Strong[c]
Negativistic	Weak	Average	Average	Strong	Average[c]	Weak[c]
Depressive	Weak	Strong	Strong	Average	Average	Average
Sadistic	Average[a]	Strong[a]	Weak	Strong	Average	Weak
Masochistic	Weak[a]	Strong[a]	Strong	Average	Weak	Average

[a] Reversal between polarities. [b] Blocks between polarities. [c] Conflict between polarities.

balance—marked by a relative midpoint between each of the poles. It is unlikely that any person would be able to maintain an absolute balance between the poles. Yet the longer one remains near the center, the more one approximates a consistent state of adaptive functioning called *mental health* (Millon, 1991b). Table 2.1 presents the relative balance for each of the personality prototypes discussed in later chapters.

This perspective on mental health provides the cognitive–behavioral therapist with a foundation for client conceptualization. The therapist may ask, "How do the symptoms relate to the individual's imperative orientation?" or "In what way are these symptoms adaptive to this individual?" In this context, depression, for instance, is not simply a disorder that has befallen an otherwise healthy individual, but is an element of that individual's "overall orchestration" relative to existential challenges (Millon, 1999). This approach is not novel. Beck described the cognitive model as evolution based and the primal modes (discussed later in this chapter) as based on threats to one's existence (see Beck & Weishaar, 2000). Similarly, Ellis tied all thoughts and actions to evolution-based adaptations (see, e.g., Ellis, 1973, 1988; Ruth, 1992). The constructivists also argued that all cognitive processes are connected to the need to survive (Mahoney, 1991, 1995).

In recent publications, Gilbert and others discussed the adaptive purposes of many clinical conditions in evolutionary terms (e.g., Gilbert, 2002a, 2002b; Gilbert & Bailey, 2000; Nesse & Williams, 1994). Nesse and Williams observed that "each emotion is a specialized state that simultaneously adjusts cognition, physiology, subjective experience and behavior, so that the organism can respond effectively in a particular kind of situation" (p. 210). The noted emotions scholar Robert Plutchik (2003) discussed emotions from an adaptive perspective, and evolutionary theorists Cosmides and Tooby (1995, 2000) described the role of emotional expression in meeting evolutionary demands. The conceptual and theoretical foundation provided in this discussion is broadly held and has been well articulated. In a simple, conceptual summary, one might argue that the problems clients present with are not so much their problems as their maladaptive solutions to evolutionary challenges. Adler, in 1932, suggested that "all neurotic symptoms are safeguards of persons who do not feel adequately equipped or prepared for the problems of life" (Adler, 1932/1979, p. 95).

From a cognitive–behavioral perspective, this evolution-based foundation allows the clinician to take a top-down approach to understanding the client. Rather than starting at the symptom and conceptualizing upward to automatic thoughts and schema-based beliefs, with only cursory attention to the concept of personality, this approach provides a ready foundation for the clinician to understand the client first and to conceptualize the symptoms relative to that derived understanding. From this foundation, the clinician is able to build an understanding of how the symptoms may contribute to the client's adaptive enterprise. Symptoms of depression are an example; although a clinician might simply look at the biological processes of depression and treat the condition medically, if the depression is serving an important adaptive purpose, the medical treatment may not be effective, or new symptoms may develop to compensate for the affective response targeted by the medication. This is a common situation in the pharmacotherapy of depression (Bothwell & Scott, 1997; Paykel, 1994a, 1994b; Scott, 1988; Thase, 1994).

The clinician might also identify the depressed client's automatic thoughts and introduce metacognitive processes to alter the connection between thought and affect. But the need for the emotion to drive withdrawal behaviors may undercut the value of the metacognitive process. Thinking about the role depression plays in this individual's orientation to existential demands, however, provides the opportunity to address the root factors contributing to both cognitive and biological outcomes. For the negativistic individual who desires to avoid the inevitable unpleasantness of engaging with others, depression serves the useful purpose of compelling a retreat from social engagements. Similarly, for a person with a compulsive personality, depression may contribute to a constraining of environmental opportunity, thus rendering life more manageable. The personality-guided approach provides opportunities to consider the syndrome in its entirety. The symptoms are viewed as part of the overall orchestration of the individual (survival adaptation), rather than simply as the consequence of a specific dysfunctional process.

Of particular value in this approach is the potential reduction in resistance to treatment. To the extent that symptoms are serving some adaptive purpose, without adequate alternatives it is unlikely that the person will abandon the symptoms simply at the direction of the therapist (Rasmussen, 2002). Understanding the role of the symptoms in the client's efforts to meet imperative challenges, the therapist and client can explore more adaptive means to meet the imperative demands. In this discussion, the evolutionary imperatives create the critical foundation for understanding the client and developing effective treatments.

PERSONALITY

Personality is the defining theme of the person that reflects his or her orientation to the evolutionary imperatives and the ways that he or she has come to satisfy the existential challenge. According to Millon and Davis (2000),

> Rather than being limited to a single trait, *personality* refers to the total configuration of the person's characteristics: interpersonal, cognitive, psychodynamic and biological. Each trait reinforces the others in perpetuating the stability and behavioral consistency of the total personality structure. (p. 10)

Defined by and oriented toward the survival challenge, personality comprises all the interactive attributes that enable the individual to adapt to environmental circumstance in his or her own idiosyncratic style. Understanding a client's personality, in its multiple facets and relative to the survival imperative, gives the clinician a perspective on all roads related to where the individual is traveling. In other words, the clinician can understand the client's goals and what means he or she uses to arrive at those goals. In this regard, understanding how the attributes interact provides a thorough comprehension of those qualities of the individual that contribute to pathological conditions, subsequently revealing the routes toward effective therapeutic outcomes.

Personality Structures and Functions

Each person is naturally equipped with various attributes that allow him or her to meet the existence and reproductive imperatives, albeit in

TABLE 2.2
Personality Structures and Functions

Structures	Functions
Self-image The view and opinion of the self	Expressive behaviors How the person has come to act in response to external contingencies
Object representations View of the external world based on previous experience	Interpersonal conduct The ways in which the person engages and interacts with others
Morphological organization Consistency in schema-based orientation to external and internal experience	Cognitive style Focus and allocation of attention, attributional style, and cognitive biases
Mood and temperament Baseline mood state and style of affective reactivity	Regulatory mechanism Strategies for maintaining integrity in the face of threat

erratically adaptive fashion. These attributes define the style and focus of adaptation and include personality structures (aspects of the personality that remain generally constant, exist inside the person, and affect how information is processed) and personality functions (aspects of the personality that are dynamic and relied on to meet existential challenges). One might think of these attributes as the tools a person possesses for dealing with imperative challenges—they are what the individual uses in the task of adaptation, and although all of these attributes are adaptive, often the adaptiveness is relative only to an immediate challenge, and only in the subjective judgment of the individual. Likewise, the attributes may contribute to an immediate adaptation to a situational demand (e.g., avoidance of a threatening social situation), but may be ultimately quite maladaptive (e.g., compromising to rewarding social affiliations). Each of the structures and functions is listed and described in Table 2.2.

In a subsequent section of this chapter, I will revisit the role of personality structures and functions as they relate to core beliefs and mode reactions. In the section that follows, I present components of the cognitive model and describe how they interface with the personologic view.

Schema and Core Beliefs

The term *schema* describes the organizational processes that provide a guiding frame of reference for how events will be interpreted and processed relative to situational demands. Conceptually, schemas are cognitive structures that hold functional information. The term *structure* refers to something that exists, and the term *function* refers to something that is done. One can think of a schema as similar to a file folder labeled according to its contents. Within a filing cabinet, a multitude of files might exist, each with a specific label corresponding to the functional significance of the contents. For any given situation, a particular file may be most relevant, and the individual pulls it for its functional purpose. Similarly, multiple files may be relevant to the immediate circumstance in complementary, contradictory, or confusing fashion.

In their discussion of schemas, Young and his colleagues identified numerous schemas, all of which hold particular information that is functionally useful to the individual across many situations (e.g., McGinn & Young, 1996; Young, 1999). The expectations related to each of the schemas provide the individual with a frame of reference for managing a situation. On the basis of the schemas, the person expects certain things to occur and responds affectively and behaviorally in ways that best serve to protect the individual from potential or inevitable pain and other unpleasantness or to maximize the enhancing benefit of the situation.

Although schemas may be independent of one another and generally specific to a situation, most schemas maintain a degree of similarity that can be observed across situations and different schemas (Mischel, 1981). This similarity is defined by the core beliefs corresponding to the schemas and is generally consistent with the individual's orientation to the existence imperative. For instance, one who is highly focused on self-protection at the sacrifice of pleasure will hold schemas that are associated with self-protective mode responses. One who is oriented more toward pleasure, regardless of the risks, holds schemas related to enhancing outcomes. It is this commonality between schemas that lends itself to discussion of personality. Consideration of Young's (1999) list of early maladaptive schemas illustrates well the relationship between schemas, beliefs, and the existence imperative. In Table 2.3, each of Young's 18 maladaptive schemas is listed with a brief description of the survival concern. Returning to the file metaphor, the schema is the file, and the survival-related beliefs constitute the file contents.

Core beliefs are the contents of the schema and represent the specific attitude one has regarding the self, the world, and the future (called the *cognitive triad*) relative to the immediate situational occurrence. Core beliefs are analogous to the informational documents held in the file (schema). Like the information in the file, the core beliefs serve to orient and guide the individual relative to the situation that stimulated the activation of that schema (or pulling of that file). Core beliefs, rather than being random cognitive occurrences or mere genetic outcomes, develop in response to past existential challenges and serve in the immediate circumstance to guide behaviors relevant to an immediate challenge (i.e., to meeting survival challenges and reproductive focus). Thus, core beliefs relate to survival

TABLE 2.3
Young's Early Maladaptive Schema

Early maladaptive schema	Survival concern
Abandonment/instability	"I must protect myself from abandonment by others." "Without others, I may not survive."
Mistrust/abuse	"I must protect myself from the mistreatment of others."
Emotional deprivation	"Others will not treat me as I need to be treated."
Defectiveness/shame	"I must protect myself from the rejection of others by hiding my defectiveness."
Social isolation/alienation	"I am not part of the social world." "People do not desire my company."
Dependence/incompetence	"I cannot function without others." "I must keep others invested in me."
Vulnerability to harm or illness	"Something bad is going to happen!"
Enmeshment/undeveloped self	"My pleasure and safety come from others."
Failure	"I am inept."
Entitlement/grandiosity	"I should get all the pleasures I desire."
Insufficient self-control/ self-discipline	"I can have what I want."
Subjugation	"Others are more important than me."
Self-sacrifice	"I must not hurt or distress others."
Approval-seeking/recognition-seeking	"My pleasure comes from others." "I must keep others impressed with me."
Negativity/pessimism	"It's all painful."
Emotional inhibition	"Emotional expression will lead to painful outcomes."
Unrelenting standards/ hypercriticalness	"I can never be good enough."
Punitiveness	"I deserve pain."

concerns, as experienced by the individual. For some, those concerns will be related more to preservation of well-being (pain avoidance), and for others the concerns will relate more to enhancement of well-being (pleasure procurement).

Core beliefs are influenced by the individual's stage of development and cultural pressures and relate to what one must do to ensure optimal survival given maturational limitation, environmental options, and perceived contingencies. Thus, what a child does to maximize positive experiences and to minimize negative experiences is typically different than what an adolescent or adult would do because of the differences in thinking, physical strength, and environmental constraints. Yet a common theme may often be observed across developmental stages as older individuals implement perceptive and reactive processes in current challenges that had been effective in previous circumstances. For instance, a child who is able to effectively circumvent responsibilities through displays of anger and aggression may come to rely on these same responses in later situations, albeit in a manner that reflects age-consistent options. Whereas a child may lie down and throw a tantrum, an adolescent may scream obscenities, and an adult may threaten physical harm. Core beliefs relating to one's view of the self and view of the world are conceptually equivalent to the personality structures of *self-image* and *object representations*, respectively, as described in the personologic model (Millon, 1999).

The third component of the cognitive triad, one's view of the future, is not so immediately complemented by a personality attribute. Nonetheless, it can be discussed relative to the goal orientation described by the existence imperative. The goal is survival (enhancement and protection), and future projections are made relative to that imperative. In this regard, one's view of the future is relative to one's future projections concerning survival threats and opportunities (see Figure 2.1). Although one may of necessity contend with immediate survival challenges and opportunities, one must also anticipate existential challenges. The goal of optimal survival then necessitates future projections.

Intermediate Beliefs

Intermediate beliefs are cognitive attitudes that derive from core beliefs and are intermediate between core beliefs and automatic thoughts (Needleman, 1999). Intermediate beliefs include conditional assumptions, central goals, and implicit rules.

Conditional assumptions are beliefs concerning what must occur in order for the world to be satisfying (or unpleasant) or safe (or threatening). Conditional assumptions are often described as "if . . . then" conclusions. If one condition occurs, the individual reasons, then another will follow. For instance, persons with a histrionic style maintain a belief that the world is safe and pleasurable as long as they get the attention they want. Likewise, a person with an antisocial style believes that the world is acceptable if they get what they want without having to answer to anyone or do anything they do not want to do. In both cases, there are conditions that must exist in order for the individual to feel that his or her existence is optimized.

In the integrated perspective, conditional assumptions are concerns related to the survival task. In order for the existence imperative to be satisfied, these conditions must be met. If these conditions are not met, an

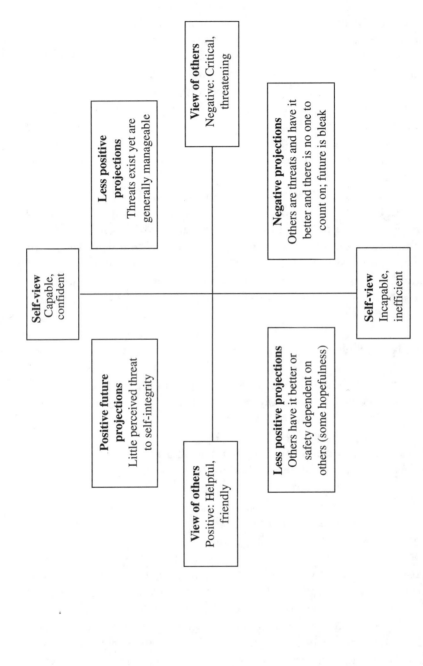

Figure 2.1. The cognitive triad and the existence imperative.

existential challenge exists, thereby prompting an adaptive response. In therapy, instigating change in these conditional assumptions is often critical to treatment success. Failure to change these assumptions may contribute to therapeutic resistance when the client maintains assumptions despite other changes. For instance, despite the development of effective social skills, if an individual with an avoidant style maintains the belief "If I don't say all the right things, then others will think me an idiot and reject me," then that individual may resist entering social engagements regardless of actual social skill.

Central goals are outcomes for which one strives and are often tied to familial and cultural values (Needleman, 1999). They are what one must do to achieve pleasurable outcomes and to avoid painful consequences. For instance, in order to experience the self as capable or worthy of respect and the admiration of others, an individual may strive for a material position that advertises financial potency. For this individual, the central goal is social status, and success is defined in large part by the individual's adherence to culturally defined success criteria. For others, the goal may be safety. They may believe that they cannot measure up to external expectations and therefore strive to remain safe from the rejection and rebuke of those perceived as more accomplished. Within the integrated model, central goals relate naturally to the survival task; essentially, central goals reflect the condition that must be met to provide enhancement or protection, or both.

Although central goals and *morphological organization*[1] are not conceptually equivalent, central goals can be considered critical aspects of one's morphological organization (Millon, 1999) in that they serve to guide choices and actions as part of the individual's survival imperative. This relationship is perhaps more clear when one considers the impact of central goals. For some individuals, central goals may be somewhat variable, whereas for others the central goals may be more consistent and better described by a singular, superordinate goal. Those with a simple and specific goal organize themselves relative to the attainment of that goal and act predictably across situations because actions are directed at satisfying that single, consolidated goal. Others may have goals that are relative to the immediate situation or that change as subtle aspects of a circumstance change. In the first example, one's morphological organization is tighter, less variable, and thus more predictable and defining of the individual. In the second example, organization is looser, more variable, and less predictable. For instance, the central goal of an individual with a compulsive style may be to avoid imperfection, which contributes to a very tight, compartmentalized morphological

---

[1] Discussed in greater detail in a later section, *morphological organization* is a term used to describe one's internal organization of the mind.

organization. For the individual with a borderline personality style, one central goal may be to keep others invested, and another might be to avoid being taken advantage of by others. These conflicting goals contribute to a morphological organization that is often chaotic as the two goals compete and conflict with one another.

Implicit rules are the codes of conduct for self and others, most often tied to core beliefs and central goals. They are the beliefs regarding what one and others should or should not do relative to the individual's survival orientation. The person with a compulsive disorder must, as should others, act according to the established rules (as he or she perceives them). For the individual with a borderline personality style, one must do what is necessary to invest another, and that other must value and protect the individual. The individual with a histrionic personality must be popular among others, and others should appreciate and be impressed by his or her attributes. The critical term in this description is *should*. Implicit rules are often reflected in automatic thoughts in the form of *shoulds, musts,* and *oughts* (Beck, 1976; Freeman, Pretzer, Fleming, & Simon, 1990). In sum, what any individual believes that he or she and others must do to satisfy the existence imperative are the implicit rules. Violation of these rules will invariably prompt a reaction oriented to making the circumstance be as it "should." Clearly, one's view of the way things should be has significant implications for the emergence of reactive and clinical conditions and is an important target in a cognitive intervention.

Automatic Thoughts

Core beliefs and intermediate beliefs contribute to the nature of automatic thoughts. *Automatic thoughts* are the quick cognitive reactions prompted by situational events that orient the individual to the demands of the situation. They are one's best-guess conclusions concerning a situation (Beck, 1976). Gilbert (2001) referred to these automatic cognitions as "pop-up thoughts." Although these thoughts are part of one's awareness, they are not processes that involve much, if any, reflection or controlled cognitive processes. According to Gilbert (2002b), automatic thoughts are implemented on the principle of "better safe than sorry." In this sense, they serve the purpose of a quick assessment that allows the individual to size up a situation and minimize the risk of negative outcomes. For some, the compulsion to avoid danger is not as well developed, and automatic thoughts may reflect more of a "devil may care" principle in which the opportunity for enhancement is perceived prior to any assessment of risk.

These thoughts expose one's position on the survival bipolarity. The focus on better safe than sorry reflects a concern with maximum safety, even at the expense of virtually all enhancements. The individual with a

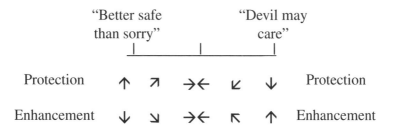

Figure 2.2. The existence bipolarity. ↑ = strong on this dimension; ↓ = weak on this dimension; → and ← = equal or balanced on this dimension; ↗ and ↘ = the midpoint between strong or weak extremes and neutrality.

dependent style, for instance, may forgo any pleasure to maintain security. At the opposite pole, an individual attends to enhancement opportunity without concern for the danger or consequences. Such an orientation is observed in impulsive individuals, thrill-seekers, and often those with an antisocial style of personality. Not surprising, perhaps, the devil may care orientation may be less common; thrill-seekers and sociopaths are more likely to die prematurely, lowering their contribution to the gene pool. Our ancestors were more likely to be those who used some degree of caution in life. That the devil may care attribute has not been bred out of the species may be because these high-risk, impulsive individuals reproduce early and often. As illustrated in Figure 2.2, an individual may be more toward one extreme or the other on either of the polarities.

Automatic thoughts may be cryptic, but they represent some complete thought. For instance, Needleman (1999) pointed out that the automatic thought "Oh no!" may relate to a more elaborate thought, such as "Oh no! Here we go, I'm going to make a fool of myself in front of the whole class again" (p. 29); this automatic thought prompts a better safe than sorry reaction. Such thoughts orient the individual to the need to react to protect the self from social scorn and rejection. Likewise, the automatic thought "Oh, boy!" may belie a more involved thought, such as "Oh, boy! That looks like a lot of fun! I want to do it, too!"

Thus, automatic thoughts are connected to quick emotional reactions implemented to energize reactant behaviors. For the individual with a compulsive style who worries about doing something wrong, the "better safe than sorry" principle is associated with anxiety and behaviors enacted to prevent the negative outcome from occurring. For the individual with a borderline personality style introduced to a new social group, the thought of "Oh, boy; that looks like fun" is associated with positive excitement and impulsive engagement in the situational task, without concern for the consequences. Thus, given how he or she evaluates the situation, the individual reacts emotionally and behaviorally to best deal with or revel in the circumstance. It is important to note that the emotion gets woven into the experience and furthers the automatic processing related to the event. For instance, the excitement felt by the individual with a borderline personality style influences how he or she perceives and reacts to other events. In this sense, one becomes caught up in the situation. The person with an anxious–compulsive style may become so concerned about potential dangers that he or she commits an entire day to activities enacted to remain safe (e.g., compulsive washing).

Priming is the term used to describe the process in which a schema is increasingly activated by circumstantial events, mediated by automatic thoughts and schemas. Triggering is the point at which a schema is activated. Whether a schema is activated or not depends on several factors, including the importance of the issues related to the schema, current emotional state, and nature of the situational event. It is at the point of triggering that the critical cognitive shift occurs—that is, a pathologic process is initiated, and thinking changes from neutral to biased (Beck, 1996). As long as the individual is in a conscious or semiconscious state, a schema is active. The active schema serves to prime the activation of a more specific schema.

Orienting Schemas

The orienting schema, which has been described as the "gatekeeper" for a mode (Needleman, 1999, p. 34), orients the individual to enhancement opportunities and threats and activates the mode response given the schema activated (i.e., by prevalent schemas). Primed by automatic processes, the orienting schema activates the schema and mode pertinent to the existential challenge at hand. Even when engaged in a singular task, one continues to attend to other stimuli in the environment. The orienting schema serves as the information-processing mechanism that attends to whether threatening or enhancing situations arise to which the individual can or must respond.

One's orienting schema is influenced by one's bias to expect and perceive threats or enhancement opportunities. When adequately primed and stimulated, the orienting schema triggers a specific orientation to the existential demand. This orientation, which serves as the organizing frame of reference for that situation, constitutes the schema. At any one time, a person experiences a frame of reference based on schema components (core beliefs, intermediate beliefs, modes) that serves to maximize the individual's adaptive reaction to the circumstantial event. However, as previously discussed, the notion of adaptive is relative to the immediate and optimal goals. Thus, one may engage in behaviors that enhance one's social position in the current or immediate situation; gossiping about others with a group of friends is an example. Although engaging in the gossip enhances one's position among the immediate group and provides a sense of superiority relative to those who are the target of the gossip, ultimately such behaviors may contribute to negative feelings about the self and strained interpersonal relationships, which contribute to the experience of various emotional conditions, including anxiety and depression. This may occur when the gossip spreads after one member of the initial group joins a new group and shares comments from the old group.

Casual and impulsive substance abuse or sexual promiscuity would also provide good examples of such problems. Although engaging in social activity connected with substance abuse is enhancing, and engaging in a sexual act is validating and pleasurable and thus adaptive in the immediate situation, both actions may contribute to later problems. As another example, although it is optimally maladaptive to be depressed, the withdrawal prompted by depression may be very adaptive in an immediate situation. Thus, what is adaptive in one situation may be quite maladaptive in another.

Personology and Schemas

Personality can be described as a *superordinate schema* in which personality is the prototypal summary of the combined schemas. Thus, one's personality reflects a descriptively unifying summary of one's prototypical schemata. In a psychometric sense, personality can be portrayed as the single best predictor of the theme of any single schema. Although there will certainly be exceptions, the risk of error in describing any single schema is reduced by considering the personality. Of course, the expression of responses both internally and externally occurs within the situational context. Consistent with Lewin's (1946) argument that behavior is a function of the person by situation interaction ($B = P * S$), using the described model, one can understand the person component relative to the situational demands. For instance, understanding that one client's personality is prototypically most similar to a histrionic style and another's is most consistent with a borderline style, the clinician can predict differences in how the individuals will react given the objective situation. More important, the clinician can understand the client's presenting clinical condition relative to personality and situational factors.

The more one's personality is consistent with a specific prototype, which may then fit best a *Diagnostic and Statistical Manual of Mental Disorders* (4th ed., text revision; DSM–IV–TR; American Psychiatric Association, 2000) categorical description of personality disorder, the less the error variability in making such predictions, indicating a greater commonality in schema theme across situations. The less one's personality fits a specific prototype, the greater the probability that schema themes differ. At this point we can again consider the personologic concept of morphological organization. To the extent that schemas are variable in theme, it is likely that there is inconsistency in one's organization. Indeed, the lack of a unifying theme may be indicative of a psychotic or delusional condition. Essentially, this implies that all individuals who display a relative capacity to function in the social world have some defining theme that guides their reactions and is reflected in specific schemas.

It is important to point out that consistency in schema theme does not necessarily imply mental or emotional health. A healthy prototype would suggest relative consistency across situations, but that consistency would be further defined by a general balance across the imperatives. Consistency that is marked by imperative biases or imbalances suggests only a degree of consistency, perhaps in the nature and frequency of subsequent reactions and clinical conditions.

As a final point, just as a specific schema can be defined by one's orientation to the evolutionary imperatives, so too can one's personality. Subsequently, given the adaptive purpose of schemas and their defining role in personality, personality will reflect one's orientation to the evolutionary imperatives. Figure 2.3 illustrates the relationships among personality, schema, situational demands, and the survival imperative. In this model, the superordinate task is survival (implied in the model by the large arrow, which is used to suggest an overarching motivator), including the avoidance of pain and pursuit of pleasurable outcomes. The adaptive and reproductive focus is represented in the individual's personality style, defined by the collective schema themes. Thus, an individual schema associated with specific circumstances, as well as the collection of schemas, reflect the individual's style of adaptive functioning (passive vs. active) and reproductive focus (self- vs. other-orientation). Finally, one's schemas are understood to include core beliefs and intermediate beliefs, as well as mode components.

Modes and Mode Activation

As presented in Figure 2.3, modes are aspects of schemas. When a schema is activated, so are mode-based reactions, in varying degree. As the term implies, *modes* are ways or methods of functioning and acting. For instance, mode of transportation refers to how a person travels from point A to point B. Law enforcement professionals use the term *modus operandi* (i.e., mode of operation) to describe a criminal's way or style of conducting a crime. In describing a client's way of reacting to a circumstantial event, one describes his or her modes of reaction. In this context, modes represent the person's way or style of reacting to and dealing with existential challenges (i.e., survival and reproduction). In his description of schema-based modes, Beck (1996) defined *mode* as "an integrated network of cognitive, affective, motivational, and behavioral components" (p. 2). Bearing in mind the

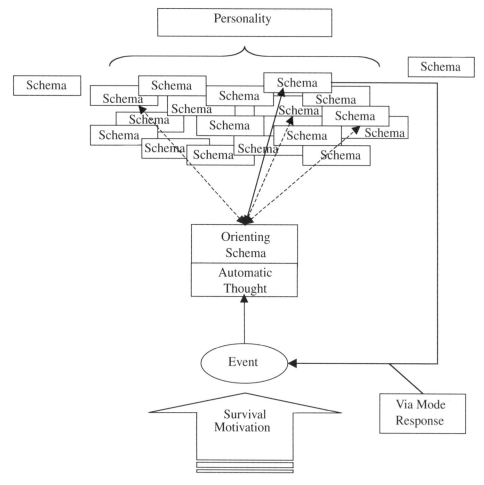

Figure 2.3. The personality-guided cognitive–behavioral model.

relationship to schema, a mode reflects one's personality. Knowing a person's personality then provides a best-guess model for describing the ways that he or she will react to challenges and opportunities.

Although a clinician could construct a sense of a client's personality by combining the various ways of reacting across different circumstances, such a strategy would be both labor intensive and time consuming, as well as prone to error, as the clinician gets drawn into unwarranted elaboration on seemingly critical aspects that prove to have little significance after further appraisal (the "red herring" effect; Dumont & Lecomte, 1987). A more practical strategy is to assess personality in a manner that allows the clinician to estimate specific mode responses, which he or she can then evaluate relative to their specific contribution to the presenting problem.

Mode responses are specifically defined by personality structures and functions, which are the attributes the individual relies on to manage existential challenges. In the following sections, mode systems are discussed relative to the personologic model. Beck (1996) discussed modes in relation to personality and psychopathology. It is noteworthy that in his 1996 publication, Beck used the terms *structure* and *function* to describe the schema (structure) and the activity (function) carried out relative to the situation. According to Beck's theory, one has a cognitive schema or structure that includes cognitive processes, an affective schema that includes affective processes, and a behavioral schema that includes behavioral functions. Unfortunately, Beck's and Millon's views of structure and function are conceptually similar, but not equivalent. Nonetheless, discussion of Beck's mode descriptions relative to Millon's view of personality structures and functions yields an enhanced understanding of personality, schema activation, and style of reaction to evolutionary demands. Beck (1996) presented six separate systems "participating in a mode" (p. 6): the cognitive, affective, physiological, behavioral, conscious, and motivational control systems. These systems are organized and coordinated by the demands of the evolutionary challenge in a way that maximizes protection or minimizes the potential of pain.

The *cognitive system* accounts for the way in which information is processed. This includes "assignment of meanings, selection of data, attention, interpretation (meaning assignment), memory, and recall" (Beck, 1996, p. 5). The cognitive system includes all the thought processes that occur in the mind. The cognitive system, like other systems, is not random or chaotic, but is organized around structural and functional (Beck's terms) themes related to the evolutionary objectives. Millon described the way of processing information as *cognitive style*. The Millon Index of Personality Styles (Millon, Weiss, Millon, & Davis, 1994) and the Millon Personality Diagnostic Checklist (see Tringone, 1997) both provide data corresponding to the examinee's cognitive style. One's cognitive style can be characterized by one of the descriptors Millon and his colleagues used to distinguish the thinking style of individuals with the various prototypal personality styles (Millon, 1999; Millon & Davis, 2000). These styles are summarized in Table 2.4.

The *affective system* relates to how the person feels and responds affectively. The affective reaction energizes behaviors enacted to communicate with others and to bring about a change in circumstance. Without the emotional component, the behaviors would be enacted without urgency or passion, if at all (Plutchik, 1980, 1984, 2000, 2003). In addition, the affective system provides feedback concerning the immediate situation; one evaluates pleasure and pain by how one feels at the moment. Thus, although one may cognitively conclude that the state of affairs is good, unless it is felt as good, it is not experienced as such.

TABLE 2.4
The Cognitive Styles

Cognitive style	Functional characteristics
Schizoid Impoverished	Thinking is limited, nonreflective, and concrete; associated with difficulties generating insights, alternatives, empathy, and so forth
Avoidant Distracted	Thinking is easily distracted by internal and external cues, including interpersonal actions and prompted memories
Depressive Pessimistic	Cognitive processes are biased to perceive events in their bleakest form
Dependent Naïve	Thinking is oriented to avoiding and denying trouble; simplistic, naïve, and trusting (Pollyannaish)
Histrionic Flighty	Externally focused, noninsightful, scattered
Narcissistic Expansive	Biased to self-aggrandizement; self-glorifying
Antisocial Deviant	Egocentric, antagonistic, unconventional
Sadistic Dogmatic	Narrowly opinionated, close-minded, obstinate, intolerant, and judgmental
Compulsive Constricted	Rule-driven, absolute, concrete, unyielding
Negativistic Skeptical	Cynical and doubting; biased to look at situations in a negative fashion
Masochistic Diffident	Hesitant, self-defeating, deferring
Schizotypal Autistic	Odd, self-absorbed, magical, tangential, and fantasy oriented
Borderline Capricious	Fluctuating, inconsistent, emotion-based, conflicting
Paranoid Suspicious	Skeptical, cynical, mistrusting, conspiratorial; finds hidden meaning

Cognitions and affect most often correspond, but to the extent that there is inconsistency, cognitive process may very well be affected by emotions. Indeed, contemporary psychoanalytic theorists argue that affect is the motivator influencing cognition (Westen & Gabbard, 1999). The relevance of this argument to the cognitive therapeutic model is that changes in cognitive process may be critically dependent on or limited by changes in affective processes. The affective processes of the individual are primarily a function of the mood and temperament attributes of the individual's personality. Table 2.5 lists the various attributes corresponding to each of the personality prototypes.

Affective processes are also influenced by personality attributes. The affect that an individual displays is a component of his or her efforts to cope with a situational demand. As an example, an individual with a sadistic personality style maintains a baseline mood state of irritability and contentiousness. When presented with a situation that conflicts with the individual's view of the optimal circumstance (core belief), he or she may rely heavily on affectively driven displays of behavior implemented to alter the unacceptable circumstance. Thus, such an individual may rely on anger to induce compliance in others. Similarly, a person with a depressive style may effectively avoid threats of failure or obligation by withdrawing into a greater state of depression. In this regard, the affective process helps the individual to meet (i.e., avoid) and contend with the existential challenges faced.

The *physiological system* comprises the physical systems that allow for the activation and regulation of all other systems and processes. The physiological system includes the central nervous system, the autonomic nervous system, the sympathetic and parasympathetic nervous systems, the motor system, and the sensory system. The functioning of all other processes is limited by the functioning of these systems. Factors such as incurred and genetically mediated organic abnormalities, metabolic processes, and exertion factors all influence the reaction of the individual to the immediate existential demand. As an example, a person oriented to pleasurable outcomes may pass up the opportunity for pleasure because of fatigue. Similarly, someone with a pain avoidance orientation may be inclined to react in extreme ways to physical sensations, resulting in somatic and psychosomatic conditions.

Unfortunately, the line between psychological and physiological processes is not clear. Physiological processes place limits on and prime psychological processes, and psychological processes affect physiological states. Further, many psychological processes have significant physiological indexes. For instance, depression that is an adaptive reaction to a hopeless situation has a significant impact on the physiological system, perhaps most notably the hypothalamic-pituitary-adrenal system (Heuser, 1998). In the current model, physiological dysfunction contributes most specifically to simple clinical reactions that develop relatively independent of personality (Millon, 1999).

The *behavioral system* is involved in what the person expresses or how the person acts outwardly. To varying degrees, these behavioral reactions are automatic, such as the behaviors observed in a spontaneous defensive reaction mediated by the fight-or-flight reflex and in various conditioned reactions. It also includes less automatic reactive responses that are quickly

TABLE 2.5
The Affective Processes

Mood or temperament	Functional characteristics
Schizoid Apathetic	Unexcitable, cold, emotionless
Avoidant Anguished	Undercurrent of tension, sadness, and anger; vacillates between hope and desire and fear; may become numb
Depressive Melancholy	Woeful, gloomy, tearful, joyless, and morose; worrisome, dysphoric
Dependent Pacific	Warm, tender, and noncompetitive; timid and conflict avoidant
Histrionic Fickle	Shifting and shallow, vivacious, animated, impetuous; easily enthused, angered, and bored
Narcissistic Insouciant	Nonchalance, imperturbability, feigned tranquility; unimpressionable or buoyantly optimistic, critical, prone to rage and shame
Antisocial Callous	Insensitive, irritable, and aggressive; lack of compassion and empathy
Sadistic Hostile	Excitable, irritable, contentious, belligerent, cruel, and mean-spirited
Compulsive Solemn	Tense, joyless, and grim; restrains warm feelings, keeps emotions under control
Negativistic Irritable	Touchy, temperamental, peevish; petulant and impatient, easily annoyed and frustrated
Masochistic Dysphoric	Mixed emotions; anxious and forlorn, anguished and tormented, guilt-inducing
Schizotypal Distraught or Insentient	Apprehensive, agitated and anxious, suspicious, or deficit in emotional expression
Borderline Labile	Variable and reactive, extreme or intense; varies from anger to euphoria
Paranoid Irascible	Cold, sullen, humorless, edgy, envious, jealous, defensive

implemented to satisfy the imperative challenge. Often, in retrospect, a person may wish that he or she had reacted differently in the situation, but at the time the behavior was determined at some level of consciousness as the best response.

The behavioral system includes the personality attributes labeled *expressive behaviors* and *style of interpersonal conduct*. These personality functions describe the modal manner of reacting that is consistent with the personality style. Table 2.6 identifies and describes typical expressive behaviors and interpersonal conduct for each of the personality styles. As an example, a person with a histrionic style tends to be dramatic in the expression of behaviors, implying that behaviors are expressed with excessive spectacle. Furthermore, the histrionic individual acts in interpersonal affairs in such a way to ensure that attention is directed to the self.

The *conscious control* system refers to the extent to which the individual is functioning with an awareness of his or her own reactive tendencies. For instance, people may be more or less aware of factors that elicit particular emotional responses in themselves, and they may be able to use that awareness to control those reactions. This system can be defined by the extent to which a person is operating on automatic processes versus slower, reflective, and controlled cognitive processes (Gilbert, 2000, 2002a, 2002b). Furthermore, although this system affects the expression of personality attributes, it is not itself one of the attributes Millon described. Nonetheless, one's morphological organization and regulatory mechanisms can be discussed relative to one's conscious control. Indeed, through metacognitive processes, the task of therapy is to increase the client's awareness of his or her regulatory efforts and to promote greater control over the client's morphological organization.

The *motivational system* includes the impact and constant reassessment of the survival imperative. One's status relative to the survival imperative is constantly being reevaluated through cognitive processes that influence emotional state and expressive behaviors. When the imperative is satisfied, emotions change and alter expressive behaviors. In essence, there are three components of this motivational system: (a) If the threat or opportunity persists, the individual continues adaptive efforts; (b) if the situation is viewed as hopeless, the individual terminates adaptive efforts and turns attention to a new task; or (c) the individual completes the task and ceases adaptive efforts. No doubt, this system relies heavily on the feedback mediated by the affective system.

Each of these modes contributes to the individual's ability to meet existential demands consistent with his or her personality and schema-based modes related to enhancement and protection. Essentially, modes are the resources one brings to the task of survival. In the next section, I describe

TABLE 2.6
Expressive Behaviors and Interpersonal Style

Personality	Expressive behavior	Interpersonal conduct
Schizoid	Impassive: Lacks engagement in life activities	Unengaged: Recognizes no obligation or commitment
Avoidant	Fretful: Covers all contingencies; seeks safety	Aversive: Keeps others at a distance
Depressive	Disconsolate: Is dejected, gloomy, detached from external experiences	Defensive: Awaits rejection
Dependent	Incompetent: Does not meet life expectations	Submissive: Does what is necessary to keep others invested
Histrionic	Dramatic: Does everything in an extreme way	Attention-seeking: Seeks to keep others invested on his or her terms
Narcissistic	Haughty: Remains detached from external activities via contempt	Exploitative: Takes advantage of others for personal gain
Antisocial	Impulsive: Pursues more immediately rewarding activity	Irresponsible: Is engaged only to the point of personal gain
Sadistic	Precipitate: Creates situations that signify or provide opportunity for domination	Abrasive: Seeks to dominate and defend against control, leading to defensiveness
Compulsive	Disciplined: Demands that everything be done correctly	Respectful: Demands that people be treated "right"
Negativistic	Resentful: Does not want to be bothered	Contrary: Desires to escape or avoid interpersonal obligation
Masochistic	Abstinent: Should not indulge	Deferential: Allows no interpersonal aggrandizement
Schizotypal	Eccentric: Wants things done his or her own way, against convention	Secretive: Avoids the criticism of others
Borderline	Spasmodic: Reacts to every event	Paradoxical: Loves and hates based on immediate situation
Paranoid	Defensive: Is always on guard	Provocative: Is defensive and concerned over power hierarchy, contributing to hostile defensiveness

the process by which these mode reactions contribute to clinical reactions and complex disorders.

Pathologic Process

Clinical syndromes develop when pathologic processes become part of the adaptive course—that is, when pathologic processes take on adaptive functions. The term *pathologic process* thus refers to adaptive processes that create recurrent problems in meeting life responsibilities and that compromise one's quality of life (e.g., by causing emotional distress). Everyone occasionally experiences simple clinical reactions that involve relatively short-term patterns of reaction and that are generally unpleasant and could lead to additional problems if not resolved. As an example, metabolic changes brought about by acute or chronic illness could contribute to lethargy or anxiety, which could become integrated into the individual's adaptive processes corresponding to situational demands. In such cases, it is not the personality attributes that need to be immediately targeted, but the physical condition and the source of the stress (e.g., the viral or bacterial pathogen).

If the illness is sustained, however, the adaptive processes could become woven into schema-based mode reactions and thereby contribute to clinical conditions independent of the direct impact of the physical condition. For instance, in the case of chronic fatigue brought about by endocrine system pathology, the individual may come to view the self as inefficient and others as self-centered, demanding, and unsupportive. Such changes in core beliefs could continue even after the medical condition resolves. For this reason, it is important that the clinician be attentive to the contribution of current or previous medical conditions in initiating and maintaining the clinical condition. In Figure 2.4, the relationship between stress and the different outcomes is depicted relative to the role of personality.

Complex clinical syndromes are more dependent than simple clinical reactions on schemas that involve pathologic processes. In the case of complex clinical syndromes, aspects of the schema, including the various mode reactions, contribute in critical ways to the condition. For instance, an individual with a seemingly healthy cognitive triad—that is, core beliefs that include a view of the self as capable, of others as less capable, and of the future as full of promise—may be susceptible to anxious and depressed affect when faced with situations that challenge these core beliefs. As an example, a young college student with a history of considerable academic success is enrolled at a competitive college. He struggles to maintain a positive academic self-view when faced with evidence that his academic skills are not sufficient to maintain the level of success previously achieved. This student finds himself unable to maintain a level of academic

Simple Clinical Reaction

Stress   ⇨   Clinical Reaction

Pathogen   Illness

Loss of loved one   Sadness

Complex Clinical Syndrome

Stress ⇦⇨ *Personality* ⇨ *Clinical Condition*

                 (Core belief)   (Low to moderate

Academic "failure"   "I want to be the best"   probability)

                                            Anxiety and depression

Personality Disorder

Stress ⇦⇨ *Personality* ⇨ *Clinical Condition*

                 (Core belief)   (Moderate to high probability)

Academic "failure"   "I must be the best"   Anxiety and depression

Figure 2.4. The pathologic process and the contribution of personality.

performance superior to his peers, who appear to be more capable in meeting the new academic demands.

By itself, this circumstance is likely to contribute to an anxious reaction, which is justifiable given the threat. How this individual deals with this circumstance is influenced by schema-based reactions. More focused attention to academics, for example, would be both an immediately and ultimately adaptive reaction. But there are other reactions that are immediately adaptive yet optimally maladaptive. For instance, cheating as a response to the perceived threat to self-integrity may enable the student to maintain a superior level of performance relative to peers; however, that student may then have to contend with an altered self-view, a lack of academic mastery, and potentially the consequences of being caught. In this situation, the pathologic process is the confrontation of the self-view with external realities and the means for dealing with anxiety created by that confrontation. Successful treatment will require a change in self-view relative to others and a more optimally adaptive means for dealing with anxiety.

Taking this example further, the student may react to the disappointment of not measuring up to personal standards by becoming hopeless and withdrawing into depression. Although this could contribute to greater academic failure, it might also provide relief from the ongoing battle to stay ahead; once depressed, the person is no longer immediately confronted with the need to stay ahead of others, and depression may serve to elicit sympathy from others, perhaps from those whom the person was trying to impress, such as teachers, peers, parents, and siblings. Although the depression may be unpleasant, to this individual it is better than continued failures associated with the goal of being academically superior to others. My intention is not to imply that depression in such a case is feigned or contrived, but to describe the adaptive value of the depression. As suggested by Gilbert (2000), depression can serve to keep the person from fighting a fight he or she is not going to win. For the student in the example, not being the best student is indeed depressing, and continuing to try to be the best is destined to further failure. The fact is that if a person is doing as well as he or she expected, depression would not be needed; it is the interpreted failure that precipitates the depression. In this situation, the withdrawal into a depressed state and the adaptive value of this withdrawal constitute the pathologic process.

How an individual reacts is a function of the current situation and his or her past experience with challenging and frustrating situations. If the student decides to cheat, it is likely that he or she has taken desperate measures in desperate situations in the past, and cheating is now the desperate response. If the student becomes depressed, withdrawal has been an adaptive reaction in the past. In addition, how the individual responds to a new challenge may set in motion a style of adaptation that contributes to later problems. This student's current clinical condition was brought about by vulnerabilities created earlier in life that were not problematic until activated by current life circumstances.

In another example, an individual with a history of subtle verbal abuse and social awkwardness has developed a view of the self as inept and others as hypercritical. As a child, her symptoms were not clearly observed. Teachers and others described her as shy or quiet. The person was able to get enough schoolwork done to avoid being labeled learning disabled. This child played with a couple of friends at recess, albeit in a disengaged and peripheral fashion. At home, the child played computer games, watched television, and interacted with siblings. Her parents tended to be critical in their interactions with their children, focusing on what had not been accomplished rather than on what had been done well. The siblings interacted in a critical manner with one another.

From these experiences, the child develops the view of the self as not good with others and of people as sources of ridicule and scorn. This individual may go through life relatively free of clinical problems if she is able to avoid interactions with others that do not go well and is able to be content in life without close social and intimate relationships. However, the demands of life are likely to create situations for this individual that may prompt a clinical reaction. For instance, hopelessness and depression may set in during young adulthood if the person cannot find the courage to approach someone for a date, let alone foster a relationship that leads to marriage and intimacy. If she is able to find a mate, the expectations that go along with being a spouse, wage earner, and parent may be more than she feels prepared for, which may prompt depression allowing a retreat from hopeless situations. By avoiding social relationships throughout most of life, this individual is able to avoid painful experiences, yet she has experienced recurrent anxiety throughout life when faced with social engagements. Later in life, the demands of social affiliations may not be adequately avoided, and the anxiety may prompt other reactions that keep the individual safe from immediate demands (e.g., somatic symptoms), but these reactions become a pathologic process contributing to recurrent problems.

In these examples, the pathologic process is not a function of a personality disorder per se, but it is rather created by aspects of the personality that could best be described relative to a particular personality prototype. A *personality disorder* implies a predominance of pathologic schemas defined by the overarching theme of personality. For an individual with a personality disorder, the personality is so broadly defined by pathologic schemas that he or she is frequently faced with clinical conditions, and these clinical conditions become a significant dimension of the person's personality. To say that someone has a personality disorder is to suggest that his or her schemas are predominately pathologic.

Pathologic processes may predominate as the result of constant or recurrent activation. Activation occurs when the individual is faced with recurrent situational demands (narrow range of activating events) and subsequently displays responses that are ultimately maladaptive. The more that an activated schema is consistent with a pathologic personality, the more the individual can be said to have a disordered personality, which suggests that pathologic reactions have become part of his or her adaptive process. The individual's schemas may be highly variable in theme, and most may not involve a pathologic process. The more adaptive the schemas making up the personality, the less likely it is that active pathologic processes and clinical outcomes will occur. Thus, healthy personality is defined by a greater proportion of balanced and optimally adaptive schemas.

Personality and the Cognitive Model

The personologic model provides an appealing and simple conceptual model for understanding the nature and impact of cognitive processes, including schemas, core beliefs, and mode reactions. In this context, information processing is carried out in a manner that is specifically connected to one's imperative balance and derived personality style. For some people the role of personality attributes is more significant than for others. As well, certain clinical conditions may emerge because of specific schemas that are not consistent with one's personality. Personality, then, reflects one's relative imperative balance and thus defines one's orientation to life in the broadest sense, including one's relationship with the self, with others, with situational circumstance, and with the task of growth and maturation. Starting at the point of personality, the clinician can consider an individual's general orientation to events and make predictions regarding how he or she will interpret and deal with circumstances. By understanding the client and the role of the clinical condition in his or her constant task of adaptation, the clinician is in the best conceptual position to introduce meaningful change strategies.

Although there are various ways to conceptualize the personality to understand the client and his or her problem, the discussion in this volume relies on the model of personality devised by Millon and his colleagues and associates. This model serves as the foundation for the Millon Clinical Multiaxial Inventory (MCMI–III; Millon, 1997), which provides the clinician with a quantitative appraisal of the individual's specific and pertinent personality attributes and associated clinical conditions. Intended as a source of hypothesis, the MCMI–III provides the initial foundation for conceptualizing the client. The clinician may choose to limit his or her assessments to the MCMI–III, but other inventories in the Millon arsenal can provide a broader and more complete assessment of the construct described in his model. For instance, the Millon Index of Personality Styles (Millon et al., 1994; see Appendix A) produces scores reflecting an individual's position on each of the imperative poles, in addition to descriptions of his or her cognitive and interpersonal style. The Millon Personality Diagnostic Checklist (Tringone, 1997; see Appendix A) provides scores reflecting several of the personality attributes described in the current chapter.

TREATMENT IMPLICATIONS

From a cognitive–behavioral perspective, the task of therapy is to alter information processing in such a way that the client is able to prevent the cognitive shift that occurs when a maladaptive schema is triggered and protective or opportunistic mode responses are activated. By altering the cognitive processes, mode-based affective and behavioral reactions are likewise modified, thereby decreasing the client's state of distress. A combination of the two models provides the cognitive–behavioral therapist with quick access to client personality attributes contributing to cognitive processes and mode-based reactions and, thus, to the pathologic process. Treatment success is demonstrated by changes in the polarity balances accomplished through alteration in the client's core beliefs related to self-view, view of others, and future projections—in other words, to changes in self-image, object representation, and perceptions of existential challenges. Thus, what was a threat relative to the client's self-image and perception of the world comes to be perceived as less threatening and manageable, and perhaps even enhancing. The client can then reflect on what appears to be an opportunity for enhancement relative to the consequences and cost of engagement.

Changes in core beliefs can best be accomplished through consideration of personality attributes that contribute to the maintenance of the core beliefs. Although it may in some cases be sufficient to confront core beliefs with metacognitive processes, without changes in underlying attributes, core beliefs may not shift in any consistent or permanent fashion. As a result, changes in core beliefs are most likely to occur as the result of accommodations based on alteration of other personality attributes.

For instance, it will be easier for the individual with an antisocial personality style to alter a core belief related to autonomy when he or she is able to derive pleasurable outcomes based on prosocial behaviors. The individual with an avoidant orientation will be able to alter views of the self as socially inept if he or she is able to observe in him- or herself the development of functional social skills that lead to pleasurable social encounters. Thus, consideration of the underlying personality attributes yields avenues for addressing and altering the more substantial core beliefs.

Knowing, for instance, that a client is pleasure seeking, low in pain avoidance, active, and self-focused gives the clinician a good sense of the personality attributes that contribute to the client's pathologic process and clinical condition. Effective treatment will require that this individual become more attentive to the needs and feelings of others, more concerned with consequences, and perhaps more patient and contemplative.

Treatment involves identifying the pathologic process and the personality attributes contributing to that pathologic process and then introducing strategies for altering those attributes. The clinician identifies these processes and attributes by considering the client's imperative polarity balances and the personality dimensions contributing to those balances. This integrated model establishes a foundation the clinician can use in considering a client's behavior relative to his or her orientation to the existence imperative and stylistic manner of satisfying the existential challenge. Thus, what a client does is most typically related to his or her need for protection or enhancement and is observed through the active or passive efforts the client enacts to bring about a desired outcome. By considering first the client's orientation to the imperatives, the clinician gains a broad conceptual understanding of that client that leads to specific treatment goals. For instance, by knowing that a client is high on pain avoidance and low on pleasure seeking, the clinician already understands the general nature of treatment. By understanding that the client tends to be passive and self-focused, the clinician can identify more clearly the nature of the individual's condition.

In the following chapters, I discuss each of the *DSM–IV–TR* personality disorders relative to the integrated model. I conclude with a description of personality disorders discussed by Millon that do not exist as specific conditions in the *DSM–IV–TR*. Although I rely on the classification of personality disorders as my organizing scheme, I approach each classification as a prototype rather than as a category. Appendix A describes a sample of the Millon inventories, and Appendix B outlines a conceptual scheme for conducting a clinical assessment, and Appendix C provides a case example.

SUMMARY OF THE INTEGRATED MODEL

Each person is oriented to life through a descriptive balance on the evolutionary imperatives. Thus, one is oriented to survival by maximizing enhancing outcomes and minimizing threatening and otherwise painful outcomes, thus maximizing one's sense of well-being. How one goes about meeting this objective is reflected in adaptive style and focus.

The imperative balance is reflected in one's personality. Thus, how one goes about meeting the existence imperative is reflected in a characteristic style of engagement with the world. For some this style is more distinctive than it is for others.

Personality reflects a thematic consolidation of situational schemas. Schemas reflect core beliefs, intermediate beliefs, and mode reactions, all of which are oriented around the imperative task of survival (i.e., maximizing well-being).

Personality structures and functions are captured in beliefs and modes. Thus, the personologic model and cognitive–behavioral therapy come conveniently together at the point of personality attributes and schema and mode reactions. Personality and mode reactions contribute to the pathologic process contributing to the clinical condition. Consistent with the immune system metaphor, stress is a function of the true valence of the stress and one's personality-based interpretation of that stress. Further, how one reacts or responds to perceived stress is a function of personality-based attributes. Although most responses are in some capacity adaptive, in the long term many reactions contribute to various clinical conditions. Treatment of the clinical condition requires attention to the personality-based attributes contributing to the pathologic process.

3

THE PARANOID PROTOTYPE

Key phrase: Mistrust
Evolutionary focus: Defensive, protection from others

The paranoid style of personality is marked by a unique polarity balance characterized by a "rigid compartmentalization" (Millon, 1999, p. 679; see Figure 3.1) of thoughts and feelings. Individuals with this personality style do not characteristically ignore painful consequences in their quest for pleasurable outcomes, but they are attentive to the social and physical implications of their desires and intentions. As a result, they tend to be rather guarded in what they express openly and are selective about whom they associate with and to whom they are more open regarding personal thoughts and feelings. Despite their guardedness, they can endure various painful consequences if pursuing an outcome in which they are particularly invested. For instance, although an individual with a paranoid orientation may be guarded and reserved in his or her interactions with employment supervisors and may strive to keep a low profile at work to avoid criticism or control, he or she can be tenacious and dominating when pursuing status within a different social group.

As an example, Peter worked at the corporate office of a national insurance company. He went to work each day and did his job without bringing unnecessary attention to himself. He was rather standoffish and curt with coworkers, with whom he had fostered no meaningful social relationships. Peter viewed work as a necessary annoyance and looked forward to the day he could retire.

Peter was also involved with a Southern Heritage organization and had organized a local chapter, about which he felt proprietary, and he strove

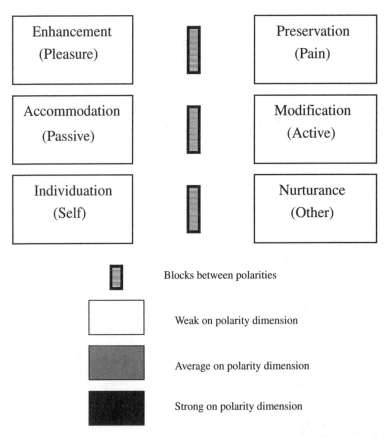

Figure 3.1. Polarity balance of the paranoid prototype. From *Personality-Guided Therapy* (p. 680), by T. Millon, 1999, New York: Guilford Press. Copyright 1999 by John Wiley & Sons, Inc. Reprinted with permission.

to maintain control over the focus and direction of the chapter, making certain that the causes he felt were important were pursued. He encountered opposition from other members of the chapter, who he felt were failing to understand the importance of his causes and trying to undermine his right as the founder to determine the focus of chapter activities. Thus, although he maintained a low profile at work, in his chapter activities Peter had a high profile and was known to be very active and confrontational. Thus, Peter was pain avoidant in one circumstance but more enhancement seeking in a different environment.

The individual with a paranoid style may at times focus on the personal implications of circumstantial events (a self-focus), feeling victimized or unfairly treated, or he or she may focus on the behaviors and intentions of others more or less as independent of him- or herself (a focus on others). For instance, Peter might obsess over the implications of an employment decision only as it affects him and him alone, whereas at other times he speculates on the intentions and actions of others without specific attention to any personal implications. As an example, his attention may be on the unfairness of corporate heads, with whom he has no affiliation.

Those with the paranoid prototype personality can be stubbornly resistant and passive when asked to cooperate or contribute to an externally imposed demand or expectation. Yet they may pursue an activity that serves their own purpose with great energy. Thus, the individual with a paranoid style is neither active nor passive but is capable of being either as the situation and intention require.

PERSONALITY-GUIDED COGNITIVE–BEHAVIORAL CONCEPTUALIZATION

For Millon and colleagues (Millon, 1999; Millon & Davis, 2000), the paranoid personality reflects a profile of intrapersonal and interpersonal attributes that define the individual's stylistic manner of perceiving the self and interacting with the world. The personality structures and functions of individuals with the paranoid prototype style, and their associated liabilities, are presented in Table 3.1. Although paranoia may not characterize all or even most of the situational schemas, for those with the paranoid prototype personality, mistrust is the predominant theme of most schemas. As a result, these individuals are more likely to be suspicious of others and to take on a caustic, defensive posture in both immediate and indirect interpersonal relationships.

The self-image of these individuals is one of *inviolability*, a term that represents the rigidity of the individual's perceptions and opinions and reflects the individual's efforts to avoid threats to self-esteem or self-integrity. These individuals often assume that other people are the source of bad events in the world, particularly those that relate directly to them. They are convinced that their view of the world is the valid view and feel threatened by and contempt for those who view the world differently. They are often stubborn and will frequently hold to an indefensible argument even in the face of clearly disconfirming evidence. When rational argument will not suffice to defend a position, the person with a paranoid style may turn to hostility and attacks on the integrity of the other individual. Indeed, his or her need to maintain an indefensible position may contribute to the display of clear irrationality suggestive of a delusional or psychotic state (Millon, 1999).

TABLE 3.1
Structures and Functions of the Paranoid Prototype
and Associated Liabilities

Personality domain	Liability
Self-image Inviolable	Unwillingness to contribute to social undertakings or to cooperate with others in a common cause
Object representations Unalterable	Expectation of harm, exploitation, or deception by others
Morphological organization Inelastic	Considerable treatment resistance; any call to change attitudes and interpersonal style considered an invitation and vulnerability to exploitation and harm
Mood and temperament Irascible	Objectionable demeanor leading to strained interpersonal relationships as others avoid and potentially undermine the person, thus justifying the paranoid orientation
Behavioral acts Defensive	Defensiveness that is aversive to social partners and contributes to an undermining of interpersonal relationship and affiliation
Interpersonal conduct Provocative	Strained interpersonal relationships and avoidance and rejection by others
Cognitive style Suspicious	Defensiveness in interpersonal interactions and suspicious minidelusions
Regulatory mechanism Projection	Decreased sense of personal responsibility and increased paranoid ideations

Behind the inviolable self-image of a person with a paranoid style is a powerful concern with the external world, including people and events. Such individuals are hypersensitive to immediate or potential threats to their personal integrity. The rigidity of their self-image bolsters their defense against external threats. To be weak in opinion or values is to be open to exploitation and external control. The rigidity of the self-image also contributes to a defensive posture against demands and expectations. Rather than giving in to the mistreatment, exploitation, or unwarranted influence of others (which better characterizes a dependent style) or being indifferent to the actions of others (such as seen in a schizoid personality style), the paranoid prototype contributes to a defensive rigidity enacted to resist external influences and other threats to self-esteem.

The core beliefs and cognitive style (see Beck & Freeman, 1990) of the individual with a paranoid style are represented by such self-statements as "I am vulnerable to other people," "Other people cannot be trusted," and "They are out to get me." Related to these core beliefs, conditional beliefs such as "If I let my guard down, they will take advantage of me" or "If someone is nice, they must want something from me" contribute to the individual's interpersonal orientation. Instrumentally, the individual maintains a cautious, self-protective, and mistrusting demeanor reflected in instrumental attitudes such as "I need to keep my guard up," "Don't trust anybody," and "I can't give other people a chance to take advantage of me." Such attitudes contribute to the irascible mood and to provocative and defensive behaviors.

The automatic thoughts of individuals with a paranoid style are associated with immediate perceptions of threat, which orient them through schema activation to a suspicious and defensive posture complete with mode reactions necessary to defend against the perceived threat. Maintaining this suspicious and defensive posture, the individual provokes others into defensive positions, which then reaffirms the individual's view of others as threatening.

Behaviorally, individuals with a paranoid personality are characterized by a *defensive* posture and a *provocative* interpersonal style. Their actions are oriented toward defending (i.e., protecting) the self from interpersonal affronts. Their defensiveness is often perceived by others as being provocative. In fact, others frequently feel threatened and provoked by individuals with a paranoid orientation. These individuals' manner of relating to people often leads others to avoid them and to the likelihood that others will in fact conspire against them (e.g., talk disparagingly about them to others), thus contributing to the individual's paranoia.

The cognitive style of the paranoid personality is *suspicious*. Even kind gestures by others may be interpreted as having hidden and malicious intent. Thus, it is difficult for an individual with a paranoid style to accept a gift or compliment without concern over the intent. Indeed, Kinderman and Bentall (1996, 1997) described the attribution patterns of the individual as characterized by a tendency to attribute negative outcomes to the actions of others.

The mood and temperamental attitude of individuals with paranoid styles are characterized by *irascibility*. They maintain a defensive and hostile posture that serves to keep them prepared for the attacks and affronts they believe to be inevitable. Those with a paranoid style expect that others will attempt to exploit them in some way, and thus they remain prepared to defend themselves at all times.

PATHOLOGIC PROCESS OF THE PARANOID PATTERN

To those with the paranoid prototype personality, stress is experienced in situations that they perceive hold the potential for exploitation. In stressful situations, these individuals are inclined to react in a defensive and provocative manner, which provides a sense of protection but often makes matters worse by creating interpersonal conflicts. The more the individual is defined by paranoid-style attributes and schemas, the more pervasive is the paranoid interpretation of stressful situations. How the individual responds to that stress is frequently reflected in the clinical condition.

As a result of their attitudes toward others and their own felt vulnerabilities, individuals with a paranoid orientation are forced into a constant state of suspiciousness and defensiveness and are subsequently prone to both anxiety and anger. Indeed, suspiciousness requires a degree of anxiety (Öhman, 2000) to drive the hypervigilance to signs of external threats. Through defensive display of anger and hostility, such individuals are able to deal with immediate threats and affronts. Unfortunately, both of these reactions are associated with a host of negative and, thus, paranoia-perpetuating consequences (i.e., anxiety and hostility). These individuals may also be vulnerable to episodes of depression when they feel overwhelmed and helpless relative to perceived threats and social isolation. Finally, in situations marked by immediate and extreme threats, individuals with a paranoid prototype personality may experience manic reactions to ward off the threat and may become delusional or even psychotic in their thinking.

The following section identifies the various clinical vulnerabilities associated with the paranoid prototype. Although this list is not exhaustive, it does highlight the role of these *Diagnostic and Statistical Manual of Mental Disorders* (4th ed., text revision [*DSM–IV–TR*]; American Psychiatric Association, 2000) Axis I clinical outcomes in the pathologic process of the paranoid prototype. Thus, rather than standing by themselves as simply biochemical abnormalities, the conditions are understood relative to the objectives of the individual.

AXIS I VULNERABILITIES

Generalized Anxiety Disorder

For individuals with a paranoid style, the world provides constant threat, requiring that they be on guard at all times to prevent others from taking advantage of them and their resources. These individuals worry about things and events that are of little concern to others. For instance, an individual with a paranoid style worries that the bank is not trustworthy, that employers "have it in" for him or her, that his or her spouse is unfaithful, or that others are conspiring against or hiding true feelings from him or her. Although individuals with a paranoid personality disorder are convinced of the dishonesty and ill intent of others, those with a paranoid style experience a more or less constant or recurrent concern that may intensify under certain situations. These thoughts and associated anxiety contribute to their defensive posture, which is easily interpreted by others as being provocative.

Work may be a constant source of anxiety for the person with a paranoid style, who perceives the workplace as a hostile environment in which the others are incompetent yet aligned against him or her. The individual interprets quiet conversations among fellow workers as evidence that they are talking disparagingly about him or her. Although not necessarily delusional in thinking, the individual interprets such interactions between coworkers as maliciousness. Often the person is concerned that superiors are conspiring against him or her. Similarly, the individual is frequently fearful that his or her spouse is secretly involved or wishing to be involved with another and is remaining with him for ingenuine purposes, such as for money or some other form of security.

Panic Disorder

When anxiety mounts as the result of internal processes or external events, the individual with a paranoid orientation may experience acute anxiety or a panic reaction (Bermanzohn, Arlow, Albert, & Siris, 1999; Millon, 1999). Reich and Braginsky (1994) argued that individuals with a paranoid style are particularly vulnerable to panic disorder. Being under a constant state of siege and feeling unprepared to cope with unforeseen dangers, the individual is vulnerable to situations in which he or she feels threatened and perceives no escape or defense (Bermanzohn et al., 1999).

Obsessive–Compulsive Disorder

As part of their concern with the actions of others, individuals with a paranoid style are vulnerable to the development of an obsessive–compulsive condition (Kimble, 2000). Their obsessions may relate to their preoccupation with others' ill intent toward them. The anxiety associated with these obsessional concerns is combined with thoughts and feelings associated with their self-righteousness and contempt for others. In the face of these anxieties, the person may engage in compulsive behaviors in efforts to counteract or defend against affronts. In some cases, the compulsive behaviors may be enacted as a safeguard against future interactions. For instance, compulsive cleaning may provide the individual with a distraction from interpersonal interactions perceived as threatening and confrontational, while at the same time providing some relief from the threat of criticism (e.g., concerning a dirty house). Likewise, the compulsive behaviors may be enacted as a means of staying ahead of criticism or as a means of displaying a sense of superiority over others. In either case, the obsessive–compulsive condition is a component of the paranoid orientation.

Anger and Depression

In the face of a hopeless situation, the individual with a paranoid style may develop depressive symptoms or a depressive disorder. However, unlike those who attribute failures to personal shortcomings, the individual with a paranoid style attributes failures to the actions of others (Kinderman & Bentall, 1997), and hopelessness is associated with the constant state of threat or failure of others to act in a more pleasing manner. Although the individual may display evidence of depression, the more prevalent emotion is likely to be anger (Millon & Kotik-Harper, 1995). Hopelessness may be associated with feelings of isolation, inferiority, or frustrations related to the person's inability to convince others of his or her point of view. Such individuals may be more vulnerable to anger displays than to the withdrawal associated with depression, but their preoccupation with how others treat them nevertheless renders them vulnerable to depressive episodes, enabling them to retreat from conflicts they perceive as unsolvable. Similarly, they become vulnerable to depressive symptoms when their attributional process turns to personal shortcomings (Bodner & Mikulincer, 1998). In a sense, the external, suspicious focus of individuals with a paranoid style may serve to decrease vulnerability to depression, yet the line between external blame and personal responsibility and contempt may be quite thin.

It is also important to consider the role of anger and depression as they relate to the individual's ability to manage interpersonal relationships when experiencing paranoia. Anger is specifically implemented as a means of countering interpersonal affronts (see Arsenio & Lemerise, 2001). For such individuals, interpersonal affronts occur in the form of direct and indirect attacks on their physical or psychological security, but also as the result of others' failure to adhere to their idiosyncratic expectations. Although the value of anger is relatively clear, the value of depression in this regard is less obvious. Depression may represent a withdrawal from a hopeless situation, but it is also a powerful source of interpersonal control, which may be particularly effective for the individual with a paranoid style. In this sense, the sympathy received and constant investment of others may prove highly reinforcing to the individual. For instance, depression may enable the individual to retain the constant investment of a spouse whose loyalty and honesty he or she questions. Thus, anxieties over the spouse's infidelities, for example, are effectively allayed through the spouse's attention to the individual's depression. Although this may not describe the typical depression in a client with a paranoid orientation, the secondary gain of the depression should be carefully considered.

Bipolar Disorder

Persons with a paranoid style may experience manic episodes reflecting their active efforts to deal with perceived affronts (Akiskal, Azorin, & Hantouche, 2003; Kellerman, 1990). Although mania may be more common in persons characterized by a paranoid disorder (i.e., personality disorder, delusional or psychotic disorder) during times of intensified threat and stress, individuals with a paranoid style may be inclined to hostile reactions that are consistent with a manic or hypomanic condition. Because depression increases the individual's perceived vulnerability to the actions of others (Millon & Kotik-Harper, 1995), withdrawal into a major depression may be unlikely. Rather, the person with a paranoid style is more inclined to react with anger and hostility to defend against a perceived threat. Indeed, Millon (1999) described the bipolar pattern of such an individual as one of hostility rather than euphoria. Although hopelessness may underlie the expression, the individual with a paranoid style is more likely to "go down fighting." The recurrent periods of active confrontation may suggest a manic or hypomanic episode, which may be followed by a withdrawal into social isolation.

Paranoid Schizophrenia

In some cases of paranoia, the individual may be vulnerable to reactive episodes of psychotic thinking. Considering that individuals with a paranoid style often behave in ways that lead others to avoid interactions with them and to have negative impressions of them, their suspicions are often justified and reinforced by the reactions of others. To the extent that the reactions of others have significant implications for the safety and welfare of the individual with a paranoid orientation and his or her dependents, the pattern of paranoid thinking may evolve from heightened sensitivities to delusions and eventually to a full-blown psychotic episode.

VARIATIONS ON THE TRADITIONAL PARANOID PERSONALITY

Millon and his colleagues (Millon, 1999; Millon & Davis, 2000) described five variants of the paranoid orientation. Although each is very similar to the traditional concept of the paranoid personality, differences are observed that render each style more or less vulnerable to various clinical outcomes.

Individuals with the *insular paranoid* personality style, which includes characteristics of both the avoidant and schizoid personalities, find social encounters threatening and generally unpleasant, and thus avoid social interactions. Rather than remaining in an encounter while exhibiting a stubborn and irascible demeanor, they avoid social affiliations and exist in their own personally conceived world. However, dissimilar to the schizoid and more similar to the avoidant style, individuals with an insular paranoid style are psychologically invested in the behaviors and intentions of others. Indeed, their own world may be defined in a socially contrary fashion. As a result of their general avoidance and relative indifference to others, these individuals may be less vulnerable to anxiety than other paranoid variants, but perhaps more vulnerable to episodes of depression associated with isolation or to delusional and psychotic episodes. Unlike the classic avoidant style, individuals with an insular paranoid style are not interested in positive intimate relationships as much as in creating their own idealized environments, including, perhaps, compliant others.

The *malignant paranoid* personality style includes sadistic attributes; this style of paranoid personality is associated with the most hostile actions and reactions. The person with this variant of the paranoid style expects malevolence from others, is nearly always on the defensive, and desires revenge for perceived wrongs. Although in most cases the revenge is typically fantasized and outward expressions typically do not go beyond belligerence and argumentativeness, this revenge may be reflected in a variety of reactions to perceived threats. For instance, the individual with a malignant paranoid personality may directly confront another but may more often strive to undermine the other's status among peers. For example, a college professor who felt that others in his department were conspiring to deny him tenure went on a crusade to undermine the status of departmental colleagues among students and other staff and faculty of the institution. Once confronted, he attempted to sue the university for breach of contract. In the extreme, individuals with this personality style may strive to induce emotional, economic, or physical harm on another who they feel has wronged them in some way. The malignant paranoid personality may be vulnerable to numerous clinical conditions, perhaps most notably obsessive–compulsive or manic conditions.

The *obdurate paranoid* personality style combines the characteristics of the paranoid personality with the attributes of the compulsive personality. In this personality style, individuals are rule driven and often rigid and self-righteous. They have, in a sense, resigned themselves to an external authority structure, but rather than following rules for the sake of doing what they are "supposed" to do, they use rules as a means of establishing status over others. In fact, they may resent and conspire against the "rules" when they do not fit their own perceptions of how things should go. Nonetheless, they believe that others should comply with the rules, and they strive to assure adherence by others to their idiosyncratic view of the rules. They tend to be very judgmental and to look down on those who do not live life as they believe others should. They criticize people for their weaknesses and failure to live a structured and disciplined life (Millon & Davis, 2000, p. 380). The individual with an obdurate paranoid personality is vulnerable to anxiety, obsessions, recurrent depression, mania, delusions, and, potentially, psychotic episodes.

The obdurate paranoid personality may be observed in individuals who form their own social organizations that are on the fringes of acceptable society and that may have as a focus criticism of the more established social order. For instance, a person with an obdurate paranoid style may be identified in both the leaders and followers of militia organizations and other similar groups.

The *querulous paranoid* personality style includes features of the negativistic personality. Individuals with this style are caustic and cynical. They perceive others as receiving unfair advantages and feel resentful and jealous of others. They are accusatory and prone to take various actions, including unwarranted legal action, to correct the wrongs they believe they have endured. They grumble and complain and rarely have close or fulfilling relationships with others (Millon & Davis, 2000, p. 381). Individuals with the querulous paranoid style may be particularly vulnerable to recurrent depression as a result of their lack of success in interpersonal relationships. Through the experience of depression, they retreat from and avoid interpersonal engagements that are the source of unpleasant emotion. As an example, an individual with the querulous paranoid style was perceived by coworkers as very cantankerous and unpleasant and as frequently accusing others of doing something to make her job and life more difficult. Her own belief was that others at work treated her unfairly and that if she was not on guard, someone would do something to get her fired or to dump an unfair proportion of the work on her.

The *fanatical paranoid* personality style includes features of the narcissistic personality. However, unlike those with a narcissist style, who can claim some accomplishment upon which to rely for feelings of superiority over others, individuals with the fanatical paranoid style have no real claim to power or success and create for themselves an illusory sense of superiority. They may be most prone to delusions of grandeur and strive to counter the evils of the world. Individuals with the fanatical paranoid style may develop elaborate schemes for coping with a world gone awry and recruit followers into their scheme. Millon and Davis (2000) described the religious leader

Jim Jones, who led his followers to mass suicide in 1978, as an example of someone with the fanatical paranoid style. Paranoid delusions, mania, and psychotic episodes may be more common among such individuals.

CASE EXAMPLE

Mark is a 41-year-old warehouse manager for a national distribution center. He is currently in a second marriage, which has lasted 2 years. His recent marriage followed an 11-year period after his divorce in which he dated very little. His first marriage was at age 19 and lasted for 9 years. The relationship was often tumultuous but was also marked by periods of pleasure and security. This relationship deteriorated as the result of repeated periods of conflict, which eventually led his wife to request a separation that ultimately resulted in divorce. He presents for therapy with his new wife, at her insistence, because problems are beginning to occur in the current relationship.

Two factors contributed to Mark's new wife, Marie's insistence that Mark seek therapy. First, although she loves Mark, she is becoming increasingly frustrated with his constant criticism and questioning. By her report, Mark has a very specific view concerning marriage and each partner's role in the relationship. Although he is certain that he is fulfilling his role—to the point of accepting no criticism from Marie—he frequently tells her what to do and checks up on her to make sure she is doing what he thinks she should be doing. When she fails to live up to one of his expectations, he is hypercritical and insulting.

The second topic of concern is that Mark calls Marie at her workplace at least four times each day. Although the conversations are not typically confrontational, the purpose of these calls, as Marie sees them, is to check up on her and to make sure that she is not doing something that Mark does not want her to do. Mark is somewhat hesitant to agree, but he admits that he calls to see how she is doing and that it gives him reassurance to talk to her. He reports that he has tried several times to resist the urge to call, but he just gets more anxious and desperate to call. Over the past year, Marie has tried to negotiate a schedule in which Mark could call twice each day, but any agreement was short lived.

On the Millon Clinical Multiphasic Inventory (MCMI–III; Millon, 1997), Mark's scores revealed a profile most suggestive of the paranoid prototype. Not surprisingly, scores were also elevated slightly on compulsive personality and narcissistic personality. Nonetheless, paranoid personality was the more representative elevation. Also, the MCMI–III scores suggested a generalized anxiety condition with some evidence of an obsessive–compulsive pattern. Although Mark failed to meet DSM–IV–TR criteria for any one personality disorder, his profile was most consistent with a paranoid prototype.

Although Mark does not meet criteria for a paranoid personality disorder as defined by the *DSM–IV–TR*, his personality is prototypically paranoid and contributes to the experience of the clinical conditions. Effective treatment would require several specific outcomes. The optimal outcomes, given the presenting circumstance (i.e., marital conflict), would be an enhancement in the relationship between Mark and Marie and a decrease in Mark's anxiety and obsessive concerns. These changes will require attention to Mark's paranoid style.

TREATMENT OF THE PARANOID PROTOTYPE

The task in treating individuals with the paranoid style of personality is to alter their interpretation of threatening interpersonal encounters. For these individuals, biased interpretations set the stage for anxious and aggressive emotions and provocative and defensive behavioral reactions. As a result, before behavioral expressions can be addressed, it is necessary to lessen the suspicious cognitive style.

Individuals with paranoid personalities do not often come to therapy with the intention of getting help for their paranoia (Freeman, Pretzer, Fleming, & Simon, 1990). Although some individuals with a mildly or moderately paranoid style may report feeling overly sensitive to what others think and feel about them, the greater the paranoid makeup of the personality, the less the likelihood that paranoia or sensitivity will be the presenting complaint. It may be the case that most individuals with a paranoid orientation come to the attention of mental health workers as the result of a third party. For instance, a child or spouse may present with problems that are associated with their connection to the individual. A boss may be instrumental in referring an employee for treatment as a result of the stress created by that individual's provocative demeanor with coworkers. It is possible that the individual with a paranoid style may come to see a mental health professional with complaints about another person, with the hope of getting the therapist to validate his or her claims and accusations regarding that other person or, perhaps, group of people. In any of these cases, attention to paranoid personality attributes may not conveniently be the initial target of treatment.

The Therapeutic Relationship

The first task in treating the individual with a paranoid style is to establish a safe therapeutic relationship. Generally, such individuals do not make willing and enthusiastic psychotherapy clients (see Bernstein, 2001; Chiesa, 1996; Hamberger, Lohr, & Gottlieb, 2000). Their inviolable self-image renders them naturally resistant to the process of psychotherapy, and their view of others as incompetent, self-serving, and untrustworthy puts them in their defensive and provocative position. In the case example of Mark and Marie, any effort to get Mark to relax control over Marie's choices and behaviors would almost certainly lead Mark to a defensive and resistant position concerning therapy. Before any legitimate therapy can be pursued, the therapist must first create an environment where the client feels safe in relaxing his or her guardedness and is able to consider his or her suspicious-ness and defensiveness from new perspectives.

To foster a safe therapeutic environment for the client with a paranoid style, it is first important to allow the client time and opportunity to vent frustrations and concerns and to express personal perspectives on the present-ing problems. Because such clients typically offer a variety of irrational beliefs and conclusions, it is easy for the therapist to jump at any of a number of irrational distortions as a focus of cognitive therapy. For in-stance, a therapist could readily challenge Mark regarding his narrow view of marriage. However, jumping too quickly to challenge the client may prompt a self-protective, defensive reaction and a retreat from treatment. Although the client will tend to externalize problems during the initial phases of therapy, speculating on the motives, intentions, and faults of others, challenges to these externalizations offered too soon will not be beneficial. However, validating the client's claims may also create a perceived alliance that the therapist may have to violate or alter later, thereby threat-ening the therapeutic relationship. In the example of Mark and Marie, validating Mark's view of marriage may create problems later when the therapist confronts the rigidity of his views. The challenge is to strike a balance between confrontation and validation of concerns related to biased perceptions.

Second, to avoid a misrepresentative alliance, the therapist can validate the client's emotions related to his or her paranoid beliefs without validating the beliefs themselves. The therapist can "go with it," a phrase that refers to a practice of accepting every idea and belief expressed by the client as a possibility. By not confronting or challenging the client, but going with the belief as a possibility, the therapist takes a position of alliance from which to redirect the client's schema orientation. The following dialogues contain examples of a therapist's going with it:

> Client: I know that everyone at my office thinks that I should be fired.

> Therapist: No doubt that makes going to work very difficult.

* * *

> *Client:* My wife thinks I'm an idiot, and I know she wishes she had married someone else. I'm convinced she is trying to find an excuse to contact her old college boyfriend to see if he is unattached.
>
> *Therapist:* So, you're convinced that she is considering her options.
>
> *   *   *
>
> *Client:* Do *you* think my wife is having an affair?!
>
> *Therapist:* It does happen that wives have affairs, and I can see that this is very unsettling to you, but before assuming she is having an affair, let's consider all the information.

In these examples, the therapist has avoided an active confrontation of the client's belief by validating the affect and other consequences associated with those beliefs without validating the veracity of the belief. Through such responses, the therapist minimizes the chances of the client feeling threatened and defensive and maximizes the chances of creating an environment conducive to challenging the individual's paranoid schemas.

Balancing Imperative Polarities

The individual with a paranoid orientation is characterized by weaknesses on both self-enhancement and self-protection. The task of therapy is to decrease the client's perception of threat and defensiveness and to increase perceptions of and participation in pleasurable social and intimate activities. Thus, the individual's weakness on protection and enhancement must be bolstered. The adaptation level does not need to be significantly altered, but it is necessary to attend to periods of excessive activity and passivity, such as passive avoidance of social affiliation and intimacy and manic hostilities enacted as a means of self-protection. To alter the client's survival orientation, attention to his or her reproductive focus may also be necessary. This effort will involve increasing the client's concern for the perspectives of others to understand how others are perceiving and reacting to his or her personal behaviors. Indeed, one of the common characteristics of the individual with a paranoid style is quick speculation regarding the thoughts and intentions of others, typically biased toward the assumption of ill feeling and ill intent. Attention to automatic thoughts and to social perceptiveness and functioning should adequately resolve this imbalance.

Treatment Focus

To effectively alter the polarity balance and subsequently improve social and intimate functioning, several counteractive perpetuations must be addressed. It is necessary to deal effectively with the individual's suspiciousness and often delusional thinking, as well as with the associated interpersonal provocativeness and social avoidance. None of this, however, can be accomplished in the absence of a solid therapeutic relationship.

Cognitive Goals

Once the relationship is formed, the therapist can begin to prepare the client for the work of therapy. At this point, the goal is to help the person understand the advantages of abandoning the paranoid orientation. Unless the person comes to see advantages to processing social information differently, he or she is not likely to benefit from treatment. It may be useful to begin inviting the client to speculate with the therapist on how the client's beliefs originated, how his or her behaviors are perceived by others, and the possible motives behind the objectionable behaviors of others discussed by the client. As the client comes to consider these speculations presented by the therapist, the therapist can embellish the speculations, maintaining vigilance as to how the client is reacting to the speculations.

> *Therapist:* It seems that in many of the interactions and relationships you've described, there is a lot of concern over the motives of the person that you're interacting with.
>
> *Mark:* I don't usually trust other people to do the right thing.
>
> *Therapist:* That must make it hard to simply enjoy the interaction.
>
> *Mark:* I don't know, sometimes I enjoy others, often I don't . . . . It does seem to depend on whether or not they're doing what I think they should be doing.

Once this topic has been presented and the client is able to recognize his or her sensitivities to others, the therapist may then initiate some discussion concerning where those sensitivities may have originated, providing an opportunity to discuss childhood experiences that may have contributed to the paranoid makeup.

> *Therapist:* I can't help but to wonder where your concerns originated. Perhaps there were times in your younger life where it was very important that you watched out for yourself by watching out for others.
>
> *Mark:* I have had to watch out for myself my entire life!
>
> *Therapist:* This must have been quite difficult to do.
>
> *Mark:* I've gotten pretty good at it.
>
> *Therapist:* Have you ever imagined what it would be like to be able to simply relax and enjoy relationships?

Mark: I am sometimes able to do that.

Therapist: I wonder what gets in the way of your being able to do it all of the time.

Through such dialogue, the therapist is able to move the client into discussion of interpersonal sensitivities without provoking a defensive reaction. In the above exchange, the therapist has introduced the possibility of exploring early experiences and other factors that contribute to recurrent interpersonal problems. Either direction may be useful; a discussion of current problems may be more economical and less threatening, but consideration of childhood origins can contribute to a greater appreciation of current patterns of behavior and may prove to be a safer area of discussion for the client because no immediate threats are being activated. It may be most beneficial to allow the client to determine the direction of subsequent sessions, choosing between exploration of childhood origins and discussion of current interactions. For the client with a paranoid style, being allowed to determine the direction of treatment can minimize the impact of the concern these individuals have about the intentions of other people.

Although not necessarily critical to effective interventions, discussion of past experiences can help the client to understand that his or her orientation to situational demands reflects a pattern of childhood reactions implemented with the intent of adapting to situational demands. Through this discussion, the client may come to see his or her orientation to external realities as the outdated strategies developed in childhood as a means of remaining safe in a difficult and threatening environment. In this way, the client can develop some psychological distance between how the world is and his or her current perceptions. The therapist needs to be sensitive to the level of understanding available to the client; although some clients are readily able to explore the origins of their attitudes and orientation to situational demands, others are not psychologically prepared, willing, or even capable of thinking in such terms.

For many people with a paranoid orientation, a host of developmental factors have contributed to the paranoid makeup. Haynes (1986) listed seven specific historical contributions and four nonspecific historical determinants. Specific factors include

1. direct modeling of paranoia (e.g., a parent with a paranoid personality blaming others for his or her problems),
2. reinforcement of paranoid reactions (e.g., agreeing with the child who externalizes problems),
3. prompting of paranoid behaviors (e.g., blaming a teacher for a child's bad grades),
4. insufficient punishment of paranoid behaviors,

5. insufficient reinforcement for nonparanoid behaviors,
6. situational control of paranoid behaviors (e.g., reinforcing paranoia in specific circumstances), and
7. a history of confirmed suspicions.

Nonspecific factors include (a) living in an insular family, (b) aversive parent–child interaction, (c) inconsistency of behavior or stimulus–response chains, and (d) lack of reinforcement of appropriate social behaviors. Other factors discussed by Haynes included the impact of paranoid behaviors on others, contingency control of paranoia, disrupted social feedback system, and social skills deficits.

Discussion of these factors can be initiated and enhanced through administration and discussion of the Young Early Maladaptive Schema Questionnaire (Young, Klosko, & Weishaar, 2003). Identifying a maladaptive schema provides a focus for discussion and speculation concerning the origins of that schema orientation. For instance, Mark had high scores on the Mistrust/Abuse schema. According to Young et al., "patients with the Mistrust/Abuse schema expect others to lie, manipulate, cheat, or in other ways to take advantage of them, and in the most extreme form of the schema, try to humiliate or abuse them" (p. 211).

> *Therapist:* Your scores on the questionnaire appear to be consistent with the sensitivities to others that we have talked about. I wonder how this might have developed.

Therapist and client can then discuss early developmental influences, including family dynamics associated with mistrust and mistreatment, that may have contributed to this orientation.

Paranoia as Strategy

Either as a complement to or independent of the discussion of childhood experiences, the client and therapist can discuss the adaptive value of the client's hypersensitivities and defensiveness. In this discussion, the paranoia is described as a strategy rather than a core attribute—a strategy that is adaptive and in many ways quite reasonable, albeit overly active. The important advantage of this approach is that the paranoia is conceptualized as a strategy rather than as a defining feature of the individual, thereby decreasing the probability of defensiveness and resistance to therapy.

In addition to discussion of how the irascible mood, suspiciousness, and defensiveness are adaptive, client and therapist can also consider the consequences of this orientation. Essentially, the client and therapist conduct a cost–benefit analysis of the suspicious orientation. In fact, the client's commitment to therapy and change can be assessed by his or her willingness to consider alternative ways of processing information and interacting with others. To the extent that the client remains hesitant, the therapist can go with the client's concerns but remind him or her of the cost of that orientation.

At this point in the therapeutic progression, the clinician reveals the initial aspect of the pathologic process. In specific situations, the client jumps to rapid, automatic conclusions oriented to keeping him or her safe from sources of psychic or physical harm. Once activated, schema-based mode reactions are implemented, which include distorted thoughts and motives and ultimately maladaptive affective and behavioral reactions that are consistent with the various clinical conditions. By remaining ever attentive (i.e., oriented) to signs of threat, the individual with a paranoid orientation is constantly prepared to deal with those threats when they exist, an adaptive orientation given the expectation of harm. The problems lie in the perception of dangers that do not exist and the extreme reactions to any subtle threats that may occur. As a result, the automatic thoughts of these individuals are oriented to keeping them safe from exploitation and are thus biased to perceive threats where none exist (at least, of any substantial significance). Because these thoughts contribute to an increase in irascibility and provocativeness, alteration of these thoughts takes on primary importance in the sequencing of treatment.

From a cognitive–behavioral therapy perspective, several strategies are useful in ferreting out biased and problematic automatic thoughts. Guided discovery and a collaborative effort to discover the thoughts associated with recurrent feelings and reactions can lead the client to recognition of how immediate thoughts prompt more extreme and consolidated emotional and behavioral reactions. Therapist and client can then consider the evidence relative to the conclusions the client has drawn, trustworthiness of the information source, validity of the data, alternative pieces of data, and the like (see Freeman et al., 1990). The goal of this collaborative effort is to increase the client's awareness of his or her automatic appraisals of threatening circumstances. By considering the data and alternative explanations of information, the client is able to understand the arbitrary nature of past appraisals. To the extent that the client has come to distance him- or herself from the paranoia, the ability to challenge these rapid appraisals is tremendously enhanced.

Several distortions may be identified in the individual's automatic thoughts. For instance, *arbitrary inference* refers to the tendency to form extreme conclusions in the absence of confirming evidence. Similarly, the tendency to consider limited types or amounts of information reflects a *selective abstraction* distortion. In addition to other distortions, the individual with a paranoid style is prone to *dichotomous thinking*, such that events are either safe and predictable or severely threatening. In this context, people are good or bad, friend or enemy. Such polarized thinking is observed in the case example of Mark, who sees Marie as a good wife or harlot.

Several strategies may be useful for altering the individual's minidelusions. The term *minidelusion* describes the individual's tendency to form false beliefs that contribute to maladaptive reactions. These delusional thoughts constitute violations of core beliefs and conditional assumptions. For instance, in the example of Mark and Marie, Mark believes that others, his wife in particular, should be loyal and defer to him. However, he also believes others to be inherently untrustworthy. Thus, he expects his wife to violate his belief about how wives should behave. Further, he believes that if he is not constantly vigilant of her behavior, she will violate his code of wifely conduct. Although an understanding of the source and implications of a hypersensitive orientation may lead to a decrease in the paranoid orientation, it may be necessary to more specifically attend to the persistent minidelusions.

For instance, Baker and Morrison (1998) described a verbal reattribution procedure for treating delusional thoughts that coincides well with the personality-guided model described in the current volume. In this process, the clinician would direct Mark to generate alternative explanations and conclusions concerning Marie's behavior anytime he experiences anxiety associated with Marie's untrustworthiness. Mark could be directed to monitor threat-activating thoughts to identify the belief and to generate a rebuttal to the delusional belief that helps to create a less threatening reaction. Mark could be instructed to monitor those situations that prompt the minidelusions, identify the associated emotion, and generate a cognitive rebuttal to the initial thought, noting as well the subsequent emotion. This procedure is effectively paired with efforts to alter the irascible mood of the client.

Through use of this procedure, Mark would be able to develop greater control over his cognitive and emotional reactions and subsequently over his impulsive behavioral reactions. To the extent that his emotional reactions reflect specific Axis I conditions, this procedure leads to direct relief from the affectively experienced clinical condition. If Mark has already created some psychological distance from his paranoid orientation, the benefit of this procedure would be tremendously enhanced.

When the client fits a paranoid style, the clinical conditions are part of the individual's efforts at self-protection and enhancement. For Mark, efforts were directed at enhancing the pleasure he received from his marriage by actively managing his wife's behaviors and by protecting himself from the pain associated with his wife's violations of his expectations. In important ways, the clinical conditions such as anxiety, depression, hostility, and so forth are the affective components of behaviors Mark implemented to provide some form of protection or to secure some form of pleasure. Subsequently, to simply target the symptoms of the clinical condition without altering the underlying personality attributes creates an uphill clinical challenge marked by client resistance and poor treatment outcomes. Understanding the personality attributes contributing to those clinical conditions directs therapy to the core factors contributing to the clinical condition.

Behavioral Goals

If the therapeutic relationship is secure, the therapist may provide the client with feedback on his or her interpersonal style, and role-play scenarios can be introduced as both example and change practice (Freeman et al., 1990). It may also be useful to ask the client to solicit feedback from close others whose opinion he would respect and not feel threatened by. As another strategy, the therapist, after securing the permission and comfort of the client, may elect to use in-session videotaping with immediate feedback as a means of discussing the client's interpersonal style. For those clients with greater amounts of paranoia, the therapist can provide the client with the videocassette at the end of the session, perhaps adding the task of watching the video between sessions. The importance of this task is to have the client understand his or her own contribution to problematic interactions and to adjust his or her interpersonal style in such a way that the probability of a positive engagement is maximized.

Once the client has come to feel some degree of security in interpersonal relationships, he or she can be encouraged to venture out and seek pleasurable interactions with others. It is most beneficial to have the client focus on safe targets, or persons around whom he or she generally feels safe and who therefore pose little threat. In the case of the prototypical paranoid personality, such targets are generally available, whereas for those with a more severe personality disorder, safe targets may not exist outside of the therapist's office. In marital situations, the target is most often the spouse; however, when the spouse is the source of paranoid ideations, a safer target may be preferred. A friend, family member, or specific coworker may be a good target. This task may require preliminary discussion of basic social skills that the client with a paranoid personality may lack. Indeed, if the client has nurtured a paranoid orientation, it is quite probable that he or she has not had the opportunity to develop appropriate social skills. In this regard, it is best to offer the client direction in social skills that have the greatest likelihood of leading to positive reactions from others. Although assertiveness is indeed a valued attribute in most cases, for the individual with a paranoid style assertiveness may appear too readily as defensiveness and provocativeness. Skills that foster positive interpersonal relationships would be more valuable.

Equipped with cognitive rebuttal strategies for fending off feelings of interpersonal concern and sensitivity, the client can learn to engage others in a positive form of discourse and to interact with others in a more positive, gracious, and prosocial manner. Often it is useful to have these clients do thought experiments, in which they imagine the outcome of different ways of interacting with others. In this process, the client is encouraged to "try on" different interpersonal strategies and, importantly, to consider how a particular style of interaction would be interpreted and responded to by others. Through this exercise, the client develops adaptive interpersonal skills that contribute to an increase in the pleasure orientation and greater empathy and interpersonal awareness that contribute to a greater balance on the reproduction imperative.

Success in therapy requires that the client with a paranoid style develop realistic expectations concerning what is to be gained in the interactions and a repertoire of responses to the common discourse of interpersonal engagement. In many cases, the individual may have a skewed perspective regarding what is to be gained in a relationship with others, thinking that each interaction is a competition for dominance. In such situations, conversation with the client is typically sufficient to encourage an adjustment in his or her attitude. In more serious cases, particularly when the paranoid style begins to approximate a personality disorder, more specific measures may be necessary to prompt a change in a competitive attitude.

Because the client has developed a pattern of social avoidance, as therapy progresses the client may frequently escape or avoid interactions that he or she finds threatening in some way. The therapist should prepare the client to enter threatening interactions equipped with realistic expectations and a repertoire of coping reactions in case things do not go well. Because it is highly likely that the client will encounter others who are themselves critical and caustic, it is necessary that treatment involve discussion and practice of strategies for coping with such inevitabilities.

CONCLUSION

The paranoid prototype is characterized by a general feeling of distrust. In subtle form, individuals with a paranoid style may possess relatively minor fears that others will harm, exploit, or deceive them; in more blatant form, they possess obsessional certainties that others will act in harmful, exploitive, or deceptive ways. As a result of these suspicious concerns, those with the paranoid prototype personality develop a protective resolve in their self-image, rigidity in their view of others, and an ever-ready affective tone necessary to drive defensive reactions. Indeed, they live life under a constant state of siege and must maintain a defense of their fragile sense of self-integrity. As part of their suspicious and defensive posture, these individuals are particularly vulnerable to several clinical conditions, including anxiety, panic, anger, depression, and delusional thinking.

Successful treatment of clients with a paranoid personality requires an alteration of the paranoid orientation, which can be accomplished only with careful consideration of the therapeutic relationship and sensitivity to the reactant style of the client. In a safe therapeutic environment, the client can be guided through a discovery of the source of his or her paranoid-styled orientation, the adaptive nature of the orientation, and the associated interpersonal and clinical consequences. Subsequently, the therapist can assist the client in altering biased assumptions and in developing more adaptive forms of behavioral expression and interpersonal engagement.

4

THE SCHIZOID PROTOTYPE

Key phrase: Indifference
Evolutionary focus: Autonomy, detachment

The general indifference to life felt and expressed by the individual with a schizoid style is seen in the balance of the imperative structures (see Figure 4.1). The schizoid personality is weak on both self-enhancement and self-protection. Such individuals neither watch for painful outcomes nor seek pleasurable opportunities. They are passive adapters who simply react to events as they occur and take very little proactive action to create a more hospitable environment or to protect or defend personal rights. Unlike the individual with a paranoid style of personality, persons with a schizoid style of personality do not vacillate between protection and enhancement but remain at the lower ends on each pole. They have an average orientation toward the self; they attend to basic needs and show little concern with the attitudes, intentions, or needs of others. Similarly, they see others as providing essentially no rewarding value. Their lack of concern with others may make them more vulnerable to exploitation. Because they tend to be nonconfrontational, other people may not hesitate to make unreasonable requests or demands or to treat them with disrespect.

As an example, Alice, a 24-year-old college graduate currently working in an art studio, is pursuing therapy because of depression. Alice has never been strongly interested in social relationships, being more interested in the arts and in solitary activities. She has found, however, that interactions with others are difficult to avoid. Recently, social engagements have been expected at work, and she has come to see herself as socially defective. The

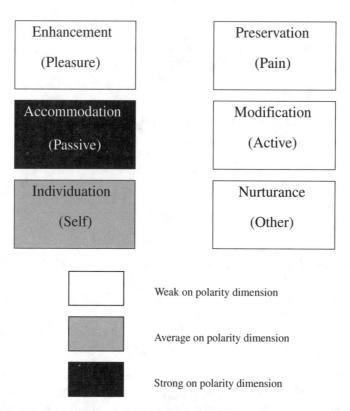

Enhancement (Pleasure)	Preservation (Pain)
Accommodation (Passive)	Modification (Active)
Individuation (Self)	Nurturance (Other)

Weak on polarity dimension

Average on polarity dimension

Strong on polarity dimension

Figure 4.1. Polarity balance of the schizoid style. From *Personality-Guided Therapy* (p. 285), by T. Millon, 1999, New York: Guilford Press. Copyright 1999 by John Wiley & Sons, Inc. Reprinted with permission.

studio where she works occasionally holds exhibits for local artists, and the staff of the studio take on the responsibility of hosting receptions for the artists. The two times that she has been involved, Alice completed the task without enthusiasm and was not proactive in socializing with the artist and patrons of the exhibit. The studio owner confronted her on her lack of enthusiasm on both occasions. Alice is concerned that her job may be in jeopardy. Another exhibition is coming up in the next few weeks, and she is not optimistic that she will do better in this next opportunity to host the exhibit.

PERSONALITY-GUIDED COGNITIVE–BEHAVIORAL CONCEPTUALIZATION

The personality attributes of the schizoid prototype and their possible liabilities are presented in Table 4.1. The schizoid personality is associated

TABLE 4.1
Structures and Functions of the Schizoid Prototype and Associated Liabilities

Personality domain	Liability
Self-image Complacent	Lack of ability to see the self as in need of change; little self-reflective thought
Object representations Meager	Few intimate or meaningful relationships with others; no perceived value of interpersonal relationships
Morphological organization Undifferentiated	No clearly defined sense of interest or purpose guiding life decisions; tendency to go with the immediate situational flow in a disengaged manner
Mood and temperament Apathy	Emotional unexcitability; action compelled by desires, urges, or impulses, not emotions; typical lack of reactiveness to subtle or critical situational demands
Behavioral acts Impassive	Little passion, enthusiasm, fear, or other strong emotion in carrying out actions
Interpersonal conduct Unengaged	General lack of interaction with others except in curious, obligatory fashion
Cognitive style Impoverished	Absence of thinking in terms of implications and options; tendency to interpret and respond to events with concrete, narrow, indifferent frame of reference; schemata not clearly defined or extensive
Regulatory mechanism Intellectualization	Little emotional investment in dealing with more complex concerns; matter of factness; black-and-white thinking

with a *complacent* self-view. Such individuals are not generally dissatisfied with themselves and resist the efforts of others to engage or motivate them. Unlike avoidant personalities, those with a schizoid personality prefer to be left alone. They view others as intrusive and are unengaged in interpersonal relationships. Individuals with a schizoid style of personality are commonly found in jobs that require very little interaction with others, such as independent laboratory work, computer programming, and the like. Those who are required to work with these individuals find them difficult to motivate and often frustrating to be around, although easy to exploit.

The core beliefs of the schizoid personality (see Beck, Freeman, & Associates, 1990) are characterized by such statements as "I am basically alone," "Close relationships with other people are unrewarding and messy,"

"I can do things better if I'm not encumbered by other people," and "Other people only get in the way." There is a relative absence of the anguished thoughts or associated feelings that characterize the avoidant personality. When the schizoid makeup is not so severe as to constitute a personality disorder, the apathy may be accompanied by various feelings of anguish, self-contempt, or longing.

The intermediate beliefs of the schizoid personality include conditional beliefs related to the implications of getting too close to others or to others getting too close. For instance, a person with a schizoid personality may believe, "If I get too close to people, they will get their hooks in me" or "I can't be happy unless I have complete mobility" (Beck et al., 1990, pp. 51–52). The instrumental beliefs include, "Don't get too close" and "Don't get involved" (p. 52). By maintaining their distance from others, individuals with a schizoid style are able to remain detached from relationships, intimacies, and obligations.

The typical affective tone of individuals with a schizoid personality is *apathy*, which underscores their general demeanor of indifference. There is simply not much that these individuals get excited about. Although they are often unhappy and may in fact display a generally flat, somewhat dysphoric affect, they perceive isolation as preferable to interaction. They may get together with others for specific reasons, such as for occupational activities, but otherwise they prefer to remain distant. However, when forced into social interaction, these individuals may feel anxious and even panicky, not necessarily because they do not perceive themselves as having what it takes to function socially but, rather, because they find it burdensome. They are quickly threatened by any actions that represent encroachment by others.

Individuals with a schizoid personality style are not as much avoidant as indifferent—they do not think about interacting with others and would prefer not to. Their cognitive style tends to be *impoverished*; these individuals are not inclined toward introspection and are not attentive to subtle or even many blatant social cues. Individuals with a schizoid personality are *impassive* in their actions. They are not proactive and are often stubborn in their willingness to act on their own or another's behalf. Considering these characteristics, it is not surprising that these individuals are not often seen in individual therapy.

PATHOLOGIC PROCESS OF THE SCHIZOID PATTERN

For individuals whose schizoid style of personality falls short of meeting the *Diagnostic and Statistical Manual of Mental Disorders* (4th ed., text revision; American Psychiatric Association, 2000) criteria for the disordered condition, matters are both better and worse than for those with full-blown schizoid personality, for whom the world and its varieties are so removed from their experiences as to be meaningless and thus nonproblematic, at least in a direct manner. As the result of detachment from the self, there is minimal anguish over unfulfilled desires and goals. For those with a schizoid style, there is enough interaction with the social world to render them susceptible to the impact of unpredictable and sometimes volatile interpersonal events. Similarly, with some greater degree of self-awareness and introspectiveness, those with a schizoid style must cope with greater intrapersonal thought and anguish.

Because of the general indifference expressed by those with a schizoid personality and the detachment they feel from their emotions, they are not commonly seen in outpatient settings, although as Millon pointed out, they may be seen in halfway houses that cater to the homeless population (Millon, 1999). When they do appear in outpatient settings, it is typically through the actions of others and is not self-initiated. For instance, a frustrated wife who married the man she did because of his "easygoing" disposition comes with her husband for marital therapy because of her frustration with his lack of intimate engagement or lack of initiative, or an employee is referred for evaluation and treatment by her employer, who is concerned that she is being taken advantage of by other workers. Clients with a schizoid personality style, particularly those with the remote variation (described later in this chap.), may be seen in community mental health programs, likely through the action of a community worker who came in contact with the individual through a non–mental health program, such as a soup kitchen or shelter. Nonetheless, the individual with a schizoid style is vulnerable to various clinical syndromes that emerge as a consequence of the personality style.

AXIS I VULNERABILITIES

For individuals with a schizoid style, clinical conditions emerge relative to their felt obligation or desire to interact more interpersonally. For instance, they may experience anxiety because of their perceived obligation to function at a higher social level or as the outcome of their own sense of social alienation.

Generalized Anxiety Disorder

Although not generally common among those with the schizoid personality, the individual may develop symptoms characteristic of a general anxiety syndrome when pressured at work or by other obligations to interact and function in a broader social environment. The anxiety in this case serves to fuel the hypervigilance the individual feels relative to the threatening situation. Often this vigilance relates to feelings of frustration related to the obligation and the desire to be left alone. In the case of the schizoid personality disorder, the degree of detachment may be so great that the individual reacts even to forced interactions in a disengaged and indifferent manner. In the case of the schizoid style, the individual does not maintain the extent or degree of detachment and subsequently is more vulnerable to the subtle implications of social responsibility and social failures. The individual with a schizoid style may retreat from activities in response to anxiety. In such cases, retreat provides a sense of relief from the felt obligations and thus a reduction in anxiety. His or her general indifference to life contributes to the ease of retreat, as he or she may have little personal investment in the job, activity, or affiliation.

Somatoform Disorder

The general detachment of the individual with a schizoid style of personality may be reflected in somatic complaints. Indeed, somatic concerns may stem from anxieties felt in social situations and can serve multiple adaptive purposes. For instance, the somatic symptoms may provide some sense of meaning or focus in an otherwise barren existence. Further, the somatic complaints, which may be associated with the anxiety related to interpersonal or occupational expectations and pressure, may provide opportunity for disengagement. Unlike others with somatic complaints, the individual with a schizoid orientation is not likely to complain to others about somatic symptoms, except to report to a superior the reason for work absence, but instead keeps the symptoms to him- or herself and provides self-directed treatments. By nurturing the condition, the individual is provided some relief from other obligations.

Obsessive–Compulsive Disorder

Obsessional concerns occupy the time and experience of the individual with schizoid personality style, independent of social stimuli. Indeed, the indifference to social activities that is common with the schizoid style leads to a cognitive void that may be filled by nonsocial obsessional thoughts. In fact, these obsessions and the associated compulsions may serve as an avoidant strategy that releases the individual from the need to affiliate more in burdensome social and intimate relationships. The reclusive hoarder may be more common among those with a schizoid personality style; the preoccupation with objects of obsession may provide relief from the aversiveness of greater social participation and a sense of immediate enhancement in the absence of other forms of pleasure (Rosenthal, Stelian, & Wagner, 1999; Vostanis & Dean, 1992).

Depression and Dysthymia

The general demeanor of indifference and complacent self-image of the schizoid personality may create a degree of immunity to reactive depression. If one cares little about issues of social affiliation or personal advancement and status, there is little to become depressed about. However, for those with a schizoid personality style, rather than the personality disorder, resiliency to depression may not be as strong. These individuals may judge themselves harshly at times as they reflect on their meager interpersonal relationships, and they may at times feel isolated and lonely, which may contribute to episodes of depression. In addition, the treatment they receive from others could contribute to their perception of themselves as defective and thus stimulate thoughts associated with depressed affect. The example of Alice shows the relationship between the schizoid style and depression.

For Alice, the task of hosting the reception is a daunting and unpleasant responsibility. Although she initially took on the hosting job without genuine concern for its success, now that criticisms have developed concerning her performance, the undertaking has taken on greater magnitude. Although she had not typically given much thought to her general indifference to social affiliations, the current situation put her in a position in which she thought a great deal about her disdain for social activities. Her thoughts were associated with feelings of self-contempt ("What is wrong with me? Why can't I do this?") and frustration with the necessity of the task ("I don't care about the stupid reception. Why do I have to do it?"). These thoughts contributed to a feeling of hopelessness and a disengagement from the job. Although the depressed symptoms were unpleasant, the depressed feeling resulted in an inability to challenge her self-view and interpersonal tendencies and enabled her to pass the task to another staff member. In this context, Alice's depression was associated with her personality style and contributed to her ability to protect herself from an unpleasant task. For some, the withdrawal of the schizoid style is associated with a more general dysthymia.

Bipolar Disorder

Similar to the avoidant personality, the individual with a schizoid personality style may experience occasional bursts of energy and engagement that contrast with the person's typical demeanor. These bursts of engagement may emerge during times of high social demand or opportunity that the individual finds hopeful and enjoyable or as hostile defensiveness to perceived exploitations or heightened responsibilities (Millon, 1999). Although the reaction may be mediated by specific biological processes, for the individual with a schizoid orientation the manic or hypomanic reaction reflects a more or less spontaneous reaction to a circumstantial event. For instance, a 46-year-old tax attorney who had worked for years in a corporate office without ever socializing with his fellow attorneys erupted in a hostile rage when passed over for a partner's position that was given to a younger associate. His reaction was completely unexpected, considering his general demeanor. When discussing the eruption with his therapist, the attorney said, "I work my entire career doing a good job and not causing any trouble and just because I don't do dinner parties, I get passed over for a promotion I deserved. I had to let them know that it wasn't right."

For this individual, the assumption that his career success was based entirely on his productivity was justifiable, albeit somewhat naive. He had failed to consider and appreciate that the decision to offer an associate attorney a partnership was also a function of social factors and relationships. In addition, his failure to be more socially involved made it easy for him to be overlooked by the partners of the law firm. By quietly doing his work day in and day out, he had simply not made his way into the consciousness of the partners considering promotion. That he reacted to the disappointment with a hypomanic reaction reflected his polarized engagement with the world. He was either disengaged or ready to attack. He had no experience with reactions between the two extremes.

Depersonalization

As suggested by Beck et al. (1990), depersonalization may occur as a result of living a peripheral existence and of feeling isolated and emotionally distant from others. Individuals with a schizoid style of personality may experience a distorted sense of themselves and their surroundings (see Mellor, 1988; Rosenfeld, 1947). They may report that they feel "like a robot" or are "going through life in a dream." The depersonalization experienced by the individual may be a function of neurological processes similar to those observed in autism or schizophrenia. Depersonalization may also reflect the episodic extremes of the individual's disengagement with the world. When faced with circumstances that the individual feels some affective connection with, yet is unprepared to manage, depersonalization may provide relief from any sense of obligation to act in a way outside of the typical pattern of social disengagement. Indeed, a problem is not seen as a problem if it is not cognitively or affectively processed as such.

VARIATIONS ON THE TRADITIONAL SCHIZOID PERSONALITY

Although each of the schizoid varieties includes the social detachment and relative indifference of the schizoid prototype, each differs in terms of the degree of social participation or isolation and relative to the pathologic process and clinical outcomes. In the paragraphs that follow, each of the varieties is discussed in relation to those differences.

The *affectless schizoid* personality style displays compulsive features and maintains an almost autistic orientation to the social environment, which may suggest critical genetic and neurological involvement (Siever, 1992). Individuals with this style are somewhat singular in their focus on activities and rarely turn away from those activities to interact with people. They are very content living in the world that they create for themselves, focusing their attention on specific tasks. Their range of emotional expression is severely constricted and nearly nonexistent, as they are apathetic about almost everything. If they do not come to appreciate the adaptive value of social affiliation, they will develop little interest in therapy. The affectless individual is not highly susceptible to many clinical conditions. However, their "easygoing" indifference may lead others to take advantage of their tendency to avoid conflict. When exploited by others, the individual with an affectless schizoid style may become filled with personal or interpersonal frustrations that may fuel depressive, agitated, or even enraged expressions.

The *languid schizoid* personality style combines features of the depressive personality, including anhedonia, fatigability, deficient initiative, slow motoric and cognitive tempo, and lack of interest in socialization. Others may perceive persons with the languid schizoid orientation as lazy or colorless. They have few interests about which they feel excitement. Unlike the pure form of the schizoid personality, the individual with this style experiences a greater degree of emotional anguish, yet not to the extent that one might expect given the dearth of substance in the person's life, nor as great as experienced by those with a depressive personality. Such individuals may possess some degree of interest in social affiliations, but they perceive themselves as deficient in social appeal or skills and withdraw into a state of relative indifference, rather than anguishing over their lack of social affiliation. The person with a languid schizoid style of personality may experience anxious and depressive affect that should resolve once he or she develops greater social skill and confidence with his or her ability to foster rewarding social affiliations and intimacies.

The *depersonalized schizoid* personality style, as the name suggests, maintains attributes found in depersonalization disorder—that is, features often found in a schizotypal personality. Individuals with this style are disengaged from others and from the self. They appear distant and dreamy. They are rather void of thought, having little cognitive engagement with the outside world or with an internal world of thought and feeling. It is possible that the individual with the depersonalized schizoid personality style has developed a strategy of disengagement with the social environment that has served to provide some distraction from social threat or despair. For instance, in the face of perceived social expectation, individuals with a depersonalized schizoid prototype personality may disengage from reality and the demands of the circumstance. For these individuals, the task of therapy is to increase social engagement and decrease depersonalization. For instance, by teaching these clients adaptive social skills, along with increasing appreciation for the value of social participation, depersonalization becomes less necessary as a coping strategy.

The *remote schizoid* personality style combines features of the avoidant personality and, in some cases, the schizotypal personality. Distinctive to this schizoid style is a history of intense hostility and rejection that contributes to a profound repression of emotional experience and a general withdrawal from pleasurable activities. Thus, similar to the avoidant style of personality, the remote schizoid style of personality associates interpersonal interactions and relationships with painful emotions; yet, unlike the avoidant style, this personality has abandoned any desire to be more socially accepted and engaged. Millon suggested that the remote personality is often found in homeless people and in those who are chronically hospitalized and living on the margins of society. The task of therapy is to engage such individuals with social activities.

TREATMENT OF THE SCHIZOID PROTOTYPE

Treating the individual with a schizoid style of personality yields a host of unique therapeutic challenges. First, because the individual does not typically present for treatment on his or her own, motivation for treatment is not strong. Second, because the individual does not desire greater social affiliations and finds little pleasure in other activities, there are few incentives to keep the client invested in the therapeutic process. Finally, as Beck et al. (1990) pointed out, even when the individual with a schizoid style of personality does present with Axis I symptoms, there is typically little motivation to pursue remedial attention to deeper personality attributes; thus, the client may not be interested in addressing issues related to his or her personality. Successful treatment of the client thus involves ongoing attention to the client's appreciation for the value of therapy.

The Therapeutic Relationship

As is the case with most clients, attention to and concern with the nature of the therapeutic relationship are important (Beck et al.,

1990; Freeman, Pretzer, Fleming, & Simon, 1990). This concern takes on particular relevance in the treatment of clients with a schizoid style because of their general indifference and lack of motivation for change and the process of therapy. Unlike treatment of most clients, treatment of clients with a schizoid style of personality must include selling them on the value of therapy (exceptions to this often include the antisocial, sadistic, and dependent styles). This need creates a unique ethical issue: Although the therapist may be able to explain how personality attributes contribute to the clinical syndrome that motivated the initial presentation for treatment and how attention to these factors can lead to enhancing outcomes, it is up to the individual to determine whether to undertake additional work.

Whereas most clients are motivated for treatment by the lack of meaningful social relationships and intimacies and by the aversiveness of the Axis I syndromes, the individual with a schizoid personality style is relatively indifferent to social relationships, so this source of motivation is weak or absent. In addition, the therapist does not automatically become a meaningful source of human connection. It is the challenge of the therapist working with these clients to provide a positive and encouraging environment that will maintain the client's motivation for treatment without overtaxing his or her tolerance of unpleasant encounters and situations. The challenge to the client with a schizoid style is to increase interest and engagement in pleasurable activities, to take greater adaptive initiative to avoid painful encounters and experiences (e.g., to avoid and counter negative behaviors of others), to increase active participation in enhancing life events, and to develop a greater concern for personal matters along with a greater sensitivity to the needs and ambitions of others.

The ambivalence of the client with a schizoid style regarding interpersonal relationships must be addressed prior to any deeper therapeutic effort. To this end, the therapist must be able to demonstrate the safety and reward of intimacies, which can best be accomplished by the therapist's demonstration of warmth and acceptance, thereby offering a positive side of human connection. At a minimum, the client should come to appreciate that although a relationship with another person may not be optimally necessary or critical, it can enhance, in multiple ways, the quality of his or her own existence. For instance, the client may come to appreciate the value of interpersonal relationships as they relate to occupational success and advancement, to improved familial relationships, and to greater proactive control over occupational, familial, and social choices. In fact, this can prove to be one of the more powerful motivators for clients with a schizoid style, because their general indifference often puts them in a position to be taken advantage of in various ways by others.

CASE EXAMPLE

Stanley was a 31-year-old laboratory worker in a university extension office that provided services to local poultry farmers. He was a conscientious worker and had held the same position for several years before problems began to emerge. He was referred for treatment by his boss, who was concerned that Stanley had become a "powder keg waiting to explode." These concerns stemmed from the boss's observations that Stanley was becoming increasingly frustrated by coworkers' tendency to pass on unpleasant tasks to him and to take advantage of him in various other ways (e.g., telling him to clean and lock up at the end of the day so they could leave early). The boss had observed this pattern for some time but had initially thought that if it really concerned Stanley, Stanley himself would say something about it.

However, Stanley was showing other signs of becoming increasingly frustrated. For instance, the boss had observed Stanley slam down a piece of laboratory equipment one afternoon, and he interpreted this as a sign of impending trouble. This episode compelled the boss to talk to Stanley about seeing a therapist. Stanley's willingness to come to see the therapist was consistent with his tendency to simply accept others' directions. He was not enthusiastic about the visit but did not put up any objection, and he did show up at the appointed hour. When the therapist discussed the situation behind the referral with Stanley, it was apparent that he was indeed getting very frustrated and that he felt ill equipped to do anything about the situations that he faced. In response to his building frustration, Stanley was contemplating quitting his job. He was not considering other work options, only quitting his current job.

The therapist discussed with Stanley the advantages of becoming more proactive in fending off abuses and finding pleasures outside of work:

Therapist: It seems like your coworkers have come to assume that you don't have anything else going on, so they may as well ask you to stay later or do the unpleasant jobs.

Stanley: Yeah, probably.

Therapist: I wonder if they've simply figured out that all they need to do is ask you, and you'll agree to do those jobs they don't like.

Stanley: Yeah, I'm sure they do.

Therapist: It would seem that our spending time talking about how to avoid being taken advantage of by your coworkers would be time well spent.

Stanley: Yeah, I guess so.

Therapist:	I wonder too if it would be useful if we talked about things that you do outside of work. I suppose that if you had things that you enjoyed outside of work, it would not be as easy for you to agree to do the extra work.
Stanley:	Yes, I'm sure you're right. I always agree to do the work because I know that I don't have anything better to do, and they do.
Therapist:	I wondered if that might be the situation. It would make sense then that we also talk about things that you would find enjoyable.
Stanley:	I don't know what they would be, but I guess we could talk about it.

To connect the client with the value of interpersonal relationships, the therapist and client, as suggested by Beck et al. (1990, p. 130), can discuss the functional and dysfunctional aspects of social isolation and indifference. For instance, although it is the case that isolation keeps one safe from the criticism and demands of others and from the need to coordinate one's own choices and actions with those of others, the practical value of relationships is lost. By having such clients observe others, which they are often not used to doing, the therapist and client can discuss the practical value of having others upon whom one can depend for assistance and encouragement.

Assuming that the client works in an environment with others, opportunities for observation should be readily available. Should those opportunities not be available, the client can make casual observations of others in public, or the therapist and client can discuss the practical value of relationships observed in television programs or movies. It may be helpful to assign the client the task of watching a particular film that depicts social affiliations that the therapist is familiar with and then to discuss the social relationships shown in the film (see Sharp, Smith, & Cole, 2002; Wedding & Niemiec, 2003). Through the interactions with the therapist and discussion of the functional value of relationships, the individual with a schizoid personality style will be in a better position to tolerate the tasks necessary for greater gains associated with changes in the personality style.

Therapist:	Were you able to watch the film I suggested last week?
Client:	Yes, I watched it.
Therapist:	Did any of the characters stand out for you?
Client:	Not really, maybe the guy somewhat.
Therapist:	Do you mean Oscar, the man who fell in love at the end?

Client: Yes, that's the one.

Therapist: Let's talk for a bit about what was going on with Oscar.

Through discussion of the character in the movie, the therapist and client can identify the value and necessity of relationships and the challenges faced by each of the characters relative to relationship maintenance. Throughout this focus, the therapist needs to be careful not to be too casual about the ease of fostering relationships and should present topics and suggest changes at a pace that is challenging to the client without being overwhelming.

These discussions should also reveal the client's cognitive triad. Once revealed, the therapist and client can discuss strategies for altering these beliefs. It is important for the therapist to keep in mind that the client's willingness to commit to the treatment program is dependent on his or her increasing appreciation for the value of intimacies. Once the individual has gained some appreciation for the value of relationships, he or she can be encouraged to venture into other interpersonal encounters. In order not to overwhelm the client, a gradual increase can be arranged in such a way that the odds of successful interaction can be maximized. For instance, the therapist may arrange for the person's involvement in a group therapy encounter.

Because of the aversiveness of early socialization experiences and the absence of subsequent socialization opportunities, the individual with a schizoid personality style may be lacking in basic social skills. The therapist can assess the client's social skills by having the client role-play various social situations in session. If deficits are noted, the therapist can focus on the client's acquisition of social skills. Once these skills are established, the client will be better prepared to pursue pleasurable outcomes with the greatest probability for success.

With an emerging appreciation for a connection with others and developed social skills, the client is now prepared for greater social interactions. At this point in therapy, the therapist can have the client complete a thought log to monitor self-statements and other cognitions that can be addressed in session. If the therapist has done an adequate job of establishing the foundation for the value of relationships and intimacies, these cognitions can now be discussed relative to those earlier points of discussion.

As the client begins to approach more social interactions, previously unacknowledged painful emotions and Axis I symptoms may emerge. The therapist and client will need to anticipate these events and discuss means for countering unpleasant feelings. For instance, as the client is encouraged to engage more with others, it is likely that anxious emotions will emerge. The client should understand that this is to be expected and should be reminded of the purpose of anxiety (i.e., heightened vigilance). Also, contingency plans should be arranged in case the anxiety becomes overwhelming. In this case, the means for an appropriate exit from the interaction, complete with adaptive self- and other statements and gracious and confident behaviors, can be discussed and designed. By making these preparations, the individual is less inclined to leave an interaction with self-defeating and externally critical attitudes that may undermine future efforts to broaden his or her social interactions and compromise his or her motivation for therapy.

Through these efforts, the client will develop a more active participation in life. This participation can be accentuated through discussion and focused treatment oriented at increasing active modification and decreasing passive acceptance of environmental events. Further, this treatment approach also increases the client's sense of self-awareness and of the intentions and behaviors of others with whom he or she interacts.

CONCLUSION

The schizoid personality prototype is characterized by a complacent self-image, interpersonal indifference, and generally apathetic mood. Individuals with a schizoid style are typically not interested in intimate or otherwise enhancing interpersonal relationships. They tend toward great passivity and look only to themselves as sources of validation and enhancement. As the result of their general indifference to social matters and passive orientation, they are somewhat immune to the negative consequences of greater interpersonal affiliation and social participation. However, their lack of positive affiliations and affective indifference often put them in a position to be easily taken advantage of by others, and at times they may struggle with personal feelings of isolation and social alienation.

At the level of a personality style best characterized by the schizoid prototype, these individuals may be described as calm and easygoing, slow to anger, and often very accommodating. At a stylistic level, these persons may seek out and enjoy social and intimate affiliation, but typically not with a great deal of concern. When social affiliations go awry, individuals with the schizoid personality may take it well in stride. However, as the style is characterized more by a schizoid disorder, the sense of alienation felt and tendency to be isolated, overlooked, or exploited increase, bringing a greater potential for various clinical outcomes. Treatment of this client population targets the development of a greater appreciation for the value of social participation and enhanced ability to function in the interpersonal world. The task of therapy is often to convince these clients of the benefit of greater social participation.

5

THE SCHIZOTYPAL PROTOTYPE

Key phrase: Eccentric
Evolutionary focus: Independence, estrangement

The defining pattern of the schizotypal polarity balance is an unstable weakness at each of the polarities (see Figure 5.1). Individuals with a schizotypal style are not compelled by a specific pleasure orientation or general pain avoidance but vacillate between high and low ends on both poles. They may impulsively jump at opportunities for activities that appear fun or interesting, with little concern over the consequences or implications. Their passivity underscores their lack of proactive initiative and lack of clearly defined goals or ambitions. They tend to go with the flow of the social current they find themselves in, which most often involves affiliation with individuals who are similarly disenfranchised or disassociated with the common or popular social culture. At times, they may act on opportunities for pleasurable and enhancing activities and display a highly active engagement with situations related to that activity.

For example, William is a 24-year-old who quit going to college two courses short of graduation. When asked why he stopped, he replied, "I don't know, I guess I just got bored." His college performance had been less than impressive, and he had never been able to settle on a major. When he stopped, he had no specific plans and spent his time "hanging around with friends." He was able to sustain himself by getting occasional support from his parents and through a series of jobs at local restaurants, usually doing dishes or other menial work. He was reasonably content with this level of subsistence, but when the opportunity to teach English to children

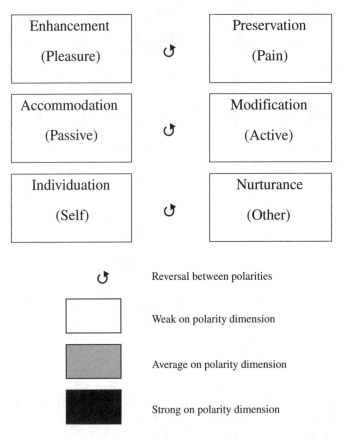

Figure 5.1. Polarity balance of the schizotypal style. From *Personality-Guided Therapy* (p. 618), by T. Millon, 1999, New York: Guilford Press. Copyright 1999 by John Wiley & Sons, Inc. Reprinted with permission.

in Kenya came up, he jumped at the opportunity without thinking about his qualifications, the actual task facing him, or the requirements of travel to Africa. He proved to be a less-than-optimal teacher. He did not take the task very seriously, and after repeated efforts by the administrators of the school to get him to prepare his lessons, they eventually asked him to return home.

Although individuals with a schizotypal style are not strongly oriented to deriving pleasurable outcomes or maintaining self-protection, they may act with some intensity to derive pleasure or to avoid aversiveness given the situational demands. Similarly, their focus may cycle between high and low self- or other focus. Thus, at one point they may attend to personal thoughts, including fantasies and images, and at another time focus on the behaviors and presumed intent of others. Predicting the orientation of such individuals is quite challenging; if they are anything consistently, it is eccentric and unpredictable.

PERSONALITY-GUIDED COGNITIVE–BEHAVIORAL CONCEPTUALIZATION

The attributes of the schizotypal personality are shown in Table 5.1. The individual with a schizotypal style maintains a self-image that is difficult to pinpoint and describe. As explained by Millon and Davis (2000), the self-image of the individual is *estranged*, a term that identifies the lack of a specific and defining self-view. The sense of self is most often defined by current perceptions and interpretations, which are typically judged by others as strange and only tangentially, if at all, related to the circumstance. It is not uncommon for the individual with a schizotypal personality style to experience periods of depersonalization, derealization, or dissociation (Wolfradt & Watzke, 1999), all of which underscore the strangeness of this personality style and the estranged sense of self of individuals with this style.

One individual with a schizotypal orientation being treated in an inpatient facility concluded that he was in fact dead and was living in a state of metaphysical limbo. Multiple times during the day he would present to his therapist looking for confirmation of whether he was either dead or alive; he sensed that he was dead. Such individuals' view of others is similarly estranged; they see others as "different than me" and as "potentially dangerous." This view underscores the source of anxiety that these individuals feel in social interactions and the hypervigilance they maintain regarding others.

The core beliefs of the individual with a schizotypal style relate to this sense of estrangement. For instance, the individual may believe, "I don't fit in with others," "I need to keep myself safe," "I live in my own world," or "Friendships are for other people." Conditional beliefs relate to the threat they feel from the external world. For instance, they may believe, "If I interact with others, they will be able to sense my feelings and thoughts" or "If I engage with people, I may become lost." Subsequently, they develop instrumental beliefs related to remaining safe from these external threats. For instance, they may believe, "If I create my own world, I will not have to deal with the other world." Because of these individuals' self-estrangement, they may have a difficult time developing insights into their own core beliefs. In fact, the core beliefs of the individual may not be very stable or well defined, making it difficult to target specific cognitive errors and distortions.

The schizotypal personality is expressively *eccentric*. Others are inclined to view the behaviors of these individuals as strange, odd, or peculiar; they simply act in ways that are curious and strange to others. This eccentricity

TABLE 5.1
Structures and Functions of the Schizotypal Prototype and Associated Liabilities

Personality domain	Liability
Self-image Estranged	No clear, defining sense of purpose or value, possibly contributing to feelings of depersonalization, forlornness, and emptiness
Object representations Chaotic	Lack of a history of consistent and self-defining relationships, resulting in failure to derive a clear sense of self; inability to identify self via association with others or create own sense and definition of identity
Morphological organization Fragmented	Loose ego boundaries; easily influenced character, vacillation between different ideas and motives; impulsivity
Mood and temperament Distraught or insentient	Feelings of isolation and hopelessness; general indifference and imperviousness to people and events
Behavioral acts Eccentric	Engagement in actions viewed by others as strange and peculiar; intentional or naive violations of social norms
Interpersonal conduct Secretive	Lack of pursuit of social engagements; tendency toward isolation and avoidance; preference for activities that are low profile
Cognitive style Autistic	Poor social perceptiveness; inability to read interpersonal cues well; tendency to draw bizarre or strange conclusions about others; attention to senses rather than memory or logic
Regulatory mechanism Undoing	Use of appeals to unconventional resources to deal with stress; impulsive, emotionally based (sensed) reactions to circumstantial events

is often seen in their awkward interpersonal style, which frequently includes bizarre, idiosyncratic phrases and gestures. Their attire is also unique. For instance, one man with a schizotypal personality wore women's capri pants that he had purchased at a second-hand store, along with mismatched basketball shoes. When asked about his unique attire, he would comment, "I don't know, I just felt like wearing it." This phrase, although somewhat dismissive, may be reasonably close to the truth. Individuals with this style of personality often do things that are judged as strange by others, just because they "feel like it." They are not necessarily looking to prompt critical reactions in others, although some may enjoy this more than others.

Persons with a schizotypal orientation are interpersonally *secretive*, preferring private activities and peripheral vocational roles. They are often uneasy in interactions with others and unskilled in common social discourse, which contributes to their tendency to be awkward and bizarre. Rather than engaging in common discourse about personal matters, these individuals may give a bizarre response that serves to evade personal discussion. Their cognitive style can be described as *autistic*, a term Millon used to reflect the ambivalence concerning social interactions, poor social perceptiveness, and limited social acumen of these individuals. The person with a schizotypal style often knows that others view him or her as strange yet does not fully appreciate the negative impact of his or her behavior; one individual, reporting how he had failed to secure a job following a recent interview, was surprised when the therapist suggested that the attire he had chosen to wear to the interview might have been judged negatively.

Millon described the affective nature of a person with schizotypal personality as *distraught* and *insentient*, terms that describe the agitation and mental conflict characteristic of such individuals. They are uncertain of themselves relative to the broader world and are ambivalent about participating with the social world, feeling on one hand that social affiliations are unavoidable and on the other that they would like to avoid them all. Their inability to foster meaningful and consistent relationships contributes to their feelings of social isolation and recurrent despair associated with social exclusion.

PATHOLOGIC PROCESS OF THE SCHIZOTYPAL PATTERN

The passivity and comparative lack of concern over self-protective and enhancing outcomes puts those with the schizotypal personality in a vulnerable position relative to the pathologic process and clinical outcomes. In many situations, they remain more or less indifferent to consequences related to social affiliations and basic survival concerns. Others who are concerned about these individuals are more distressed than the individuals themselves. At other times, these individuals may be very aware of their social alienation and may struggle with feelings of anxiety and self-contemptuous despair. Indeed, some struggle recurrently with feelings of meaninglessness. When this occurs, symptoms of anxiety, episodes of depression, and periods of dissociation may arise. Awareness of their estranged social position contributes to feelings of anxiety, which may then be followed by depressed feelings and potentially by a cognitive and affective denial derived through dissociation. As a final point, the secretiveness and eccentric behaviors often contribute to legitimate problems in interpersonal affairs, and the social awkwardness these individuals exhibit can contribute to a cascading assortment of personal and interpersonal reactions culminating in various clinical outcomes.

AXIS I VULNERABILITIES

For individuals with a schizotypal prototype personality, clinical conditions emerge relative to the distress associated with social participation and social estrangement. Being unable to create a sense of purpose and meaning through their relationships, they struggle with feelings of isolation and estrangement.

Generalized Anxiety Disorder

Of all Axis I clinical syndromes, the individual with a schizotypal style may be most vulnerable to generalized anxiety, although not necessarily of a chronic variety (Millon, 1999). Anxiety symptoms are most likely to develop at two relatively distinct periods. First, when the individual perceives threats from the social environment, anxiety is probable, particularly in circumstances in which he or she faces demands or expectations with which he or she feels unprepared to cope. Second, when the individual senses his or her estrangement from the self and from others, periods of anxiety may develop. Anxiety is most likely what motivates the individual to present for treatment. The anxiety may be experienced as some form of somatic complaint or phobic condition, both of which may serve to detach the individual from social discourse and the felt obligation to pursue greater interpersonal intimacies. In this way, the person remains relatively safe from painful social encounters.

Depression

Those with the schizotypal personality may be vulnerable to depressive conditions associated with their lack of fulfilling social participation and lack of life meaning. Depression serves a particular role in keeping the individual safe from social threats and failures, although not without the disappointment of social isolation and absence of meaningfulness. Given their unique and eccentric persona, these individuals often do not fit in well with a typical social group and are subsequently vulnerable to conditions associated with perceptions and feelings of social isolation.

Depersonalization

Individuals with a schizotypal personality style live in a semidepersonalized state, which means that they do not connect well with the social environment and feel generally estranged from others. These feelings of estrangement from self and others may be expressed as depersonalization (Wolfradt & Watzke, 1999). Considering such individuals' uncertainty and anxiety in social situations, combined with a tendency toward fantasy, recurrent depersonalization seems reasonable and probable.

Disorganized Schizophrenia

The person with a schizotypal style is particularly subject to disorganized schizophrenic disorders (Millon, 1999). The disorganization and social estrangement characteristic may develop into a disorganized form of psychosis. Indeed, the line between schizotypal personality and schizophrenia may be quite thin (see Johnson, Tuulio-Henriksson, & Pirkola, 2003; Tienari, Wynne, & Laksy, 2003).

VARIATIONS ON THE TRADITIONAL SCHIZOTYPAL PERSONALITY

Each of the schizotypal varieties includes the social detachment and relative indifference of the schizotypal prototype, but they differ in terms of the degree of social participation or isolation of the individual and relative to the specific nature of the pathologic process and clinical outcomes.

The *insipid schizotypal* personality style includes features of the schizoid, depressive, and dependent personality styles. Individuals with this style display a pervasive and seemingly bizarre detachment from the external world, marked by occasional reactions to a reality that they feel threatened by and unprepared to manage. They appear to others as physical entities more than social partners. In the extreme, disordered version of the insipid schizotypal personality, another person may look the individual right in the eye and feel no sense of another person looking back, only a disconcerting feeling that something is amiss. Similarly, the individual with an insipid schizotypal style may feel no personal connection with the self. As described by Millon and Davis (2000), some individuals with a schizotypal style feel "hollow" or "dead" or like "automatons." They feel little connection with the outside world or with any inner experience that would define an identity. These individuals exist in a type of depersonalized state, detached from an internal or external reality. The individual described earlier who felt that he might be dead is an example of an individual with the insipid schizotypal style. As a result of their lack of a sense of self, and without a clear external source of identity, such individuals become passively dependent and must rely on others for sustenance. They may occasionally struggle with bouts of severe depression associated with their sense of alienation from the world. During periods of isolation and despair, these individuals may consider suicide as a means of dealing with their sense of estrangement (Overholser, Stockmeier, Dilley, & Freiheit, 2002).

The *timorous schizotypal* personality style combines avoidant and negativistic features. Unlike individuals with the insipid schizotypal style, individuals with the timorous schizotypal orientation are somewhat more connected with the external social world. However, they are apprehensive and suspicious, remaining guarded in their interactions with others. These individuals use apathy and indifference as a way to cope with their social anxieties. Being more aware of and engaged with, albeit anxious about, the social world, these individuals maintain a degree of hypervigilance characteristic of the avoidant personality that enables them to stay attentive to threats from others.

As part of the unique thinking style, individuals with a timorous schizotypal personality style may attend to things in the social world that others miss and that may be unrelated or only remotely related to social issues. For instance, such individuals may remain highly attentive to the temperature of a room as a means of determining the attitudes of others toward them. Likewise, they may engage in somewhat bizarre behaviors as a means of remaining safe—for example, keeping their muscles stiff throughout the duration of an engagement. Feeling estranged from the social world, individuals with a timorous schizotypal style are likely to create a unique, internal fantasy world. For instance, a fascination with metaphysical phenomena leads an individual to imagine teleporting to distant countries and planets, occupying him or her in a manner that is independent of and safe from actual human social engagement.

TREATMENT OF THE SCHIZOTYPAL PROTOTYPE

Individuals with a schizotypal personality style do not often present for therapy; however, self-referral for therapy may be more common than referral by others, reflecting the awareness of many of these individuals of their social estrangement and awkwardness and the disappointments associated with a meaningless existence. In such cases, the task of therapy is to help the individual function better in a social environment. For example, Michael presented for therapy with symptoms of social phobia. He reported that other people frequently commented that he was strange and that he, personally, had always felt different from others and that he just did not fit in well. He added that he did not, however, want to be like everyone else and that he felt frustrated that others seemed to want him to conform to their ways of living. He admitted that this created a conflict, but he indicated that he would like to have adult relationships. Michael and his therapist agreed to a treatment plan that involved attention to his social relationships with the intent of improving their quality and quantity. They also agreed that they would discuss and negotiate the changes to be made, working to find the balance between healthy affiliation and the maintenance of Michael's unique identity. In this arrangement, it was necessary for the therapist not only to maintain an open mind regarding Michael's ideals but also to foster and maintain a trusting relationship that would allow her to challenge Michael's hesitations and irrationalities.

To promote social participation and affiliation, the individual with a schizotypal style must be able to derive greater pleasure from interpersonal activities and to avoid the scorn and ridicule of those with whom he or she associates. Because such individuals are rather indifferent to how they display themselves to others or may even attempt to present themselves in a somewhat outlandish fashion, they are targets for criticism, avoidance, and rejection. Although some may revel in this rejection, others are more distressed by it and struggle with recurrent feelings of dysphoria. To help decrease that vulnerability, the therapist can encourage the client to be somewhat more attentive to issues related to hygiene, grooming, and social presentation (Freeman, Pretzer, Fleming, & Simon, 1990). It may be necessary to build the case for these changes because the client may perceive such suggestions as an assault on his or her identity and as acquiescence to social standards he or she personally rejects. As another example, Alice was a college student at a select university where most students were very conservative in attitudes and attire. Alice saw herself as different and did not want to be "a sheep like all the other students." She tended to dress in ways viewed as bizarre by the other students. She often wore mismatching socks and did not wash her hair, which she usually wore in mismatched pigtails fixed by various rubber bands and other accessories. She frequently wore shirts that displayed political attitudes that were contradictory to the general attitudes of the student body, and she found pleasure in making comments that others were either confused or amused by.

The therapist pointed out to Alice that given the culture she found herself in, it may be unrealistic to think that she could win the acceptance of the others while also promoting her own self-focused ideals. The therapist made it clear that this did not mean that she needed to simply conform like all the other students in terms of attire and political attitude and observed that it would be helpful to be sensitive to how she is presenting herself so that she can maximize the benefit of social affiliations while promoting her own identity and values. The therapist presented these ideas to Alice as a means of striking a balance of cooperation and mutual respect.

In addition to interpersonal adjustments, the therapist could also implement specific cognitive strategies. Freeman and colleagues (1990) pointed out that treating the individual with a schizotypal style often relies more on behavioral interventions than cognitive strategies, but that thinking is not so bizarre or delusional that cognitive interventions are doomed to being lost in the maze of peculiar cognitions. It is useful to these individuals to develop a keener understanding of how their thoughts are unique and how they contribute to various interpersonal problems and negative emotional states. It is particularly beneficial to have these clients monitor their thoughts and behaviors in a log, making note also of the reactions of others. Completed monitoring forms can then be used for in-session discussion. Discussion in session that helps link the clients' perceptions with their emotions and actions can contribute to a greater understanding of their own contribution to interpersonal problems and can provide opportunity for discussion of change options and opportunities.

Because individuals with a schizotypal prototype personality tend to wander into fantasy, which contributes to their inability to follow and maintain common and appropriate social discourse, it is often necessary to implement specific strategies to control fanciful thinking. For instance, to help Michael control his distracted thinking style, he and the therapist could role-play repeated social interactions, having Michael monitor his tendency to go off task and prompt himself to remain on task. Michael could also practice staying on task and engaged in role-play scenarios by asking appropriate questions concerning a topic presented by the therapist as a topic of social discourse. Through this approach, Michael could develop greater skill and confidence concerning social affiliation. Similarly, this approach should decrease his tendency to wander into cognitive fantasies that distract him from the flow of the social discourse. For instance, he observed his own tendency to wonder about the other person's life away from the conversation, including speculation about the person's hobbies, childhood experiences, and other possibilities.

In situations in which the individual's thoughts become delusional or psychotic, the therapist could introduce treatment strategies useful in controlling the thoughts of people with schizophrenia. For instance, Baker and Morrison (1998) reported a verbal reattribution strategy implemented to help patients with schizophrenia gain increasing control over psychotic thoughts.

One of the defining features of the individual with a schizotypal orientation is lack of social skills, most notably, perhaps, a lack of social perceptiveness. Such individuals are often either unaware of how their behaviors and appearance are perceived by others or simply indifferent to or humored by it. Often, individuals with a schizotypal personality will gravitate to sub-cultures in which their peculiar demeanor, behaviors, and attire do not stand out as noticeably. Although this may provide somewhat of a buffer to recurrent social rejection, the individual may, even in these cultures, struggle in interpersonal relationships and occupational activities.

Because of these individuals' eccentric and peculiar ways, it is often necessary to direct a large amount of attention to social skills training, including attention to social perceptiveness. It may be useful to videotape sessions for immediate playback and discussion to prompt the client's aware-ness of how he or she is perceived by others.

CONCLUSION

The schizotypal prototype is characterized by a general sense of es-trangement from others, eccentric and secretive behaviors, and a history of awkward and unfulfilling social affiliations and intimacies. The behavior of individuals with a schizotypal style is often unpredictable, and they frequently engage in behaviors that appear inconsistent and counterproductive. At the level of personality disorder, these individuals may be seriously handicapped by personality features associated with dissociative experiences, failure to accept and maintain reasonable responsibilities, and a chronic sense of social estrangement. At less severe levels, the schizotypal personality is associated with eccentric behaviors that may be a source of connection with others who enjoy the entertainment value of the eccentric style. At any level of severity, however, the schizotypal prototype personality contributes to the individual's sense of social alienation, which may be manifested in episodes of anxiety, states of depression, and periods of dissociation.

Successful treatment of clients with a schizotypal personality requires that they develop an appreciation for the value of social affiliation and take greater initiative in fostering more adaptive interpersonal relationships. It is often difficult to treat these individuals because their eccentricities often interfere with the therapeutic process by making it difficult to remain on task. To the extent that they are feeling some degree of despair as the result of social estrangement, individuals with a schizotypal style may express greater motivation for therapy. Nevertheless, the presence of a patient and nonjudgmental therapist is critical in providing a therapeutic environment in which these clients can confront and alter their idiosyncratic style of engagement and disengagement from the world.

6

THE ANTISOCIAL PROTOTYPE

Key phrase: All for me, to hell with you
Evolutionary focus: Freedom, pleasure, and predation

The polarity balances of the antisocial prototype are displayed in Figure 6.1. The antisocial personality is marked by a weak orientation on pain avoidance and self-preservation. Indeed, a common feature of this personality is the apparent indifference to punishment and other negative consequences. These individuals simply do not react to punishment in an optimally adaptive way, nor do they anticipate the punishing consequences of their actions. Their orientation to positive, pleasurable outcomes is approximately average, yet their pursuit of enhancing outcomes is more impulsive and less inhibited than that of others. Those with an antisocial personality do not reflect long on their decision to pursue an enhancing outcome and are relatively indifferent to the potential consequences of those decisions, both for themselves and for others.

When in pursuit of a pleasurable outcome, individuals with an antisocial style can be very active. Indeed, in extreme cases, they may go to considerable lengths to bring about a desired outcome. Their focus of attention is on personal gain. They do not think about how their behavior will affect others and often think of others only as obstacles or assets related to personal gain. At the point that others cease to be of some advantage to the individual with a severe antisocial orientation, he or she will end the affiliation. In less severe cases, an individual with an antisocial style of personality may not fully abandon a relationship but may meet only rudimentary aspects of responsibility to that relationship.

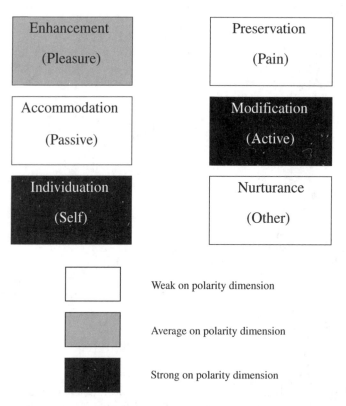

Enhancement (Pleasure)	Preservation (Pain)
Accommodation (Passive)	Modification (Active)
Individuation (Self)	Nurturance (Other)

Weak on polarity dimension

Average on polarity dimension

Strong on polarity dimension

Figure 6.1. Polarity balance of the antisocial prototype. From *Personality-Guided Therapy* (p. 466), by T. Millon, 1999, New York: Guilford Press. Copyright 1999 by John Wiley & Sons, Inc. Reprinted with permission.

For instance, Marilyn was a 36-year-old woman and parent of two. She was a less than ideal parent. Although she would see to it that her children were fed and clothed, she demonstrated little investment in the task of parenting beyond these basic behaviors. However, when the task of being an invested parent appeared to be advantageous to her, Marilyn's investment greatly improved—at least for the length of perceived benefit. Once the benefit ended, Marilyn again turned her attention to other, more personally enhancing activities.

Considering their imperative orientation, it is not surprising that individuals with an antisocial peronality are inclined to act aggressively toward others. They simply want things to go their way (i.e., in a personally enhancing way) and are willing to act out in aggressive and ethically dubious ways when events do not go the way they want. Similarly, when confronted by others regarding their inappropriate behavior or need to meet some socially consensual responsibility, they will implement whatever strategy necessary to avoid or escape that obligation, including manipulating others, lying, and conveniently forgetting.

PERSONALITY-GUIDED COGNITIVE–BEHAVIORAL CONCEPTUALIZATION

The self-image of the individual with an antisocial style is one of *autonomy* and self-advocacy (Table 6.1). He or she sees life as a competitive battle and views others as adversaries in his or her pursuit of pleasurable outcomes. The individual lives an antagonistic existence, constantly on

TABLE 6.1
Structures and Functions of the Paranoid Prototype and Associated Liabilities

Personality domain	Liability
Self-image Autonomous	Lack of thought about the impact of own behavior on others or welfare of others; no sense of obligation to conform to social rules or responsibilities
Object representations Debased	History of bad relationships leading to a feeling of entitlement or revenge
Morphological organization Unruly	High reactivity to environmental events, most typically social occurrences; poor reaction control
Mood and temperament Callous	Insensitivity to others, lack of compassion; tendency to be mean, hostile, and exploitative
Behavioral acts Impulsive	Poor behavior regulation; impulsive reactions with little concern for personal and interpersonal consequences
Interpersonal conduct Irresponsible	Lack of concern with interpersonal obligation and responsibilities
Cognitive style Deviant	Thought processes primarily in terms of personal benefit; rejection of conventional norms related to work and relationships
Regulatory mechanism Acting out	Lack of remorse following acting out; extreme responses to perceived criticisms and affronts

guard against affronts and the "unfair" treatment of others. The individual with an antisocial style is a master at externalizing problems. Often such individuals feel that they have been given a bad deal in life and are therefore justified in pursuing their desired ends by whatever means possible. Life is a battle to get what they want before others beat them to it. They do not care or think about the welfare of others or pursue interactions and activities for their own benefit, and they are not empathetic. They do not work well in a collaborative endeavor and do not give assistance without expecting reciprocation or compensation.

Needing to keep an advantage or defensive posture against others, the individual with an antisocial style relies on hostile, angry, and defensive emotions, including contempt and anger. Emotionally, the antisocial personality style is characterized by *callousness*. Individuals with an antisocial personality style are generally indifferent to the needs and feelings of others and can be vicious and sadistic without sympathy. Because guilty and remorseful feelings require a sense of obligation to others, these individuals either have never developed this capacity or have abandoned the effort to hold these feelings. Likewise, they have little capacity for empathy, seeing only how things affect them personally. Even when the adverse effects of their behaviors on others are pointed out, these individuals typically feel and demonstrate very little insight or concern.

The core beliefs of individuals with an antisocial personality style are not as specific as they might be in those with other personality styles. However, they likely relate to the belief that "I should be able to have what I want" or "It is everyone for him- or herself." The conditional beliefs of these individuals relate to their self-centered and defensive attitude. They may believe, "If I don't take what I want, someone else will take it" or "If I give others a chance, they will take what I deserve." The instrumental beliefs relate to the defensive posture of the individual; the statement, "I should take [or get] what I want" reveals the common attitude of those with the antisocial personality.

The beliefs of individuals with an antisocial style are associated with an *impulsive* behavioral style. These individuals do not think about the implications of their behaviors beyond the satisfaction of immediate needs and desires. They are *irresponsible* in interpersonal conduct, failing and refusing to accept or be concerned about the immediate or long-term implications of their behavior for others—at least the implications that are not directly related to them. Their cognitive style can be characterized as *deviant*, reflecting the individual's nearly constant concern with negotiating and manipulating a situation to his or her personal gain. This trait, in particular, renders individuals with an antisocial personality untrustworthy, although their deviant efforts can include an ingenuine social charm. Indeed, a socially adroit and charming individual can be very effective in winning the admiration and trust of others, only to exploit that trust later.

PATHOLOGIC PROCESS OF THE ANTISOCIAL PATTERN

Individuals with an antisocial personality encounter stress when their freedom or desires are threatened. These individuals are willing to go to relative extremes to bring about their desires, which may be material possessions, status, or freedom from responsibility. When events occur that threaten procurement of the desired outcomes, these individuals seek to protect their personal desires. The antisocial pattern is most typically observed when obstacles develop that thwart their ability to obtain a desired and pleasurable outcome or when others place on them burdens of obligation. Either condition will prompt a defensive or proactive reaction to ward off the threat or obligation. Psychopathology emerges, then, relative to the encountered obstacles and obligations.

The individual with an antisocial orientation wants to be able to work without obligation and criticism. Thus, he or she desires freedom from work obligations. When confronted by a superior to perform at a higher productivity level, this individual may perceive a threat to his or her freedom and may react to defend against the unwanted burden of responsibility. He or she may fend off criticism in an impulsive, aggressive, and callous manner. In addition, the individual may be oriented more to the attainment of pleasurable outcomes and may shirk responsibility to pursue that pleasure, independent of concern for others. For instance, one who desires sexual gratification or the intoxicating effects of alcohol and drugs may abandon family or employment obligations to pursue those pleasures. He or she ignores or minimizes the importance of responsibility and obligation through denial or rationalization.

Some individuals with an antisocial personality style may receive a diagnosis of impulsive disorder. However, it is notable that the diagnosis is not typically made until they are confronted with the consequences of the impulsive behavior. In the face of those consequences, these individuals may engage in a host of emotional and behavioral reactions, typically involving a negative and hostile response, that serve to defend against the threat of negative consequences. For instance, anxiety may be experienced in the form of hypervigilance to the negative consequences of antisocial acts (e.g., a paternity suit or litigation); anger may be implemented as a means of countering criticism; hostile mania may be expressed as a means of warding off multiple sources of consequence; and dissociation and somatization may be expressed as means of escaping consequence and obligation.

AXIS I VULNERABILITIES

As a result of their self-serving and confrontational style of engagement with the world, those with an antisocial personality style are vulnerable to numerous clinical conditions. In part, the extreme emotional and behavioral responses are enacted as a means to procure desirable outcomes and to deal with the consequences of their self-serving actions. The following sections describe the various clinical outcomes relative to the role in the pathologic process of the antisocial prototype.

Generalized Anxiety Disorder

Because those with the antisocial prototype personality view life as a competition in which they must get theirs before others take it from them, their lives are fraught with anxieties. Unlike anxieties observed in other personality styles that are characterized by the fear of negative events, these individuals are more inclined to fear that others will get advantages that they feel entitled to or simply want. Further, these individuals may encounter anxiety when forced to face the consequences of their actions. For instance, the consequences of legal action, financial crisis, or family collapse may precipitate tremendous anxiety symptoms in these individuals. They may respond with anger and resentment to confrontation, but anxiety may characterize their responses to unavoidable or impending consequences and responsibilities. It is also possible that the anxiety they experience is associated, directly (as physiological effect) and indirectly (through concern with legal consequence), with their frequent use of legally controlled substances.

Substance-Related Syndromes

For several reasons, the antisocial personality style is associated with various forms of substance use and abuse (von Knorring, von Knorring, Smigan, Lindberg, & Edholm, 1987; Whitters, Troughton, Cadoret, & Widmer, 1984). Indeed, their lack of concern with consequences renders these individuals highly susceptible to the use and abuse of mind- and mood-altering substances. Further, their high activity, need for excitement, and often extroverted demeanor frequently put them in environments where illegal substances are readily available. Substance abuse problems often contribute to poorer outcomes relative to other clinical conditions. When the individual is currently contending with a substance abuse problem, other concerns may have to be put on hold until the substance abuse problem is resolved.

Bipolar Disorder

As a result of their behaviors, individuals with an antisocial orientation are frequently forced to face unpleasant consequences. They are not likely to be overwhelmed by feelings of guilt or remorse, but they may still be forced to face aversive consequences from an unhappy spouse or other family member, a dissatisfied employer, a debt collector, or a legal authority. Because their prime intent is to protect themselves from negative consequences, these individuals may implement a host of manic-type reactions to avoid or counter negative consequences (Blackburn & Lee-Evans, 1985) or to manage circumstances related to pleasurable procurement. To be sure, when goal oriented, whether toward pleasure or protection, their behavior may very well fit a hypomanic pattern. The depressed phase of a bipolar condition may often be marked by periods of social withdrawal and binge substance abuse (e.g., Skinstad & Swain, 2001).

Somatoform Disorder

Somatic complaints have been shown to be associated with the antisocial personality style (Lilienfeld, 1992). One of the cardinal features of the antisocial style is the failure to accept personal responsibility for one's actions and the failure to accept responsibility for specific life obligations, such as wage earning and raising a family. For those with an antisocial style of personality, somatic complaints provide a convenient means of escaping critical life responsibilities and of securing the support and assistance of others (Lilienfeld, 1992). In some cases, the stress associated with the externally imposed obligation to meet life responsibilities may precipitate the somatic complaint and be maintained through secondary gain processes. In other cases, the somatic complaints may reflect either a factitious condition or malingering. In any case, the somatic complaints expressed by those with an antisocial personality are very often associated with their desire to avoid accepting important life responsibilities.

Dissociative Disorder

Similar to the process contributing to somatic conditions, individuals with an antisocial prototype personality may be vulnerable to the development of a dissociative condition. Indeed, the active denial of personal responsibility that characterizes the antisocial style is closely aligned with dissociation. When faced with responsibilities and obligations, the individual with an antisocial style may escape through dissociation. The release from perceived responsibility through episodic amnesia or fugue is quite consistent with a pattern of reaction seen with the antisocial prototype. The extent to which the dissociation is a genuine dissociative state versus malingering may be difficult to ascertain. Nonetheless, dissociation may prove to be an immediately adaptive response to unwanted responsibility and accountability.

VARIATIONS ON THE TRADITIONAL ANTISOCIAL PERSONALITY

Millon (see Millon, 1999; Millon & Davis, 2000) described several varieties of the antisocial style. In each of the variants, the style of interaction with the social environment is unique, as is the nature of the information attended to and processed. These differences create subtle differences in clinical vulnerability and introduce unique clinical challenges to which the therapist should attend.

The *covetous antisocial* personality style is a subtle variation on the traditional form and combines features of the narcissistic personality. The defining feature of this antisocial style is the sense of envy and entitlement. Those with this orientation feel that they were not given a fair advantage in life or that they have been deprived. Subsequently, they are determined to wrest from life all the bounty to which they feel entitled. A defining term for this group of individuals is *compensation*. Because they believe they were not given the advantages and resources they should have been, they dedicate themselves to making up for those disadvantages. Some enact this compensation through blatant criminal behaviors, and others do so by becoming entrepreneurs who use their business acumen to accumulate wealth and possessions and who may exploit and manipulate others for their own benefit and amusement.

Even without great economic success, these individuals will attempt to show off their accomplishments through pretentious materialistic displays. When creditors seek payments that the individual with a covetous antisocial personality style does not have, he or she may react with anger over the unfairness of the world. Because of their chronic feelings of emptiness and fragile feelings of self-worth, no matter what these individuals achieve or possess, as long as others have something more, they struggle with feelings of inadequacy and a desire to possess more. During periods of felt inadequacy, these individuals will direct angry and contemptuous emotions at those whom they feel responsible for their position in life, including parents and those who received the benefits that they did not.

Individuals with the covetous style are particularly prone to negative emotions such as frustration, contempt, and anger. Their quest for possession and its associated validation may contribute to manic displays of behavior.

When obstacles arise in their path, they may react with intense anger and aggressiveness, enacted directly (e.g., violence) or indirectly (e.g., passive-aggressiveness, manipulation, and lying). When events do not turn out as they might like, these individuals may become hopeless and depressed. However, their depression may not typically be of the passive–withdrawal type but is characterized more by expressed complaint and as justification for extreme actions and the avoidance of responsibility.

For example, Bill grew up in an economically disadvantaged home. His father abandoned the family when he was a child, and his mother remarried twice and, at different times, had three live-in boyfriends during his childhood. As a youngster Bill vowed that he would not be poor. He was able to get through college, although he was inclined to cheat on exams and papers, and after college he was able to secure a job with a national marketing firm. He was tireless in his quest for financial gain and advancement. He occasionally misrepresented figures on financial documents both to increase the appearance of company profit and to maximize his financial benefit. He encountered trouble on the job when a coworker accused him of taking credit for one of her accounts. When first approached about the situation, Bill was very defensive, lied about his handling of the situation, and generated numerous counteraccusations against the person bringing the complaint against him. He was seen in therapy through the company's employee assistance program, having been referred because of his anger. He felt that his forced involvement with the counseling office was unjust and refused to commit to further sessions.

The *nomadic antisocial* personality style combines features of the avoidant and schizoid personalities. Individuals with this style feel a general sense of alienation from the world of other people and form very few, if any, close or intimate relationships. They are most likely to be found living along the margins of society. As the name implies, they may often be among the vagabonds and drifters who live on the streets. The antisocial features are evident in their lack of concern for their own welfare and for how their behaviors affect others. They are inclined to act on opportunities that present themselves during their travels, which often include theft, prostitution, or some other illegal activity. They may also be found making use of homeless shelters, soup kitchens, and other social service providers, yet they are most typically physically and intellectually capable of holding full-time employment.

An example of the nomadic pattern is the case of Dwayne, who is 26 years old and has never held a job for more than a few weeks, typically with job service programs or restaurants. He has never quit a job by working out a notice; he simply leaves the job when he does not feel like returning. He has had periods in which he has stayed with someone who felt either an obligation or a desire to be helpful to him. Most often, these arrangements ended because Dwayne either stopped returning or was asked to leave. He was referred to therapy by a pastor at a soup kitchen who felt that Dwayne had many redeeming qualities and would benefit from efforts to help him "get focused."

The *malevolent antisocial* personality style combines features of the paranoid and sadistic personalities and is, in Millon's words, "the least attractive antisocial" (Millon, 1999, p. 112). (Considering the general unattractiveness of the antisocial personality, to be the least attractive of the group is a point of disreputable distinction.) Individuals with a malevolent antisocial personality style go through life with hostility and vengefulness that permeates nearly all aspects of their lives. They are constantly defensive and react aggressively to perceived affronts; they may escalate a conflict to whatever level necessary to come out on top. They are not opposed to physical aggression and may implement either direct confrontations and assaults or secretive attacks. They expect others to mistreat them and often deal with potential interpersonal threats by mistreating others first. When the sadistic features are more prominent, these individuals take pleasure in victimizing others (Millon, 1999).

The malevolent antisocial style is associated with various negative emotions, particularly frustration, anger, and hostility. Depression observed in individuals with this personality style often reflects a somewhat intentional effort to avoid or escape responsibility for a misdeed. They may also display episodes of mania reflecting efforts to procure some desirable outcome. When pursuing a goal, the ends justify the means, and these individuals will do what it takes to attain what they seek, even when this includes violating social norms and legal limits. Martin provides an example of the malevolent antisocial style; at age 24 he had already had several run-ins with legal authorities. He had been married for a short time, but he had gotten angry on several occasions and hit his wife, and the marriage ended after a major confrontation with his wife's father, who had aggressively confronted Martin about the way he treated his wife. Martin viewed himself as a rebel and everyone else as out to get him. He was quick to take offense to anything anyone said that sounded derogatory, and his defensiveness could easily turn to anger and violence. He entered treatment as part of a pretrial intervention program that followed a conflict he had encountered on a temporary job. Before being fired from his job, he had been accused of having taken tools from the job site.

The *risk-taking antisocial* personality style includes features of the histrionic personality. The antisocial features contribute to a devil-may-care attitude toward dangerous and risky behaviors that both shock and amaze others. Individuals with this personality style enjoy the attention they receive for engaging in behaviors others find too risky or dangerous. They revel in the opportunity to display and boast about their feats of daring and risk.

The individual with a risk-taking antisocial personality style will put others at risk to elicit the attention he or she desires. Although others are often amazed at the behaviors of these individuals, what they often fail to adequately comprehend is that their audience views the behavior as stupid, irresponsible, and foolhardy; if these views are expressed to the individual, he or she likely responds with satisfaction. Except for those with a similar fascination with danger, most people learn quickly to avoid interaction with these individuals.

The risk-taking antisocial style may be particularly associated with episodes of mania related to the quest for excitement. In such episodes, the implications and consequences of the activity are of little concern. Depression may be observed when the consequences come to fruition. Francis's behavior exemplifies a risk-taking antisocial pattern. She has always been drawn to adventure. She is an ultralite pilot, a skydiver, a BASE jumper, and a participant in a variety of other high-risk behaviors. In her mind, if she doesn't get "amped" by an activity, it is not worth doing. Her risk-taking behavior has gotten her into various forms of trouble. For instance, she has been arrested twice for illegally jumping off of a tower and a building. Her two marriages failed after each husband became intolerant of her adventure seeking and, in her case, its associated irresponsibility. She was forced to declare bankruptcy, and she has been treated twice for alcoholism and is a regular user of marijuana. Her employment history is also irregular. She has been in numerous automobile accidents, and several of these have resulted in injuries to others as well as to herself. Not surprising, Francis has recently been diagnosed with bipolar disorder.

The *reputation-defending antisocial* personality style includes sadistic features. An individual with this style takes defensiveness to its highest level. Needing the admiration of others, he or she will engage in behaviors thought to best lead to the validation and respect of the group to whom he or she is affiliated. When the admiration is not forthcoming, the individual may erupt into an angry and violent tirade meant to punish and scorn those who have failed to provide the respect and validation sought. Millon described the phenomenon of the "alpha male" as an example of the reputation-seeking antisocial orientation (Millon & Davis, 1999). For such individuals, it is critical to be "top dog" among the group, and they will use whatever means necessary to establish and maintain that position. The individual with a reputation-defending antisocial pattern may be prone to substance abuse problems, legal entanglements, euphoric and hostile manic episodes, and episodic depression.

As an example, Donna is a terrific hostess. She is a member of a number of social clubs and takes great pride in her home and garden. She is also a country club member and very active in club functions. She also likes for things to go her way. When others disagree with her, or even when they fail to validate her choices, she becomes mean and vindictive. She has a reputation that others often find intimidating, and she knows it and uses it to her advantage. She has been instrumental in having members expelled from the club and other organizations. When she has it in for someone, she will go to great lengths to meet her desired outcomes.

TREATMENT OF THE ANTISOCIAL PROTOTYPE

The individual with an antisocial personality style does not usually present for treatment unless he or she is forced to do so by others. Because such individuals are very good at externalizing blame for any difficulty they encounter, they see little use for personal psychotherapy. When they do seek therapy, it is most often because they have been ordered to do so by the courts or compelled by ultimatum to seek therapy by some significant other person, such as a family member or employer (Beck, Freeman, & Associates, 1990).

A debate exists concerning whether those with an antisocial personality disorder can or should be treated using psychotherapeutic procedures in an outpatient setting (see Freeman, Pretzer, Fleming, & Simon, 1990). In fact, some have suggested that to consider these individuals mentally disordered misrepresents the circumstance, and that *criminal* would be more appropriate (Freeman et al., 1990; Frosch, 1983). Although those with serious antisocial personality disorders may, in many ways, be hopeless candidates for genuinely effective psychotherapy, individuals who are closer to the antisocial prototype may benefit from therapy. Millon (1999) suggested that the defining feature of those with the antisocial prototype is their irresponsibility and impulsive acting out, rather than their maliciousness and cruelty. Helping these individuals to accept more responsibility, to be more cooperative and less defensive, and to develop greater behavioral and emotional self-control can result in significant therapeutic gains.

The Therapeutic Relationship

Treating the client with an antisocial personality style can be a considerable challenge. Although each client presents unique relationship challenges, clients with an antisocial style are particularly difficult because of their resistance to therapy, especially as this relates to their unwillingness to be sensitive to the needs and concerns of others, to accept personal responsibility for the outcome of therapy, and to accept occupational and social obligations. The therapist may develop a certain degree of dislike for such clients, particularly when their behaviors are self-serving, unethical, immoral, or otherwise reprehensible. Although this is more of a difficulty for the patient with a serious personality disorder, those with the antisocial style can also present hardship in fostering a therapeutic relationship.

It is helpful for the therapist to consider that the individual with an antisocial personality style has developed the most effective means available to him or her for deriving a sense of enhancement. Although these means are misguided, the desire for enhancement is not itself condemnable. Thus, the task of therapy is to help the individual develop more adaptive and respectful means of deriving desired feelings of enhancement.

Because an individual with an antisocial orientation typically has a history of problematic interpersonal relationships (object representations), problems may emerge in the therapeutic relationship. The therapist needs to be concerned with the possibility of being manipulated by the client, but it is also important to avoid the creation of a mistrusting and confrontational therapeutic atmosphere. It may be beneficial to assume that the client will misrepresent information. Although this should not lead the therapist to assume that everything the client says is a misrepresentation of the truth, it does imply that the therapist not take information obtained from the client too literally. When the client's efforts to deceive are blatant, the therapist can discuss with the client the disadvantage of such misrepresentation given the goals of therapy. If the therapist has created a good working relationship with the client and has presented the advantages of therapy, misrepresentations may be less frequent. The following are recommendations for working with this style of individual:

- Emphasize the collaborative nature of the therapeutic enterprise.
- Maintain a focus on the therapeutic task, staying vigilant to efforts to redirect or sidestep treatment issues.
- Avoid direct confrontation.
- Monitor one's own feelings to maintain control over and reflection on one's responses to the client's behavior.

As long as individuals with an antisocial style can do whatever they desire without obstacle or negative consequence, their lives progress smoothly. Unfortunately, because of the nature of life activities and the necessity of accepting responsibilities, these individuals are forced to manage the various obstacles to their autonomy and to manage the consequences of their indifference to the welfare of others. This description highlights the mediating role of personality in the perception of stressors and in the affective and behavioral endpoints implemented in response to threat. Individuals with an antisocial orientation are reactive to perceived threats to autonomy, and the actions they implement in response to those threats are often associated with various clinical conditions. Threats to autonomy occur relative to the desire to engage in a desired activity, avoid an unwanted obligation, or procure a desired object or substance. Effective treatment must then lead to a decrease in impulsive behaviors leading to aversive personal and interpersonal consequences, an increased sense and display of interpersonal responsibility, and an alteration of deviant cognitive interpretations.

Because those with an antisocial prototype are often impulsive in their efforts to protect autonomy, they are frequently confronted with the consequences of those impulsive actions; this confrontation often results in the cascading effects of repeated reactivity. Several cognitive–behavioral therapy strategies may be effective with these individuals as a means of decreasing reactive impulsivity.

Treatment of the Antisocial Pattern

The goals of treatment revolve around increasing the individual's awareness and control of self-serving impulsive actions and the associated interpersonal consequences and, subsequently, increasing behavioral self-control and interpersonal cooperation. The strategies described in this section are taken from the list of cognitive–behavioral strategies provided by Freeman and colleagues (1990). Although these strategies can be effective with numerous conditions described in this volume, they are highlighted here relative to the antisocial prototype.

Anticipating the Consequences

In the cognitive strategy of anticipating the consequences, the client discusses with the therapist future encounters, drawing on experiences from the past to anticipate possible reactions to situational events. Most important, the discussion focuses on the possible and likely consequences of impulsive behaviors. Particularly useful with this strategy is identification of important signs of impulsivity. For instance, the client may be encouraged to focus on the subtle reactions of others indicating that the behavior is problematic. Similarly, the client can be encouraged to focus on internal markers (e.g., accelerated heart rate) of excitement or anxiety, which often precede impulsive reactions. In either situation, client and therapist discuss the prompts to increase their saliencies and thus to increase the probability that the client will reflect on impulsive behaviors in those situations where impulsivity may be problematic.

Cued Awareness

The cued awareness technique involves the use of environmental manipulations designed to increase cognitive awareness of impulsivity. Based on the old strategy of tying a string around the finger, the intent is to introduce environmental signs that will capture the individual's awareness during those times that impulsive behaviors are likely. One individual inclined to angry outbursts at employees purchased a gaudy desk ornament that he could not fail to notice while looking across his desk at an employee. The purpose of the ornament was to remind him to control his impulse to yell. Another person placed a small blue dot (i.e., a piece of blue-colored tape cut into a small circle) in the center of her analog watch to remind her to think about her choices and her behaviors. Because she looked at her watch repeatedly throughout the day, she was regularly reminded to be cautious about her impulses. In both cases, the cue served as a discriminative stimulus for alternative behaviors. In implementing this strategy, therapist and client can collaborate to determine an effective cue.

Self-Instructional Training

Self-instructional training, described by Meichenbaum (1977), encourages greater self-initiative in monitoring ongoing behaviors. In this strategy, the client has the opportunity to develop a more pronounced internal dialogue guiding behavioral decisions by talking the self through a new activity. In this way, actions are more "thoughtful" and less impulsive. Gilbert and Bailey (2000) discussed the internal dialogue as a critical aspect of behavioral self-control. By way of self-instructional training, the individual with an antisocial orientation can develop greater internal control over impulsive, predatory activities. Through the expression of greater control of impulsive behaviors, the individual is able to avoid the necessity of dealing with the negative consequences of impulsive behaviors.

Acting "As If"

In the acting "as if" strategy, the individual can be encouraged to engage in behaviors that are inconsistent with his or her impulsive tendencies. Although individuals with an antisocial prototype personality may typically act on their own impulses, independent of others, they can act instead as would a person with greater concern for others. This strategy requires that the individual be invested in taking greater responsibility for fostering positive interpersonal relationships; it can be an effective means for developing greater impulse control and greater social sensitivity. For instance, the client can act "as if" he or she genuinely cared about the feelings or concerns of another person. Therapist and client can then discuss the outcomes associated with different ways of acting.

Empathy Training

In many cases, individuals with an antisocial orientation, as reflected in their object representations, do not encounter situations in which they are encouraged to think about the feelings of others and encounter, instead, situations in which they need to watch out for themselves. Several strategies may be useful in altering their interpersonal focus.

To get the individual with an antisocial style to take more responsibility for fostering good relationships and meeting interpersonal obligations, it is beneficial to increase his or her awareness of and appreciation for how others respond to and feel about a circumstance common to the individual with an antisocial orientation. Two strategies—taking another's perspective and film viewing—can foster greater empathy in these clients.

In taking another's perspective, therapist and client discuss various interpersonal situations, drawing from either common or personal (i.e., the client's) experience. The client is encouraged to consider the unique situation from the perspective of the different participants. This procedure places the client in the novel position of reflecting on other individuals' perspectives on a situation. This technique is enhanced by the degree to which the individual is able to connect affectively with the perspective of the other individual. Consideration of how the client might feel him- or herself in a given situation may be useful in this regard. This procedure is helpful in fostering greater interpersonal sensitivity and in creating better impulse control. Indeed, it is more difficult to act impulsively when one is aware of the implications of one's impulses.

With film viewing, client and therapist discuss characters depicted in a popular film. The advantage of this strategy is that it avoids personal defensiveness that might be elicited when discussing the client's personal interactions, and it provides targets for discussion that are often presented in very salient form, thus providing convenient opportunity for reflection and discussion. In many cases, the client, as a function of his or her callous temperament, may be inclined to be harsh, cynical, and judgmental. The client can be encouraged to consider the motives of the characters relative to a desire to procure self-esteem–enhancing outcomes, promoting the development of greater interpersonal understanding and sensitivity.

Other Treatment Strategies

As with other personality styles, it is often quite helpful if the individual is able to understand how his or her orientation to life is largely a function of a learned style of interaction with the environment and is not necessarily a reflection of inherent attributes that are not amenable to change. This understanding can be facilitated by helping the individual identify those developmental factors that contributed to the emergence of his or her personality style. The history of many individuals with the antisocial prototype is characterized by an emotionally and materially deprived background in which they had to fight for enhancement and protection; many others come from a background marked by pampered, self-centered indulgence. The outcome of these influences is the detached object-relations feelings and perceptions characteristic of individuals with an antisocial prototype personality. Through discussion of his or her historical influences, the client should be able to appreciate the relatively arbitrary manner in which he or she developed means for procuring enhancing outcomes and protecting the self from perceived threats.

Within this context, it is also useful for the individual to consider the cost–benefit outcomes associated with the antisocial pattern. By engaging in carefully directed discussion, therapist and client can consider the history of negative outcomes associated with the antisocial style and discuss future projections associated with a more other-focused, prosocial style. It is often helpful to have clients reflect on personal feelings relative to interpersonal affronts, as this helps them to take the emotional perspective of others. Although these suggested strategies are often not effective when treating an individual with an entrenched and personality-disordered antisocial orientation, it can be very effective in those with a nondisordered antisocial style.

Once the client has come to appreciate the value of changes in his or her interpersonal orientation and has developed a greater sense of responsibility for altering the interpersonal style, the therapist can introduce specific cognitive and behavioral strategies to help him or her develop greater emotional and behavioral self-control. The introduction of specific prosocial behaviors can further increase the client's resiliency to the various clinical conditions. The therapist can use two techniques to help the individual learn to control impulsive and provocative behaviors:

Social Skills Training. In many cases, the individual with an antisocial personality lacks basic social skills. Training may be required for such basic skills as eye contact, hand shakes, greetings, and the like or for more sophisticated social skills such as how to perform in a job interview. The primary objective is to help the client acquire the skills necessary to function appropriately in social situations.

Graduated Task Assignments. The therapist encourages the client to go out and build rewarding social affiliations and relationships. A significant component of this procedure is social skills training; however, it goes beyond social skills training in that the individual is assigned specific tasks requiring higher level social skill. For instance, the client may be assigned the task of doing a kind deed for another individual.

Because individuals with an antisocial orientation tend to interpret events in a self-serving manner, it is often necessary to introduce specific exercises for altering biased and self-serving cognitive interpretations. Individuals with the antisocial prototype personality often display problematic reactions based on problematic interpretations mediated by biased and distorted automatic, core, and intermediate beliefs. Two cognitive strategies may be useful in helping these clients alter deviant cognitions:

Challenging Absolutes. The core beliefs of the antisocial style typically reflect a sense of autonomy and entitlement. Beck et al. (1990) identified the core beliefs of the antisocial personality: "I need to look out for myself" and "I need to be the aggressor or I will be the victim." Reflected in these beliefs are absolutes that leave little room for exception and that often motivate self-centered and socially irresponsible acts. By challenging these absolute beliefs, the individual is able to consider situations from a renewed perspective and with less self-serving certainty. The challenging absolutes strategy can be implemented through in-session verbal discourse and reflection on data collected from cognitive self-monitoring procedures. The task is to help the client identify the absolute conclusions in automatic thoughts and core beliefs and to be able to generate alternative cognitions to counter those beliefs. Indeed, to the extent that the individual has come to accept responsibility for contributing in prosocial ways to interpersonal interaction and to appreciate the value of positive affiliations, this task is made more effective.

Labeling Distortions. Because the individual with an antisocial style is prone to various cognitive distortions, having the client learn to identify his or her distortions and to offer appropriate and optimally adaptive rebuttals can prompt schema changes. The client can maintain a cognitive log, and therapist and client can subsequently discuss the nature of the distortions. Once the client is able to identify the common distortions promoting self-serving reactions, he or she can engage in in-session rebuttals and in homework assignments in which he or she records and rebuts identified biases.

In treatment, the task is to help the individual with an antisocial orientation to develop renewed ways of interpreting external and internal events and to generate alternative strategies for responding to circumstantial events. Consistent with the immune system metaphor, by altering the interpretation of threatening situations by altering personality attributes, clinical outcomes are affected in positive and adaptive fashion. The following section provides a case example of an individual with an antisocial prototype personality.

CASE EXAMPLE

Bill, previously introduced in the description of the covetous form of antisocial personality, would fail to meet diagnostic criteria for an antisocial personality disorder, but he does present with an antisocial prototype, including features of the narcissistic prototype, as evidenced by his Millon Clinical

Multiphasic Inventory (Millon, 1997) profile. His Axis I condition is consistent with an adjustment disorder and impulsive anger (intermittent explosive disorder, or possibly bipolar disorder). Bill's anxiety stems from the precarious position that he finds himself in at work. His impulsive condition reflects his tendency to be reactive when his self-serving autonomy is threatened. In fact, his accusation of his coworker is an example of this impulsivity. Bill's anxiety and impulsivity are mediated by his unique personality attributes; were it not for his tendency to manipulate situations to his advantage, his anxiety and the specific impulsive patterns would not be evident.

To treat Bill's anxiety and impulsivity, the therapist sought an understanding of his antisocial prototype personality. Bill's core beliefs reflect his view of himself as autonomous. He has taken the initiative to escape his childhood background and to be successful, even if that means cutting a few corners and taking advantage of a few people. His impulsivity contributes to his tendency to make decisions that are self-serving without giving much consideration to the ethical and professional implications of his choices. His view of others is that they are both obstacles to his accomplishments and resources for his benefit. He strives for a sense of interpersonal superiority through financial gain. He interprets situations relative to his own benefit, with limited concern about others. When confronted, he responds by counterattacking, which he hopes will quell the attack and circumvent undesirable consequences.

The target of treatment was Bill's impulsive anger and current anxieties. It is important to note that the therapist did not challenge Bill's desire for status and advancement. The therapist suggested, however, that his strategies for achieving his goals were problematic because they put him in a position of recurrent reprisal by others. Had Bill's antisocial traits been more pronounced, he might have rejected these suggestions and ultimately the need for treatment. However, given the moderate extent of his antisocial attributes and his current situation, he was in a position to reconsider his life goals, cognitive beliefs, and behavioral tendencies.

Bill was first invited to consider the impact of his childhood experiences. Through this discussion, he was able to recognize how he had developed a reactive orientation against being poor and a dedication to financial gain. This discussion was important for two reasons. First, it helped to foster the therapeutic relationship, and second, it created a cognitive distance from the core beliefs. In this context, Bill was able to understand how his orientation emerged as a result of childhood experiences and was not simply an inherited and unalterable disposition.

It was determined that Bill's anger emerged as a means of removing obstacles to the outcomes he desired—in the recent circumstance, this included financial gain and freedom from confrontation by others. Bill recognized the functional value of his anger, and through discussion of the consequences of his anger expression he was able to understand the maladaptiveness of his callousness and hostility. In addition, he was able to recognize the internal cues preceding an anger response, which for Bill included a feeling of tension and hotness. The therapist encouraged Bill to respond to this cue by using a list of self-instructional statements to counter the anger response and to change his internal dialogue. The therapist might also introduce efforts to address cognitive distortions and challenge absolutes at this point.

In addition, Bill and the therapist discussed the likely responses of others to his anger. They recognized this anger as a relatively effective means for compelling capitulation in others, but also as entailing consequences, typically in the form of retaliation or relationship damage. To complement and build on the insights gained, Bill and the therapist discussed alternative reactions that would serve to enhance Bill's status and likely successes without the negative consequences. In this sense, enhancement was maximized and threat minimized. Various homework assignments were suggested to solidify those changes.

CONCLUSION

Clients with an antisocial prototype personality view themselves as independent of other people. Their thinking is typically self-serving and deviant from norms of social discourse and cooperation. They are often irresponsible and impulsive, and they may react aggressively to the demands and expectations of others. Their affective callousness contributes to distressed interpersonal relationships and a propensity for hostility. These individuals often find themselves having to contend with the consequences of their impulsive, callous, irresponsible, and self-serving actions. Spouses are often frustrated and angered by their actions, as are employers and coworkers. Individuals with an antisocial style see themselves as above the need to accept interpersonal responsibilities and are often indifferent to the hardship or inconveniences they create for others.

Although the antisocial prototype introduces unique clinical challenges, successful treatment can be accomplished by paying careful attention to the therapeutic relationship and structuring treatment in a way to minimize reactant resistance and treatment retreat. Successful treatment of those with the antisocial prototype personality involves the establishment of greater interpersonal sensitivities and personal responsibility. This can frequently be accomplished through cognitive–behavioral strategies that involve the development of new perspectives on interpersonal sensitivity and social discourse.

7

THE BORDERLINE PROTOTYPE

Key phrase: Don't abandon me
Evolutionary focus: Connection

The borderline prototype is marked by conflict between the polarities (see Figure 7.1). Stemming from their lack of a defining self-identity, individuals with a borderline personality style do not become settled at one end of a polarity or another but vacillate in a reactive and conflicted manner between extremes. These individuals may passively imbibe the pleasures of an intimate or social relationship but react with active hostility when ideals are challenged or threatened. For a period of time, their focus may be on the pleasurable and self-esteem-enhancing benefits of a particular relationship, but their focus can turn quickly to signs of abandonment, leading to impulsive and often extreme defensive and protective reactions. At times, actions are directed at securing a threatened relationship, and the focus is on the needs and actions of the other person or group of people. At other times, the focus may be specific to personal needs and feelings, with little concern for the feelings or reactions of others.

Although individuals with a borderline personality style maintain an overall average balance across polarity dimensions, they vacillate between extremes dependent on social and interpersonal circumstance. For instance, these individuals may pursue pleasurable outcomes with some degree of reckless abandon in situations in which they feel safe; but they may then experience tremendous distress over the possible implications of those behaviors and become obsessed with protective, pain-avoidant behaviors. Likewise, they may vacillate between periods of helpless dependence and active,

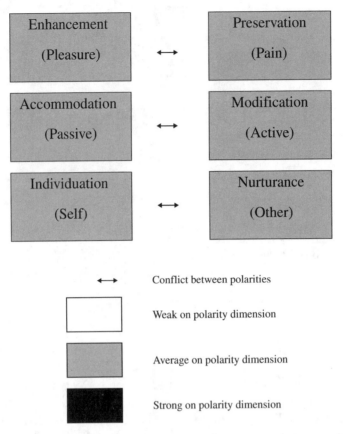

Figure 7.1. Polarity balance of the borderline prototype. From *Personality-Guided Therapy* (p. 642), by T. Millon, 1999, New York: Guilford Press. Copyright 1999 by John Wiley & Sons, Inc. Reprinted with permission.

manipulative efforts directed at maintaining a relationship or defending the self from rejection and abandonment. Although consistently attentive to their own emotional states, individuals with a borderline style also vacillate between a focus on themselves and their internal states and a focus on the behaviors, intentions, and feelings of others. In all situations, the vacillation reflects their dichotomous orientation to events; they are either all of one polarity or all of another, but neither for extended periods of time.

PERSONALITY-GUIDED COGNITIVE–BEHAVIORAL CONCEPTUALIZATION

Despite the fact that individuals with a borderline style of personality occasionally act with boldness and assertiveness, which might suggest confidence, they more typically struggle with recurrent and intense feelings of fear, anxiety, and despair, all of which underscore the uncertain self-image (Millon, 1999). Their labile feelings reflect their chronic struggle with feelings of worthlessness and self-contempt, which compels them to turn to others for nurturance and protection. However, they also expect to be mistreated and ultimately abandoned by those they turn to for safety and validation. As suggested by Millon, although individuals with a borderline style want to feel accepted and validated by others, they do not see how others could accept them; this reflects their fragile sense of self-esteem and their incessant vigilance to signs of rejection.

Millon used the term *uncertain* to describe these individuals' history with others. They fear rejection, like those with an avoidant style, yet individuals with a borderline orientation hold some hope and expectation that others will provide validation. Beck, Freeman, and Associates (1990) suggested, "They vacillate between autonomy and dependence, without being able to rely on either" (p. 187). Considering this orientation to the world and to the self, it is not surprising that the borderline style is known for inconsistent, chaotic, and often frantic interpersonal behaviors. The personality attributes and associated liabilities are reflected in Table 7.1.

According to Beck et al.'s (1990) description, the borderline personality style is characterized by core beliefs such as, "The world is dangerous and malevolent," "I must have someone I trust that I can turn to," and "I cannot manage on my own." Unfortunately, the view of others is that they are mean, controlling, unfair, and hostile. Thus, to individuals with a borderline style, the world is dangerous, they are relatively powerless, and they need others, but the others will ultimately let them down. Subsequently, the borderline style is marked by chronic tension and anxiety, vigilance for danger, and guardedness in relationships (Beck et al., 1990). Conditional beliefs are often as follows: "If I don't have someone to depend on, I cannot survive" or "If I am not the most important thing to another person, I am the least important!" Instrumentally, the individual believes, "I must remain the most important!" and "I cannot let him or her abandon me!"

Because individuals with a borderline style of personality expect rejection and abandonment, they are not able to relax in relationships with others and must be constantly on guard for subtle signs of rejection, which they must then manage. Their reactions, unfortunately, are often chaotic, impulsive, manipulative, and in other ways maladaptive. Thus, their efforts to protect their sense of integrity and manage relationships are *spasmodic* (emotional and impulsive) and *paradoxical* (i.e., ultimately maladaptive). Having failed to develop a clear and stable sense of personal values and identity, persons with a borderline style are easily drawn into the principles and activities of people to whom they turn for protection and validation. As a result, these individuals may become involved in various contradictory

TABLE 7.1
Structures and Functions of the Borderline Prototype
and Associated Liabilities

Personality domain	Liability
Self-image Uncertain	Lack of clearly defined sense of self upon which to rely to guide choices and relationships
Object representations Incompatible	Expectation that others will reject and abandon them but craving for deep and nurturing relationships, conflicting attitudes that contribute to the splitting that often occurs in relationships
Morphological organization Split	Overidealization of others; reliance on someone else to provide a defining identity; periods of contempt and devaluation when rejection is sensed
Mood and temperament Labile	Moods relative to circumstance—pleasant and content when feeling enthusiastic and safe, defensive and hostile when perceiving a threat to security
Behavioral acts Spasmodic	Behavior driven by emotional reactions; tendency to display whatever behavior is necessary to satisfy pleasurable desires and the need for safety and integrity
Interpersonal conduct Paradoxical	Behavior takes one form in a relationship at one time and a completely opposite form in another relationship or time
Cognitive style Capricious	Hypervigilance to signs of rejection and constant processing of plans of reaction, preventing focus on a task
Regulatory mechanism Regression	In times of threat, regression to childlike behaviors implemented to bring about positive changes in events

activities and adhere to discrepant ideals, all in an effort to secure a safe and dependable relationship with others.

For instance, a college student becomes involved in a sorority organization, which she commits to with enthusiastic zeal. However, when her relationships in the sorority go bad, which often occurs with individuals with a borderline style, the student may turn her needs and attention to a group of social outcasts who adhere to values quite discrepant from those of the sorority. Thus, she may go from one organization and personal identity in which very conservative values are the norm to another in which the ideals are at the opposite end of the spectrum.

One of the hallmarks of the borderline pattern is dichotomous thinking (Beck, Rush, Shaw, & Emery, 1979). To clients with a borderline personality style, there is no gray area. Things are "great, wonderful, the best ever" or "horrible, terrible, the worst it could be." Opinions change as the quality of relationships change. To the extent that they are able to rely on others and receive constant attention and validation from them, the world is "terrific!" As soon as problems develop, which are inevitable in most interpersonal relationships (particularly for those with a borderline style), these individuals will conclude that things are "terrible," and rather than making subtle efforts at relationship repair or enhancement, they will express extreme reactive emotions and behaviors in an effort to retain the relationships.

For instance, a person with the borderline style of personality may react to subtle rejection by pouting and when this does not lead to changes in the relationship, may intensify the reaction by expressing frustrations through criticism or accusations. Depending on the response of the other, if the person with a borderline orientation is not satisfied, he or she may then express anger in an attempt to elicit greater responsiveness and compliance, which may turn into an uncontrolled rage characterized by frantic and extreme reactions, including suicidal threats and various other dangerous and impulsive behaviors (e.g., reckless driving). If still not satisfied, the individual may strive to take some degree of revenge for perceived mistreatments. Because others often find such individuals difficult to affiliate with, primarily as a result of their constant demands and clinginess, rejection by others is a recurrent experience. Subsequently, the fears of rejection and abandonment these individuals feel are not unfounded. Many individuals, as the result of repeated bad experiences, come to understand how their own personal behaviors contribute to interpersonal problems. But they may keep their fears and frustrations to themselves rather than express their concerns to those on whom they have come to depend. In such cases, the individuals are vulnerable to self-contemptuous feelings, often including suicidal ideations.

When the individual with a borderline style is without a defining and secure relationship, feelings of fear, despair, and self-contempt are typically present. Often, these individuals describe themselves as feeling empty or void, underscoring the lack of defining identity they feel when not connected with a defining person or group. During these empty periods, individuals may engage in various impulsive behaviors as a means of creating feeling and escaping psychic pain. Many clients have described the self-injurious cutting that is not uncommon in patients with a borderline style as serving to provide some feeling in an otherwise empty existence (Kemperman, Russ, & Shearin, 1997; Shearer, 1994). Others describe these behaviors as justifiable self-destruction, considering their perceived worthlessness and the hopelessness of their situation.

Individuals with the borderline style of personality struggle to manage their emotional reactions. They engage in emotional reasoning, assuming that if they feel something, it must be so. Even when they have greater cognitive awareness of the nature of interpersonal affairs and personal needs and desires, they struggle to control their emotional reactions. They vacillate between periods of self-blame in which they hold themselves responsible for negative experiences and periods of externalizing the blame. In either case, they use extreme emotional reactions in response to the conclusions formed. They will turn those emotional reactions on themselves in self-contemptuous rages, marked by impulsive and self-injurious acts, or direct them at others in the form of sulkiness, tantrums, or tirades.

Individuals with a borderline orientation are masters of emotional extortion, using their emotional reactions to control relationships. Because periods of moodiness, rage, and self-contempt often result in supportive, sympathetic responses from others, those reactions are in various ways reinforced; at a minimum, they are able to revel in some degree of victimization. Unfortunately, others eventually tire of their chaotic emotionality, and the abandonment they fear recurs; thus, the fear behind the reactions is frequently realized, in large part, because of the very manner in which they attempt to deal with that fear.

PATHOLOGIC PROCESS OF THE BORDERLINE PATTERN

Individuals with a borderline prototype personality are vulnerable to a host of clinical conditions mediated by personality attributes. For these individuals, stress is often encountered in the form of threat to their self-defining sense of intimacy with others. As long as these individuals are able to foster and maintain validating interpersonal relationships, they function reasonably well. Unfortunately, when the relationships they depend on for their sense of self-worth and identity are compromised in any fashion, their fragile self-esteem is threatened, thus compelling compensatory, protective reactions. Further, because these individuals often have high expectations for the enhancing contribution of interpersonal interactions, they may be easily disappointed, and their current affiliation may feel overburdened by their neediness and reactivity. As a result, problems are often recurrent. How these individuals come to respond to those threats and interpersonal conflicts contributes to the specific nature of the clinical condition. Although in any one individual the specific processes may change, the underlying aspect of the pathologic process is the frantic reactions to relationship threats.

AXIS I VULNERABILITIES

The borderline prototype creates considerable vulnerability to various clinical outcomes. Reactions expressed by individuals with a borderline style to manage interpersonal relationships and respond to interpersonal frustrations can take the form of several clinical conditions. Several of these conditions are described in this section, but the borderline prototype sets the foundation for recurrent emotional distress and reactive behaviors, many of which do not reflect a specific clinical disorder.

Anxiety Disorders

The chronic fear experienced by individuals with the borderline orientation regarding abandonment by others contributes to their experience of anxiety. Although the severity of the anxiety symptoms may wax and wane, these individuals frequently struggle with some degree of anxiety, which may be manifested as a generalized anxiety, panic, phobic condition, obsessive–compulsive condition, or posttraumatic stress disorder (Zimmerman & Mattia, 1999).

Even when relationships are going relatively well, the individual with a borderline personality style is anxious about the security of that relationship and the ulterior motives or desires of the person to whom he or she has become attached. For instance, the individual may be in a relatively stable relationship yet may assume, without evidence, that the relationship partner would prefer to be elsewhere or prefer to be with someone else. These beliefs compel anxiety and increased vigilance to all aspects of the relationship. The initial experience of anxiety may develop into an extreme anxiety reaction, which may develop into a brief panic or psychotic episode. To be sure, helping the individual manage anxiety is a critical determinant of successful therapeutic outcomes (Linehan, Cochran, Kehrer, 2001; Wildgoose, Clarke, & Waller, 2001).

Dissociative Disorder

During periods of intense anxiety and anger that surface at times of perceived threat to relationships with and dependence on others, various dissociative experiences may emerge. When the individual with a borderline style perceives no behavioral options for dealing with intense emotions, he or she may experience a dissociative state—an emotional shutdown that satisfies the imperative need for self-protection. Dissociation thus provides the opportunity for some degree of emotional calm in an otherwise emotionally violent and intense episode. During these periods of dissociation, the individual may withdraw into a trancelike state or fugue. The fugue may represent a means of doing something, even if that something is of no value other than removing the person from the immediate source of distress. It is during dissociative experiences that some with the borderline orientation engage in self-injurious behaviors (Bohus et al., 2000).

Somatoform Disorder

Being vulnerable to intense anxiety and angry feelings renders the individual with a borderline style of personality susceptible to various somatoform conditions (Perugi & Akiskal, 2002; Perugi et al., 1998; Zimmerman & Mattia, 1999). As Millon (1999) suggested, the advantage of somatic complaints is that they block the true source of the individual's distress from awareness. By focusing his or her attention on somatic complaints, the individual does not have to face other concerns, such as those that relate to the fragility of interpersonal relationships. Thus, somatoform symptoms may be negatively reinforcing, apart from the fact that the symptoms may themselves be distressing. In addition, somatic concerns also serve the adaptive purpose of decreasing one's obligation to various aspects of relationship maintenance (e.g., cooperation with responsibilities, activity participation, and sexual intimacy). Finally, somatic symptoms may be positively reinforced by the care and attention the individual is able to elicit from others.

Dysthymia

Dysthymia, similar to full depression, serves the purpose of "stopping us [from] chasing rainbows" (Gilbert, 2001, p. 31), or as Nesse and Williams (1994) suggested, "disengag[ing] us from a hopeless enterprise" (p. 217). In the case of the borderline personality style, dysthymia reflects a general resignation to the fact that life is fraught with peril and that the individual is poorly equipped to deal effectively with those perils. When the person with a borderline style becomes aware that problems are frequently the result of his or her own inherent qualities, he or she may prefer to essentially "lay low," and dysthymia provides this form of disengagement from the external world (Vollrath, Togersen, & Alnaes, 1998). Millon (1999) described dysthymia as a means of anger control derived by turning feelings of resentment inward. From a cognitive–behavioral perspective, the individual realizes the dangers inherent in expressing various strong emotions and is able to derive some relief from the pain of these emotional experiences through the withdrawal and disengagement of dysthymia. In addition, dysthymia also provides a signal to others of his or her need for attention, caring, and patience. Thus, by displaying a general disengagement, the likelihood of others making demands on the individual are decreased, thereby providing relief from the threat of these potentially painful outcomes. Nonetheless, a hallmark of the borderline style may be an individual's ability to react in ways uncharacteristic of dysthymia when the situation or opportunity calls for a different mood.

Major Depression

Similar to dysthymia, the individual with a borderline orientation is prone to episodes of major depression (Zimmerman & Mattia, 1999). These episodes, although potentially reflecting a biological vulnerability, also indicate an agitated form of withdrawal from activities and efforts the person has come to view as hopeless. It is important to note that efforts to bring about positive outcomes are abandoned not with benign acceptance but, rather, with frustration and resentment, thereby contributing to the degree of agitation seen in these individuals' depression. It simply is not in the repertoire of those with a borderline personality style to accept things as "just the way they are" or as "just part of life." Instead, frustrations and disappointments are viewed as continuing evidence of how the world is against them and how others cannot be trusted to be helpful and reliable. Although they experience rage and engage in blatantly manipulative and vengeful behaviors, they will not express these emotions unless they have given up hope or impulsively conclude that the reactions have the potential for bringing about more positive, enhancing outcomes.

When the individual with a borderline style is lacking in confidence, his or her inability to accept the inevitable frustrations that occur in life may be expressed in an agitated form of depression, marked by anxiety, desperation, and the hallmark features of depression, including apathy, anhedonia, dysphoria, suicidal ideation, and perhaps suicidal gesture (see Gilbert, 2001; Gilbert & Allan, 1998). Furthermore, the hopelessness of depression may contribute to the display of several impulsive and pseudo-suicidal behaviors. Through the depression, individuals with a borderline orientation may judge themselves as justified in implementing any of a host of desperate behaviors in an attempt to ease their emotional pain.

Bipolar Disorder

Considering the core beliefs of clients with a borderline orientation, life is a constant struggle for the investment of others who will provide a sense of identity, validation, and protection. At times, these individuals are more confident of having relationships that will satisfy that self-defining need. However, because of the animosity these individuals have for the self and their lack of self-confidence and positive self-regard, they are unable to relax and simply enjoy interpersonal affiliations and remain ever vigilant to signs of rejection and abandonment. These feelings of profound self-contempt, marked by periods of contempt for others, render them particularly vulnerable to recurrent episodes of extreme affect and expressive and impulsive behaviors consistent with a bipolar condition (i.e., of the hostile variety; see Millon, 1999). Of all clinical conditions, the various forms of bipolar disorder (i.e., cyclothymia, bipolar I and II) are perhaps the most common in clients with a borderline personality style (Uecok, Karaveli, Kundakci, & Yazici, 1998).

Feelings of deep anguish and contempt for the self are extremely distressing. To deal with these feelings, the individual with a borderline orientation will turn his or her attention to others for the protection and validation of worth he or she desperately seeks. When opportunities present themselves, in either reality or fantasy, for deriving feelings of validation and protection, the individual may impulsively embrace those opportunities in an excessively enthusiastic manner. Because they tend to see things in dichotomous terms, such individuals see these opportunities as the Holy Grail to their quest for identity and validation. The enthusiasm and impulsivity with which they pursue these activities and opportunities are manic in their expression. Facing the inevitable failures and disappointments that occur in most manic episodes and that typically follow the emotional neediness and impulsivity of the borderline style, these individuals are then faced with the consequences of their actions. When signs of failure begin to appear, individuals with an enthusiastic and manic borderline style may externalize problems and act out toward others whom they perceive as obstacles to their desired states. As they become increasingly hopeless and self-blaming, outwardly expressed anger becomes internalized in the form of an agitated and hopeless depression.

VARIATIONS ON THE TRADITIONAL
BORDERLINE PERSONALITY

Millon (1999; Millon & Davis, 2000) described several variations on the borderline theme. The difference between the unique variations exists in the focus of attention and reactive style displayed. For some, the source of distress is external, whereas for others, the distress is more internal.

The *discouraged borderline* personality style is a combination of the borderline style, the avoidant style, and the depressive or dependent style of personality. In any of these combinations, the critical feature is the individual's need for attachment, submissiveness, and clinginess to others. Individuals with a discouraged borderline orientation put "all their eggs in one basket," relying on just one person to provide for them their sense of identity and safety (Millon & Davis, 2000, p. 418). However, they are not able to relax completely and must remain vigilant to signs of rejection in that relationship. As a result, they display a host of behaviors and emotions, all enacted and experienced in the service of remaining safe within the relationship. Unfortunately for these individuals, the behaviors they display often damage the relationship, which perpetuates a pattern of reaction and re-reaction that can escalate into a crisis situation that may include suicidal and pseudosuicidal behaviors. In addition, as these individuals go through repeated cycles and relationships, they may become hopeless and increasingly discouraged, which increases the probability of self-destructiveness and depression. Not surprising, those with the discouraged borderline personality are particularly vulnerable to repeated major depressive episodes and suicidal ideations, gestures, and attempts (Millon, 1999; Millon & Davis, 2000).

The *impulsive borderline* personality style includes a combination of the histrionic or antisocial styles. Poor emotional regulation and a recurrent fear of rejection and abandonment define the borderline aspects of this variation, while the seductive, gregarious, and impulsive attention-seeking define the histrionic contribution. Impulsivity, capriciousness, and moral and legal irresponsibility define the antisocial dimension. Although some individuals may have more of the histrionic flavor and others more of the antisocial flavor, others may combine all three. The character Alex in the film *Fatal Attraction* (Jaffe, Lansing, & Lyne, 1987) may well characterize the impulsive borderline style. In all cases, the defining attributes include emotional deregulation, fear of abandonment, and impulsive and chaotic efforts to elicit and maintain the investment and protection of those on whom they hope to depend. The impulsivity characterizing this style of borderline expression may be consistent with symptoms of an impulsive disorder, adjustment disorder, or manic episode of a bipolar disorder. Furthermore, in the face of the interpersonal conflicts caused by the impulsive behaviors, these individuals may be vulnerable to recurrent episodes of anxiety and depression.

The *petulant borderline* personality style combines borderline and negativistic features. This pattern describes an individual who is "unpredictable, restless, irritable, impatient, complaining, disgruntled, stubborn, sullen, pessimistic, resentful and envious" (Millon & Davis, 2000, p. 420). Not surprising, the individual with a petulant borderline style has particular difficulty fostering and maintaining interpersonal relationships. Whereas those with other variations of the borderline style retain some qualities that might connect them with others (nonargumentativeness in the discouraged, gregarious in the impulsive, and conformity in the self-destructive), individuals with the petulant borderline personality style are characterized by few qualities that would win the investment and protection of others. These individuals tend to be demanding in relationships and use their emotions as weapons to control the behaviors of others. As long as they have another person at whom to direct their angry and hostile feelings, they do not turn that rage on themselves. However, because people attempt to avoid and escape their negativity, individuals with a petulant borderline style are almost inevitably required to deal with the fact that they have been abandoned by others. When this occurs, the rage and hostility may turn to pleading and despair and eventually back to rage directed at the self, manifested as self-contempt, self-harm, depression, and suicidality.

The *self-destructive borderline* personality style includes depressive or masochistic features, or both. Individuals with this borderline style are most at risk for self-injury, suicidal attempt, and ultimately suicide. They are more hopeless, pessimistic, and self-contemptuous and hold themselves more responsible for negative events than do those of the other borderline variations. Unlike the other borderline styles, in which the individual may turn frustration and other negative emotions on others, the self-destructive borderline personality turns these emotions on the self. Individuals with the self-destructive prototype are particularly vulnerable to a variety of psychiatric, medical, and emergency conditions.

TREATMENT OF THE BORDERLINE PROTOTYPE

The primary goal in treating the individual with a borderline personality style is stabilization of the conflict between the imperative polarities. Thus, the task is to settle the client into a more stable and consistent pattern of interpersonal relationships and to decrease the extreme emotional and behavioral reactions. Without a defining sense of self, individuals with a borderline prototype personality are susceptible to being drawn into opposing social circumstances. Indeed, the goal in treating these individuals is to decrease their dependence on others for self-defining ideals, which implies helping to increase their internalized self-identity.

With clients characterized by a borderline personality disorder, it may be necessary to consider inpatient treatment because the patterns of reactivity (e.g., pseudosuicidal behaviors) are often more than can be managed in an outpatient setting. Even when the personality style is prototypically borderline, without being disordered as defined by the *Diagnostic and Statistical Manual of Mental Disorders* (4th ed., text revision; American Psychiatric Association, 2000) criteria, the therapeutic challenges may be considerable. However, because reactions are not as extreme in the client with a borderline style, outpatient treatment should most often be sufficient.

As emphasized by Linehan (1993a, 1993b) and others (Beck et al., 1990; Freeman, Pretzer, Fleming, & Simon, 1990; Young, 1994), attention to the therapeutic relationship is critical in treating the individual with a borderline orientation. Therapist and client must make a commitment to treatment yet also set limits concerning the availability of the therapist, including phone calls and unscheduled office visits. Although suicidal gestures are likely to be less common in those with a borderline style than in those with a borderline personality disorder, suicidal gestures and threats (subtle and blatant) may emerge. It is important for the therapist to set limits on how to respond to those gestures. Although suicidal ideations and gestures must be taken seriously, it is important that the client not be allowed to use suicidality as a means of managing the relationship with the therapist. As Linehan (1987) suggested, a plan can be devised for dealing with suicidal gestures that includes emergency services and hospitalization but not the direct involvement of the therapist. Suicidal thoughts can be talked about as part of the therapeutic process, but suicidal gestures can be separated from ongoing treatment.

As an example, Michelle was being seen for treatment in an outpatient setting, and one day she came to the session after having taken an undetermined number of sleeping pills. When the therapist recognized her disorientation and Michelle had admitted to the act, the therapist calmly called for an ambulance that took Michelle to the hospital, where she was admitted and treated for short-term stabilization. Although the therapist followed up with the hospital, as per his agreement with Michelle, he did not visit the hospital and suspended his ongoing treatment until her release. Once resumed, treatment was taken up at the point at which it had been suspended, with appropriate attention to issues contributing to the suicidal gesture.

In this example, by following through with the agreement not to react beyond her immediate safety, Michelle's suicidal gesture was not allowed to detract from ongoing treatment efforts. Upon her return to treatment, the motives and purpose of the suicidal gesture were discussed, but relative to current topics in treatment. Michelle's treatment had been going quite well, and the therapist had mentioned the possibility of increasing the time between sessions. Michelle initially took this as a sign of her improvement, but she began to dwell on the threat of ending therapy and of no longer having the therapist in her life. These thoughts were coupled with anguished and dysphoric feelings. Whether intentional or not, Michelle recognized the coincidence and convenience of her having taken the pills just prior to her session. This prompted useful discussion regarding the value of therapy, the ultimate goal of her independence from therapy, and an agreement to talk about fears of independence rather than allowing her emotions to get so extreme as to prompt a suicidal gesture or attempt.

Clients often form a bond with their therapists that is not unlike the intense feelings the clients have for others. Thus, when treating an individual with a borderline style, the therapist must be careful to manage the client's idealization and be appropriately responsive to the negative, defensive, and retaliatory reactions that may emerge when he or she becomes disenchanted with the previously idealized therapist. In dealing with these possible outcomes, the therapist can set the stage for these developments by discussing with the client his or her possible reactions and making a plan for dealing with them should they arise. In this way, if such patterns do emerge, they will come as no surprise to the client or therapist, and appropriate, planned reactions can be implemented to deal with the momentary event. In Linehan's dialectic behavior therapy model (1993a), the therapist is encouraged to interact with the client in an accepting manner, (i.e., as an individual struggling to make changes), to remain "unwaveringly centered" (p. 110), yet with "compassionate flexibility" (p. 109), and to be "benevolently demanding" (p. 111).

With the establishment of a working therapeutic alliance, the therapist and client can design a treatment plan to counter the perpetuating tendencies that have previously proved so problematic for the client. One of the first tasks of therapy is to stabilize the paradoxical interpersonal behaviors and decrease dichotomous and capricious thinking. As is true with other conditions, it is often helpful to have the client consider the origins of the interpersonal style and its purpose and relative adaptiveness given childhood experiences. Through this discussion, the client is able to create some degree of separation between how the world naturally is and how he or she has come to view it. It is also beneficial to consider what the client seeks through the paradoxical behaviors, a discussion that typically will lead to conversation about validating and secure relationships.

Once the client recognizes that his or her quest is for a sense of connection with and validation from others, the therapist and client can agree to work on the skills associated with improved relationships with others and on improved self-protection. With the goal of fostering relationships, the therapist can explain that emotional upheaval is still possible yet can be far less probable. To maintain the therapeutic relationship and prevent reactions from the client, the therapist can take the time in initial phases of therapy to focus on the client's emotional reactions, with discussion of the purpose behind emotional expressions (see Rasmussen, 2003a). The therapist should be careful not to minimize the client's emotional distress and should validate the difficulty of fostering perfect relationships. It is useful to validate the client's intentions and desires, while pointing out the futility of the manifested behaviors.

> Client: I was so extremely angry, livid! I wanted to just tear his head off!
>
> Therapist: I can tell by your reaction how difficult that must have been.
>
> Client: It was horrible, just horrible!
>
> Therapist: And all you wanted was for him to say, or at least to imply, that you were important.

Client:	Yes, but all he wanted was sex!
Therapist:	So, sex didn't win him over, and it seems that a direct confrontation didn't work either.
Client:	Sounds pretty hopeless, doesn't it?
Therapist:	I guess that using those strategies it does. Perhaps we could talk about other strategies.

Such interactions with the client create opportunity to discuss the purpose and maladaptiveness of current emotional displays. Although by itself such discussion will not decrease the emotional intensity that the individual feels, it will introduce a new level of cognitive processing in the face of frustrating situations that typically elicit extreme and maladaptive reactions. As these discussions become more commonplace, the client is now in a position to begin considering attitudes and other cognitive processes that contribute to the emotional displays.

Therapist:	So, what you hope for is a reliable and supportive relationship that you can relax and enjoy?
Client:	It'll probably never happen, but it would be nice.
Therapist:	Considering our recent discussions, it would seem that the strategies that you have implemented to create those relationships are not working, and may even make matters worse.
Client:	Yep, I'm pretty pathetic, aren't I?
Therapist:	You seem more frustrated than pathetic. Do you feel pathetic?
Client:	Most of the time.
Therapist:	Let's talk about how it is that you think about these interactions, and maybe we'll understand better why you get so frustrated or, to use your term, "pathetic."

The therapist can engage the client in a collaborative process of exploring the cognitive processes that typically precede the emotional reaction, when possible identifying the logical nature of the emotional reaction given the cognitive conclusion.

Client:	I want him to give a damn about me, but I know that he's going to reject me. Like every other guy, he just wants to screw.
Therapist:	So, you have sex and get hopeful about a relationship, while at the same time expecting to be rejected.
Client:	That's it.

Therapist: I think I can understand your frustration better. You have a hope and expectation and after having engaged in a sexual relationship, you believe that you are in ways entitled to a deeper relationship.

Client: Yeah, pretty much.

Therapist: Then, when you suspect that he is not as invested in the relationship as you'd like him to be, you feel frustrated.

Client: Yes.

Therapist: Tell me more about how you display that frustration.

Once this connection is made, therapist and client can begin to discuss and implement strategies for altering attitudes.

Therapist: It seems from your description that you often expect rejection, and the ways that you react almost guarantee rejection. In fact, it seems that you may even at times create the rejection first. Sort of like a "quit before I get fired" approach.

Client: Yes.

Therapist: So, it's time to try new approaches.

Client: Please.

These discussions can also focus on the dichotomous thinking that often characterizes the client with a borderline style. In this example, the client is beginning to understand the motives behind her emotional reactions and the extreme and dichotomous thoughts preceding those extreme reactions.

Therapist: As we talk about the situations that you have found yourself facing and the emotional reactions you have expressed, let's take some time to consider the thoughts that seem to be behind the reactions.

Client: There are a lot of thoughts.

Therapist: You were telling me a while ago about how you and Steven met. You described it with a big smile on your face. It was clear that was a very nice time in your life.

Client: Oh, yes. I was pretty excited about it. He was so handsome and kind, and exciting to be around (*smiling*). I really thought that I had found the person for me.

Therapist: Let's stay on this for a bit and think about the thoughts that were going on in your head at the time. So, here he is, handsome, kind, exciting. Put yourself back in that time, if you can, and tell me the thoughts you had about it.

Client:	Like I said, I was thinking, "Finally, I've found him. The perfect guy for me. And he is interested in me!"
Therapist:	Can you take those thoughts further and talk about what that meant, to have found the perfect guy for you?
Client:	I remember it pretty well. After our first date, he was all I could think about. I thought about the things we could do together. I imagined places we would travel, things we would see, and the fun stuff we would do together.
Therapist:	Anything else?
Client:	Heck, yes, I had already figured out how many children we were going to have, what their names were, and even what they'd look like—blonde hair and blue eyes. One boy and one girl.
Therapist:	It sounds like you really ran with it.
Client:	Oh, yeah (*sigh*), I did.
Therapist:	I can't blame you, it seemed pretty right to you—why wouldn't you dream about the possibilities? It seems like I remember you telling me something about him being involved with someone at the time when you met him.
Client:	Oh, yes. He was semiengaged. But I didn't let that bother me too much.
Therapist:	You two made love that first night, is that right?
Client:	Yep! Jumped right into bed with him. Couldn't help myself.
Therapist:	As I listen, it seems that you went pretty quickly from he's handsome, kind, and exciting to images of marriage, children, and "happy ever after."
Client:	That does seem to be my style.
Therapist:	I can appreciate the joy of it, but what's the cost? Does it set you up for disappointment?
Client:	No doubt.
Therapist:	Can we follow this a bit more?
Client:	I guess.
Therapist:	You saw him a few more times during that initial week and continued to revel in the experience . . .
Client:	(*with a sly smile*) Oh, yes!
Therapist:	What happened that night he broke it off with you?

Client: We were at the restaurant for what I thought to be the start of another wonderful evening. He had that look in his eyes that said something was up. I could just tell something was up.

Therapist: What happened to you? What did you feel?

Client: I remember feeling a surge of heat overcome my entire body. It was like in the old cartoons where the red starts at the feet and rises to the head and smoke shoots out of the ears. I wasn't at the point of smoke shooting from my ears, but I could feel it coming.

Therapist: Am I right in recalling that he had not said anything at this point? Your feeling was based only on that look you saw in his eyes?

Client: That was all I needed.

Therapist: OK, let's stay with that. There must have been a lot going on inside your head to have prompted such an extreme reaction. Can you put words to the thoughts behind that feeling?

Client: I don't know, I was pretty focused on the feeling. I do know it was related to wanting to kill him before he could say anything.

Therapist: It seems like you had an idea about what was coming. What was that idea?

Client: I knew that I was going to get the standard line, "I really like you, but I can't see you anymore; I hope we will be able to be friends." *Friends!* We'd been screwing every day for a week, and now he wanted to "just be friends!"

Therapist: But he never actually said that, this is just what you thought and what compelled that flush of anger you felt.

Client: Yeah, that's right.

Therapist: You then got up and left, right?

Client: Yep! Left him just sitting there!

Therapist: And you haven't had contact with him since.

Client: Nope.

Therapist: Without discussing whether your assumptions were true or not, let's talk for a minute about what you experienced and try to tie it all together. When you first met him, you concluded that he was handsome, nice, and exciting, and you imagined all sorts of wonderful outcomes associated with the relationship. For that first week, you reveled in passion, particularly the sexual aspects of the relationship; then, without any direct evidence, other than a look in his eyes, you assumed the worst. It seems like you went from one extreme to another, without much in between.

Client: I can see that.

Therapist and client are now in an ideal situation to discuss the client's dichotomous and capricious thinking and its association with extreme and distressing emotions and spasmodic behaviors. Recognition of the desire that the individual has for meaningful and validating emotions is very important. With a focus on the desire to foster rewarding relationships, therapist and client can now engage in discussions regarding the client's interpretation of events and stylistic manner of responding to those interpretations. The client can be instructed in various self-monitoring procedures to test his or her speculations and to practice new styles of interpersonal interaction.

A defining feature of the borderline personality is inconsistency, which is observed relative to self-view, expectations, social relationships, and occupational status. Individuals with this style seek stable, validating relationships, but they believe that such relationships are unavailable, either because they do not deserve the investment of others or because others are simply unwilling or unlikely to provide the investment they seek. This uncertainty, matched by impulsive reactions to subtle and blatant interpersonal affronts, contributes to the capriciousness in behaviors and emotions characteristic of individuals with a borderline style. The challenge in treating these clients is to help them remain more emotionally stable and consistent across situational circumstances.

The conflict between active and passive adaptation underscores the general inconsistency of the borderline pattern. At times they may take a very passive role and expect others to accommodate them. Indeed, the need for a self-defining identity often contributes to a passive adaptation in which individuals with a borderline orientation essentially go with the flow of interpersonal relationships, often in such a way that they find themselves in difficult situations. As an example, a college student who is enamored by the seductions of her suitors may find herself in a crisis when drawn into a dangerous intimate situation. To prevent such occurrences, it is necessary to help the individual anticipate such situations and develop a repertoire for dealing with them. Discussion of previous and possible events can help the client to anticipate consequences. Furthermore, using Meichenbaum and Cameron's (1974) self-instructional techniques, the client with a borderline personality can be assisted in developing greater control over impulsiveness. The closer the anticipated situations are to actual events, the greater the probability that the client will be able to catch him- or herself prior to an impulsive act. The opposite extreme is active efforts to win the investment of others or to avoid the insult of rejection. The individual with a borderline style may make active efforts to avoid or mask feelings of emptiness and despair and may engage in active and impulsive reactions, such as shoplifting, reckless driving, promiscuity, and the like.

To reduce the conflict between the active and passive reactivity, the therapist and client can engage in guided discovery, looking to find the connections between events, thoughts, affective reactions, and impulsive behavioral expressions. Because individuals with a borderline orientation are so quick to react to events in an extreme fashion, it is particularly helpful to focus on those automatic thoughts that activate schema-based reactions. Several cognitive techniques are helpful in this regard. Acting as an unbiased observer, the therapist can offer observations and ask questions that will help the client to see the relationship between rapid, impulsive thoughts and the various mode-based reactions. To decrease the individual's defensiveness, the therapist may validate the reactions based on the automatic thoughts identified. Indeed, given the rapid conclusions drawn by the individual, extreme reactions can appear justified. However, further consideration of the circumstance should reveal the ultimate maladaptiveness inherent in the reaction. Several techniques can be particularly useful in helping the individual with a borderline style identify problematic automatic thoughts.

Using current conflicts, the client can be assisted in examining the evidence (Freeman et al., 1990) relative to the recent event. At issue is whether the objective evidence supports the conclusions drawn by the client, or whether other conclusions may have been equally or potentially more valid. As an example, individuals with a borderline prototype personality frequently jump to extreme conclusions concerning another's intentions; typically, the client readily perceives rejection and reacts with self-esteem-defending reactions. Working through the events of the situation to consider the source and validity of the information and the role of information previously overlooked, the client may come to see that the conclusions drawn were biased. Unfortunately, individuals with a borderline style are at times correct in their conclusions—they do tend to have strained relationships. Given this reality, the therapist can use the information as a means of introducing more positive social skills. The therapist can use the client's desire for validating, enhancing relationships as a foundation and an opportunity to discuss interpersonal skills.

Individuals with a borderline personality style are particularly prone to absolute thinking. Through guided discovery, the therapist can help the individual flush out dichotomous conclusions by looking for "toxic" terms such as *always, never, everyone, no one,* and the like. The client can be reminded that using such terms may prompt extreme emotional and behavioral reactions. Examining the evidence, however, the client can see that the absolutes are typically not well supported, although there may be some grains of truth. Similarly, the therapist could help the client consider the odds of dreaded outcomes (see Freeman et al., 1990). Often the absolute thinking relates to low-probability outcomes. However, because of the client's interpersonal style, the probability may not be as low as it would be for others. This provides an opportunity to discuss means for lowering the probabilities. Indeed, such conversation can help the individual develop a more balanced and realistic expectation concerning interpersonal relationships.

The conflict between the pain–pleasure polarities must also be addressed in therapy, specifically in relation to the dichotomous thinking that characterizes the client with a borderline orientation. To this client, the world is full of either unbearable pain or wondrous joy; these extremes are invariably related to interpersonal relationships and feelings of inclusion, validation, and acceptance—on terms defined by the individual. In therapy, the client needs to develop more realistic, balanced expectations concerning pleasure and pain. To help these individuals, several strategies can be implemented as a means of decreasing impulsive pleasure seeking and reactive pain avoidance.

Reducing the conflict between self–other polarities will involve helping the client process concerns related to both self and others, rather than focusing only on the self or on others. In times of threat, the individual with a borderline style is inclined to think of the implications of an event for the self, rather than how things are perceived or felt by others. Likewise, her or she is inclined to internalize or externalize blame for negative events and emotions, rather than considering the contribution of all parties. By encouraging the client to process information relative to everyone involved, this conflict can be reduced. Thought experiments in which the client is encouraged to process information from another individual's perspective can help develop this interpersonal skill (see Freeman et al., 1990).

Because individuals with the borderline prototype personality are prone to impulsive and extreme emotional reactions, specific attention to emotional control strategies is very important. Medications may be useful to help moderate emotional reactions, as might relaxation procedures. As implied in previous sections, a metaemotional understanding of how emotional reactions serve an immediately adaptive purpose should help these individuals gain greater emotional self-reliance and control.

Several techniques can help the individual with a borderline style gain greater emotional self-reliance and self-control. In one procedure, the client is oriented to the adaptive purpose of emotional expression and introduced to a technique for monitoring his or her emotional reactions over a period of time, recording the objectives behind the emotional expression (what the individual was hoping to gain), and generating alternative reactions that do not require extreme emotional reactions or self-defeating actions (Rasmussen, 2003a, 2003b). It is important that the client understand both the purpose and the impact of the emotional response and accept responsibility for controlling his or her emotional reactions. Through this procedure, the client uses emotional reactions as a means of reconsidering cognitive intent and behavioral alternatives. In this way, the emotion is not given more meaning than being a motivator of behavior in the service of an attitude.

CASE EXAMPLE

Meeca is a 31-year-old wife and mother of two. She has a degree in education, but she has not held a consistent teaching assignment since her graduation from college 9 years earlier. She has a history of anorexia and has been treated in outpatient settings at various times since high school. She is presenting for treatment at this time because she is unhappy in her marriage and is again beginning to constrict her food intake. Meeca describes a pattern of feelings and behaviors over the last year that is suggestive of a borderline personality style. Meeca revealed to the therapist that since her marriage, she has reunited on a few occasions with an old boyfriend and engaged in sexual relations. Typically the meetings have been spontaneous, but on occasion she has initiated the meetings. She has a number of friends, but her relationships with them tend to be sporadic. At times she spends a great deal of time with her friends, and at other times she wants nothing to do with them.

In addition to sporadic interactions with her friends, Meeca's relationship with her husband is currently strained. They have had numerous fights over the past year, some of which have led Meeca to extreme reactions. On one occasion, she began hitting her husband with one of their children's toys. On another, she left the house and did not return until the next morning (she had gone to see her old boyfriend). Her husband claims to still love her but admits that it is hard remaining married to her. Her attention to her responsibilities as mother is generally consistent and positive. She is generally pleasant in her interactions with her children, although she tends to be somewhat overindulgent with them.

Although Meeca does not meet the criteria for a borderline personality disorder, her prototype personality is most consistent with a borderline style. In addition, she appears to be returning to an anorexic condition and is displaying evidence of a bipolar condition. In the cognitive–behavioral conceptualization, Meeca's mood volatility and her food intake restriction stem from her borderline style. Her mood fluctuations occur in a pattern consistent with her level of satisfaction and dissatisfaction with her relationships. Her current period of food restriction relates to her desire to remain sexually desirable and to her loss of appetite associated with her mood changes.

Meeca's view of herself is variable (uncertain). At times she sees herself in very positive terms, such as when she is being nurtured by her husband or seduced by her boyfriend. At other times, she views herself in very objectionable terms. Following periods of anticipated or enacted extramarital engagements, she views herself as being a "horrible" individual worthy of punishment or rejection. She wants to see herself as a good wife and mother but struggles with a desire to be an unburdened free spirit. Her mood is labile and vacillates with her attitudes toward herself and toward others in her life. Similarly, her capricious thoughts reflect her belief that "to be loved, one should be made a fuss over by others," which conflicts with her view that "to be a good wife and mother, one must make sacrifices." Her conflicting thoughts and chaotic emotions contribute to mode-based reactions characteristic of a borderline pattern. As her husband suggests, "it is really hard keeping up with her moods."

Meeca defines herself through her relationship with others. However, she finds herself feeling bored, resentful, or threatened in her relationships and turns to other relationships when the current relationship is unsatisfying or when she is feeling criticized. A pattern was identified in which Meeca would create a crisis before engaging in extreme behaviors. For instance, when she desired a dalliance with her boyfriend, she would pick fights with her husband that would justify her contacting the boyfriend. Similarly, during times of engagement with her friends, when she felt that her place among the group was threatened in some way, she would find herself in an argument with one of the friends, compelling a hopeless cry to her husband, who would provide sympathy and reassurance.

It was initially important for Meeca to make a decision regarding whether she wanted to remain in her marriage or leave the relationship. She was quick to state that she wanted to remain in the marriage, and she subsequently took the initiative to break off the relationship with the old boyfriend. Concern with her food intake was not initially addressed because she had not experienced significant weight loss and because her current caloric intake appeared to be minimally sufficient to maintain her health. Concern with an exacerbation of her eating disorder warranted regular reassessment of weight and eating behaviors. Similarly, the specific aspects of the bipolar condition were not addressed independent of the personality attributes.

As a foundation to therapy, Meeca focused on aspects of her relationship with her husband. She acknowledged the importance of this relationship to her and set out to improve the marriage. The therapist made clear to

Meeca that throughout treatment, she would likely feel impulses to rekindle her relationship with her boyfriend and potentially to pick a fight with her husband. She agreed to talk to the therapist about such feelings before acting on an impulse. The therapist agreed not to prevent her from contacting the old boyfriend, thereby minimizing the need for Meeca to hide her rendezvous. Nonetheless, the therapist reminded her that such contacts would have implications for the success of therapy.

To minimize her impulsive and seemingly chaotic behaviors, Meeca focused initially on identifying those events in her marriage and interpersonal relationships that prompted strong emotional reactions. Through a process of guided discovery, she was able to recognize patterns of dissatisfaction and fears of rejection. In session, she discussed cognitive rebuttals and alternative reactions to implement at times that she recognized the reactant emotions and cognitive conclusions. For several weeks, Meeca monitored ongoing thoughts, feelings, and behaviors, including the identification of impulsive reactions and alternative responses useful to fostering an improved relationship with her husband. It was also useful at one point in treatment to include her husband to inform him of the changes Meeca would be making and to enlist his assistance in improving the relationship. This was important because her husband, although supportive, had developed a critical style of interaction with Meeca. It was left up to Meeca to determine whether to discuss with her husband her relationship with the old boyfriend.

Throughout the course of treatment, Meeca did experience periods of frustration with her husband and with therapy. The therapist reminded Meeca that she could change her mind but that the focus of treatment was on her patterns of reactivity relative to an improved marital relationship. The intent was to help stabilize her self-view by remaining focused on a single aspect of her life. As her marital relationship improved, her desire for the carefree, uncommitted life decreased, and her commitment to her role as wife and mother increased. Important for Meeca, she developed strategies for addressing fears and concerns with her husband, and subsequently her friends, rather than allowing herself to enter into crises that justified her acting out. As treatment progressed, food intake was continually monitored and did not prove to warrant specific treatment. In managing her food intake, Meeca consulted information she had been given during a previous period of treatment for her eating disorder.

Important in Meeca's treatment was her ability to take appropriate responsibility for fostering a fulfilling relationship with her husband. It was necessary at times for her to consider the appropriateness of her expectations and reactions, and it was necessary for her to make unwanted sacrifices at times. Nonetheless, she was able to gain greater control over her cognitive conclusions and the resultant emotional and behavioral expressions.

CONCLUSION

The borderline personality is one of the most challenging of the personality prototypes. In fact, it is not uncommon to come across therapists who refuse to take on such challenging clients. It may not have been until the emergence of dialectical behavior therapy, developed by Linehan (1987), that clinicians began to develop some confidence that this personality disorder could be successfully treated. The personality attributes defining this prototype reveal a pattern characterized by extreme reactivity. Clients with a borderline prototype personality are hypersensitive to signs of rejections by others and respond with frantic efforts to prevent abandonment, or to at least save a sense of self-integrity. Their reactive nature contributes to the difficulties they have in committing to a treatment regimen.

The more intensely a client is characterized by the borderline disorder, the greater are the treatment demands and often the need for inpatient treatment or more concerted and intense outpatient treatment, such as that using the dialectical–behavioral approach (Linehan, 1993a). Even when the borderline style is merely prototypal rather than floridly disordered, treatment challenges can be considerable. However, the individual with a borderline style is often able to cope with great uncertainty and to control emotional reactions such that recurrent interpersonal problems are less common and less severe.

Because the individual with a borderline style of personality maintains such a strong desire for self-fulfilling interpersonal relations, treatment that provides a consistent and supportive atmosphere in which the client can reconsider uncertain cognitive assumptions and learn to regulate labile affective states should be most effective. Considering the adaptive purpose of the borderline attributes relative to the imperative polarities, treatment can be focused in such a way that the individual is able to develop behavioral resources that allow for greater emotional calm and a more stable self-view.

8

THE HISTRIONIC PROTOTYPE

Key phrase: Drama
Evolutionary focus: Exhibitionism, attention

The polarity balance of the histrionic style is depicted in Figure 8.1. Individuals with a histrionic personality style maintain a relative balance on enhancement and preservation that reflects their need for attention and approval. In addition, they are often willing and able to endure some degree of pain, in various forms, in the service of positive experiences. The experience of pain and discomfort may be a direct route to self-enhancement, which is derived from the attention of others. For instance, somatic suffering, martyrdom, victimization, and emotional sensitivities can all serve to invest others in these individuals' distress and crises. Without suffering, they may not get attention from others, or at least not a satisfying amount. A minor crisis may be blown tremendously out of proportion to elicit desired attention. When unable to win the investment of others in more socially approved fashion, the individual with a histrionic style will use any available opportunity.

Consider the example of Mary. Mary was talking with a coworker who described her current emotional and financial predicament. Upon hearing that her coworker did not have the money to pay her bills, had just broken up with her boyfriend, and was dealing with a child with academic and discipline problems, Mary broke into tears. She hugged the coworker while expressing her sadness and concern amid her tears. Soon, the troubled coworker was consoling Mary. For the next 2 days, Mary took every opportunity to talk to other coworkers about the woman's desperate situation. For

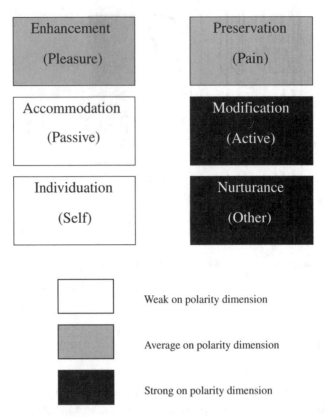

Enhancement (Pleasure)	Preservation (Pain)
Accommodation (Passive)	Modification (Active)
Individuation (Self)	Nurturance (Other)

Weak on polarity dimension

Average on polarity dimension

Strong on polarity dimension

Figure 8.1. Polarity balance of the histrionic prototype. From *Personality-Guided Therapy* (p. 400), by T. Millon, 1999, New York: Guilford Press. Copyright 1999 by John Wiley & Sons, Inc. Reprinted with permission.

Mary, the other woman's circumstance provided opportunity for her to elicit the attention of others.

Individuals with a histrionic style are willing to sacrifice some pleasures in the service of pain avoidance; pain typically takes the form of social disapproval or rejection. For example, a person with a histrionic style may avoid a social encounter when she knows that she may be upstaged by another individual. Although the engagement might have been very enjoyable, the threat of being one-upped by one perceived as more skilled in some critical capacity is more significant as a behavioral motivator than is the opportunity for attention. When upstaged by another, the individual with a histrionic prototype personality is placed in a position in which some form of compensatory reaction is necessary to reestablish the external approval desired. In such situations, it may not be uncommon to see the individual's protective reaction being directed at attention seeking. For instance, in response to the threat of interpersonal inferiority, the person with a histrionic style may express somatic complaints prompting avoidance of that activity, while securing the validating attention of others at the same time.

As implied by this description, the individual with a histrionic orientation is very active and will aggressively take whatever steps necessary to win attention or to avoid or compensate for disapproval. Similar to those with the dependent style, individuals with the histrionic style are dependent on others for attention and affection, but unlike individuals with a dependent orientation, who tend to be very passive in their dependency, these individuals work diligently to establish and maintain the investment of others. As Freeman, Pretzer, Fleming, and Simon (1990) suggested, individuals with a histrionic prototype personality cannot leave the acquisition of approval to chance and must work to ensure the attention they need. When the fraternity brother of a college student with a histrionic style leaned way out over a hotel railing on the 30th floor, the student reacted by standing on the railing, thereby regaining the attention of his peers. Another individual with a histrionic style may throw emotional fits or retaliate aggressively in an effort to counter an insult or to secure attention and approval. The energy and vivaciousness of these individuals underscore this active style of engagement with the world; such individuals are likely to be the life of the party or the burdensome pest in social situations. The one thing that they will not be is ignored.

The activity of individuals with a histrionic style of personality is characteristically directed at others. These individuals are more interested and invested in the actions of others than they are aware of their own internal motives. Their general orientation to the world is characterized by attention and reaction to others. In the example of the risk-taking college student, this individual overlooked the risk to his physical safety in his quest to win back the validating attention of his peers. In disordered form, this orientation characterizes a frantic need for the attention and investment of others. At the prototypal level, the individual with a histrionic orientation may be very personable and sensitive to the subtleties of interpersonal interactions, and he or she may use nonextreme and even prosocial actions to gain attention. As an example, when feeling ignored in a social interaction, the individual may interrupt to see who needs a drink or to see if the group wants to hear different music. Although not blatantly intrusive, these actions are effective as means of maintaining the attention and validation of the group and are particularly effective in providing the opportunity to change the topic of discussion from something that was not of interest to the individual to a topic that is more validating.

The symptoms of a histrionic style are qualitatively as well as quantitatively different from those of a diagnosable personality disorder. For some individuals with a histrionic personality style, the nature of the symptoms may simply be less dramatic. For others, the nature of the attention seeking and emotionality may be somewhat unique. For instance, the histrionic style may underlie the person's lack of emotional self-reliance. In such cases, the actively dependent individual relies on others to create opportunity for positive emotion or relief from negative emotion. This dependency creates an intensified sense of interpersonal intimacy in which the individual with a histrionic style expects greater intimacy than the other person may be prepared or willing to provide. Further, the histrionic style may be evidenced in the individual's strong reliance on emotional expression as a means of interpersonal communication. For instance, the wife of a man with a histrionic orientation felt that she was being "extorted" by her husband's willingness to use strong emotion when he did not get his way.

PERSONALITY-GUIDED COGNITIVE–BEHAVIORAL CONCEPTUALIZATION

Individuals with a histrionic personality style tend to believe that for life to be worthwhile, it should be entertaining, enjoyable, and filled with people who are engaging and validating. They see themselves as glamorous and deserving of the attention they seek. Millon (1999) described the self-image of the histrionic style as *gregarious* (see Table 8.1), a term that underscores these individuals' enhancement orientation and external focus. They depend and thrive on the social aspects of life; in fact, it is often difficult for them to stay engaged in a nonsocial task because the desire for social engagement is such a powerful influence. Indeed, the histrionic style may interfere in serious ways with the individual's ability to meet the demands of the academic enterprise. For college students with a histrionic style, the monotony of schoolwork may be highly unattractive but the social opportunities intoxicating. As one father described, "My daughter majored in sorority." Similar problems may occur in work settings or other activities in which the person with a histrionic style must contend with nonsocial activities and responsibilities.

The conditional beliefs of those with a histrionic orientation relate to their need for attention. For instance, such individuals may view life as meaningless and painful unless they are able to keep others invested or unless others are impressed with them. For some, the belief may be that unless others are showing constant attention and admiration, they are going to leave. The ability to maintain validating attention is critical and may be perceived as contingent on their ability to display specific qualities. For instance, the belief that one would be rejected or overlooked by others if not dressed fashionably puts the person in a position of recurrent threat that emerges whenever the opportunity or necessity for social engagement arises. Such behaviors characterize the *attention-seeking* interpersonal con-

TABLE 8.1
Structures and Functions of the Histrionic Prototype and Associated Liabilities

Personality domain	Liability
Self-image Gregarious	View of the self as glamorous, sociable, and deserving of the attention and validation of others
Object representations Shallow	Lack of thought about relationships beyond the immediate and superficial aspects of the immediate engagement; tendency to be insensitive to internal motives, drives, ambitions, and so forth
Morphological organization Disjointed	Tendency to react to immediate situations without a guiding frame of reference beyond immediate validation; interpretation of most events is relative to immediate desires
Mood and temperament Fickle	Regular mood shifts, typically corresponding to immediacy of the situation and current cognitive interpretation
Behavioral acts Dramatic	Behaviors expressed with dramatic flair; common behaviors enacted with extravagance
Interpersonal conduct Attention seeking	Need for attention and investment of others to thrive; willingness to act in extreme fashion in order to solicit that attention
Cognitive style Flighty	Typical thought processes involve only immediate circumstance and immediate need to invest the attention of others
Regulatory mechanism Dissociation	Tendency to avoid thinking about things that are unpleasant and uncontrollable

duct described by Millon (1999). For these individuals, the task of life is to win and retain the attention of others. Unlike the narcissistic personality, the individual with a histrionic orientation does not necessarily need to feel superior to others; they simply desire to have others attending to them.

Instrumental beliefs are of the following type: "I must trust my feelings," "Be entertaining," and "Strive to insist on or demonstrate superiority." With these beliefs, individuals with a histrionic prototype personality strive to do whatever possible to keep others engaged with and invested in them.

Although they are clearly oriented toward other people, intimacy and genuine concern are generally lacking. In describing the interpersonal relationships of an individual with a histrionic style, Millon (1999) used the term *shallow*. His or her interpersonal history may be based more on appearance than on intimacy. For instance, the relationship the individual has with a parent may be based on a common interest in superficial activities such as shopping and beauty tips, athletic accomplishment, and so forth, and not on issues of fears, ambitions, and other intimate concerns. It is also not uncommon for such individuals to have a history in which their status among others was dependent on their appearance or ability to keep others invested (e.g., through athletic, musical, or theatrical pursuits).

As discussed earlier in the description of Mary, behaviorally the individual with a histrionic style is *dramatic*. Reactions are often more extreme and expressive than the circumstance warrants. The dramatic characteristic of these individuals contributes to the extreme reactions to circumstantial events. Interpersonally, the individual is attention seeking. The dramatic flair that characterizes the individual serves his or her need for attention. In one-on-one interactions and in group settings, the individual keeps the attention on him- or herself and will implement a host of behaviors in this regard. It is not unusual to observe such a person go from being loud and effervescent to hurt and tearful in a short period, all enacted to keep the attention of the audience. The cognitive style is *flighty*, shifting with perceived changes in interests and investments of the audience (person or group). These individuals are highly sensitive to the attentional focus of the group and display an incredible ability to keep the attention directed toward them, regardless of the topic. Because of this constant redirection, the individual appears overly spontaneous and sporadic. They are *fickle* in mood and temperament, with affect changing according to the needs of the circumstance. It is not uncommon for an individual with a histrionic style to be described as moody by others, with the shifting mood serving to manage the attention of others.

PATHOLOGIC PROCESS OF THE HISTRIONIC PATTERN

Individuals with a histrionic prototype personality encounter stress when interpersonal attention is not, or may not be, focused on them. In such situations, they will engage in immediate, preemptive, and anticipatory ways to ensure that they receive the attention and investment of others that they desire. Although some individuals may take a very aggressive approach to deriving attention, others may be more subtle and may seek to secure the investment and validation of others through their naiveté, innocence, or helplessness. In many cases, the various clinical conditions exhibited by these individuals reflect adaptive means of securing the enhancing investment of others. For instance, the anguish associated with a depressed or anxious state would not typically be quietly endured, but rather vigorously expressed to those who will listen.

AXIS I VULNERABILITIES

The individual with a histrionic style is vulnerable to a host of clinical conditions stemming from the exhibitionistic orientation to the world. On one hand, the absence of validating attention or the failure to elicit desired attention can itself lead to stress manifested in various clinical conditions, including anxiety, depression, eating disorders, somatic conditions, and others. On the other hand, the display of the clinical conditions may also serve as means of securing the desired attention and investment of others. As a result, the individual is uniquely susceptible to a host of clinical conditions. The following are several of the common conditions associated with the histrionic prototype.

Generalized Anxiety Disorder

Because individuals with a histrionic orientation define self-worth through the attention and investment of others, they are vulnerable to periods of anxiety when not in a validating interaction or relationship. It may be during times of social isolation that the individual presents for treatment, complaining of nonspecific anxiety symptoms. Even among a group at a festive engagement, the individual is vulnerable to anxiety when the attention shifts to someone else. For some individuals, the anxiety itself may become a source of attention seeking. To be sure, any acute crisis or other distress can turn the attention away from others and back to the individual with a histrionic style. Although some cases of anxiety and other distress may be feigned, the lack of attention is indeed painful to the individual, and the anxiety symptoms are convenient means to elicit the attention of others.

Panic Disorder

To persons with a histrionic orientation, phobia provides an opportunity to invest others in their distress. Although the conditioned emotional component of the phobic condition may develop as any conditioned emotional response, the phobic disorder is maintained not only by the negative reinforcement derived through escape and avoidance but also by the reinforcing value of attention from others. For instance, a woman with a histrionic style who has a fear of snakes not only avoids areas where snakes might be found but also makes a theatrical fuss any time she is brought into the proximity of a grassy or forested area. At any time the opportunity develops to talk about her fear of snakes, she will do so with great detail and intensity.

Dissociative Disorder

Dissociation is a condition that emerges apart from neurological pathology when an observed reality exists that the individual perceives to be unmanageable or unacceptable and that can be more or less effectively denied through dissociation (Candel, Merckelbach, & Kuijpers, 2003; Steiner, Carrion, Plattner, & Koopman, 2003). Because individuals with a histrionic personality style lack an independent sense of self-identity, dissociation may prove to be an adaptive reaction when others are unavailable to them. As an example, one woman with a histrionic personality disorder said that during the weekends that her husband was away she would lose all track of time, immersing herself in housework that she would not even recall having done after her husband returned.

Furthermore, the secondary gain from dissociative states may occur in the form of soliciting desired attention and dependence or not being required to attend to tasks that these individuals find unpleasant but that others expect them to complete. In either case, the dissociation proves to be an adaptive response to several situations. As an example, the infamous histrionic character of Scarlet O'Hara in Margaret Mitchell's saga *Gone With the Wind* (1936) proclaimed, "I won't think of that now. . . . If I think of it now, it will upset me" (pp. 72–73).

Obsessive–Compulsive Disorder

Faced with painful feelings of isolation and self-contempt, the individual with a histrionic style may come to rely on obsessive–compulsive symptoms as a means of avoiding deeper, distressing thoughts and feelings. Furthermore, an individual with "obsessive–compulsive disorder" invests others in his or her "illness," but on his or her own terms. In some cases, the symptoms may develop as obsessional thoughts related to sexual or hostile feelings toward others. In this situation, the obsession is related to potential sources of attention and may be combined with compulsive and impulsive behaviors enacted to bring the potential outcome to fruition. For the individual with a histrionic style in need of perfection, obsessions and compulsive behaviors can range from excessive attention to detail to incapacitation by the need to be perfect.

Somatoform Disorder

As Millon and Davis (2000) observed, individuals with a histrionic orientation "utilize hypochondriacal and somatization symptoms as instruments for attracting attention and nurturance" (p. 222). The chronic concerns and ailments of somatoform disorders provide ample and consistent means of soliciting the attention of others. Although their concerns over health-related matters, including aches and pains, may be very legitimate, the use of these symptoms as means for eliciting the attention and investment of others is a hallmark of the histrionic personality. In the case of someone with a disingenuous histrionic personality, somatic complaints may serve as the primary source for exploiting the patience and good intentions of others. For many with a histrionic style, were it not for the constant physical aches and pains they experience, they would have little to invest others. As with other somatoform disorders, conversion symptoms prove to be very effective means for winning the investment of others. For individuals with a histrionic prototype personality, both positive and negative reinforcement provides a powerful behavioral incentive. Through their physical symptoms, these individuals gains relief from isolation and boredom and the reward of attention from others.

Depression and Dysthymia

When an individual with a histrionic orientation experiences depression, it is not typically of the retarded variety (see Millon, 1999). Rather, such individuals are more likely to express the agitated variety in which the depressed affect is advertised to others. Although in some cases the depression may be more feigned than real, the histrionic style leaves them vulnerable to a hopeless depression stemming from the alienation they have created and these exhaustion of available relationships. In the case of these hopeless feelings, these individuals display distress in a way consistent with the personality style, which is in the form of a complaining, expressive type of suffering.

Although it is not unlikely that an individual with a histrionic orientation would display symptoms of dysthymia, this condition is somewhat inconsistent with the histrionic style. Because the individual relies, in large part, on upbeat and attention-seeking behaviors, dysthymia would not prove to be an effective strategy for winning the investment of others. However, the individual may display dysthymic symptoms in certain circumstances. For instance, the individual may connect with a group of people who are disenchanted with dominant cultural values. Within this group, being the most disgruntled and emotionally caustic may prove very adaptive for someone who needs the attention and validation of others.

Likewise, the individual who is feeling some sense of hopelessness relative to social and cultural values may rely on those feelings as a means to invest others, including the therapist. For instance, Millon and Davis (2000) suggested that some individuals with a histrionic style express their emotional distress in popular jargon that reflects a certain emotional pretentiousness. As an example, one struggling with dysthymia is not "sad," but rather "fighting an existential crisis in this age of mass society" (p. 242). In another case, one who is unable to maintain the investment of others because of excessive attention seeking may withdraw into a dysthymic condition in the form of social withdrawal. However, for this individual, should opportunities change such that new or renewed opportunities for validation present themselves, the dysthymic mood may soon lift.

Bipolar Disorder

The individual with a histrionic prototype personality may be particularly vulnerable to bipolar conditions (Turley, Bates, Edwards, & Jackson, 1992). The general gregariousness of the individual and reactive tendencies are similar to the hypomanic behaviors observed in one with bipolar II disorder and cyclothymia. In fact, were the active behaviors not part of the individual's general disposition, this outgoing and often energetic behavior might be diagnosed as a bipolar condition independent of the personality. These active behaviors are particularly characteristic when things are going well for the person or when he or she needs to increase activity to win or maintain the attention of others.

VARIATIONS ON THE TRADITIONAL HISTRIONIC PERSONALITY

In each of the variations on the histrionic personality, the individual is oriented to winning and maintaining the investment of others. Differences exist relative to the beliefs the person has, perhaps reflected in core and intermediate beliefs, concerning how to establish that investment.

The *theatrical histrionic* personality style is the purest variant of the condition. Individuals with the theatrical style of the histrionic pattern win the attention of others through their ostentatious displays. They are very attentive to current cultural styles and standards and pursue those ideals with an impassioned fervor and zeal. To others, the display appears excessive and often inappropriate. Unfortunately, for these individuals there is little to define them beyond the physical display. Conversations typically do not go much deeper than the topic of fashion or style, which puts them in a dilemma when they find themselves in a situation in which mere appearance is not sufficient to win and maintain the attention of the audience. As Millon and Davis (2000) described it, individuals with a theatrical histrionic style become somewhat of a caricature of their gender stereotype. Within an evolutionary perspective, these individuals can be described as trying to win the mating challenge by being the best representative of their gender, as they perceive that role. Thus, the histrionic male personality epitomizes the culturally defined masculine ideal, whereas the histrionic female personality displays the perceived feminine ideal.

The *vivacious histrionic* personality style combines features of the narcissistic personality style. Individuals with this style live life with a tremendous, vivacious intensity. They are driven toward exciting activities and joyful outcomes and may move from one activity or one person to another on an impulsive whim. Because of their outgoing, charming, and engaging personality, they are able to enlist others in their activities, yet these relationships are prone to problems because individuals with a vivacious histrionic orientation are typically unreliable and self-centered, often leaving others to deal with the mess they created. Individuals with the vivacious histrionic style feel entitled to the attention and validation they seek and may react with petulance when it is not received.

The *infantile histrionic* personality style is a combination of the histrionic and borderline personalities. As with all varieties of the histrionic style, when attention is not centered on the individual, he or she experiences painful emotions. However, unlike the pure histrionic or vivacious histrionic orientations, characterized by intensified sociable behaviors, the infantile histrionic style is more likely to react with intense negative emotions. Similar to the borderline histrionic personality, the infantile histrionic personality may vacillate between overcompliance and resentful withdrawal and depression (Millon & Davis, 2000, p. 241). When events are not going as desired, the individual with an infantile histrionic style may react with poutiness, depression, or with a full-blown tantrum.

The *appeasing histrionic* personality style is a combination of histrionic, dependent, and compulsive styles of personality. As Millon and Davis (2000) suggested of individuals with this style, "approval is their one mission in life" (p. 242). These individuals will do whatever it takes to ensure that those on whom they have come to depend will value them and treat them well. They are overly accommodating and agreeable and avoid confrontations at all costs. They fear they may do something to warrant the rejection of others and are in a nearly constant state of damage prevention and control. When wronged by others, rather than retaliate, individuals with an appeasing histrionic orientation will take on the role of martyr or victim and in this way alter the reactions of those on whom they depend.

The *disingenuous histrionic* personality style includes histrionic and antisocial features. This style of personality is characterized by the charm and outgoing sociability of the classic histrionic, but with a more manipulative component. Individuals with this personality use their histrionic style to keep others invested, but also to exploit others for their own benefit. In some cases, the antisocial component reflects only a tendency toward the violation of social convention, broken promises, and shattered loyalties, whereas in other cases the antisocial component is more malicious and deceitful. These individuals may be inclined to factitious disorders and malingering, enacted to enlist the accommodations they seek.

The *tempestuous* personality style includes aspects of the negativistic personality. When things are going well for individuals with this orientation, they exhibit the more typical aspects of the histrionic style. However, when things are not going well, the tempestuous histrionic style is hyperreactive and overly dramatic. Such individuals externalize the problem and use their emotions to express their discontent with others and to compel others into some form of acquiescence. For these individuals, mood shifts are often rapid and unpredictable. They may become disgruntled and critical of others when they do not receive the attention and admiration they desire.

TREATMENT OF THE HISTRIONIC PROTOTYPE

Successful treatment of clients with the histrionic personality prototype requires that the client develop greater independence relative to the need for external confirmation and validation. Because these individuals tend to place responsibility for their affective experiences in the hands of others, treatment outcomes are enhanced when they develop greater emotional self-reliance and self-control. The challenge of treating those with the histrionic style emerges as a result of their hesitancy to accept this emotional responsibility.

The Therapeutic Relationship

Clients with the histrionic personality style present unique clinical challenges. On one hand, they are generally enthusiastic clients who revel in the opportunity to focus so heavily on themselves. Their typically outgoing and gregarious nature provides a regular source of energy throughout therapy. Often, these individuals strive to be their therapist's best or favorite client. However, when this is not possible, their need for validation may lead them to try being the neediest or most challenging. All too often, clients with the histrionic style pursue therapy as a means of enlisting the attention of others, and they may use therapy as a means of avoiding responsibility or securing the reassurance of people close to them. On the other hand, their need for attention and constant validation can impede therapeutic gains, and their flighty cognitive style makes it difficult to keep them on task. It is not uncommon for those with the histrionic style to seek special accommodations and concessions, such as reduced fees or special billing policies. By getting the therapist to agree to such concessions, they are able to derive, in their minds, a special relationship with the therapist (Freeman et al., 1990). These clients may also act seductively to invest the attention of the therapist. They are often so reactive to suggestions that they give up their attention-seeking behaviors. To these clients, not being the center of attention is paramount to social starvation. As a result, they may display various forms of treatment resistance. Finally, as mentioned, individuals with a histrionic style are very reluctant to accept responsibility for their own emotional reactions and rely on strong and fickle affect as a means of managing relationships with others.

To maintain a beneficial therapeutic relationship, the therapist may find it helpful to follow specific recommendations. First, it is useful to validate the individual's desire for rewarding interpersonal relationships. By doing so, the therapist is able to discuss the client's behaviors as efforts to foster close interpersonal relationships. Through a collaborative effort between therapist and client, the adaptive value of efforts the client exhibits and the rationality of his or her expectations can be considered. In this way, the defensiveness that might be elicited through more direct confrontation can be minimized. The client's goal may not involve the specific problem as much as the techniques he or she uses to derive attention and validation.

Second, to control the fickleness of the client with a histrionic proto-type personality, therapist and client must pay careful attention to specific treatment goals and adhere to the treatment plan to decrease the potential for treatment meandering in response to an immediate crisis or concern (Freeman et al., 1990). By maintaining focus on the enhancement of inter-personal relationships and greater emotional self-reliance, the therapist can bring the client's spontaneous diversions back to the ultimate treatment goals in a convenient and nonconfrontational way. By keeping the focus on relationships and how to manage them, the therapist is able to minimize resistance by focusing attention on the issues that are most relevant to the client.

An additional challenge in working with individuals with a histrionic style is that successful treatment may not offer them more than they already have. For the passive–dependent individual, such as one with the dependent personality, successful treatment promises greater engagement and fulfill-ment, albeit associated with greater risks. For the active–dependent client, such as the person with a histrionic style, change that requires sacrificing the joys of constant external validation and accepting personal responsibility for dealing with unpleasant circumstances and unpleasant emotions may not be very appealing, despite the relief he or she might gain from negative emotions. It is important that the client understands that therapy does not mean a lack of fulfillment and that social validation can still be attained. Indeed, to accomplish this goal, the individual must be able to provide self-validation and reap the benefit of more validating social interactions created by prosocial behaviors.

Successful treatment of individuals with a histrionic orientation would include greater resistance to interpersonal indifference or rejection, greater personal independence, greater emotional self-reliance, and the expression of positive, prosocial actions. One of the first concerns in treating these individuals is increasing their tolerance for not being the center of attention or not being able to rely on others for a sense of personal validation or emotional rescue. This is a daunting undertaking for many clients with a histrionic style because not being able to rely on others means being insignificant and helpless. A major obstacle in treating these individuals is that cognitive changes alone may not be enough to alter the intense emotions they might feel if they cease their attention-seeking behaviors. These individuals depend on the investment and validation of others and often have few resources for validating their self-integrity. In a metaphorical sense, they feed on the attention and reassurance of others, and to give that up would leave them with nothing else to sustain them. Not surprising, these individuals are vulnerable to a host of negative emotions when their sense of connection with others is threatened. They might react to perceived rejection or indifference with anxiety, panic, jealousy, guilt, frustration, anger, or some other affective reaction. Likewise, they are also inclined to other conditions that serve to keep others invested.

Cognitive Goals

It is very important that individuals develop an appreciation of their role in social relationships and of the impact of their behaviors on others. In addition, understanding the nature and appropriateness of their interpersonal expectations will help them justify cognitive and behavioral changes. Because these individuals regulate themselves in large part by their affective experience and do not consistently stop and reflect on their contribution to problems or alternative responses, they are often unaware of how their behaviors are perceived by others. Through the process of collaborative empiricism and guided discovery (see Freeman et al., 1990), the therapist can direct the client into discussions that should promote greater awareness and interpersonal sensitivity. The use of role-play scenarios in which the client is directed to take the perspective of a social partner can help foster greater social perceptiveness.

Once the client has come to understand and appreciate that his or her interpersonal style may be contributing to recurrent emotional distress, that individual is in the best position to begin making behavioral adjustments and accepting greater responsibility for emotional experiences. Nonetheless, even though a client has come to understand and question the appropriateness of his or her expectations of others, old assumptions will continue to emerge. To minimize the impact of these old schema-based reactions, the therapist can help equip the client with cognitive rebuttals useful for countering old conclusions. For instance, rather than allowing herself to believe "others should pay attention to me," one client learned to counter such statements by saying to herself, "Although it would be nice if everyone would do just as I pleased, it's probably unlikely that they will." In this process, she did not deny the desire, but she acknowledged it and then commented on its inappropriateness and unlikelihood. By adding to this an appreciation for the value of prosocial behaviors, the client is in the best position to foster rewarding interpersonal relationships.

Behavioral Goals

Because individuals with a histrionic orientation are naturally very social, it is unreasonable to suggest that they give up their social investment. In fact, their natural social orientation can be used to help them develop behavioral skills that are more optimally adaptive through an increase in prosocial behavior and a decrease in dramatic, attention-seeking behaviors. Using role-play scenarios, the therapist can help the client develop greater sensitivity to how others are reacting to their behaviors and develop more adaptive interpersonal skills (i.e., that are less likely to lead to negative reactions by others or to lead to further dependency). Once the client feels comfortable with the role-playing, he or she can practice those behaviors in ongoing interpersonal interactions.

Changes in interpersonal behaviors require that the client develop a greater willingness to accept personal responsibility for fostering positive interpersonal relationships and personal emotional reactions. Without these cognitive adjustments, the suggestion of behavioral changes will likely lead to a deterioration in the therapeutic relationship as the client comes to feel that the therapist is failing to understand the problem—that is, other people's unwillingness to be more accommodating. It is often necessary to introduce specific behavioral interventions to alter behavioral habits, such as impulsive spending and eating disorders, that are often associated with the histrionic style.

Affective Changes

Perhaps more than with any other personality style, with the exception of the borderline prototype personality, individuals with a histrionic personality style rely on emotional expression as a means of managing relationships with other people. In addition, they are often very much inclined to place responsibility for their affective reactions on others. Thus, if they are feeling distressed in any way, it is someone else's fault and someone else's—not necessarily the same person's—responsibility to make them feel better. Their affective reactions compel behaviors that are dramatic and often distressing to others. As a result of their emotional dependency, they are inclined to extreme reactions when others do not provide for them the validation or assistance they seek. To decrease their emotional dependency, the therapist can introduce metaemotional processes to assist them in developing a greater understanding of what they hope to accomplish with their emotional reactions and in considering alternative reactions. In fact, emotions can serve as the cue to consider cognitively their interpersonal motives and as an indication to consider alternative reactions.

To foster positive relationships with others and control his or her own emotional reactions, the client with a histrionic style can monitor ongoing cognitive, affective, and behavioral reactions. In this task, the client monitors reactions to situational events by acknowledging the desired outcome, reflecting on the appropriateness of that desire, and then considering alternative courses of action and associated affect to create a positive interpersonal engagement. The client can bring completed forms to subsequent sessions to use as a source of discussion and refinement (see also Rasmussen, 2003b).

CASE EXAMPLE

Louise is a 28-year-old woman presenting for treatment secondary to nonspecific emotional distress. She is married with no children and works part time as a sales associate at a major department store. She is pursuing treatment at the request of her husband, who has grown tired of her impulsive spending and her emotional reactivity. He has talked about separation and divorce. She was diagnosed by a psychiatrist as having bipolar II disorder 2 years previously and has been treated pharmacologically since the diagnosis. She reports some benefit from the medicine, but she has continued to struggle despite the medical treatment. She was diagnosed with cyclothymia while in high school and also treated medically at that time.

Her emotional reactions and manipulations have contributed to strain in her marriage. She is prone to emotional extremes, and her emotional expressions typically precede a brief period of episodic depression. Her initial reaction is to counterattack when confronted by her husband regarding her spending, then to claim she does what she does for him, and finally to retreat into a state of victimization. Fortunately, her depressed periods are relatively short in duration. By her own report, substantiated by her spouse, "my joy for living gets me out of the depression." She is extremely attentive to her attire, and her tendency to overspend on clothing has contributed to her marital conflicts. When confronted about her spending by her husband, she is emotionally very reactive. She frequently gets angry and then tearful. She and her husband have also fought over her tendency to be flirtatious in her interactions with other men. She insists that she has been loyal to her marital vows and sees his accusations as unfounded; she sees herself as just being friendly.

Louise's goal in therapy is to gain greater control over her emotions and to improve her marital relationship. However, as Louise described her situation, it seemed clear that her hope was to get others to be more protective of her emotions, most specifically her husband. Thus, greater control appeared to mean greater ability to control others. The Millon Clinical Multiaxial Inventory (MCMI–III; Millon, 1997) assessment suggested a histrionic style. Her scores were also suggestive of depressive and dependent features, yet the histrionic prototype was most specific; Axis I symptoms suggested by the MCMI–III included anxiety, depression, and potential for substance abuse. Louise was optimistic about therapy but also hesitant, thinking that her symptoms suggested a chemical imbalance that could be treated only by medicine. Louise's style of personality best fits the appeasing histrionic style.

Louise has various personality attributes that contribute to her emotional reactivity. Her need for attention and validation from others (attention-seeking interpersonal style) puts her in a precarious position. To her, validation is derived through her appearance, and this is the predominant focus in her life (shallow object relations). In fact, she defers to others on most other life issues to attend to her own appearance and to her home decorations. Although she is pleased with her personal appearance and the appearance of her home, her focus is on impressing others and receiving validation from others. If others do not comment on her appearance, she feels insulted. Although her husband feels pride in her appearance and the attractiveness of their home, her spending has created financial problems.

Louise is not as gregarious as many individuals with a histrionic style. In fact, her social engagements are in many ways more imagined than realized. Yet during interpersonal engagements, her efforts to maintain the attention and validation of others are apparent. For instance, when interacting with men, she behaves in a flirtatious manner to keep them invested (attention seeking). In addition, her lack of investment in the marriage, including issues of emotional and physical intimacy, has frustrated her husband. He is also interested in starting a family, and she is hesitant to do so. She views herself as pretty and fashionwise, but also as inept in many areas, which is consistent with the dependent qualities. Her core beliefs include, "I must look attractive" and "others won't like me if I don't look good." These beliefs fuel her intermediate and instrumental beliefs. For instance, Louise believes, "If I don't look good, people will not like me; therefore, I have to look good." Likewise, she believes, "I must do whatever it takes to keep up appearances." This belief in particular has contributed to her manipulations and impulsive spending and to her inattention to her marriage.

When confronted by her husband on issues of concern in the marriage (a source of stress), Louise does not consider very deeply the justification of his concerns (shallow representation) and reacts impulsively with defensive anger and sulkiness (dramatic and attention-seeking behavior). As a result, problems are not resolved. Typically, she rebounds quickly from her depression and ignores the conflict that had preceded the argument (mild dissociation as a regulatory mechanism).

For Louise, the pathologic process is activated in numerous circumstances. She does not regulate her emotions well when confronted with a desire to possess a new item for the house or a personal item or when confronted or ignored by others. These experiences prompt extreme emotional and behavioral reactions, which define the bipolar pattern. During these times, she becomes emotionally reactive. The behaviors compelled by her emotions are immediately effective means for justifying purchases, eliciting desired attention, and fending off perceived criticisms and affronts.

The primary goal of treatment, as expressed by Louise, is the development of greater emotional self-control. Although pharmacological means have been tried, the reality of her interpersonal circumstance necessitates the reemergence of her emotional reactions. In her efforts to maintain and bolster her physical appearance, Louise frequently puts herself in a position in which she must manipulate financial matters to procure the items she desires. The guilt felt by Louise following her impulsive spending and subsequent efforts to hide or justify her spending, together with the frustrations felt by her husband and his subsequent confrontations, compel her extreme emotional reactions. Although therapeutic attention could be focused specifically on the behavioral control of impulsive spending or on metaemotional processes, as long as Louise perceives her worth and integrity to be dependent on appearance, she will continue to feel compelled to procure more appearance-validating items.

Although it is unlikely that she will abandon her concern over physical appearances, it is possible that Louise can increase her satisfaction with less and derive greater satisfaction from other outcomes. Through guided discovery, the therapist encouraged Louise to consider the nature of her dependency on physical appearance. She recognized the emergence of this trend in childhood. Louise reported a childhood atmosphere of perceived inadequacy where other families had more than her family. From a young age, she perceived worth to be based on physical images depicted in magazines and on television.

In addition, Louise was able to recognize the cost of her impulsive spending and its relationship to her emotional reactions. For instance, she recognized the pattern of emotions she felt, beginning with envy and jealousy, that compelled her impulsive spending. She was able to identify the cognitive dialogue she had with herself that would eventually lead to her justifying a purchase. Following the purchase, she was racked with feelings of guilt and fear (related to her husband's reactions), and she would implement efforts to hide the purchase from her husband. When confronted, she often felt deprived and would defend herself by getting angry and pouting. In fact, she was able to report that her guilt put her in a bad mood, which she would use to prompt a fight with her husband about unrelated issues. By her report, she then felt justified in having made the purchase.

This pattern of emotional reactivity underscored the bipolar diagnosis. Efforts were initiated to stop the process at its origin by helping Louise control what became known in her therapy as a "crisis of want," which was described as an emotional crisis related to her disparate desire to buy something new. In this regard, efforts were directed at generating specific cognitive responses when such crises occurred. For instance, to minimize the feeling of deprivation that often followed her own refusal to buy an item, she simply said to herself, "I can have this if I want it, but I have to wait until tomorrow." The inside joke to Louise was that tomorrow would never arrive.

In addition, efforts were directed at enhancing Louise's investment in her marriage and in her friendships, with some discussion on altering or abandoning those relationships that tended to fuel her "crisis of want." Attention to these matters was important to provide Louise with enhancing life experiences independent of physical appearance and material acquisition. Throughout this process, Louise implemented various cognitive strategies for countering feelings of insecurity and for regulating her emotional reactions. Although other issues remained for Louise and her husband, her ability to control her spending and dramatic emotional reactions constituted a significant therapeutic gain.

CONCLUSION

The individual with a histrionic orientation displays an active dependency characterized by a strong need for external validation in the form of interpersonal attention, support, and reassurance. Such individuals tend to respond to life according to their own emotional reactions and to place a great deal of the responsibility for their feelings on others. As a result, they are put in the position of needing to manage interpersonal relationships in such a way that others are available to them and react to them in a way that provides the attention and reassurance the individual desires. Unfortunately, others often feel burdened and annoyed by these individuals' manipulative and emotional reactions. In their efforts to secure the investment of others, the individual with a histrionic style is prone to a host of negative emotional reactions that contribute to the experience of Axis I clinical conditions.

Successful treatment of these clients requires that they develop greater, genuine sensitivity and concern for the feelings of others, take greater responsibility for their own emotional reactions, and decrease their reliance on emotional displays as a means of controlling others. Fortunately, their natural social inclinations can be used as a means of redirecting their interpersonal energies in such a way that interpersonal relationships are enhanced.

9

THE NARCISSISTIC PROTOTYPE

Key phrase: Admire me
Evolutionary focus: Competitiveness

The narcissistic style of personality is characterized by a relative balance on the enhancement and protection bipolarities (see Figure 9.1). Individuals with a narcissistic personality style desire validation and attention and are thus oriented to enhancing and pleasurable outcomes, but they are also attentive to threats to their status and integrity and are thus likewise oriented to protection. Often this orientation is observed in their occasional efforts to elicit compliments from others or to create an appearance of superiority over others. They may also express efforts to avoid negative social interactions in which they are not, to their minds, the most impressive—which may relate to being the most attractive, most intelligent, most athletic, most traveled, and so forth. In situations in which they are successfully one-upped by another individual, they are compelled to enact any of numerous techniques for putting the person down, including the following:

- responding directly (e.g., personal verbal attack),
- responding indirectly (e.g., behind the person's back, with gossip and criticism),
- one-upping the other individual, or
- retreating from the competition.

Any of these actions may be accompanied by a caustic and cutting remark. Alternatively, an individual with a narcissistic style may display a smug disposition and derive a sense of superiority through his or her lack of

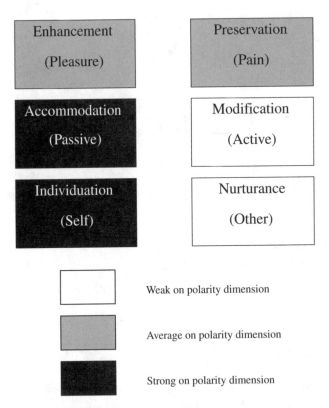

Figure 9.1. Polarity balance of the narcissistic prototype. From *Personality-Guided Therapy* (p. 435), by T. Millon, 1999, New York: Guilford Press. Copyright 1999 by John Wiley & Sons, Inc. Reprinted with permission.

engagement in the competitive one-upmanship. However, even in such an attempt, there is typically some effort, albeit subtle, to establish a sense or an impression of superiority. For instance, one may offer a subtle yet insulting remark, claim to have better things to do, or simply leave the interaction with no explanation.

Millon (1999) described individuals with a narcissistic orientation as passive–independent. Viewing themselves as better than others and deserving of admiration, these individuals tend toward passivity. Essentially, there is nothing they need or should do to win the investment and validation of others; others should simply provide those outcomes. Nonetheless, the individual is episodically active, as necessitated by the need to counter an attack to status and to reestablish a position of superiority. In most situations, however, the individual may be more inclined toward a smug indifference characteristic of their passive style of adaptation.

Individuals with a narcissistic prototype personality are highly self-focused. To them, they are the center of the universe. They typically consider only how events affect them personally, and they are generally indifferent to the joys or suffering of others. In their description of the individual with a narcissistic style, Maxmen and Ward (1995) told the anecdote of the client who insisted on being given a tissue for her runny nose by one of the hospital staff, who was currently attempting to resuscitate a dying client in the next bed. Although this description may be somewhat extreme, it underscores the lack of empathy and insight into the needs and concerns of others. Whereas these individuals may be attentive to others, most typically their concerns are with the attributes and accomplishments of others relative to their own attributes and accomplishments.

As an example, Sally was a member of a social group affiliated with her church. When the group would get together, Sally was very attentive to the activities of the other group members. She listened very attentively to everything others would say. But anytime one of the other members of the group mentioned something positive that he or she had done, Sally experienced a pang of anxiety, as if she has been personally insulted. Her typical response was to find reason to minimize the accomplishment of the other person, or she would share a personal anecdote that effectively minimized the other person's success. For example, one woman talked of her family's enjoyable trip to Maine. Sally countered by describing her family's intended trip to France. Once she had countered the other person's accomplishment, Sally's feeling of distress dissipated.

It is, perhaps, the self-focus and passivity that most marks the narcissistic style. For those with a narcissistic orientation who do not meet the *Diagnostic and Statistical Manual of Mental Disorders* (4th ed., text revision; American Psychiatric Association, 2000) criteria for the disorder, the general expectation that others should accommodate them in various ways (e.g., be nice to them, not treat them "badly," or not ask too much of them), independent of what they have done for anyone, may be the feature that contributes most to the individual's vulnerability to various clinical conditions.

PERSONALITY-GUIDED COGNITIVE–BEHAVIORAL CONCEPTUALIZATION

Individuals with a narcissistic personality style are defined by a self-view of *admiration* (Millon, 1999). They view themselves as special and unique and deserving of validation from others and of special privileges and freedoms (Beck, Freeman, & Associates, 1990). In extremes, this includes delusions of grandeur and the universal admiration of others; in less extreme, stylistic form, this involves a sense that one is more capable or gifted than others and thus entitled to special privilege and opportunity. Phil is an example of an individual with a narcissistic style. He is an attractive 20-year-old college junior. He comes from an affluent home where his parents are both professionals who make very good salaries. He is not flashy or obnoxious but views himself as better than the other students at the university. He is convinced that most of the girls find him attractive and that the other male students are intimidated by him. He does not feel much need to practice common courtesies, and he is often rather smug in his demeanor.

Individuals with the narcissistic style see others as being less important or less capable or gifted than they are, and consequently they expect others to be both impressed with them and willing to provide them the validation and accommodation they believe they deserve. They do not feel much, if any, obligation to foster positive relationships. This sense of indifference to personal social responsibility is often expressed as *haughtiness* in the extreme and as conceit or arrogance in those less characterized by the narcissistic style. For instance, although the individual with a narcissistic disorder may literally stick his nose up at another person, the individual with a narcissistic style will act with a detached superficiality while interacting with another person, unless talking about him- or herself, when the degree of enthusiasm can be observed to rise considerably.

Individuals with a narcissistic orientation expect the world to be accommodating and thus view themselves as having a rather bright future. Unfortunately, their bright future is dependent on whether the environment provides them the validation and accommodation they believe they deserve. As long as the external environment is providing the resources desired, these individuals can do quite well. Indeed, such individuals with unique intellectual, artistic, or athletic talents may be quite successful, with a minimum of effort, in deriving the admiration, affirmation, and accommodation from others that they desire. For those less able to derive the constant or satisfying admiration and accommodation of others, the narcissistic style can contribute to considerable vulnerabilities as the individual is unable to thrive in an unaccommodating environment.

When others fail to provide individuals with a narcissistic prototype personality the admiration sought, they are forced into a compensatory position in which they must incite others to fulfill what they believe is their obligation to accommodate them. Similarly, when such individuals' status is threatened or compromised, they must act in a way to protect or reestablish a sense of superiority relative to others. For many individuals with a narcissistic style, others are simply unwilling to provide constant validation. Subsequently, they face adaptive challenges that require the manipulation or exploitation of people and resources.

Table 9.1 lists the personality attributes of the individual with a narcissistic orientation. Notable in these attributes is the lack of prosocial skills. The individual is clearly oriented toward self-protection and self-promotion

TABLE 9.1
Structures and Functions of the Narcissistic Prototype and Associated Liabilities

Personality domain	Liability
Self-image Admirable	View of the self in more positive terms than others; failure to see or accept one's equality with others
Object representations Contrived	Relationships and intimacies generally more fantasy than reality; assumption of more prestige and reason for admiration than exist in reality
Morphological organization Spurious	Ability to manage image and relationships better at some times than at others; inclination to be reactive to perceived threats or opportunities for enhancement and admiration
Mood and temperament Insouciant	Some degree of smugness or arrogant indifference; viewed by others as arrogant and conceited
Behavioral acts Haughty	Condescension in interpersonal relationships; treatment of others as inferiors
Interpersonal conduct Exploitative	Sense of entitlement, leading to ignoring or rejection of others' rights and opportunities; use of others for self-promotion, either as audience or source of comparison
Cognitive style Expansive	Undisciplined imagination; invention of fantastic stories for self-promotion; preoccupation with images of personal superiority
Regulatory mechanism Rationalization	Self-deception; ability to construct justification for exploitation and inconsiderateness

and is willing and able to manipulate a situation to maximize personal gains. In the individual with a narcissistic style, there is often greater attention to and concern with social relationships than in those with a narcissistic personality disorder; nonetheless, the bias remains promotion of the self and avoidance of undesired social obligation and responsibility.

The core beliefs of the individual with a narcissistic personality style, according to Beck et al. (1990, pp. 49–50), are along the lines of, "Since I am special, I deserve special dispensations, privileges, and prerogatives"; "I am superior to others, and they should acknowledge this"; and "I am above the rules." Conditional beliefs are of the following nature: "If others don't recognize my special status, they should be punished" and "If I am to maintain my superior status, I should expect others' subservience." Instrumental beliefs include "strive to insist upon or demonstrate superiority." With these beliefs, individuals with a narcissistic style strive to do whatever they can to promote their status among others. These individuals may seek "glory, wealth, position, power, and prestige as a way of reinforcing their superior image" (Beck et al., 1990, p. 50). They are often competitive with others who claim an equally high status, and they will resort to manipulative strategies to gain their ends. They do not have a cynical view of the rules, but they see themselves as above them. They regard themselves as part of society, but at the top stratum (Beck et al., 1990).

PATHOLOGIC PROCESS OF THE NARCISSISTIC PATTERN

The narcissistic style is captured in schemas that relate to concerns with status, defensiveness, and competitiveness. When defensive schemas are activated, individuals with a narcissistic style are prone to a variety of mode-based reactions implemented to protect or maintain a sense of superiority over others. For instance, in the face of being upstaged by others, the core beliefs of these individuals are activated, and mode reactions are implemented to meet the competitive challenge. For individuals with a narcissistic orientation who find themselves in a nonaccommodating environment, compensatory and defensive reactions can become quite common.

AXIS I VULNERABILITIES

As suggested in discussion of the pathologic process, the narcissistic prototype leaves one vulnerable to various clinical endpoints. Living life in competition for external praise and respect places these individuals in situations in which there is necessity for anxiety-mediated hypervigilance and anger-mediated aggressiveness and in which disappointments contributing to depressed affect are nearly unavoidable. The following sections describe several clinical conditions relative to their place in the narcissistic pathologic process.

Anxiety Disorders

Because individuals with a narcissistic prototype personality are dependent on the validation and accommodation of others who may be generally unwilling to provide them with the constant admiration they desire, anxiety may be a common reaction. In those situations in which they are upstaged by others and their status is on the line, anxiety fueling hypervigilance and quick reactance to social circumstance may be quite adaptive, albeit unpleasant. Such reactions may be more common in the individual with a compensatory narcissistic style, who holds deeper concerns about status. For these individuals, the potential of being upstaged, revealed as an "imposter," or obligated to perform in an undesirable fashion or at a threatening level may all contribute to considerable anxieties.

In some situations, the fear of exposure and embarrassment may contribute to a social phobic condition. In other situations, because individuals with a narcissistic orientation do not often possess the degree of indifference to social norms as do those with an antisocial personality, anxiety may be experienced as an outcome of threats brought about through the individual's exploitation of others who are now in a position to retaliate. As an example, Michelle had been shirking her responsibilities in the law firm in which she was employed. Because her grandfather was a founding partner of the firm, she felt that she did not need to work as hard for promotion as did the other law associates in the firm. She assumed that her family connection would be enough to get her through.

What Michelle failed to appreciate was that her grandfather had been gone for a very long time, and the current managing partners were not as interested in her lineage as they were in her productivity. Michelle received notice at her annual review that her position with the firm was now probationary and that she was to meet a target level of productivity by her next review in 6 months. She was initially angered, but her anger soon dissipated as the implications of the situation sank in. Over the next several weeks her anxiety increased to the point that she was unable to do any work related to her target goal. While trying to work, Michelle was overwhelmed by two issues. First, she hated the work she was required to do, and second, she was concerned with the implications of being terminated from her grandfather's law firm. When Michelle was terminated from the firm 1 year later, she attributed her dismissal to her anxiety disorder, which the partners failed to allow for.

Somatoform Disorder

Related to the experience of anxiety, individuals with a narcissistic style may experience various somatic complaints. For these individuals, somatic symptoms may serve multiple purposes. It is the goal of the individual to receive special treatment from others and to avoid the responsibilities of cooperation in social, occupational, and avocational activities. Somatic concerns, which may be legitimate somatic complaints or factitious symptoms, may emerge as the individual feels more obligations to act cooperatively with others. Further, somatic concerns provide the justification necessary to avoid cooperative responsibility and to elicit sympathy and assistance. For individuals with a narcissistic style, the somatic concerns may stem specifically from a stressful situation, while also providing an opportunity for relief from that very situation.

As an example of such a pattern of reactivity, the reader is referred to the character of Ignatius J. Riley in John Kennedy Toole's (1980) novel *A Confederacy of Dunces*. Riley, who possessed a tremendous sense of self-importance, was able to effectively avoid most life responsibilities and thus retain his childhood dependency by the fortuitous activity of digestive problems. In such situations, the task of engaging in an undesirable activity can serve as stimulus for a conditioned emotional reaction that involves various somatic symptoms. When the somatic complaints lead to the escape from or avoidance of a dreaded activity, those somatic complaints are reinforced. For someone who desires the avoidance of social obligation and interpersonal accommodation, somatic symptoms may be readily conditioned (see Van den Bergh, Stegen, & Van de Woestijne, 1997).

Dysthymia

To the extent that dysthymia represents a general detachment from social obligations, it seems reasonable to expect to see dysthymia in individuals with a narcissistic prototype personality. The fact is that such individuals are generally not good social partners. Subsequently, they are susceptible to various forms of social rejection. Because this constitutes a chronic circumstance, the implications may be felt as a consistent sense of isolation and hopelessness. Indeed, the hopelessness may relate to their desire for unconditional validation and freedom from social responsibility. Further, the social detachment that accompanies a dysthymic orientation provides the entitled individual with a ready available reason to avoid greater social participation and cooperation.

Depression

The need for validation and accommodation renders the individual with a narcissistic style vulnerable to episodes of depression. The central goals of the individual relate to deriving the admiration of others. Because his or her sense of self-importance is in large part dependent on the reactions of others, to the extent that the individual with a narcissistic prototype personality is unable to derive the accommodation and validation of others, feelings of hopelessness may ensue. Similarly, because of his or her condescending demeanor, others may come to avoid and even disparage the individual, leading to feelings of isolation and despair.

When a client who is depressed displays evidence of a narcissistic style of personality, it is important to assess the extent to which personality factors are contributing to interpersonal problems. It may be common for the individual to minimize the role or importance of strained social relationships, as this would suggest that social affiliations are more meaningful to the person than he or she would like to admit. Likewise, a depressed client who blames others for causing his or her depression may have a narcissistic orientation. Although not limited to the narcissistic personality style, the tendency to put the burden of positive emotions in the hands of others typically renders one susceptible to disappointment. With the more exacting standards and expectations for how one expects to be treated by others of the narcissistic makeup, this vulnerability is increased.

Finally, because the individual with a narcissistic style may not externalize problems to the extent that the disordered individual does, he or she may be more inclined to internalize the source of interpersonal conflicts. Thus, although striving to impress others, the individual may be very in tune to the fragility of his or her interpersonal status and may react to failure to impress with hopeless withdrawal. In this context, the individual may be particularly vulnerable to suicidal ideation and suicidal attempt as the result of the hopelessness that is often inevitable given his or her high expectations of the world. Indeed, for one who believes that others should provide unyielding praise and admiration, life may become quite hopeless.

Bipolar Disorder

Anger and hostility may be the most defining emotional reactions of the individual with a narcissistic style of personality. Needing to maintain a sense of superiority over others, and feeling entitled to the admiration and assistance of others, the individual may need to resort to anger and other contemptuous emotions when the validation he or she feels entitled to is not forthcoming. When these emotions are expressed with great intensity or are of a prolonged duration, the symptomatic pattern may fit a bipolar description. For instance, if one feels entitled to a particular outcome that is not forthcoming, anger and hostility may be effective means for securing that desired outcome, albeit not without inflicting serious damage on the relationship.

Marty, for instance, fits the description of an individual with an elitist style of narcissism. Generally, this style reflects itself in a general snobbishness and strong sense of entitlement. He is a member of a prestigious fraternity at his college. He has a reputation of not holding up his end of the responsibilities in fraternity social service projects, and he has been accused of being in the fraternity simply for the parties. His fraternity brothers have approached and confronted him on many occasions about his lack of contribution. When confronted, he has consistently gotten defensive and argued that he does his share and should not have to do more. Finally, the brothers decided to kick Marty out of the fraternity. When he was confronted with this news, Marty went into a rage that involved efforts to undermine the fraternity with the school administration, interference in the relationships of his fraternity brothers with their girlfriends, and even calls to the national fraternity office to attempt to have the campus chapter president kicked out of office.

Schulte, Hall, and Crosby (1994) suggested that individuals with a narcissistic personality may be at higher risk for violent reactions as a result of the failure of others to meet the individuals' expectations. In their report, individuals who encountered a "narcissistic injury" were more likely to react impulsively and in ways strongly suggestive of potential harm to the self and to others (e.g., purchase of a gun, suicidal gesture).

VARIATIONS ON THE TRADITIONAL NARCISSISTIC PERSONALITY

The variations on the narcissistic theme (Millon, 1999; Millon & Davis, 2000) represent differences in the ways that the individual seeks to derive the investment and validation of others and the manner in which they react to slights and insults. In all variations, the individual believes the self to be deserving of external validation, more or less independent of actions, and has a basic lack of concern for the feelings or welfare of others.

The *elitist narcissistic* personality style is the pure variant of the narcissistic style (Millon, 1999; Millon & Davis, 2000). Such individuals feel privileged and empowered by virtue of their special childhood status and their pseudoachievements; their status and achievements are, however, typically either fabricated or overstated. They seek the favored and good life, are upwardly mobile, and attempt to create special status and advantages through their interpersonal associations. These persons may become distraught when others fail to provide them the validation or assistance they believe themselves to deserve. They may become angry to elicit the compliance and accommodation of others, to derive a personally perceived sense of superiority over others, or simply as revenge. In addition, they may be inclined to depressive withdrawals in response to perceived mistreatments and disappointments.

The efforts to maintain a position of superiority over others put individuals with the elitist narcissistic personality style in a vulnerable position. Anxiety may be necessary to drive the hypervigilance to interpersonal threat. Likewise, periods of anxious distress may emerge in situations in which their status is consistently undervalued, devalued, or ignored. Indeed, in situations in which these individuals come up against the self-promotion of another individual, negative emotions may predominate. With their need to maintain a sense and image of superiority, coupled with the low likelihood that others will consistently provide the validation they seek, periods of depression may develop.

As an example, Marta was a wife and mother of two young boys. Although she did not work outside of the home, she felt that she was too busy to do housework and insisted that her husband pay to have someone clean their house. Her husband hired a woman who would come once a week to do general housecleaning, despite the fact that this put a considerable strain on their monthly budget. On the days that the housekeeper came to do her work, Marta often invited a few neighbors over to play card games. She did not see the inappropriateness of the demands that she made on the housekeeper during these times. When the housekeeper quit, she cited Marta's insistence that she make coffee and sandwiches for the guests as the reason for her quitting; she had not agreed to these responsibilities at the time of her hiring. For Marta, the chance to appear superior to her friends by flaunting her hired help, which they could not afford, was illustrative of her narcissistic style.

The *unprincipled narcissistic* personality style combines features of the antisocial prototype. This style is in many ways similar to the elitist narcissistic style, yet more malicious in intent and behavior. Individuals with an unprincipled narcissistic style possess a deficient conscience and feel little remorse over acts of interpersonal exploitation. As described by Millon (1999), these individuals may be unscrupulous, deceptive, and fraudulent in their efforts to secure prestige and validation. Whereas individuals with an elitist narcissistic style may rationalize exploitation, those with an unprincipled narcissistic style simply ignore the implications of their mistreatment of others. These individuals are among those who engage in criminal exploitation of others carried out with an entitled sense of indifference to the hardship they cause.

Ron is an example of an individual with an unprincipled narcissistic style. He was employed as an attorney and specialized in medical malpractice. His tendency was to judge cases on the basis of the promise of financial gain, rather than on the actual merits of the case and legitimacy of the wrongdoing. He had gained a reputation in his community as an attorney who did what it takes to win a case, even if that meant manipulating the system and fabricating or distorting evidence. The benefit of his efforts was the procurement of considerable financial gains, which he enjoyed flaunting to colleagues and other associates. He threw elaborate parties, always picked up the check at restaurants, and was a regular at his country club. His favorite topic of conversation was his recent purchases. He reveled in the opportunity to flaunt his new possessions.

Individuals with the unprincipled narcissistic style do not often show up in clinical settings, except when required to do so as the result of legal actions. However, when this narcissistic style is less severe (i.e., nonpersonality disordered), the antisocial features may appear as hypercriticalness, unfairness, or indifference to the welfare of close others. For instance, the therapist may meet with the spouse of an individual with an unprincipled narcissistic style who complains of being manipulated and otherwise mistreated. When not prompted into therapy by another individual, the individual with this personality style is perhaps most likely to present for therapy when his or her misdeeds have come to the attention of various authorities. In such situations, the individual often presents plagued by depression, somatic complaints, or conditions that may suggest malingering or factitiousness.

The *amorous narcissistic* personality style includes histrionic features. Although individuals with this style retain a preoccupation with the self and strive for self-promotion, they rely heavily on attributes related to physical appearance and sexual seductiveness to elicit the attention and validation of others. They tend to see themselves in positive terms in relation to physical appearance, and they invest a great deal of time, attention, and investment in promoting and accentuating their physical appearance. These individuals strive for the validation and envy of others relative to their physical appearance and sexual appeal. Individuals with an amorous style of narcissism are "sexually seductive, enticing, beguiling, tantalizing; glib and clever"; likewise, they "disincline real intimacy; indulge hedonistic desires; bewitch and inveigle the needy and naïve; and are prone to pathological lying and swindling" (Millon, 1999, p. 451).

The individual with an amorous narcissistic style, like others with a narcissistic style, generally functions well when others are providing the investment and validation he or she seeks. However, his or her interpersonal style creates opportunity for recurrent conflicts that may contribute to various clinical endpoints. For instance, Alan began having problems in his marriage as the result of his wife's frustration over his obsession with his physical appearance and his recurrent sexual flirtatiousness with other women. He repeatedly assured his wife that she had nothing to worry about, but she felt certain that he had already had an affair and would have another.

The *compensatory narcissistic* personality style has negativistic and avoidant features. Individuals with this style are marked by deep feelings of inferiority and inadequacy and compensate by creating a façade of superiority. They often see themselves as having limited resources and limited assets, and they are constantly on task in creating an image of success. Similar to individuals with a paranoid style, individuals with a compensatory narcissistic style of personality are constantly on guard to protect against flaws; as a result, they may be particularly defensive and critical. Pretense may be a defining attribute for individuals with the compensatory narcissistic style; they rely on pretensions to create an image that they believe to represent worth and superiority. These individuals may be inclined to impulsive spending and may get themselves into considerable financial trouble as the result of their efforts to purchase their way to self-importance.

For example, Marilyn was employed as a sales executive and made an annual salary of $33,000 at a time when this amount was just above the median annual income. She was 26 years old, single, and $75,000 in debt; $35,000 of this debt was direct and indirect credit card debt. Since finishing college 4 years previously, she had purchased a $40,000 European-made automobile, accumulated an extensive wardrobe, and made several trips to various exotic locations, all of which had left her with a minimum monthly debt that was approximately $500 more than her monthly income. Marilyn was consulting with a bankruptcy attorney at the same time she decided to pursue counseling to help her with her "shopping addiction." Upon assessment, the therapist determined that Marilyn's style of personality was most consistent with the narcissistic pattern. Her spending problems, the therapist judged, stemmed from her desire to compensate for her deprived status as a child, when, as she described it, "everyone had more and better things than we did." Her behaviors reflected her efforts to create an image of herself as successful within the cultural niche she valued—that of having things.

TREATMENT OF THE NARCISSISTIC PROTOTYPE

For individuals with the narcissistic style, the tendency to elicit unwarranted validation and accommodation from others (enhancing outcomes) and an unwillingness to meet interpersonal responsibilities of cooperation and respect contribute to recurrent interpersonal problems and emotional distress, both of which require protective and compensatory reactions. Successful treatment requires that individuals take a more active role in fostering cooperative interpersonal relationships. This requires, specifically, that they develop less sensitivity to status and superiority; accept their basic equality among others; become more interpersonally respectful, polite, and cooperative; take more personal responsibility for the self and for socially cooperative endeavors; and become more sensitive to the efforts and feelings of others.

Unfortunately, those with the narcissistic style of personality are not typically motivated for treatment that requires these types of changes. To accept others as equals can be particularly threatening to clients with a narcissistic prototype personality because this would imply that they are something less than they should be and because it would mean that they have less access to desirable outcomes and privileges. Likewise, the necessity of self-sacrifice and cooperation with others is often rather unpleasant for individuals with a strong sense of entitlement. Effective individuals are essentially able to make the world go their way. In the perfect world, they are the envy of all others, are free of responsibilities, and get to choose personal activities and strongly influence group activities. Even when not completely successful, individuals with a narcissistic style are able to enjoy the fantasy of a perfect world and often are able to act in ways that reinforce the narcissistic orientation. Therapy may seem to offer inferiority, the necessity of engaging in unpleasant interpersonal tasks and accepting unwanted personal responsibility, and the need to treat others in opposition to their contemptuous feelings.

Beck et al. (1990) pointed out that treating an individual with a narcissistic orientation provides the therapist with unique challenges and can be a very frustrating endeavor. It is necessary to manage not only the client's frequent attempts to undermine treatment but also the therapist's own feelings of frustration and contempt. Indeed, the feelings that the therapist may feel in reaction to the entitlement expressed by a client with a narcissistic style are similar to the feelings that others feel toward these individuals. The frustration others feel with these entitled individuals may lead them to express anger as critical and rejecting accusation; individuals with a narcissistic style typically reject this anger as something irrational about others. Others in the lives of these individuals will simply choose to avoid any further contact with them; this option is not available to the therapist. As suggested by Beck et al., "cognitive therapists must first be sensitive observers of their own thoughts, feelings, and beliefs" (p. 252).

Several factors contribute to the difficulties that emerge in treating individuals with a narcissistic style of personality. First, successful treatment requires that clients engage in numerous activities that they have typically avoided, specifically related to cooperative behaviors and interpersonal courtesy. As an example, a husband with a narcissistic prototype personality viewed taking out the trash as beneath him; yet his wife found it quite reasonable for him to perform this task. Second, such individuals are used to having other people do most of the work and may subsequently find the task of therapy to be laborious and more threatening than they had expected. Third, they do not generally have a well-developed sense of empathy that would help them to appreciate the value of change. Individuals with a narcissistic orientation enjoy the illusion of entitlement and do not consider the possibility that other people have different feelings and needs. Finally, because they often hold others in contempt, the notion of fostering a sense of equality among others can be objectionable. As one client exclaimed, "If mental health means I have to be nice to the idiots of the world, I'd rather be crazy."

The more the client is characterized by the narcissistic personality, the more these personality attributes are likely to interfere with treatment. For individuals less pervasively marked by the narcissistic style, the probability of the narcissistic attributes undermining effective treatment is lessened and the likelihood of positive treatment gains increases. The following section offers guidelines for fostering the therapeutic relationship and maintaining client motivation for change and specific strategies for prompting effective changes.

The Therapeutic Relationship

To engage the client with a narcissistic style in therapy, the therapist must convey acceptance of the individual. In addition, to take therapeutic advantage of the narcissistic style, it helps to display a degree of admiration. If the client perceives the therapist as too confrontational, he or she will feel compelled to either compete with the therapist for prestige, which may include blatant self-promotion and status demotion of the therapist ("I see that you received your degree from a state school; were you unable to get into a better one?"), or the client will simply terminate involvement in therapy. Because something has motivated the client to be in therapy, the therapist can, when appropriate, compliment the client on his or her efforts to make the best out of a difficult situation and validate the client's frustrations with things not going better. By being impressed with what the client has done thus far, the therapist fulfills the need for admiration, and the client is more likely to experience positive feelings toward the therapist. Although this is a useful strategy for many clients, it is particularly useful with the client with a narcissistic style.

Further, the therapist can offer him- or herself as a resource the client with a narcissistic prototype personality can use to determine novel ways to make the situation go better or for finding some relief from his or her distress. It is often useful to introduce the following orientation to therapy: "Together, we ought to be able to figure things out. You clearly understate yourself pretty well and have a keen insight into events, and I know a little about psychology, so working together, we should be able to sort things out." By putting the client in a position in which he or she feels some status and respect, while legitimizing the involvement of the therapist, this introduction should enable therapy to proceed with the least amount of reactive resistance. Nonetheless, with this type of client the therapist must remain vigilant to the client's investment in the therapeutic process.

Focusing on the Presenting Problem

To minimize defensive reactions in the client with a narcissistic orientation, it is helpful to stay focused on the presenting problem rather than getting too quickly invested in the client's characterological attributes. As suggested by Freeman and colleagues (1990), it is often beneficial to focus on behavioral strategies in dealing with this type of client to avoid the resistance that is likely to emerge with more cognitive or insight-oriented therapies. The therapist can invite the client to focus on the behavioral aspects of the presenting problem by discussing aspects of current situations related to the presenting complaints. As the client describes problematic situations, the therapist can offer observations and inquiry by relying on the "Colombo technique" of wondering out loud about an idea rather than stating it directly described by Freeman and colleagues (1990, p. 52). Using this strategy, the therapist can address critical ideas without being confrontational.

For instance, David was presenting for treatment of a chronic anxiety condition related most specifically to work stresses. He described a situation that had recently occurred at work that resulted in a minor panic attack. The following exchange illustrates how, as the client's investment increases, through the process of guided discovery the therapist can offer observations concerning the associations between the client's thoughts, feelings, and behaviors:

> David: So I'm talking to this applicant and I'm thinking, what an idiot this guy is. He couldn't do the job if his life depended on it. I let him talk, but I could not care less about what he was saying. I figured that I'd give him his 15 minutes and then show him the door. As he's talking, he's getting more and more excited and insulting, and by the time 10 minutes were up, I'd had enough, and I asked him to leave.

> Therapist: That was quite a situation; I can imagine that you were ready for it to be over. It was after the interview that you began to feel the anxiety set in?

> David: Yes.

At this point, the therapist could focus on the thoughts that are associated with the panic following the interview or follow up on the nature of the exchange between the client and the interviewee. With the first focus, the therapist would learn something about the thoughts associated with the panic; with the second, the therapist and client would potentially come to understand what it is about the client's interpersonal style that contributes to problem interactions. Although both would be valuable, the second line of thought has the greater potential for providing insights into the client's characterological vulnerability to panic and anxiety.

> Therapist: Before talking more about the panic itself, could we talk for a minute about the interview?

> David: Sure, I guess.

> Therapist: I can't help but wonder about what it was that was getting the interviewee so excited.

David:	Who knows?
Therapist:	You indicated that he wasn't upset or excited at first, but got increasingly excited as he talked to you. I have to wonder what he was seeing that was getting him so excited.

In this interaction, the client is indirectly prompted to consider what it was he was doing to contribute to a bad interaction. Once he recognizes his contribution, therapist and client can consider the associated automatic thoughts and other cognitive factors contributing to the breakdown of the interpersonal interaction and, eventually, talk about the ultimate outcome of that breakdown.

David:	Well, he could probably tell that I was somewhat less than enthusiastic about the conversation. It was a waste of my time!
Therapist:	That's what I was wondering. What do you think he observed exactly?
David:	I don't know.
Therapist:	I know that when I have felt that someone wasn't listening to me, I got that sense from the fact that the person was not making eye contact. In fact, the person was looking at other things. I wonder if something like that was going on.

The therapist can follow this line of questioning with specific discussion of the panic. Given that the panic was associated with the implications of a failed interview, failure to fulfill a job vacancy, and the possibility of the interviewee complaining about something the person did, the connection between David's behavior and the subsequent panic attack can be made.

Because the client desires outcomes that reinforce his or her status, the therapist can introduce treatment topics as means for helping to ensure positive, status-enhancing outcomes. Once the client comes to entertain the idea that his or her own behavior may have contributed to the problem, therapist and client can then discuss the commonality of such problems for the client and discuss the advantages and disadvantages of being dismissive of others.

Fostering Greater Empathy

Perhaps the most important goal in treating clients with a narcissistic personality style is increasing their interpersonal skills, including social cooperation and empathy. To increase the client's empathy for others, it is useful to have him or her consider how the other individual experienced the interaction. Using a guided discovery technique, therapist and client can consider the implications of acting with narcissistic motives.

Beyond guided discovery, the therapist can help the client to anticipate the consequences of various actions and to consider the odds relative to positive and negative outcomes given different behaviors. In this strategy, the therapist is not being directive but, rather, is providing the client the opportunity in a safe environment to consider outcomes and then to make informed decisions about how best to act in interpersonal affairs. Although some clients may choose to act in a self-centered manner, they will be unable to do so with the benefit of ignorance. In this situation, the therapist need not be judgmental and can simply let the probabilities play out depending on how the client chooses to act. The therapist can also introduce dissonance-inducing strategies by having the client, as an experiment, act in ways that are dissonant to the narcissistic and entitled style. In this way, the client is put into a position of cognitive conflict and can make renewed attributions regarding attitudes toward him- or herself and others. In addition, the therapist and client can reflect on the outcomes of this exercise and consider the cost–benefit outcomes relative to different styles of interpersonal behavior.

If the client is unable to put him- or herself in the other person's situation, a role-play scenario may be helpful in which the therapist plays the dismissive role and the client monitors his or her own feelings related to the dismissive attitude of the therapist. In this way, the client can develop greater insight into his or her own behavior and its impact on others. Once the client is able to develop some insight into his or her own behaviors, the therapist may invite him or her to consider these issues further. For the willing client, several strategies can be implemented to expand his or her interpersonal awareness and sensitivities. For instance, the therapist might videotape role-play scenarios for immediate playback. In this strategy, the client receives immediate feedback concerning his or her interpersonal style. Similarly, the client can be asked to obtain feedback from particular others in the environment who would provide objective insights. Therapist and client can identify useful targets, and the client can collect information for discussion in the subsequent session.

Interaction between the therapist and the client with a narcissistic orientation can introduce aspects of the client's interpersonal style that prove problematic and provide opportunity to discuss more directly the client's grandiosity, entitlement, hypersensitivity, and lack of empathy. Throughout the process, it is useful for the therapist to continue to reinforce the client's investment; in this way, the client's need for admiration is fulfilled. Indeed, the client's need for admiration is not itself the problem, but rather the ways that he or she goes about getting that admiration. Discussing with the client his or her problematic interpersonal interactions will provide opportunities to discuss the client's own negative contributions to those interactions; rather than simply pointing out to the client how he or she creates his or her own problems, the therapist can continue to validate the client's desire for admiration while helping to identify circumstances that interfere with this objective and helping the client develop more rewarding social behaviors.

Specific situations to target in therapy are those in which the client felt sensitive to the actions or accomplishments of others. These situations can be identified by having the client monitor ongoing interactions, paying particular attention to those that prompt an anxious and defensive posture. These interactions can then be used as focal topics in subsequent sessions, with the objective being how those interactions could have been made to go better. The therapist can prompt the client to consider the ideal outcomes in the various interactions, validating the benefit of having things always go one's way, while commenting on the unlikelihood of such outcomes and considering how to make the best of the situation given that the ideal outcome is typically not available. It is useful to consider the client's absolutes and to examine the evidence concerning the conclusions that he or she often draws. For instance, individuals with a narcissistic personality style often interpret the accomplishments of others as evidence of their own inferiority. The therapist and client can consider the evidence concerning whether a particular accomplishment compromises his or her status or not. These conversations often help to reveal the client's grandiosity, without any need for the therapist to bring up the term or idea. Simply validating the client's desire to have things always go his or her way is enough to identify the attribute. Once the client comes to see the low probability of such outcomes actually occurring, he or she and the therapist can devise the best alternatives, which will by necessity require greater responsibility and interpersonal sensitivity.

Decreasing Grandiosity and Hypersensitivity

Before addressing the client's grandiosity and hypersensitivity, and the associated illusions and exploitations, the therapist must prepare the client to consider characterological issues. To the extent that therapist and client have had success in addressing factors that contribute to problems in interpersonal interactions, the client is better prepared to address specific characterological concerns.

Any time that characterological issues are addressed, it is often helpful to have the client consider the childhood origins of their current orientation. The advantage of discussing his or her childhood is that is allows the individual to derive a degree of separation between his or her sense of self and problematic attitudes. When the person sees that his or her current orientation originated, in large part, in childhood experiences, he or she is better able to entertain alterations to that general orientation. Once the client is prepared to address issues related to his or her grandiosity, several procedures can be introduced to assess the impact of this orientation and to prompt recognition and alternative behaviors. For example, the client could monitor ongoing thoughts to identify the grandiose and egocentric qualities. These thoughts can then be discussed in therapy relative to their contribution to recurrent problems. The client can then be instructed in various cognitive strategies implemented to change core beliefs and underlying assumptions. For instance, the client could engage in various imagery techniques in which prosocial behaviors are associated with positive, self-esteem enhancing outcomes. Similarly, the client could rewrite identified cognitive assumptions in ways that reflect greater self-confidence and prosocial concerns.

CASE EXAMPLE

Kenneth, a 21-year-old college senior, is the only child of a wealthy banker father and attorney mother. He was referred for treatment by his college counselor following a panic attack that prevented him from completing his midterm examinations. This was not the first time that Kenneth had experienced panic symptoms. During his junior high school years, he had had periods of mild to moderate panic at what seemed to be random times. He had a few episodes during high school, but never enough to warrant concern in his parents. While in college, he had experienced a few bouts of panic, once while going through his fraternity rush and again following a date.

Kenneth is exceptionally bright and capable and has also done very well academically. He sees himself as being very smart and has taken pride in the fact that he has never had to work very hard to get good grades. He did fine during his freshman year, but his grades began to drop during his sophomore year. The drop appeared to be clearly related to the fact that Kenneth was not doing the work, and the courses were getting increasingly difficult. His attitude was that the work was beneath him. He thought he could do well on the exams without studying and that doing well on the exams was all that mattered. Kenneth has consistently been unconcerned about his drop in performance, assuming that ultimately his grades are not really that important. His parents, alternatively, have been very concerned and have talked with his counselor and others at the college to determine what could be done to help Kenneth improve his performance. Arrangements were made for him to receive academic counseling through a special needs counselor, and testing was undertaken to determine whether an undetected learning disability might explain his poor academic performance.

Throughout this process, Kenneth has gone along with the recommendations of the various people who have intervened to help, but he has not taken the initiative to work harder and has been rather passive throughout the process. During his junior year, his grades were so poor that he was placed on academic probation. The panic symptoms Kenneth displayed corresponded to his awareness that failure to do well on the midterm exams would lead to his expulsion from the college and to the unhappiness of his parents. Unfortunately, Kenneth had done nothing to increase the chances of doing well on the exams. Discussion with Kenneth revealed that he had developed a rather smug attitude concerning education, expecting to do well without having to work, and consequently he had failed to develop the studying skills and habits necessary to do well in a competitive college environment.

Although Kenneth presented with evidence of panic symptoms, he did not have the recurrent pattern of panic attacks warranting the diagnosis of panic disorder. Although there was no specific Axis I condition, Kenneth's parents and treating professionals had over the past 2 years considered generalized anxiety, attention-deficit/hyperactivity disorder (predominantly inattentive type), and dyslexia, but none of these conditions appeared to adequately describe Kenneth's condition or to explain his lack of academic achievement. The Millon Clinical Multiaxial Inventory (Millon, 1997) assessment suggested vulnerability to anxiety symptoms and to somatic disturbances, as well as a narcissistic personality style.

Kenneth's self-view was that he was academically and in other ways gifted, and he believed that he should not have to work as hard as others to do well (admirable self-image; contrived object relations). In fact, he viewed diligent academic work as an insult to his natural abilities. His lack of commitment and concern reflected an insouciant temperament, and his belief that his grades were unimportant reflected the expansiveness of his cognitive style. Thus, if he worked hard, it suggested that he was not as smart as he thought himself to be, and it suggested to others that he was not superior to them in academic areas.

The panic symptoms that Kenneth experienced periodically were consistent with Barlow's (2000) suggestion that panic occurs in the face of a lack of control in situations that require control. For Kenneth, midterm exams and his awareness of being unprepared put him in a position in which something needed to be done, and he had no options other than to panic. He had not developed sufficient academic discipline to prepare for his exams, he did not want to do the work, and his parents and school administrators were holding threat over his head relative to his academic performance. Indeed, panic was in many ways the only option available to Kenneth. No doubt unique and important physiological mechanisms were involved, but the circumstance Kenneth found himself in and his lack of preparedness to manage the circumstance initiated the panic reaction. In Kenneth's pathologic process, stress was encountered when he found himself in a position that he was unprepared to manage. Why he was unprepared stemmed from the passive–independent orientation that defined his personality. Kenneth needed to do well, was expected to do well, but was unprepared to do well. The clinical outcome in this circumstance was panic.

The primary goal in treating Kenneth involved development of a greater sense of personal responsibility in bringing about positive and enhancing outcomes. At this point in Kenneth's life, he had come to believe that his inherent skills and abilities were enough to carry him through the demands of life. His core beliefs of himself as superior to others had encountered obstacles as the challenges of life increased. It was necessary that Kenneth accept greater responsibility for meeting life challenges, and it was also necessary for him to acquire many of the skills that he had failed to develop earlier in life. However, before attempting to teach Kenneth deficit skills, he would first have to accept the need for those skills. His parents and school representatives had attempted to teach Kenneth deficit skills; however, he had not appreciated the value or necessity of those skills.

Cognitively, efforts were directed at altering Kenneth's perception of himself as academically superior and above the need to study. Through the process of guided discovery, Kenneth came to recognize the need to adjust his perception of himself as being above the necessity of working for desired outcomes. This did not mean that Kenneth needed to perceive himself as incapable, only that he come to perceive and appreciate the need to take more responsibility for bringing his abilities to realized fruition. Kenneth considered the accumulated evidence that clearly indicated that he was not able to maintain a superior academic position without work and study. His conditional belief that "If I have to work hard, I will appear less capable" was specifically challenged. Kenneth learned to remind himself, "To do well, I will have to work." His view of himself as superior to others was also challenged, although not by decreasing, necessarily, his positive self-view. Kenneth reminded himself that he was very intelligent, as were many others, and the critical difference was not whether one was intelligent, but how one nurtured and developed that intelligence.

Because Kenneth was deficient in basic study skills, efforts were also undertaken for him to receive the study skills trainings that he had previously been exposed to but had not taken advantage of. The history of his panic symptoms was assessed, and efforts were taken to address specific deficits in social skills. Specifically, Kenneth was taught how to interact with others in a prosocial manner. As an only child and one who felt a superior disassociation from others, he had not developed adaptive social skills. These changes were coupled with cognitive strategies emphasizing the value of positive social engagements. Similarly, Kenneth was instructed in methods for managing affective reactions, most notably anxiety reactions that occurred when he was faced with academic and social challenges.

CONCLUSION

The narcissistic personality style is characterized by passive orientation and the expectation of interpersonal validation and accommodation. Individuals with this style see themselves as superior to others and subsequently entitled to special privileges. When others fail to provide them with the validation or assistance they desire, they are inclined to become hypercritical and retaliatory. They strive for power and glory, wealth, and prestige and may be willing to manipulate people and events to bring about desired outcomes. Although they may be highly susceptible to feelings of guilt associated with their negative and exploitative treatment of others, through their well-developed sense of rationalization, they are often able to defray such feelings of guilt and personal responsibility.

Individuals with a narcissistic orientation interpret situations relative to their personal status and the potential benefit to them personally. They are attentive to both opportunity for self-enhancement and the necessity of self-protection. Enhancement is derived through their perceived superiority over others and receipt of special privileges, whereas pain is encountered in the form of common obligation and being upstaged by another. Although others may enjoy affiliation with these individuals, perhaps by deriving some sense of reflected glory, most people are not willing to provide the constant validation that persons with a narcissistic style require; thus, these individuals are vulnerable to a host of clinical conditions that emerge in the face of interpersonal conflict. They may display various anxiety symptoms associated with their fragile self-esteem, somatic symptoms, dysthymia, and depression, as well as bipolar symptoms associated with their often frantic efforts to maintain a position of superiority over others and to defend against interpersonal threats to status.

The self-centeredness and defensiveness that characterize individuals with a narcissistic prototype personality often render them resistant to treatment. Suggestions for improvements offered by a therapist are often met with a critical rejection, and contempt for the therapist frequently follows. Understanding the motives and personality style of these clients, however, provides the personality-guided cognitive–behavioral therapist with useful avenues for directing useful treatments that can sidestep the personality attributes defining the narcissistic style.

10

THE AVOIDANT PROTOTYPE

Key phrase: Please like me
Evolutionary focus: Withdrawal, play it safe

Individuals with the avoidant prototype personality are average on enhancement striving, yet very high on self-protection. They want very much to feel validated and accepted by others, but they perceive the self as possessing qualities that will ultimately lead to rejection or as not possessing the qualities necessary for acceptance. This ambivalence is felt as emotional anguish reflecting the torment of desire combined with fear. These individuals want to engage socially but feel compelled to escape or avoid social situations to protect their fragile self-integrity.

Ultimately, the individual with an avoidant style is more concerned with protecting the defective self from painful encounters and consequently displays active efforts to avoid situations that hold the potential for rejection and exclusion. By avoiding threats, the individual is able to protect and maintain some sense of personal integrity, even if felt primarily through fantasy. The focus of attention for the individual is the self. A person with an avoidant orientation does pay close attention to others, yet this attention is focused on how those others react or relate to him or her. The individual relies to a large degree on his or her own internal cues and emotions as internal barometers concerning the quality and safety of social engagements. The polarity balance of the avoidant prototype in presented in Figure 10.1.

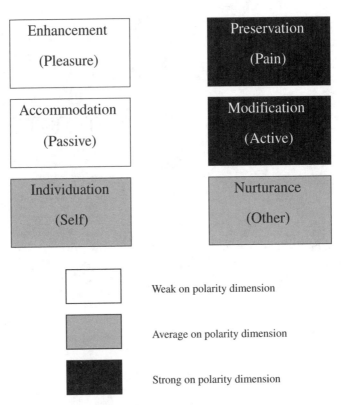

Enhancement (Pleasure)	Preservation (Pain)
Accommodation (Passive)	Modification (Active)
Individuation (Self)	Nurturance (Other)

Weak on polarity dimension

Average on polarity dimension

Strong on polarity dimension

Figure 10.1. Polarity balance of the avoidant prototype. From *Personality-Guided Therapy* (p. 310), by T. Millon, 1999, New York: Guilford Press. Copyright 1999 by John Wiley & Sons, Inc. Reprinted with permission.

PERSONALITY-GUIDED COGNITIVE–BEHAVIORAL CONCEPTUALIZATION

The self-image of those with the avoidant prototype personality is described as *alienated*, a term depicting a core belief of the self as incapable of forming social relationships. Viewing the self as socially defective, these individuals are vulnerable to numerous cognitive errors, such as overgeneralization (e.g., "No one will ever like me"), arbitrary inference ("I can tell that they don't like me"), personalization ("I did something wrong"), and other distortions. Furthermore, this view of the self leads to various cognitive assumptions and instrumental beliefs, which contribute to a pathologic process. Given their perception of defects in social functioning, those with the avoidant style believe that something would happen that would lead to embarrassment and rejection if they pursued a social activity. Therefore, to avoid such embarrassment, it is better to "just not go." In such a situation, the hopelessness felt contributes to the experience of depressed affect.

A significant influence on the self-image of an individual with an avoidant style is his or her previous experiences in social encounters. On the basis of past relationships, an individual with an avoidant prototype personality perceives social affiliations *vexatiously*, suggesting that opportunities for social interaction are marked by memories of engagements that have not gone well (see Cicchetti & Cohen, 1995; Meyer & Carver, 2000). Although there may be a preponderance of positive and rewarding interactions in the individual's past, the memories of interactions that have gone badly have stuck in the person's mind. These images serve to portend the threat inherent in current encounters. Such experiences contribute in important ways to the individual's arbitrary inference, overgeneralization, and other cognitive distortions, all of which serve to keep the individual safe from negative encounters (Gilbert, 2000).

Another influence on the information processing of the individual with an avoidant personality style is his or her morphological orientation. Although not immediately accessible to cognitive processes, the individual is vulnerable to the influence of several distressing emotions that are woven into the ongoing interpretation of environmental events and their significance to the individual. Indeed, as emotions change in response to interpretations and projections, new emotions emerge. For an individual with an avoidant orientation, a *fragile* organization renders him or her susceptible to a "complex of tortuous emotions" (Millon & Davis, 1999). One's organization is related in many ways to self-image, and how one sees the self is dependent on experiences in the past; thus, one's self-image is a function of these past interactions.

The mood state of individuals with an avoidant prototype personality is *anguished*, particularly significant when faced with the potential for social interactions. The anguish reflects their desire for fulfilling interactions and fear of humiliation and rejection. These anguished feelings contribute to the vexatious experiences and to the interpretations focusing on the potential pain inherent in social interactions. Likewise, this anguish contributes to their *fretfulness* regarding how to behave, leaving them in a constant state of turmoil regarding whether to remain or to escape or avoid the encounter. Their perception of interpersonal relations as threatening adds to their anguish and to a distracted cognitive style marked by fleeting thoughts about their own behaviors and feelings and the current and potential actions of others. As a result of their distraction to the ongoing cues during an interaction, they are less able to remain focused on the task at hand.

Individuals with an avoidant style rely heavily on *fantasy* as a regulatory mechanism. They are inclined to dream of fulfilling and rewarding social

engagements. Their fantasies contribute to the desire to pursue social relationships, yet they also contribute to fantasy-based distractions from the
social encounter. For instance, as a means of distracting themselves from
the lack of social fulfillment, they may engage in such activities as excessive
reading, television and movie viewing, and often sexual fantasy and masturbation (Arlow, 1953). In a very real sense, they would rather fantasize about
life than live it socially, thus remaining safe from social threat.

Two critical features define the core beliefs of individuals with an
avoidant orientation. First, they perceive social affiliations and intimacies
as critical to a content existence. Consequently, they deeply desire close
and meaningful relationships. Second, they perceive the self as inherently
unskilled or defective and unable to function in the social world. Specifically,
they believe that "One must be socially skilled to be worthwhile." Yet they
view the self as unlikable, inadequate, defective, and unacceptable to others.
Individuals with an avoidant prototype personality see others as socially
capable and as generally liked by others, or certainly more so than themselves.
They see the world as replete with social threat and opportunities for ridicule
and humiliation. To complete the cognitive triad, they hope for an improvement in their social relationships and even dream and fantasize about fulfilling interactions and intimacies, but they remain pessimistic about their
abilities to bring about desirable social outcomes. Considering these beliefs,
it is no wonder that individuals with an avoidant style are often characterized
and overwhelmed by social anxiety and dysphoria (Beck, Freeman, & Associates, 1990).

In addition to these core beliefs, the avoidant personality style is also
characterized by unique and thorny intermediate beliefs. In response to the
direct or indirect invitation to affiliate socially, conditional conclusions such
as "If I go, then I will make a fool of myself"; "If I go, then people
will find out that I am unlikable"; or "If I go, they will not treat me
well" are typical. These conditional assumptions elicit anxious emotions
and compel the individual with an avoidant style to find a means of
escape from and avoidance of social interactions. Instrumentally, the
individual believes that relief can be gained only by generally avoiding
social interaction or by hiding behind a contrived façade when forced
to engage with others. The personality attributes of the avoidant prototype
are summarized in Table 10.1.

PATHOLOGIC PROCESS OF THE AVOIDANT PATTERN

Stress is encountered in many, if not most social situations, ranging
from very informal and casual interactions to formal engagements. To indi-

TABLE 10.1
Structures and Functions of the Avoidant Prototype and Associated Liabilities

Personality domain	Liability
Self-image Alienated	View of self as inferior to others, socially inept, and unacceptable, leading to avoidance of social affiliation
Object representations Vexatious	Past history of painful relationships, leading to negative expectations regarding current relationships
Morphological organization Fragile	Emotional reactivity in response to social affiliations and perceived threat of rejection
Mood and temperament Anguished	Strong emotional reactions to social situations contributing to disrupted social performance and affiliation and associated with approach desires and avoidant pressure
Behavioral acts Fretful	Awkwardness in social affiliations contributing to lack of confidence and negative self-view
Interpersonal conduct Aversive	Fearfulness of social affiliations; perception of social interactions as awkward and unpleasant; aversiveness compelling avoidant behaviors
Cognitive style Distracted	Attention to multiple sources of information, preventing acquisition of guiding reference; strong genetic component
Regulatory mechanism Fantasy	Fantasy distraction, preventing engagement in adaptive behaviors and social or occupational responsibilities; ability to avoid social engagement; ability to experience moderate pleasure

viduals with an avoidant personality style, social activities provide a source of enjoyment and validation, but they are also associated with the painful experiences of anxiety and anguish. When confronted by a social situation, these individuals find themselves in an approach–avoidance conflict in which they want very much to revel in the joy of social camaraderie but are compelled to avoid or escape the threat of social failure. How they go about resolving these recurrent conflicts contributes to the clinical conditions these individuals face.

AXIS I VULNERABILITIES

Individuals with an avoidant style are particularly vulnerable to various clinical syndromes. From an evolutionary perspective, each of these syndromes reflects ways that people have come to manage the social stresses encountered. Thus, these syndromes represent stylistic and adaptive strategies for maximizing pleasure or minimizing pain, or both. In the case of individuals with an avoidant personality style, these syndromes reflect adaptive efforts to minimize the experience of pain associated with social interactions.

Anxiety Disorders

As the result of concern over social relations and affiliations, individuals with an avoidant style are particularly vulnerable to various anxiety-related conditions. This is sensible when one considers that anxiety serves the adaptive purpose of increasing vigilance to sources of threat and danger (Nesse & Williams, 1994; Öhman, 2000; Plutchik, 2003). Living in a social world that requires interaction and cooperation with other human beings proves to be a tremendous burden to persons with an avoidant orientation. To be sure, if one is worried about being criticized, rejected, embarrassed, or otherwise alienated from social affiliations, particularly when that rejection is the result of one's own failings, it is highly adaptive to remain vigilant to signs of social rejection to implement the defensive (e.g., escape or avoidance) reaction necessary to end or prevent painful outcomes.

For individuals with an avoidant prototype personality, the occurrence and severity of Axis I anxiety symptoms wax and wane with the perceived obligation to interact with others, as well as with the specific threat inherent in any given interaction. Because social obligations and affiliations are so commonplace, these individuals may come to feel a constant state of threat and anxiety sufficient to warrant the diagnosis of Generalized Anxiety Disorder. Millon (1999) described these persons as experiencing "pananxiety" (p. 312), which describes their constant state of threat. That generalized anxiety can be diagnosed independent of social anxiety and avoidance underscores the idea that Generalized Anxiety Disorder is not specific to individuals with an avoidant personality style but is a common covariate of those with an avoidant style.

The anxiety these individuals experience may also increase their distractibility and decrease their ability to remain focused on specific aspects of the task at hand, which may include simple social discourse or completing a physical task while under the scrutiny of others. Not surprising, those with the avoidant style have been described as having attention problems of the type observed in attention-deficit disorders (Tzelepis, Schubiner, & Warbasse, 1995).

Social Phobia

The relationship between social phobia and the avoidant personality is well researched (Brown, Heimberg, & Juster, 1995; Hofmann, Newman, Ehlers, & Roth, 1995; Holle, Heimberg, Sweet, & Holt, 1995; Millon, 1991a; Tillfors, Furmark, Ekselius, & Fredrikson, 2001). Indeed, for someone who has developed a personality characterized by fear of negative social relationships, the probability of an associated social phobia is quite high. Although not all social phobias are secondary to avoidant personalities, social phobia has particular adaptive value to people with an avoidant style—it allows them to avoid the phobic stimulus. Just as a person with a fear of water will avoid going to a pool or beach, a person with social phobia avoids social interactions, although he or she may not consciously understand this. For individuals with an avoidant style, social situations can have painful emotional implications sufficient to warrant a conditioned escape or avoidance response.

Panic Disorder and Agoraphobia

In the face of imminent social intimacy, dread can easily develop into a state of panic for many individuals with an avoidant style. In fact, Noyes, Reich, Suelzer, and Christiansen (1991) suggested that the avoidant personality is a classic personality in clients with panic disorder. Understanding the role of panic itself supports this view. According to Öhman (2000), panic reactions occur when one feels an impending threat of separation. The promise of social intimacy is highly rewarding; however, as the thought becomes reality and the individual feels threatened, panic sets in as he or she imagines the potential and probability of the social interaction going poorly. As in all cases of recurrent panic, the risk of developing an agoraphobic condition exists. Not surprising, as demonstrated by Brooks, Baltazar, McDowell, Munjack, and Bruns (1991), the avoidant personality is more frequently identified with panic and agoraphobia than any other personality disorder.

Obsessive–Compulsive Disorder

Obsessive–compulsive symptoms may be common in individuals with an avoidant personality style (Wewetzer et al., 2001). As part of the fantasy mechanism, individuals with an avoidant style create a world for themselves that keeps them safe from social affiliations. Engagement in compulsive behaviors may relieve the need to engage socially. In the case of a cleaning compulsion, individuals may compulsively clean the house, just in case someone was to visit. Obsessional concern with the threat of criticism, masked as fear of germs, leads to compulsive behaviors that prevent any social affiliations, either those involving visitors to one's house or visits to see another. The individual with an obsessive–compulsive avoidant style is "too busy" to socialize. Cleaning compulsions are not always motivated by an avoidant style, but a cleaning compulsion may play a role in the individual's pathological process.

Dissociative Disorders

As are individuals with chronic anxieties, individuals with an avoidant orientation are vulnerable to the development of dissociation in the face of social threat (Ellason, Ross, & Fuchs, 1995, 1996). Dissociative experiences provide relief from social threat by providing an escape from the source of distress. Consider the case of Jamie, a copy editor at a local newspaper who possesses an avoidant style. After the usual news wire person left for another job, Jamie was assigned the task of checking the wire and calling the associated news contact about potential stories. After several weeks of failing to call, even after being reminded to, another person was found to take over the wire. Jamie did not fail to remember to complete several other new responsibilities, none of which involved needing to call and speak with an unknown person who could potentially think poorly of her. Whether such forgetting is dissociative or intentional may be difficult to ascertain. In this instance, Jamie admitted to not wanting to complete the task, but her genuine intentions to call were realized only at the end of the workday, when it was too late to call. For Jamie, the thought of calling the news associate was fraught with feelings of anxiety and self-contempt. Only as long as she did not think of the need to call was she able to derive any relief from the distress of needing to make the phone call.

Somatoform Disorder

As are those with dissociative conditions mediated by anxieties, individuals with an avoidant style are more susceptible to somatic complaints. Anxiety associated with vigilance to social threat may be experienced somatically. It is important to note that attention to somatic concerns provides a distraction from the need and desire to function socially, thus providing a sense of relief from the threat of socialization. Although there are several factors contributing to the development of somatic complaints, individuals with an avoidant style are particularly vulnerable to somatic symptoms as a function of their anxiety feelings and the adaptive benefit of somatic preoccupation and incapacitation.

Mood Disorders

In the face of continued or intensified threat, the hopelessness of a situation can contribute to a recurrent pattern of social withdrawal, self-directed contempt, and other symptoms characteristic of major depression. For individuals with an avoidant style of personality, depression provides a respite or general escape from the threat of social affiliation, yet not without feelings and perceptions of alienation and failure. In fact, the more pressing and intimate the social encounter, the greater the potential need for escape.

In individuals with an avoidant orientation, a generalized sense of hopelessness may set in and thus characterize a dysthymic condition. In fact, dysthymia may reflect a general resignation to the fact that they will not fulfill social ambitions and be accepted by others. By withdrawing into a chronic state of low-grade depression, they are able to avoid social encounters and potential embarrassments yet continue to function in meeting common obligations. Unfortunately, these individuals maintain some degree of frustration with and contempt for themselves, which prevents the emergence of much positive affect. Nonetheless, the relatively minor emotional pain associated with dysthymia (e.g., isolation and unfulfilled desire of social participation) is preferable to the pain associated with social humiliation and alienation.

Individuals with an avoidant prototype personality are also vulnerable to major depressive episodes. Because they hold themselves responsible for most social failures, their focus of blame and contempt becomes the self. Because individuals cannot turn away from or reject themselves, they must retreat from the source of pain to prevent hurting themselves (Sloman, Price, Gilbert, & Gardner, 1994). However, Rossi and colleagues (2001) suggested that individuals are not inclined to display depression (if depression is viewed as a reason for scorn and rejection) because it would suggest something about their inherent weaknesses that might lead to further social scorn and ridicule. As a result, individuals with an avoidant style may mask feelings of depression, which may intensify the felt anguish. For some individuals, a retarded depression serves to keep them from continuing unsuccessful attempts at social interactions (see Gilbert, 2000). In the case of agitated depression, hope continues, yet they may feel anxious and helpless in bringing about fulfilling relationships (Millon, 1999).

Individuals with an avoidant orientation often display bipolar II and cyclothymic symptoms associated with the waxing and waning of social affiliation (Rossi et al., 2001). Ever hopeful of secure and validating social interactions, these individuals do not consistently withdraw into an isolated independence more typical of the schizoid personality. When opportunities for social affiliation present themselves, these individuals may immerse themselves in the joys of affiliation with enthusiasm and reckless abandon, only to withdraw into a depression when the nearly inevitable signs of criticalness and rejection appear. Their continuing hope of positive affiliation contributes to a recurrent vulnerability to hypomania because they remain expectant of rejection and rely on a depressive withdrawal when the threat of rejection mounts. In other situations, these individuals may erupt in hostile reaction to felt isolation and mistreatment.

Substance Abuse and Impulse Disorders

Individuals with an avoidant personality style are characteristically oriented toward the minimizing of pain that is so significant they forgo most social opportunities for pleasure. Left to themselves, these individuals may become subject to addiction and impulse disorders, conditions that serve the adaptive purpose of maintaining distance from other people while also providing some degree of pleasure or at least a decrease in pain (Skinstad & Swain, 2001). For instance, these individuals may find both relief and enjoyment in habitual pot smoking; excessive reading or television viewing; or pleasures such as excessive eating, drinking, or masturbation, all of which are pleasurable activities without direct social involvement. Their adaptive style is active, yet the activity is oriented toward the avoidance of social discomfort and aversive interpersonal interactions.

Delusional and Psychotic Disorders

The anxiety felt by individuals with an avoidant style can be so great as to prompt delusional and even psychotic reactions. Although this conjecture awaits empirical attention, these individuals, in the face of extreme social distress, may develop many of the positive symptoms of schizophrenia (Millon & Davis, 2000). Specifically, in response to the threat of emotional pain inherently associated with social interaction, the development of paranoid ideations or a general cognitive, emotional, and behavioral deterioration may serve as an adaptive defense against social humiliation. Other complex cognitive and neurological processes may be involved, but cognitive and behavioral deterioration in simple terms serves the purpose, often desperately needed, of providing escape from the anguish of social failures.

VARIATIONS ON THE TRADITIONAL
AVOIDANT PERSONALITY

Millon (1999; Millon & Davis, 2000) described four variations of the traditional avoidant style. Each is characterized by the common pattern of social avoidance and self-contempt, but they differ in terms of the covariant traits of other personality styles that contribute to unique orientations to the environment and to idiosyncratic coping strategies.

The *self-destructive avoidant* personality style includes depressive features, and individuals with this style have abandoned hope of social inclusion. They have determined that others will not rescue them from themselves and that they possess no personal resources for altering the painful experience of living. For these individuals, depression serves an important adaptive function by compelling them to remove themselves from interactions with others, which have become associated with painful outcomes. Unfortunately, such retreat renders them abandoned and isolated and without hope, and this is often more painful than the actual social encounter. Individuals with a self-destructive avoidant style are particularly vulnerable to agitated depression; they experience considerable anguish over their ambivalent feelings toward themselves and their relationships with others. Substance abuse may serve to mitigate the pain of social isolation, and suicide can be viewed as a viable source of relief from the pain of living in forced isolation.

As an example, Marcus is 33 years old and recently divorced. His marriage deteriorated over several years and primarily as the result of his wife's increasing frustration with his unwillingness to do anything to improve his situation. He is employed as a warehouse manager and has held the same position for 9 years. He sees others doing more with their lives and wishes that he could as well. Although he hates that his wife chose to leave the marriage, he cannot blame her for doing so. Each evening after work he is filled with feelings of self-contempt and anguish. He would like to go out and be with other people, but he is certain that no one wants his company. He finds that drinking alcohol and watching television usually takes his mind off this unfulfilling life. Marcus thinks of committing suicide frequently.

Treatment of a client with the self-destructive avoidant style requires intensified attention to self-defeating and dangerous behaviors. Particular attention must be paid to drug and alcohol use and abuse and to a constant assessment of suicidal ideation and intent. However, the therapist must also be careful not to reinforce suicidal ideation by allowing suicidal thoughts to be the only or primary source of validation that the client receives. Thus, it is important that the therapist be a consistent source of support and motivation independent of the client's suicidal ideation. Because the client has in many ways abandoned hope, the therapist must serve as motivator as well as therapist.

The *conflicted avoidant* personality style possesses negativistic features. A client with this avoidant style has not abandoned hope of closer social affiliations and relationships but struggles with ambivalent feelings regarding independence and a desire for greater social affiliations. For this individual, a constant conflict between approaching others and avoiding interactions creates a pattern of interactions of the type seen with a bipolar or cyclothymic condition. During times of positive affiliation, when the individual feels more certain of acceptance by others, he or she can act with abandon, reveling in social affiliation in a way that is contradictory to what might be expected in an avoidant personality. Yet when the quality of the interaction begins to sour, as it typically does as the result of the individual's sensitivity and reactant efforts to avoid and defend against affronts, the conflicted individual with an avoidant orientation will retreat into a depression, thereby avoiding any further threat of ridicule and rejection.

For example, Callie is a 19-year-old high school graduate. High school was a source of considerable distress to her, and she is exceedingly pleased to have that part of her life over. Although she did fine academically, the social aspects of high school were agonizing to her. She did not apply to college and is currently deciding whether she should go to the local community college or get a job. Her parents are supportive of either position; they are divorced, and she lives with her mother, who tends not to be very confrontational. She feels confident that her father is growing impatient with her lack of decisiveness and that he would have preferred that she had applied in time to be accepted to the state college. She is relieved that she does not talk to him very often. Most of her friends are preparing to go to college, and she feels somewhat abandoned by them.

Treatment of clients with the conflicted avoidant style requires attention to the vacillation in mood and expressive behaviors. Therapist and client can anticipate this vacillation and agree on methods for managing both the ups and downs associated with exhilaration and disappointments.

The *phobic avoidant* personality style has dependent features and individuals with this style live in a state of constant threat and apprehension regarding social affiliations. To remain safe from perceived threats, these individuals so seriously constrain interactions with the world that they may even refuse to leave their homes. They may become excessively dependent on others to provide basic survival needs. The felt obligation to interact in the social environment may precipitate a panic reaction in those vulnerable to extreme physiological states. For individuals with a phobic avoidant style, somatic complaints, conversion symptoms, and obsessive–compulsive symptoms become highly adaptive mechanisms for constraining social affiliations. Although the nature of the Axis I conditions are very real and not malingered, the adaptive value of the symptoms has been sufficiently reinforced over several years to have obfuscated the cause from the reinforcing outcome. Although an increase in social functioning may be sufficient motivation for many of these clients, pharmacological intervention may be necessary to reduce the anxiety symptoms interfering with treatment success. Indeed, from a behavioral perspective, increasing social affiliation will require a differential reinforcement of other behaviors in those situational circumstances in which avoidant behaviors have been negatively reinforced.

As an example of an individual with a phobic avoidant style, Helen is a 23-year-old college student majoring in French. She is a member of a national sorority and has several friends through her sorority. She admits that she would never have rushed the sorority had it not been for the constant prodding and encouragement by her roommate. She believes that she got into the sorority more through her association with her roommate than because of her own personality. She enjoys the social functions that go with being a member of the sorority but also struggles with feelings of dread and anguish when social occasions arise. If it were not for her friends and her ability to stay close to them, she would not likely participate in these functions. She is currently fearful that her friends are losing interest in her.

To treat the client with a phobic avoidant style, the therapist and client may consider pharmacological intervention to minimize the impact of anguished affect, particularly those feelings that emerge as the individual strives to increase social exposure. It may also be necessary to more specifically treat the clinical syndrome prior to attending to the underlying personality attributes. In this situation, the therapist may introduce various graduated exposure techniques to decrease the conditioned emotional responses characteristic of phobic and other anxiety disorders.

The *hypersensitive avoidant* personality style, which includes paranoid features, takes sensitivity to a higher degree by speculating on the rejection of others. As do individuals with a paranoid personality style, individuals with this style of the avoidant prototype personality assume that others are critical and may perceive affronts that do not exist or react in a highly defensive or deferential manner to minor slights. Being constantly on the defensive, these individuals do not make friends easily, nor do they form many positive social affiliations. Individuals with a hypersensitive avoidant orientation are perceived by others as defensive, argumentative, or moody. Potential friends and affiliates limit their interactions with these individuals, further supporting the perception that others will be rejecting. Treatment of clients with this avoidant style requires particular attention to the cognitive biases contributing to the paranoid features.

For instance, Darius is employed as a systems regulator for a power company. He is diligent at his job but is perceived by others as being rather standoffish. He has been married for 13 years, and he and his wife have very little social contact with others. At work, he attempts to do his job and avoids interacting with others. He is fearful that if he does work more closely with others, they will find reason to be critical of his job performance or will want to talk to him about things that he would just as soon not talk about; he assumes that they would be critical of his opinion, and he is reasonably certain that he would be critical of theirs. He maintains a cynical attitude toward life in general and occupies himself by engaging in activities that require very little social participation.

TREATMENT OF THE AVOIDANT PROTOTYPE

The task in treating those with an avoidant personality style is to alter their information processing in such a way that social interactions are interpreted not as threatening but more as sources of relative enhancement and enjoyment. This shift requires an improvement in the individual's willingness and ability to function interpersonally and an associated decrease in the negative feelings and reactions associated with social distress and avoidant behavior.

The Therapeutic Relationship

Individuals who have an avoidant personality style are unique in their orientation to therapy. On one hand, they are often highly motivated for treatment and hopeful of the potential relief to be gained through therapy. However, their social anxiety also contributes to numerous interpersonal and therapeutic challenges. First, their fear of confrontation and rejection may interfere with their willingness to be open and honest with the therapist. In fact, it may be common for these individuals to cancel appointments when they anticipate criticism for having not completed a treatment assignment. Likewise, if they anticipate the discussion of a sensitive topic or expect critical revelations to be made, they may feel compelled to avoid therapy. Further, their fear of social criticism may make it very difficult for them to complete specific out-of-session assignments or render them unwilling to accept clinical challenges.

In any case, the reactions and behavioral tendencies of those with the avoidant style will have to be managed in treatment. To minimize resistance to treatment, the therapist should maintain a supportive and encouraging therapeutic environment and pace therapy in such a way that gains are made without forcing the client into a defensive reaction propelled by his or her fear of failure, criticism, and rejection.

Cognitive Goals

One of the important tasks of therapy is to alter perceptions of stressful and painful social encounters. Motivated by their protective orientation, these individuals are inclined to perceive threats where none exist or overemphasize the nature and severity of mild or moderate threats. No doubt, the motto "better safe than sorry" applies to this group of clients. Unfortunately, problems rarely exist only at the cognitive level. As a result of a lifelong pattern of social avoidance, a client with the avoidant style may have failed to develop effective social skills; thus, many threats are justified as a result of the individual's lack of social aptitude. As a result, it is important to understand the extent to which interpersonal problems are the result of social skills deficits or affectively mediated implementation problems. In some cases, the individual may understand how to function interpersonally but is so distressed by the threat of negative evaluation that he or she is unable to perform effectively given the demands of the circumstance.

To the extent that social skills are enhanced and the individual is able to function effectively in interpersonal engagements, the self-view of alienation should give way to one of social participation. Likewise, as the individual develops greater confidence in the ability to find enjoyment in interpersonal relationships, the aversiveness of social participation will decline. Most important, perhaps, as the individual finds greater enjoyment in interactions with others and comes to perceive social engagements as less threatening, the necessity of pathologic reactions to social threats should decrease and may, in some cases, be eliminated. Thus, anxiety is reduced, as well as the experience of panic, depression, delusional thinking, and so forth.

In the sections that follow, specific intervention strategies are highlighted. It is important that treatments be customized to the specific needs of the individual client; thus, the suggestions are general recommendations for those providing treatment to individuals with an avoidant prototype personality.

Arranging Treatment

Several questions are relevant to treating this population of clients. Resolution of these questions has implications for the sequencing and pairing of the treatment phases and components. To begin, does the individual possess the interpersonal skills necessary to function in an interpersonal setting? If the answer is no, then initial attention must be directed at teaching adaptive social abilities. Without adequate social skills, cognitive changes are not likely to withstand the inevitable social failures brought about by insufficient social ability.

If the individual possesses adequate social skills and social awareness, attention should be directed at identifying and rectifying those cognitive or affective processes that are interfering with adaptive and rewarding social engagements. For instance, what cognitive distortions interfere with the client's willingness or ability to function interpersonally? What are the automatic thoughts mediating schema activation, and what core beliefs and intermediate beliefs associated with schema and mode activation are involved? Finally, are affective factors (anxiety or panic) interfering with appropriate behavioral displays?

It is possible that the individual is sufficiently skilled in interpersonal functioning and does not have biased cognitive processes, yet is overwhelmed by conditioned emotional responses. In such situations, can baseline and reactive anxiety be reduced through pharmacotherapy or relaxation training? In addition, can affect be altered through metaemotional processes (see Gottman, 2001; Rasmussen, 2003a, 2003b)? By carefully considering the introduction and pairing of the various aspects of treatment, the ultimate gains of therapy can be enhanced and the challenge of treatment resistance minimized.

Social Skills Assessment and Treatment

If the individual does not possess effective and adaptive social skills, changing cognitive processes is unlikely to be sufficient in bringing about clinical improvements. When social functioning is clearly deficient, attention should be given to the enhancement of social skills. To assess social skills, the therapist can discuss common social situations and how the client might respond, assessing areas of confusion, stated apprehension, or lack of knowledge. Likewise, how the individual behaves in the therapeutic session is often a good indication of basic social ability. Is the individual hesitant or awkward? Does he or she avoid eye contact or show other nonverbal signs indicating a lack of interpersonal confidence? What social activities does the client report as particularly stressful? Through in-session discussion, client and therapist can pinpoint areas of liability and work on the development of greater social skills by way of assigned readings (i.e., bibliotherapy), direct instruction, role-plays, and other exercises. Once the client is able to display appropriate social knowledge, perceptiveness, and skill, acquired skills can then be practiced out-of-session. This activity can be introduced as a graduated process in which the client practices first on relatively safe people (e.g., family members, close friends, or coworkers), moving on to less familiar people and situations as confidence increases. As the individual is directed toward greater social participation, the potential for interfering cognitions and affective reactions increases, and this must be targeted in treatment.

Cognitive Assessment and Treatment

If the individual is sufficiently knowledgeable about social skills and interpersonal dynamics but avoidant of interpersonal interaction, it is important to consider the extent to which specific cognitive or affective factors are contributing to social avoidance. Potential sources of interference include overly critical interpersonal environments, misinterpretation of social threat, misappraisal of personal resources, and interference of affective processes. Indeed, it is unwise to assume that any individual is living in a reasonable environment. It is quite conceivable that the client is living or working in a highly critical environment and that avoidant behaviors and their associated cognitive and affective processes reflect reasonable protective reactions. In such situations, the possibility of alternative living or working arrangements can be considered. When changing environments is not feasible, possible coping resources can be discussed and implemented. As the individual becomes more adept at coping with and managing the unpleasant circumstances, the need for symptoms associated with escape and avoidance behaviors should decrease.

In many situations, although the social skills of the individual are relatively adequate, he or she is biased to perceive social situations as particularly threatening and him- or herself as deficient in interpersonal skill or appeal. The associated affective distress felt in response to such appraisals is enough to compel an avoidance reaction. Several strategies are useful in ferreting out problematic distortions. Administration of the Early Maladaptive Schema Questionnaire (Young & Lindemann, 1992) may reveal specific cognitive biases associated with aversive affect and avoidant behaviors. For instance, Coon (1994) found an association between maladaptive schemas related to failure and social alienation in clients with an avoidant personality disorder. Through the process of guided discovery, client and therapist can search for the connection between cognitive distortions and social distress, highlighting the automatic thoughts and core beliefs preceding mode-based reactions. Similarly, they can examine the evidence (Freeman et al., 1990) concerning the conclusions drawn. For instance, the individual may assume that he has no social success, but through guided discovery, evidence of considerable social affiliation may be revealed.

Likewise, although the client may perceive the self as having few intrapersonal resources to draw on in social encounters, it may be discovered that he or she is in many ways quite skilled, yet unrealistic concerning social expectations. Further, in many cases the individual perceives the self as having little interpersonal appeal. One client, for instance, reported believing that others simply did not enjoy or desire her company. In such cases, the therapist can discuss with the client evidence contradicting such conclusions, emphasizing at the same time the acquisition of enhanced social skills, which would further enhance the person's social success. It is not uncommon that those who are suspicious of their own interpersonal appeal are prone to castastrophizing and overgeneralization, among other cognitive distortions. It is necessary that the therapist help the client challenge these assumptions, which is more readily accomplished as the individual develops greater confidence in his or her ability to function socially.

Cognitive monitoring procedures are also useful to help the client identify and anticipate cognitive distortions. In this procedure (see Persons, Davidson, & Tompkins, 2001), the client is instructed to monitor self-statements and to assess the associated affective and behavioral reactions. To the extent that distortions are associated with skills deficits, therapist and client should turn attention to rectifying those deficits. If social skills are sufficient, attention is given to strategies for altering distorted thoughts and affective reactions. To ensure changes in core beliefs, the therapist encourages the client to consider how changes influence core beliefs. Thus, to the extent that the client is able to derive pleasure from interpersonal engagements, the view of the self as alienated must yield to a more adaptive self-view. Similarly, positive social encounters also contradict the view of others in vexatious terms. Indeed, it is difficult to view others as harsh and rejecting if they are acting positively toward the client.

To ensure prolonged treatment gains, it is important that the client understand that not all social engagements will turn out positively, despite improved social skill and enhanced confidence. As a result, it is important that the client be prepared for the inevitable pains and disappointments that come with social affiliations. Equipping the client with interpersonal statements to counter interpersonal criticisms and self-statements to implement in the face of hurt feelings can prevent a return to old avoidant tendencies. For instance, in response to criticism, the client might say something such as, "I am sorry you feel that way" or "Everyone has a right to their opinion." In addition to these interpersonal reactions, the individual can remind him- or herself that "Sometimes things don't go as well as one hopes" and "I can handle this." The client can be reminded as well that as long as he or she continues to exhibit appropriate, positive, and respectful interpersonal behaviors, the probability of strained interpersonal relationships is minimized, albeit not eliminated.

Emotion-Based Treatments

Because the individual with an avoidant style is often compelled to act (e.g., escaping or avoiding social interactions) by aversive emotional experiences, it may be helpful to address more specifically the affective reactions that are associated with the pathologic process. In this context, attention to affective reactions complements efforts associated with cognitive and behavioral processes. At one level, the individual may be instructed in one of various forms of relaxation as a means of decreasing baseline mood state. When necessary, short-term pharmacotherapy may be helpful as a means of reducing mood state reactions that interfere with behavioral and cognitive changes. However, as the individual gains greater confidence in behavioral expressions and greater control over self-defeating cognitive processes, the necessity of continued pharmacotherapy should be reevaluated.

Metaemotional processes may also help the individual with an avoidant style gain greater emotional self-control. For instance, understanding the adaptive value of the emotional experience may help the individual develop greater objectivity concerning emotional expression. In the case of the individual with an avoidant orientation, his or her anxiety may serve to increase hypervigilance to signs of social threat and to compel reactive behaviors, including escape and avoidance associated with phobia. Episodes of depression and dysthymia reflect his or her general feelings of hopelessness and desired retreat from threatening social engagements. By understanding the adaptive purpose of the affective experience, the individual is in the best position to consider the reaction being compelled by the emotion as well as alternative reactions more consistent with the treatment program (Rasmussen, 2003a, 2003b).

When depression, obsessions, or other serious conditions interfere with treatment success, efforts to reduce the impact of these conditions may be necessary. For instance, it may be necessary to schedule involvement in pleasurable activities for those with a depressed condition or introduce exposure and response prevention procedures for those with an obsessive–compulsive condition. The ultimate goal in treating those with an avoidant style is to increase pleasure derived from social engagements and to decrease fear and avoidance associated with painful social encounters. In addition, it is often necessary to target those behaviors and activities that have served to distract the individual from his or her anguished emotions.

In many cases, the fantasy-based regulatory mechanisms of the client are themselves very rewarding. For instance, the client may find considerable pleasure in solitary activities such as reading, watching television and movies, or engaging in various vocational activities. In these situations, if possible, the therapist may introduce contingency contracts with the client in which involvement in those safer pleasures is contingent on greater social engagements. To the extent that these regulatory behaviors are pursued compulsively, the therapist may need to introduce various methods of response prevention. For example, in the case of a sexual addiction involving pornography, the therapist may introduce fantasy redirection or satiation procedures (see Rasmussen, McAnulty, & Mangum, 2001). The next section offers an example of how a personality-guided cognitive–behavioral therapy approach may help an individual with an avoidant style who is presenting with dysthymia and social phobia.

CASE EXAMPLE

Donald is a 27-year-old account executive for a national bank. He has held this position since his graduation from college 4 years previously. He graduated with a degree in consumer business after being unable to gain admittance into the more challenging and prestigious business administration program. He has remained at the same entry-level position since taking the job. Others who have come into the position more recently have received promotions from the bank or have taken better positions with other institutions. His performance reviews are marginal at best. He is criticized for not doing more to pursue new accounts. He has done relatively well managing the accounts that were given to him and those of customers he got to know before taking over their accounts; however, he struggles to make "cold calls" in pursuit of new accounts. He knows that his boss has given him a few breaks over the years, partly because he goes out of his way to be friendly and accommodating. He figures that if he can stay on good terms with his boss, his job is more secure.

However, Donald worries that his boss is beginning to lose patience with him, and he fears that at any time he may be put on probationary status, if not fired. Each day that Donald comes to work, he fears the worst. He assumes that others are talking about his performance deficiencies and asking one another why they think the boss keeps him around. Nonetheless, he strives to remain pleasant and optimistic, yet he also fears that others will see this as a façade and a lack of concern over legitimate performance issues. His days are filled with anguished emotions related to his own performance deficits, his fear of how others are viewing him, and his tremendous desire to be "one of the group" of successful young executives.

During the evenings, when he could be doing more work or socializing, he stays at home, often wishing to be invited out with the group but also thankful that he does not have to face his associates and fake being more optimistic than he is. It would be nice if they would invite him to join them, but he understands that he tends to be somewhat standoffish and does not blame them for not inviting him. The few times he has been invited, he warmly accepted the invitation and intended to go to the event, but as the time approached he became increasingly anxious and eventually concocted some reason why he could not attend. Each evening, Donald swears he is going to do more work or hang out at a nightspot, but he ends up watching television until quite late. During the time he watches television he is not thinking about work and his failing social involvements. He often has difficulty sleeping because his mind wanders to failures, shortcomings, feelings of loneliness, and impending threats. Almost inevitably he ends up falling asleep in front of the television.

Diagnostically, Donald meets criteria for dysthymia and social phobia. Although he does not meet criteria for an avoidant personality disorder, his elevation on the Millon Clinical Multiaxial Inventory (Millon, 1997) points to an avoidant prototype personality. Attention could be directed at the dysthymic and phobic conditions independently, but doing so would not necessarily address the underlying personality dimensions contributing to the clinical condition. By attending to the personality attributes and the role of the clinical conditions in meeting the survival task, treatment can produce greater gains as reflected in greater resilience to future challenges that have been dealt with in ways that involve moderate depression and anxiety.

Donald is characterized by the following personality attributes: an alienated self-image and core beliefs that include the assumptions that "I am not as good as others" and "I don't fit it with those with whom I wish to affiliate." He has a history of rejection and of not measuring up to expectations (object representations), which contributes to his view of himself as being less than adequate. He wants very desperately to fit in and be accepted, but he quickly feels threatened in social situations that he perceives as dangerous as the result of his inherent failings (interpersonal conduct). His mood is anguished as the result of the approach and avoidance conflict concerning social interactions. The only relief he feels comes from mindless attention to television and other fantasy pursuits (regulatory mechanism). Although he attempts to focus himself on the tasks he is confronted with at work, his mind wanders readily to the implications of success, which include enhanced status among others, and to the implications of failure, which include validation of his fears that he is defective and inept (distracted cognitive style). When in a social situation, Donald's anguish contributes to fretfulness (expressive behaviors) and uncertainty, which play a part in interpersonal awkwardness.

As a result of his lack of social success, he has developed a general disengagement marked by chronic feelings of mild depression (i.e., dysthymia). The anxiety that he experiences when in social interactions fits a social phobia description. Although either condition could be targeted for treatment, the underlying personality attributes will contribute to a sluggish response to treatment and may very well undermine any gains made in therapy. By attending to specific personality attributes, Donald should experience relief from his dysthymia and a decrease in social phobia and avoidance.

For Donald, the primary goal of treatment is to alter information processing in such a way that he is not compelled by the resultant anxiety to avoid social engagements. Achieving this goal is dependent on numerous factors. First, Donald must have, and perceive that he has, the requisite skills for successful social functioning. Thus, it is important to complete an adequate assessment of social functioning and to teach deficit social skills. Similarly, it is necessary for Donald to consider his suitability for the position that he holds.

Through a process of collaborative empiricism and guided discovery (see Freeman et al., 1990), it was determined that despite his lack of a business degree, Donald does indeed possess the skills necessary for job success. He is comfortable with numbers and has a good understanding of the banking business. During this process, Donald was able to appreciate how his assumptions about himself and his position with his colleagues were contributing to aversive affective reactions compelling him to avoid personal and professional affiliations and contributing to his feelings of self-doubt. Initial stages of treatment focused on Donald's basic social skills related to discourse with colleagues and clients. For instance, Donald scripted his own dialogue regarding how to make cold calls and practiced those calls as in-session role-play, and the therapist provided constructive and encouraging feedback. Potential interactions with coworkers were role-played in session as well. Once Donald developed a greater degree of confidence in his social abilities, attention was given to his automatic thoughts and core beliefs.

Initially, Donald's automatic thoughts and core beliefs were identified by way of guided discovery. The validity of those assumptions was discussed relative to information already discussed concerning his actual abilities and his recently derived social insights and acquired abilities. In addition, Donald monitored his ongoing automatic thoughts and associated schema-based core beliefs and generated alternative statements to counter the automatic thoughts on the monitoring form. It is important to note that his ability to challenge cognitive conclusions was enhanced significantly by his growing ability to function with social success, which included remaining safe and deriving enjoyment in social encounters. During the several weeks that he monitored social engagements and self-statements, various problems emerged that were the source of attention in subsequent therapy sessions; these problems were addressed consistent with the established treatment plan.

To help Donald deal with the anxiety associated with his fear of rejection, it was helpful to consider object representations and regulatory mechanisms. By understanding how current relationships reflect patterns of coping developed through previous relationships, Donald was better able to accept that current perceptions and feelings did not reflect natural and unalterable circumstances but, rather, adopted methods for protecting the self from painful experiences.

CONCLUSION

Individuals with the avoidant prototype personality are vexed by their desire for and fear of interpersonal relationships. The approach–avoidance conflict they experience is felt as anxiety and anguish and often as various forms of depression, including dysthymia, episodic depression, and periods of hypomania. The general social distress and self-contempt these individuals feel contributes to a variety of clinical conditions mediated by personality attributes. Successful treatment of the clinical conditions exhibited by those with the avoidant style requires attention to critical personality attributes and the associated beliefs leading to the clinical outcomes.

Cognitive therapy techniques have already been established as effective means for treating clients with the various clinical conditions that are commonly observed in individuals with an avoidant style of personality, as well as being effective in treating the avoidant personality disorder. Combining the cognitive and cognitive–behavioral model with the evolutionary foundation provided by the personologic view enhances the nature of treatments targeting the clinical conditions.

11

THE DEPENDENT PROTOTYPE

Key phrase: Take care of me
Evolutionary focus: Help-eliciting; clinginess

Individuals with a dependent prototype personality are willing to forgo nearly all sources of pleasure for the benefit of safety and protection. Although not necessarily passive, they tend toward submissiveness by simply responding in an accommodating way to the ebb and flow of their social and intimate affiliations. They are often unaware or indifferent to personal ambitions and desires, focusing time and resources on the satisfactions of those to whom they are emotionally attached. Thus, their self versus other focus is predominantly on the wants, needs, and reactions of others. Their self-awareness may be more emotion-based as they remain vigilant to interpersonal cues and their own negative emotional reactions. They do not believe that they can accomplish things on their own and must turn to others for advice and reassurance. Other people are viewed as stronger and more capable, and individuals with a dependent style turn to them to receive nurturance, support, and approval. As long as the caretaker is available, an individual with a dependent orientation can function adequately. However, when the caregiver becomes unavailable or inaccessible, the individual can be thrown into a panic or other emotional crisis. The polarity balances of the dependent prototype are illustrated in Figure 11.1.

As an example of the dependent style, Frank is 36 years old and lives at home with his parents. He works at a vending machine company in a job that was arranged for him several years ago by his father. After work each day, he returns home and spends the evening interacting with his

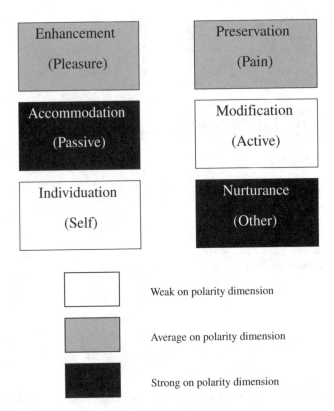

Figure 11.1. Polarity balance of the dependent prototype. From *Personality-Guided Therapy* (p. 370), by T. Millon, 1999, New York: Guilford Press. Copyright 1999 by John Wiley & Sons, Inc. Reprinted with permission.

parents, who have encouraged him for years to find a girl and get married. He has been on several dates over the years but says that he does not want to leave his parents. He was involved in one relationship that ended when his girlfriend tired of his unwillingness to commit to the relationship. He takes virtually no initiative to engage in independent activities, allowing his parents to dictate any recreational activities, which are usually related to encounters with the extended family.

PERSONALITY-GUIDED COGNITIVE–BEHAVIORAL CONCEPTUALIZATION

Persons with a dependent style typically view the self as being *inept*, or as Beck, Freeman, and Associates (1990) described it, as being needy, weak, helpless, and incompetent (see Table 11.1). Viewing themselves as

TABLE 11.1
Structures and Functions of the Dependent Prototype and Associated Liabilities

Personality domain	Liability
Self-image Inept	View of the self as helpless, incapable, and needing of others' assistance
Object representations Immature	History of pampering and overdependency; relies on others when making personal decisions
Morphological organization Inchoate	Inability to manage the self; frequent fragmentation of sense of self into identities related to what others want or need
Mood and temperament Pacific	Lack of willingness to make waves that would potentially disrupt a relationship; inability to stand up for the self and protect personal rights and limits
Behavioral acts Incompetent	Very few behavioral skills outside of responding to what close others want or need
Interpersonal conduct Submissive	Behaviors are to please or satisfy others; personal desires ignored
Cognitive style Naive	Inability to think beyond the needs of close others; inability to form independent ideas or ambitions
Regulatory mechanism Introjection	Deference to others in dealing with personal concerns and crises; internalization of emotions that might lead to behaviors that could result in abandonment

being deficient in basic skills, these individuals also believe that to survive and function, they must have other, stronger individuals on whom to rely. Their history with others (i.e., object relations) is that others are more able and can be counted on to take care of them, thus demonstrating their *immature* object relations. Frequently, they see their own ability to survive as dependent on their ability to remain connected with one or more persons who are more capable than they are. The automatic thoughts of individuals with a dependent prototype personality are oriented toward keeping them safe and invested in a protective relationship. Subsequently, they are susceptible, for instance, to arbitrary inference (e.g., "Oh, no, I can tell he is going to leave me"), catastrophizing (e.g., "I can't live without him"), dichotomous thinking (e.g., perceiving that they are either loved and protected or despised and rejectable), and magnification (e.g., assuming their mistakes to be grounds for abandonment by others).

The core beliefs of an individual with a dependent style are of the following types: "I am completely helpless," "I am all alone," or "I must have someone to take care of me." The intermediate beliefs are also consistent with the view of the self as incompetent. For instance, the conditional beliefs, as described by Beck et al. (1990), are of the following types: "I can function only if I have access to somebody competent," "If I am abandoned, I will die," and "If I am not loved, I will always be unhappy."

Consequently, the individual with a dependent personality style maintains instrumental beliefs consistent with the need to enlist and maintain the investment and engagement of others. For instance, the person maintains such instrumental beliefs as "Don't offend the caretaker," "Cultivate as intimate a relationship as possible," and "Be subservient to bind the person." As the result of this dependency on others, the individual can be highly distressed by any perceived threat to the dependent relationship. They will do all they can to maintain their dependency, believing that complete subservience and acquiescence to the wants and needs of the caretaker will maintain that caretaker's investment. The unfortunate fact is that in many cases, although the caretaker finds this subservience beneficial in many ways, the behavior is taken for granted, and the individual is devalued by the caregiver, which then prompts reactive efforts by the individual to maintain or rescue the relationship. It is not surprising that the individual is vulnerable to a host of emotional reactions related to events in their dependent relationship.

Behaviorally, individuals with a dependent style are characterized by *incompetence*. Although they may actually have greater competence than their behavior would suggest, the behaviors enacted indicate a general lack of ability to manage and care for the self. Interpersonally, they are *submissive*. These individuals compromise themselves to the needs and desires of others to maintain their care and investment. They often fear that personal demands will lead others to reject and abandon them. The unfortunate fact is that people often take these individuals for granted and frequently lose interest and respect for them. Thus, the very behaviors the person with a dependent orientation enacts to keep others invested serves to push them away.

The characteristic mood of the dependent personality is *pacific*; this term describes the passive and nonconfrontational mood of the individual with a dependent style, who seeks calmness and strives to make no waves. He or she may experience periods of joyful exuberance when a dependency-based relationship is going particularly well. However, in the face of real or perceived abandonment, the individual's calmness can give way to frantic and desperate emotions and behaviors.

PATHOLOGIC PROCESS OF THE DEPENDENT PATTERN

For those with the dependent personality style, stress is most typically encountered when faced with the threat of abandonment, rejection, or undesired independence. Unfortunately, because of their self-view and limited behavioral resources, they are inclined to perceive relatively innocuous circumstances as threatening. Thus, many situations are interpreted as possible rejection, and they are then confronted with a crisis situation requiring immediate resolution. Important in this process is the reaction to threats to dependency and the behaviors enacted to rescue a dependent relationship. Also important is the reinforcement obtained through the various behavioral and emotional responses.

AXIS I VULNERABILITIES

The dependent prototype contributes to the experience of clinical conditions as both relative cause and outcome. As a function of the dependent orientation, the individual with a dependent prototype personality perceives many circumstances as more threatening and stressful than would most other individuals. They see themselves as unable to meet many life challenges and responsibilities, and their lack of personal efficacy leaves them easily threatened and vulnerable. In addition, the reactions expressed in response to these stressors often serve the very adaptive purpose of drawing in others to provide support, reassurance, and succor. As a result, those with the dependent personality style, even in the relative absence of a diagnosable personality disorder, are highly vulnerable to clinical outcomes.

Generalized Anxiety Disorder

It is not surprising that one of the most common Axis I conditions found with the dependent personality is anxiety (Bornstein, 1995; Lilienfeld, 2001; Skodol, Gallaher, & Oldham, 1996). As Öhman (2000) described it, anxiety is the emotion that one feels when one needs to be attentive to potential dangers. For individuals with a dependent style, who view the self as functionally inept, dangers are constantly looming. Their efforts are designed and implemented for the specific purpose of keeping them safe from external threats, most typically associated with abandonment and independence. To the extent that they are unable to maintain the investment of stronger people, their survival is threatened. Further, because the possibility of rejection or abandonment is ever present and often unpredictable and uncontrollable, this reality renders them highly vulnerable to anxiety, specifically to broad, nonspecific anxiety characteristic of a generalized anxiety condition. In addition to separation-related anxieties (see Loas et al., 2002; Manicavasagar, Silove, & Curtis, 1997), individuals with a dependent orientation fear new tasks or responsibilities that might be beyond their abilities and thus threaten their status among those on whom they depend. It is important to note that the anxiety not only serves to maintain their hypervigilance to threats to their dependent relationships but also serves to reinforce their personal view of ineptness and neediness as well as to keep others, who are sympathetic to their distress, invested. However, their anxiety often comes to be a burden to others, and the reactions by others to that perceived burden may validate the individual's fear of abandonment.

Phobic Disorder

Because those with the dependent style of personality view the self as generally inept, they are likely to find many situations and objects threatening, rendering them susceptible to conditioned emotional reactions (Dyck et al., 2001). In such situations, although the fear of the phobic object is not feigned, it does emerge, in part, from one's sense of personal inadequacy and through the opportunity to avoid unpleasant circumstances and ensure the investment of significant others. Through the display of phobic symptoms, the individual is able to solicit the assistance of others who are better able to deal with those events and activities related to his or her phobic fear. Further, through a phobic response, the individual does not have to engage in activities that cause fear and must rely on others to complete the activity. In the case of phobia, the emotional reaction is fear and the need is protection, a response from others that is highly desired by the individual with a dependent orientation.

Dissociative Disorder

The objective of individuals with a dependent prototype personality is to avoid any responsibility for activities and events for which they feel unprepared or ill equipped. When faced with tasks they are unable to actively avoid, dissociation may prove particularly adaptive. Although this has not been empirically validated, through dissociation individuals with a dependent style may be able to escape responsibilities by denying the reality of those responsibilities. Similarly, amnesic episodes would allow them to avoid any undertaking for which they feel unprepared or that they find unpleasant. To the extent that such denial can be perceived by others as evidence of the dependent's fragile makeup or "illness," dissociation also provides a resource for eliciting caregiving from others.

Further, dissociation can serve to protect the individual from facing crisis situations. For instance, the husband with a dependent style whose wife is threatening divorce avoids any obligation to deal with his failure of contribution to the marriage through dissociation. This example is not to suggest a conscious manipulation of dissociative symptoms but to underscore the adaptive value of such symptoms. In the situation described, acknowledgment of the wife's dissatisfaction with the marriage puts the husband in a situation that he is unprepared to manage. Dissociation thus provides relief from a hopeless situation. To be sure, the problems in the marriage may very well continue, but he is not obligated to contend with those problems until doing so is unavoidable, such as when his wife leaves the marriage and he is forced to live independently.

Somatoform Disorder

Somatoform disorders are common among individuals with a dependent personality style (Bornstein, 1995; Garyfallos et al., 1999). Through their somatic symptoms, such individuals are able to avoid responsibilities they find unpleasant and to elicit the sympathy and nurturance they feel they need. Although somatic symptoms could be consciously feigned, the chronic separation anxiety may be manifested in various physical symptoms, which results in both positive and negative reinforcements—specifically, relief from responsibility or assistance with unpleasant tasks and the reward of sympathy and nurturance. Often, individuals with a dependent orientation who have few self-sustaining resources are able to gain relief from the incessant and often excessive demands of family members and employers through somatic complaints. Although the self-sacrificing nature of the dependent prototype personality contributes to the demanding expectations of family members, the parent with a dependent style is unable to meet those demands, is distressed by this failure, and is able to gain some relief by attending to somatic symptoms. It is important to understand that the somatic complaints may result from chronic or acute stress or may be malingered; either way, they are reinforced by relief from demands and guilt.

Individuals with a dependent personality often feel considerable frustration and resentment toward those on whom they depend. Often they perceive themselves as doing what is required to make a relationship work but others as failing to meet their responsibilities to the relationship. However, because actively expressed anger could potentially lead to rejection, they suppress their angry feelings. For these individuals, somatic complaints may represent the anger they feel toward others but are unable to express.

As an example of a somatoform disorder in an individual with a dependent style, Angela is 33 years old and the mother of three children ranging from 4 to 15 years of age. She has been married for 15 years; her husband is 10 years older and is employed by a road construction company. His job requires that he be away from home for weeks or months at a time, with irregular weekends home. To help with the finances, she works part time as a file assistant in the medical records department at a regional hospital. She finds her job very stressful and has been reprimanded on occasion for filing errors. She has asked her husband to change jobs so that he is not away as much. Although he has promised over the years to do so, he has not found the opportunity. She has struggled for years with various health-related problems that physicians have been unable to pinpoint. She has taken several types of medications, but the old problems persist and new ones crop up. She admits to being very frustrated by her husband's absence and failure to change jobs, and she feels stressed by the demands of motherhood. She would like to be more insistent that her husband change jobs and spend more time at home, but she is fearful that her insistence will "make him mad."

Obsessive–Compulsive Disorder

Individuals with a dependent personality style are prone to obsessional concerns (Skodol et al., 1996), particularly those associated with doubt and dependency. Because they doubt their ability to manage many life responsibilities and to function independently, they are inclined to obsess over the possibility of abandonment and may compulsively engage in behaviors that they believe enhance their ability to rely on others. Thus, the compulsive behaviors of many with an obsessive–compulsive disorder may reflect efforts by individuals with a dependent orientation to stave off rejection by those on whom they have come to depend. Thus, their obsession with self-doubt and separation compels those behaviors that they believe will decrease the risk of separation. Furthermore, the validation of an obsessive–compulsive condition legitimizes the person's need to be dependent and helps to secure the continued investment of those on whom he or she depends. An example of an obsessive–compulsive condition associated with the dependent style is described in the case of Marcus.

Marcus had been diagnosed as having an obsessive–compulsive disorder associated with recurrent checking. In particular, he checked and double-checked that household items were not left out, that chores were completed, and that bank accounts were balanced and sufficient. His concern was that he might overlook some detail or fail to put something away and that this would lead his wife to find him unsatisfactory and leave him. Although his wife appreciated his neatness and conscientiousness, this care was not nearly as important to her as it was to Marcus. Upon assessment, the therapist determined that Marcus's obsessive–compulsive behaviors were mediated by his dependent personality style. That his condition was worse when his wife was either annoyed with him or busily engaged in career pursuits was consistent with his introjected regulatory style and fear of inadequacy. He assumed that her lack of engagement in him was his fault and that he must do something to prove his value to her.

Major Depression

In the face of abandonment, individuals with a dependent style are vulnerable to the hopelessness and helplessness characteristic of a major depressive episode (see Akhavan, 2001; Loranger, 1996; Overholser, 1996; Widiger & Anderson, 2003; Zaretsky, Fava, Davidson, & Pava, 1997). These individuals do not often rest on their laurels and work diligently to maintain the investment of others. When their efforts prove to be ineffective and their own reactionary attempts such as intensifying efforts (i.e., trying harder) or pleading have failed, the withdrawal to depression serves to keep them from engaging in hopeless battles they will not win (see Gilbert, 2000; Nesse, 1999). In addition, the withdrawal of depression also serves to elicit caregiving attention from the one who may be attempting to leave or from others in the individual's environment who may be able to take over for the exiting caregiver (see Nesse, 1990, 2001; Plutchik, 2000).

Individuals with a dependent personality style hope that others will provide validation and protection, yet as a rule they do not perceive themselves to be in a position to insist on such treatment, and they rely instead on behaviors enacted to win and maintain the investment of others (e.g., submissiveness). When others fail to provide the desired validation and protection, the individual is vulnerable to feelings of frustration, anger, and despair. However, because they fear being rejected for acting aggressively to derive an entitled outcome, their anger is often suppressed and manifested more often as an agitated form of depression (see Zidanik, 2002).

Bipolar Disorder

When things are going well for the individual with a dependent orientation, a joyful enthusiasm for life may be evident that is not generally present when concerns over separation are more prevalent. The individual may act with more confidence and less concern over fear of rejection. However, when the individual begins to perceive reactions in a caregiver that suggest a threat to the relationship, he or she is likely to become hyperactive in an effort to avoid abandonment. During these times, the individual with a dependent style will engage in numerous activities, with seemingly inexhaustible energy and relatively little reflection, to secure the relationship. If efforts are effective, this hypomanic episode will give way to a more normal or typical mood state, one likely marked by some anxiety. If hypomanic efforts are not effective, the individual may withdraw into a retarded, helpless, or agitated depression (see Perugi, Toni, Travierso, & Akiskal, 2003). To the extent that the relationship is volatile, the probability of manic episodes may increase as the result of a greater quantity and frequency of threatening contingencies.

Catatonic Schizophrenia

In the face of absolute hopelessness, individuals with a dependent prototype personality who have not developed any confidence that they can meet the demands of life may withdraw into a catatonic state. Similar to the dissociative experience, when the reality that the individual must face is more threatening then he or she can tolerate, he or she may totally deny that reality.

VARIATIONS ON THE TRADITIONAL DEPENDENT PERSONALITY

The variations on the dependent theme (Millon, 1999; Millon & Davis, 2000) share a view of the self as inept and unable to meet life challenges independent of others and the need to enlist the investment of stronger others for a sense of protection and security. Differences exist in the ways in which each individual acts to bring about that sense of security. Reflected, perhaps, most specifically in conditional and instrumental beliefs, is the ambition expressed by each of these individuals to have others in their lives who will make life safe and comfortable.

The *immature dependent* personality style is a variation on the pure dependent pattern. Individuals with this style have essentially failed to grow and mature into functioning adults. They are nearly incapable of assuming adult responsibilities and continue to show preference for childhood activities. For instance, such individuals may fail to maintain self-sustaining employment and continue engagement in childhood activities, such as model train building, baseball card collecting, or prank playing. When pressed by others to assume greater responsibilities, they may respond with a host of emotional reactions, including anxiety, panic, temper displays, or depression. These individuals desire to remain dependent and will react in a way to avoid fulfillment of expectations when dependency is threatened.

Those with an immature form of dependency may be particularly vulnerable to various somatic complaints, psychosomatic issues (e.g., asthma, digestive problems), and other conditions that are associated with an adaptive incapacitation. In this regard, the clinical condition is adaptive by promoting dependency.

The *disquieted dependent* personality style possesses many of the qualities of the avoidant personality style. Unlike individuals with an immature dependent orientation, who do not want to abandon the pleasures of childhood dependency, individuals with a disquieted dependent style are fearful of adult responsibilities and autonomy and rely on others to meet adult responsibilities. In the extreme form, individuals with a disquieted dependent style become so extremely helpless and dependent as to require institutionalized care (Millon & Davis, 2000). For these individuals, the boundaries of institutionalized care provide relief from the demands of adult responsibilities. Unfortunately for many, they maintain awareness and understanding of the sacrifices they have made and may struggle with feelings of guilt, sadness, and despair. In less extreme cases, these individuals come to rely on others to meet their adult responsibilities, which may put them in a position to be easily exploited.

As an example, one woman described years of being put into distressing and humiliating sexual situations by her spouse, but she had felt unable to tell him of her distress for fear of being rejected. Abandonment by others is devastating to those with the disquieted dependent style, and they will precipitate extreme reactions oriented to maintaining the dependency. True abandonment may leave these individuals nearly vegetative, which may contribute to institutionalization. Those individuals who are able to escape a cycle of dependency and abandonment often are able to maintain some redeeming quality that keeps others invested in them. For instance, sexual availability, inherited financial resources, housekeeping, and meal preparation may be factors that keep others invested in individuals with a disquieted dependent prototype personality. In the absence of any redeeming qualities, the situation for these individuals is rather discouraging.

The *ineffectual dependent* personality style includes schizoid features. Individuals with this personality style display a general disengagement from adult life and responsibilities. They display a very low degree of activity and vitality. They are easily fatigued and show little spontaneity and enthusiasm. They prefer solitary activities, which may include excessive television viewing, unique hobbies that can be completed in isolation (e.g., computer games and collecting), or other independent activities. They have little motivation and are more or less content to take what life has to offer. They do not get upset or active when events turn against them. Although these individuals may not be highly susceptible to clinical conditions, their isolated and perhaps sedentary lifestyles may leave them more vulnerable to some mental and physical health-related outcomes. For instance, they may be diagnosed with panic disorder and agoraphobia that emerge during times of increased expectation and may encounter increased risk of health disease secondary to obesity and inactivity.

The *accommodating dependent* personality style includes features of the histrionic personality style. Individuals with an accommodating dependent style rely on their engaging and outgoing personality to foster relationships. They are perceived by others as gracious, agreeable, and easy to get along with. They easily slip into a submissive and accommodating role, which they are able to express with a smile and friendly word (Millon & Davis, 2000). Their main objective, as it is with other dependent styles, is to maintain the support and care of a strong person. These individuals may do well in relationships as long as this subservience is appreciated and valued. Because their behaviors are enacted to win the attention and investment of others, these individuals may become resentful and angry when the attention and appreciation they believe they deserve is not forthcoming. However, because they cannot risk the loss of the relationship, they must express their displeasure in a safe way.

Like most others with a dependent style, in the face of real or potential rejection and abandonment the individual with an accommodating dependent style may be compelled into extreme reactions to save the dependent relationship or turn to others for care and support. In fact, he or she may take on the role of victim in the face of abandonment by a caregiver, which serves to win the individual a place among others on whom to depend. As an example, a woman who accommodated her husband's verbal abuse and sexual affairs for years deteriorated into a helpless depression when her husband chose to leave her after 30 years of marriage to marry a younger woman. The abandoned wife, as the victim of years of abuse and failed appreciation, went to live with her adult son and his family, on whom she came to quickly depend and for whom she became housekeeper, cook, and babysitter.

The *selfless dependent* personality style includes features of the masochistic personality. The individual with this style of personality takes subservience to others to the extreme by sacrificing his or her sense of identity. For example, the wife who defines herself through her relationship with her husband and his career, or the mother or father who define him- or herself relative to a child's activities and accomplishments, exemplify the selfless dependent personality. For these individuals, as long as the organization or other person they have committed to values and appreciates their contributions and dedication, they can function adequately, essentially enjoying the freedom of choice that comes with effective dependency. However, if the source of dependency is lost, these individuals will be in a state of crisis, accompanied by a host of desperate emotional reactions.

TREATMENT OF THE DEPENDENT PROTOTYPE

The task in treating individuals with a dependent prototype personality is both to increase their ability to function independently and to enhance their perception of themselves as capable of functioning with greater independence. It is assumed that attention to their perception of stress will reduce the reliance on and expression of the various clinical conditions. Often, these individuals have not developed self-sustaining skills over the course of their lives and are, in reality, rather dependent on others for basic life-sustaining resources. These individuals interpret information relative to its implications for their dependent relationships. Thus, they perceive events relative to how the people close to them will react and respond, with much less thought regarding the cost to the self in terms of emotional development or optimal enjoyment.

Treating those with a dependent style introduces unique therapeutic challenges. Rarely do they come to therapy with the hope of resolving their dependency. More typically, they present for treatment with the hope of gaining relief from aversive emotions, which are associated with the dependent orientation. As is the case in most disorders, clients want relief but are often hesitant to make the changes in their lives necessary to provide that relief. This is particularly significant for individuals with a dependent orientation because relief from symptoms often requires greater independence and personal responsibility, which they are likely to see as a threat to their safety and security. As a result, they may feel obligated to undermine treatment to retain their dependency. Indeed, they may use failure in treatment as a means of demonstrating to others the dire nature of their situation and subsequently the need for them to remain invested.

Another therapeutic challenge relates to the desire of individuals with a dependent style to have others make decisions for them. Subsequently, they may come to therapy with an expectation that the therapist will do all of the work and simply make things better. They are often unprepared for the task of therapy as it relates to fostering greater personal responsibility. Thus, the task for the therapist is to manage the client's dependency in therapy. As suggested by Freeman, Pretzer, Fleming, and Simon (1990), it is reasonable to allow greater dependency early in therapy, but it is necessary to slowly decrease that dependency as treatment gains are made. To be sure, the client's dependent tendencies can contribute to his or her greater investment in therapy and greater willingness to follow treatment plans. However, the therapist will have to manage this quality carefully. If the therapist allows the client to develop a dependency on him or her, critical challenges to the therapeutic alliance are likely to emerge when it becomes necessary for the client to begin taking greater personal responsibility and initiative.

The primary goal in helping those with a dependent prototype personality is to increase their own initiative concerning personal responsibility for matters concerning the self. This includes fostering an increase in active efforts to pursue self-determined sources of pleasure and in self-initiated protective strategies and efforts. To these individuals, an independent existence is quite frightening because they do not perceive themselves as able to meet existential challenges on their own. They may feel somewhat drawn to various pleasurable outcomes, but to the extent that those inclinations might compromise their dependent relationship, they are more likely to deny the inclination. Although they tend toward passivity, they often have an active capacity as it relates to securing a dependent relationship; the implication is that they are not necessarily temperamentally passive but often more circumstantially dependent, and thus they may have the capacity for greater initiative than baseline might suggest.

The Therapeutic Relationship

In treating a client with a dependent style, it is critically important that the client believe not only that the therapist will help him or her reduce the experience of painful emotions but also that the therapist will be sensitive to the fear of abandonment and isolation. If the client perceives that the therapist is pressing for greater independence than he or she feels prepared for, the client may find reasons to abandon treatment.

It is frequently the case that the client is in a dependent relationship. Indeed, it may very well be that the individual is presenting for treatment because that dependency is threatened in some way. In such a situation, the negative emotional reactions subsequent to that threat may motivate the pursuit of treatment. It is important that therapy not threaten the security of that relationship, even when the relationship is clearly problematic. In fact, depending on the degree of the person's dependency, even in an abusive relationship, the security of that relationship should not be challenged too soon, although the therapist may want to arrange for the client's safety if he or she is in danger. Challenging the relationship too soon can easily prompt a defensive retreat from therapy, with a possible intensification of dependent behaviors.

The therapeutic relationship is often enhanced by initial attention to what the client desires in a relationship. For instance, how would his or her life be, relative to his or her relationships, if things were going better? Although this is a relatively simple question, for an individual with a dependent orientation who is used to simply responding to the needs of others, a clear sense of an improved circumstance may be lacking. They just know things are good when they feel safe. Through guided discovery, client and therapist can discuss what the client does to bring about the desired outcome and how others react. Do others respond in the manner the client hoped for? Guided discovery may help the client see that efforts to please others and to win their investment and validation are being taken for granted. Validating the client's desire for the investment of others can enhance the therapeutic relationship and decrease the potential for resistance. At this point, the therapist can encourage consideration of alternate ways of fostering closer relationships with others. By taking this approach, the client does not have to feel threatened by the process of therapy and can feel more confident that positive gains will be made.

Cognitive Goals

Increasing Active Self-Focus

As therapy progresses, the confidence gained and the benefits accrued by the client will put him or her in a position to consider an existence independent of the relationship. Through previous discussions, the client should come to see the disadvantages of relying too much on others and should see the advantage of pursuing pleasurable outcomes outside of the relationship. This does not imply that the client is intending to leave a dependent relationship—simply that the individual is considering other enhancing outcomes and experiences.

At this point in therapy, the individual with a dependent prototype personality is in the best position to begin careful consideration of personality assets and liabilities and how those attributes contribute to various clinical outcomes. Through the process of guided discovery, the client can be encouraged to consider his or her own personal desires and aspirations. In this way, his or her exclusive attention to the wants and needs of others is complemented more by personal ambitions. The client can then be assisted in deriving means for pursuing personal desires, while not being insensitive to the feelings of others. It is important that the therapist help the client manage the reactions of those who have come to depend on the client's accommodating behaviors. It is not unrealistic to expect that they are quite content with things the way they are and would not be pleased with the increased independence of the client. Thus, the therapist should discuss with the client effective means for fostering greater independence in others who have come to depend on or simply enjoy his or her submissive behaviors.

Increasing Personal Responsibility for Pleasurable Outcomes

Through guided discovery, the client can come to realize that others are invested primarily in themselves and are not oriented as a priority to protecting and validating the safety and integrity of the client. Quite often, these clients maintain a belief in contractual reciprocation. For instance, they might maintain such beliefs as the following: "If I do these things for my husband, he will love and care for me." Although this may appear reasonable, in reality it is often quite unlikely.

One of the first tasks is to increase the individual's perception of the self as able to function independently. Frequently, this requires careful and thorough consideration of the person's actual ability to function without the immediate assistance of others. Quite often, the individual with a dependent style is lacking in basic skills and developed abilities. For instance, because dependency is a personality trait that emerged in childhood, the person has most likely failed to develop skills related to work and interpersonal management, focusing instead on the formation and development of a dependent pattern. Such deficits can be dealt with in therapy.

Behavioral Goals

Because it is virtually impossible to convince clients that they possess skills they believe they do not have, an initial focus in therapy is to help them develop basic self-sustaining abilities. As an example, one woman presenting with problems related to her marital relationship demonstrated a dependent pattern in which her husband was clearly exploiting her unwillingness to confront him on his inappropriate behavior. If the therapist were to suggest that she take a stand against her husband, she might become anxious, panicky, and resistant to therapy. The therapist can instead suggest that problems in the marriage need to be addressed to improve the relationship, but that first it would be helpful to consider what might happen should the marital-focused therapy not be effective. In this way, the woman would see the early states of therapy not as a threat to marriage, but as a failsafe in case things went wrong.

The task in treating clients with a dependent orientation is to increase independent functioning and to decrease the perception that they are unable to function adequately apart from a dependent relationship. This task is made more difficult by the fact that the lifelong pattern of dependency has left these clients generally dependent on others. Consequently, it is necessary to consider skills these clients would need to develop to function independently. As a prime example, quite often the individual with a dependent style has not developed career skills necessary for financial self-sustenance. For these individuals, leaving the relationship is akin to starvation, thus necessitating that they remain in the relationship. Treatment requires that they develop the resources to generate adequate financial resources. This can seriously delay treatment as the individuals work to receive the schooling or credentialing necessary. While this is occurring, however, these clients can begin to take the initiative to follow personal interests and ambitions and to think more about personal wants and desires, independent of others.

Encouraging Adult Skills and Greater Self-Initiative

Once the client has adequately mastered basic skills that had previously been missing in his or her personal and interpersonal repertoire, more basic attention can be given to cognitive distortions and emotional reactions. At this point it is useful to have the client select various activities to pursue. Through a gradual process, the client can increase engagement in those selected, independent activities, while monitoring cognitive conclusions related to his or her perception of inadequacy and threat. Through this process, the therapist can direct the client in cognitive reorientation strategies so that cognitions are more consistent with the more active behaviors of the client.

CASE EXAMPLE

Rodney is 18 years old and recently left college after having difficulties adjusting to college life. He frequently missed classes and was not able to meet the demands of the coursework, despite having had relative academic success in high school and having done well on standardized testing. There was concern that he might have an undiagnosed learning disability or unidentified attention-deficit/hyperactivity disorder (ADHD); in Rodney's case, the concern was specifically that he had ADHD of the predominantly inattentive type. Tests were administered at the college to assess these conditions. He did not demonstrate any specific learning deficit or disabilities, but he did display moderate attention problems. Nonetheless, his symptoms did not fully correspond to the developmental pattern characteristic of ADHD. Because his early academic performance did not suggest ADHD, the counselor at the college concluded that Rodney's difficulties were a function of his immaturity and suggested that he take time away from school.

Rodney was an only child of parents who were both in their mid-40s when Rodney was born. His parents had married later in life and initially determined not to have children, but his mother unexpectedly got pregnant at age 43. After some thought about terminating the pregnancy, his parents decided that having a child would be a pleasant experience. Neither of his parents was particularly well suited for the task of parenting, and Rodney was raised with atypically high levels of assistance and accommodation. Because his parents were somewhat loners themselves, they did not take the initiative to make certain that Rodney was developing good peer relationships and social skills. Throughout most of his childhood, Rodney was content to go to school then to return home and do his homework and then spend time with his mother, who left her job when Rodney got off of school so that she would be with him. Rodney, like his parents, is moderately overweight, and they all maintain a rather sedentary lifestyle. As a child he avoided participation is sports and other forms of physical activity. While at college, Rodney's mother called him each morning to awaken him for class, despite the fact that this required his mother to get up an hour earlier than she had before Rodney started college. Typically, Rodney would wake up and then return to bed. Often, it was only after his mother called again that he would actually make it to his morning class.

Although Rodney did not meet criteria for any specific clinical disorder, he was clearly having difficulties meeting the demands of college and of life independent of his parents. Scores on the Millon Clinical Multiaxial Inventory (Millon, 1997) indicated a dependent prototype personality, with features of the schizoid pattern, suggesting an ineffectual dependent proto-type personality. Consistent with this dependent orientation is the fact that Rodney was generally content to spend his days at school playing video games and took no initiative to address what were clearly mounting academic problems. Further, his lack of concern over having been asked to leave college and of being rather indifferent to social affiliations was suggestive of schizoid features.

That Rodney is characterized more by a dependent than a schizoid style is evidenced by his reactivity when his parents attempted to encourage and require greater independence. As an example, in their previous efforts to get Rodney more involved, they had tried to force him to participate in youth activities through their church. Although he was generally compliant, he consistently refused to go on excursions unless one or both of his parents also went. When they refused, something would develop that would require that Rodney not go either. His parents found it striking that in such situations Rodney would come down with some physical ailment just prior to these church excursions.

Consistent with the dependent style, Rodney saw himself as generally unable to meet the demands of college (inept self-image), and he very much preferred the comfort of being home with his parents (introjected regulatory mechanism). Indeed, his relationship with his parents, most notably his mother, was consistent with the immature object relationships described by Millon. His relative indifference and submissiveness to the suggestions of the counselor are also indicative of the dependent orientation. From a cognitive–behavioral perspective, Rodney's core beliefs indicated an assumption that he could not do many things that others could and that ultimately he would not have to because eventually he would gain some relief from the expectation that he function at a higher level through the intervention of others. That he was eventually released from the expectation that he stay in college is consistent with this pattern.

For Rodney, the primary goal is to increase his confidence in his own ability to meet life challenges and responsibilities and to increase his independent engagement in life activities. Unless he received constant encouragement and direction from his parents, Rodney would not likely complete many activities, being content to spend his time playing video games. Because his parents continued to contribute to his dependency, it would be necessary to include them in some aspects of the treatment to avoid their actions undermining the gains Rodney could make in therapy.

To increase Rodney's personal initiative and responsibility, his parents were instructed to avoid taking initiative and responsibility for managing his activities and behaviors. Because he was now out of high school and not enrolled in college, it was expected that he would find a job. However, his general lack of self-confidence interfered with his ability and willingness to pursue employment. In fact, Rodney would have been reasonably content to simply remain at home with his parents. That they too might be comfortable with that arrangement underscores the importance of their involvement in various aspects of Rodney's treatment.

The necessity of Rodney finding employment provided a key point of focus for therapy. Because of his inept self-view and incompetent and submissive behaviors, Rodney was not likely to pursue a job or to be impressive in a job interview. Likewise, he responded to the idea of putting in job applications with expressions of anxiety, and he generated excuses for why it would be difficult to look for a job. His apprehensions served as the point of entry for discussion of his situational interpretations and subsequent affective and behavioral reactions. Rodney and the therapist considered the thoughts associated with his fears of seeking employment and concerns related to his need to find a job. Rodney was able to recognize his assumptions that he would not do well and that he would very likely be judged negatively by the interviewer. Similarly, Rodney was able to articulate his fear that he would not be able to complete the activities and responsibilities associated with the job and that this could elicit the wrath of an employer. Rodney decided that it was safer simply to remain at home. He concluded, however, that this was not a long-term strategy. He recognized this process of thinking as very similar to the thoughts associated with his failure at school. He reported feeling overwhelmed by the task of college and being fearful of not being able to manage academic demands. His preference was to return home, where life was more defined and simple.

To minimize the threat of treatment resistance, the therapist kept the pace of therapy intentionally slow. In this way, Rodney was able to manage one task before moving on to the next. The process of therapy involved challenging Rodney's belief that he could not accomplish a task and teaching those skills necessary for him to function more independently from his parents.

CONCLUSION

The dependent prototype personality is characterized by an inept self-image. Individuals with a dependent style see themselves as weak and incompetent and as needing to rely on others to survive. They are rather immature in their relationships with others, deferring to those on whom they depend and taking few self-initiated and independent actions. Their thinking is limited to the immediate concern with their dependent relationships. These individuals experience stress when they perceive the threat of rejection or abandonment by those on whom they depend. In reaction to the threats perceived, individuals with a dependent orientation encounter anxiety, often to the point of panic. In addition, their various incapacitations in the form of episodic depressions, panic disorder, somatic distress, and the like are often reinforced by the supportive and committed reactions of others.

Treatment of those with the dependent personality style is often difficult because successful therapy typically requires the development of greater independence and self-initiative. Because they perceive themselves as unable to meet the basic challenges of life, the idea of greater independence is indeed very threatening, and this often promotes therapeutic resistance. Even when the treatment is oriented toward the various Axis I conditions mediated by the dependent style, the dependent orientation may be threatened by the successful alleviation of the clinical condition. However, attention to the specific attributes associated with the dependent personality will in most situations render the clinical conditions unnecessary.

12

THE COMPULSIVE PROTOTYPE
(OBSESSIVE–COMPULSIVE)

Key phrase: Do it right!
Evolutionary focus: Ritualistic, perfection

Perhaps a hallmark feature of the compulsive personality style is sacrificing opportunities for positive, pleasurable activities to maintain a position of disciplined appropriateness. To individuals with a compulsive prototype personality, any behavior that reflects a lack of discipline or is considered inappropriate is to be avoided. In fact, to persons with a compulsive style, those who engage in pleasurable pursuits are acting frivolously and irresponsibly. They might be the first to complain about young children playing too loudly, the joyful displays of sports fans, or the raucous celebration of New Year's Eve partygoers.

Likewise, parents with a compulsive orientation are likely to be very intolerant of behaviors common to young children. Because they believe that others should adhere to their rules, and because their children are a reflection of themselves, these parents may be stern and punitive. In fact, it is not uncommon for these individuals to first come to the attention of a mental health worker at the instigation of a spouse who believes that his or her partner is too harsh and uncompromising with their children. To individuals with a compulsive style, any joyful behavior that suggests a lack of attention to "appropriate" deportment is not enacted or tolerated, particularly in those whose behavior would reflect poorly on them. To these individuals, guilt through association is still guilt.

Unlike most other *Diagnostic and Statistical Manual of Mental Disorders* (4th ed., text revision; American Psychiatric Association, 2000) Cluster C personalities, the compulsive style is not as highly pain avoidant. Individuals with this style maintain a relative balance on the preservation polarity. Thus, although they can tolerate some unpleasantness, they are attentive to behaviors that will minimize the occurrence of painful outcomes. In some situations they will tolerate a moderate level of displeasure to avoid greater displeasure. For instance, they may endure the displeasures of work assignments to avoid the personal and external scorn associated with task failure. To blatantly avoid responsibilities would be anathema to such individuals. Consequently, they inevitably face threats to their fragile sense of self-worth.

However, as an outcome of their developed skill in self-presentation, the individuals with a compulsive personality style are able to effectively defray the consequential implications of these threats through a keenly orchestrated pattern of justifications and excuses. For instance, although an employee with a compulsive style may have to face the fact that a project was not completed by the targeted date, the individual can often skillfully redirect responsibility or justify the tardiness by pointing out the failure of superiors to fully understand and appreciate the complexities of the task, something which only the individual has been able to do—or so he or she reports. Similarly, an individual with a compulsive orientation may justify the lack of leisurely family activities by pointing out the financial strain or the implications of a vacation on his or her current work assignments. Thus, although negative encounters cannot be avoided, he or she can typically face them and effectively render them unthreatening—at least for a time. Such strategies and efforts serve to keep the person from facing many of the consequences brought about by the compulsive personality style. However, as Millon (1999) suggested, "Despite the elaborate defensive strategies, compulsives tend to be among the personality styles that are most troubled by clinical syndromes" (p. 525).

On the adaptation polarity, individuals with a compulsive style maintain a passive orientation. They do not make waves. Their focus is on doing what is supposed to be done without creating havoc or controversy. Rules are not good or bad, or right or wrong; they are simply to be followed. Being conscientious, which is critically important to these individuals, requires that one accommodate to the expectations and standards of the culture in which one lives and functions. Individuals with a compulsive style feel it is important to be viewed as loyal, efficient, reliable, and so forth, even if the reality is somewhat less flattering. These individuals also prefer life to be consistent and predictable. They do not do well in novel or unfamiliar environments that call for more active adaptation; their preference is to settle in and go with the flow, as long as that flow does not threaten closely held standards and values.

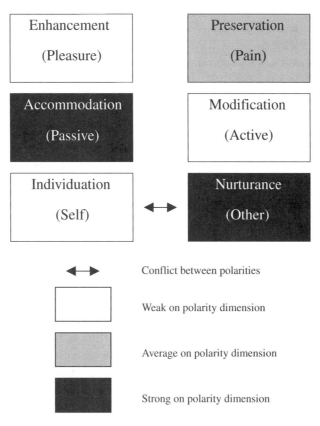

Enhancement (Pleasure)	Preservation (Pain)
Accommodation (Passive)	Modification (Active)
Individuation (Self)	Nurturance (Other)

Conflict between polarities

Weak on polarity dimension

Average on polarity dimension

Strong on polarity dimension

Figure 12.1. Polarity balance of the compulsive prototype. From *Personality-Guided Therapy* (p. 526), by T. Millon, 1999, New York: Guilford Press. Copyright 1999 by John Wiley & Sons, Inc. Reprinted with permission.

The focus of the individual with a compulsive style of personality is typically on others. They do what they do because it is expected. Because they have internalized imposed standards and values, they believe that violation of those standards will be judged harshly by others. Although relatively weak on the individuation dimension of the reproductive polarity, such individuals do at times struggle with conflicted feelings related to the need to consider the position and opinion of others in making decisions and the desire to be free of such external constraints. For instance, they may dream of being free from these constraints but are unable to muster the disinhibition to do so, certainly not without experiencing tremendous guilt as a consequence. The compulsive polarity balance is illustrated in Figure 12.1.

As an example of a person with a compulsive style of personality, Chase is 45 years old and single. He has had a few relationships, but none that developed to the point of potential marriage. Chase works as a records manager at the headquarters of an international religious organization. He has held the same position for the past 12 years. Others who have worked in the same office as Chase either have left to pursue another job or have been promoted in the church records office. Chase has been passed over for a promotion for several reasons. For instance, he is very good at what he does. Indeed, his familiarity with the job is second to none; thus, his superiors do not want to see him moved. In addition, he does not work well with others. He struggles when others deviate from his established protocol for retrieving and storing records, and his insistence that others comply with his system has contributed to occasional interpersonal conflicts. His bosses and coworkers view him as diligent, conscientious, and competent, but also as stubborn and caustic.

PERSONALITY-GUIDED COGNITIVE–BEHAVIORAL CONCEPTUALIZATION

Individuals with a compulsive prototype personality view the self as conscientious. They are responsible for doing things the way they are supposed to be done and, likewise, for seeing to it that others do it the right way as well. They are driven by the directives of *should*, *ought*, and *must*. To these individuals, failing to meet introjected standards of performance and deportment is to fail as a human being. Indeed, these individuals are characterized by dichotomized thinking and magnification. They are either good or bad; there is no in-between status. When they accomplish a task, they feel both relief and pleasure—relief from the threat of not completing it and pleasure in the accomplishment, for having done what they should have done. Although not averse to receiving compliments and recognition, individuals with a compulsive orientation are likely to respond with a matter-of-fact demeanor, implying an indifference to the praise that suggests they simply did what should have been done. The personality structures and functions of the compulsive prototype are summarized, along with their associated liabilities, in Table 12.1.

Many individuals with a compulsive style handicap themselves with their own standards. Either their standards of perfection are insurmountable or their perceptions of their inadequacies put them in a tremendous bind when they are unable to meet their own standards. In such situations, these individuals are forced into a position of either accepting blame and subsequent self-contempt or externalizing blame by finding a scapegoat or creating a sideshow in which other issues take precedence over their inability to meet their own standards of performance and accomplishment.

The view that individuals with a compulsive orientation hold of others is typically one of varying degrees of contempt. Although they are accepting

TABLE 12.1
Structures and Functions of the Compulsive Prototype
and Associated Liabilities

Personality domain	Liability
Self-image Conscientious	Feelings of being overburdened by responsibilities; neglect of pleasurable activities in order to fulfill obligations
Object representations Concealed	Narrow view of acceptable ideas; narrow range of personal and interpersonal tolerance
Morphological organization Compartmentalized	Excessive dependence on rules and regimentation contributing to a narrow-minded view characterized by inflexible, dichotomous thinking
Mood and temperament Solemn	Tight control over emotions; sacrifice of joyful, exuberant emotions for the sake of emotional control
Behavioral acts Disciplined	Concern with perfection that interferes with insightfulness, decision making, spontaneity, and task completion
Interpersonal conduct Respectful	Rigidity contributing to interpersonal discomfort
Cognitive style Constricted	Constricted ability to think expansively or with insight or empathy; egocentric thinking
Regulatory mechanism Reaction-formation	Emotional constriction; intellectualization of problems

of those whom they perceive as holding and maintaining similar values, they hold those whose standards differ from their own in contempt, viewing them as too casual, irresponsible, self-indulgent, and incompetent. To the extent that anyone holds different views, the self-view of the individual is threatened, rendering it necessary to reject those who represent the perceived threat. As Beck, Freeman, and Associates (1990) suggested, "They liberally apply the *shoulds* to others in an attempt to shore up their own weaknesses" (p. 46).

The core beliefs of the compulsive personality relate to the need to remain in control. For instance, Beck et al. (1990) suggested the following common core beliefs in the compulsive arrangement: "I could be overwhelmed"; "I am basically disorganized or disoriented"; and "I need order, systems, and rules in order to survive" (p. 47). Each of these beliefs speaks of the individual's need to remain in control to prevent the occurrence of events he or she feels unprepared to manage. The conditional beliefs are similarly focused on the prevention of negative outcomes—for instance, "If I don't have a system, everything will fall apart"; "Any flaw or defect in performance will produce a landslide"; "If I or others don't perform at the highest standards, we will fail"; and "If I fail at this, I am a failure as a person." Subsequently, the instrumental beliefs of the compulsive style relate to those efforts that must be taken to remain in control and thus avoid potentially devastating outcomes. Examples of instrumental beliefs include "I must be in control," "I must do everything just right," "I know what's best," "You have to do it my way," and "Details are crucial."

Individuals with a compulsive style are susceptible to a host of negative emotions. They experience anxiety associated with performance threat, panic in the face of impending criticism or failure, and disappointments and regrets when things turn out badly for them. Any situation where the potential exists that a job will not be done well is threatening to these individuals. These threats may be perceived as annoyances or painful catastrophes. In the face of a threat, persons with a compulsive orientation will implement strategies to prevent the consequences of failure, which might include appropriate action such as diligence and delegation or ineffective strategies such as procrastination, avoidance, or sideshow creation (e.g., creating some other issue to avoid facing a responsibility).

For individuals with a compulsive prototype personality, the behavioral tendency is disciplined, which describes their highly rule-governed behavior. Any deviations from rules, regulations, or codes are unacceptable and highly distressing. As one individual suggested, more or less in jest, "the lines in parking lots are not suggestions, they are rules sent by God Almighty concerning how people are to park." The rule governing of the compulsive personality often interferes with the ability to complete tasks and make spontaneous decisions. Interpersonally, such individuals are respectful, maintaining the proper rules of social discourse and decorum; others often find these individuals to be stuffy and boorish. Cognitive style is constricted; they do not typically think beyond the confines of the rules. The world is supposed to function in a particular manner, and individuals with a compulsive style see that it does. It should not be surprising that the compulsive personality is often found in highly committed religious individuals. The characteristic mood state of individuals with a compulsive personality is solemn.

PATHOLOGIC PROCESS OF THE COMPULSIVE PATTERN

Stressful experiences occur in response to events that threaten the individual's constricted, compartmentalized orientation to the world. For instance, the suggestion that an individual with a compulsive orientation has failed to meet an obligation could put him or her in a state of crisis. Living or working with others who fail to follow expectations of social, moral, or professional appropriateness may be highly distressing to such individuals. Likewise, failure to follow one's own code of appropriate conduct could cause distress. In all cases, stress compels the individual into compensatory efforts marked by tense, distressed emotions. How the individual deals with the encountered stresses contributes to the various clinical conditions commonly observed in those with a compulsive orientation.

AXIS I VULNERABILITIES

The individual with a compulsive style is vulnerable to several clinical conditions as a function of the compulsive personality attributes. The sections that follow identify and describe a sample of those clinical conditions. It can be reasonably argued and is frequently demonstrated that these clinical conditions reflect the individual's disparate efforts and attempts to create a state of perfection in the world, or at least in his or her own life. That such efforts are doomed to failure, or require a tremendous narrowing of one's experiences, is reflected in the nature of the clinical conditions.

Generalized Anxiety Disorder

Millon (1999) described those with the compulsive personality as "the most frequent candidates for generalized anxiety" (p. 185). Given their core beliefs, this is not surprising; being driven by *shoulds*, the world is indeed a threatening place for individuals with a compulsive prototype personality. With such high standards and the risk of failure always looming, such individuals must be ever vigilant to self-integrity threats. They may indeed be overwhelmed by personal standards, external expectations, and the perceived incompetence of others. In addition, threats also exist relative to the nature of their compulsive concerns and the fear of social condemnation for their unusual beliefs and behaviors (see Unterberg, 2003). For instance, the religious activist often feels threat and opposition from nonbelievers, and the employee with a compulsive style may fear the reactions of coworkers. In a study by Gallagher, South, and Oltmanns (2003), individuals with a compulsive personality demonstrated a greater intolerance of situational uncertainty. Dyck and colleagues (2001) identified the compulsive personality as one of the most common personality patterns associated with generalized anxiety disorder. Being anxious is simply an adaptive way to be for those with a compulsive orientation. To give up their anxiety and the associated vigilance would be to let down their guard and be forced to deal with a host of negative outcomes. For these individuals, as Öhman (2000) suggested, false positive threats are far better than false negative threats. The compulsive pattern has also been linked to agoraphobia and panic disorder (see Dyck et al., 2001; Iketani, Kiriike, & Stein, 2002; Renshaw, Chambless, & Steketee, 2003) and to general distress associated with suicidality (Haliburn, 2000).

Phobic Disorder

Individuals with a compulsive style of personality may develop a phobic response to any social activity in which their pretense of superiority over others is threatened or in which social failure is too great and the ability to sidestep responsibility too small. Millon (1999) pointed out that those with a compulsive style, like those with the avoidant style, are not likely to show or advertise these fears because this would be a sign of weakness— a chink in the armor of superiority and perfection. Thus, they must cope with these phobic anxieties in such a way that their fears will remain hidden.

Dissociative Disorder

The value of dissociation is that the person in a dissociative state does not have to deal with events that he or she finds intolerable. For the individual with a compulsive style, who must maintain a sense of superiority over others based on his or her greater commitment to a specific cause or task or simply as a function of his or her superior "moral character," the threat of failure is greater than it is for one who has not placed as much ego integrity in such superiority. The advantage of a dissociative experience is that the individual does not have to face potential failure, especially if it is obvious that he or she is the source of that failure. In addition, being plagued by chronic feelings of dread, albeit masked by compulsive attention to detail, sets a vulnerable foundation in which dissociation may be a form of collapse.

Somatoform Disorder

Somatoform conditions are particularly useful to individuals with a compulsive orientation. Needing to maintain an air of sufficiency and superiority, such individuals cannot readily abandon an undertaking, avoid responsibility, or face failure. The attitude of confidence and perfection they maintain also makes it difficult for them to express emotional distress or to take time off from responsibilities for emotional or psychological reasons. Although psychological in nature, the presentation of physical symptoms including those that escape the diagnostic skills of physicians provides these individuals respite and relief from the façade they have created for themselves. It may be a sign of weakness to have an anxiety disorder, but having stomach or pain problems may be more acceptable in their minds. Although not necessarily feigned, somatic complaints may serve a highly adaptive purpose for these individuals.

Obsessive–Compulsive Disorder

Considering their need for perfection, it is not surprising that many with a compulsive personality experience obsessive–compulsive anxiety disorder (see Nestadt et al., 2003). The obsessive–compulsive symptoms serve very useful purposes for these individuals. First, paying attention to specific details helps to ensure that they have maintained a presentation of perfection, however they may define perfection. In addition, by focusing so much attention on matters of trivial importance, these individuals are able to obtain some relief from other activities under the pretense of doing something important (e.g., cleaning the carpets) or of being "disordered." In many ways, for individuals with a compulsive style who feel a strong need for perfection, the obsessive–compulsive condition so constrains their existence that a modicum of perfection can be achieved. Unfortunately, to achieve this level of perfection, they must so constrain life that little joy is available.

Dysthymia

Individuals with a compulsive prototype personality typically fight a losing battle. In their efforts to be in complete control of themselves and often of others, success becomes impossible. The exception, perhaps, is the individual who is able to constrain his or her existence to experience consistent success. However, this typically results in curtailing most pleasurable activities. An unemotional withdrawal from efforts to manage all details of their lives is not within the repertoire of many individuals with a compulsive style. Although they could conclude that their standards have been too high, and that it is better to live and let live without insisting that others comply with their views of proper conduct and performance, such a conclusion would require them to openly admit that their life has been a scam. Thus, they cannot simply change their minds and adopt a new attitude and standard of performance.

A dysthymic condition provides individuals with a compulsive orientation an opportunity to disengage from hopeless undertakings yet avoid the implications of having to abandon their ideals and ambitions. In addition, a general withdrawal through moroseness serves to prevent possible attacks by others regarding their failure to meet their own advertised and potentially boasted standards. Their ambition is to create a world of their liking in which everyone does as they desire. Considering the unlikelihood of success in this undertaking, dysthymia may keep these individuals from putting more effort into this hopeless task. As Gilbert (2000, 2001) suggested, depression or dysthymia keeps people from chasing rainbows; for the individual with a compulsive style, the rainbow is perfection.

Major Depression

In addition to the dysthymic response, the individual with a compulsive personality is also vulnerable to periodic depressive episodes. In the case of retarded depression, the individual has given up hope, and the depression reflects the abandonment of efforts to stay in the fight, whether for personal perfection or for righteousness. Retarded depression serves multiple purposes: First, through withdrawal into depression, the person is able to abandon a losing fight without having to face full responsibility. Second, if failure is a result of depression and not personal shortcomings, he or she gains some relief from the pain of failure.

In the case of agitated depression, the individual withdraws from task involvement, but rather than withdrawing into a relative state of hopelessness and helplessness, he or she withdraws into a state of complaining and cynicism, marked by self-disparaging comments. This strategy may be implemented as a means of inspiring the self out of the depression or to enlist the attention, assistance, and support of others.

Bipolar Disorder

The bipolar displays of the individual with a compulsive orientation may manifest themselves in the form of a hyperenthused expression of pent-up emotions. Having attempted to maintain an image that is beyond reproach, the individual does not express many of the feelings and impulses that he or she actually experiences. However, at times the individual may feel pushed too far, and in an effort to maintain the image he or she has cultivated for him- or herself or to compel others into submission, the individual may display extreme, manic reactions. Indeed, the individual may vacillate between potential perfection or accomplishment that is either unachievable or contradictory, on one hand, and hopeless despair on the other. For example, a mother with a compulsive style may become hyperactive in efforts to secure opportunities and advantages for a child.

Substance-Related Syndromes

Although alcohol use contrasts with their general demeanor of control and perfection, individuals with a compulsive style may develop alcohol dependency as the outcome of efforts to control chronic feelings of anxiety (e.g., Suzuki, Muramatsu, Takeda, & Shirakura, 2002). As a result of their efforts to remain beyond criticism, they are vulnerable to chronic tension, which may be reduced through alcohol consumption. Given the chronic nature of the tension and repeated efforts at self-medication, these individuals may slowly develop a degree of alcohol dependency. As Millon (1999) pointed out, the use of alcohol may have developed initially as a form of imitation in which individuals with a compulsive orientation began to drink as a means of fulfilling a standard and lifestyle that included alcohol. Similarly, they may go through periods in which the need to perform at a particular level compels heightened activity yet prompts feelings of being overwhelmed by the mounting threat and likelihood of failure, which then compels an anguished retreat marked by alcohol or drug abuse.

Eating Disorders

Eating disorders are a common clinical outcome for many individuals, typically women, with a compulsive personality style. Numerous recent studies have chronicled this connection. For instance, in a recent investigation by Picot and Lilenfeld (2003), 10% of those with a binge-eating disorder met full criteria for obsessive–compulsive personality disorder. Similarly, the probability of a woman developing an eating disorder in adulthood was shown to increase as a function of the number of childhood signs of compulsive orientation (e.g., perfectionism and rigidity; Anderluh, Tchanturia, Rabe-Hesketh, & Treasure, 2003). In a report by Rastam, Gillberg, and Wentz (2003), one third of the anorexic patients displayed characteristics of an obsessive–compulsive personality. In a longitudinal study of adolescent girls in Germany with anorexia nervosa, the obsessive–compulsive personality was one of the most common comorbid psychiatric conditions (Herpertz-Dahlmann et al., 2001). The discipline, conscientiousness, and associated striving for perfection that characterize those with an obsessive–compulsive personality render them particularly vulnerable to the culturally defined thinness ideal. Indeed, in their quest for socially defined perfection, eating and weight regulation are readily managed targets of control and perfection.

Disorganized and Catatonic Schizophrenia

The individual with a compulsive orientation has developed a style of life that is based on the ability to maintain complete personal control. This degree of self-control masks a great deal of tension related to feelings of inadequacy and fear of failure. In the face of irrefutable failures, when the pretense of self-control can no longer defray criticisms, the individual may become vulnerable to a psychological collapse in which symptoms of a disorganized psychotic episode become evident. In such situations, the individual may display a host of bizarre and unexpected verbalizations and other reactions that appear to be the antithesis of the typical compulsive composition. The individual could potentially adopt a catatonic posture characterized by a profound passivity to external expectations and demands. In a sense, when his or her typically compulsive style of interacting with the external world fails and no options in response to an immediate crisis are perceived, the person may literally do nothing.

VARIATIONS ON THE TRADITIONAL COMPULSIVE PERSONALITY

The compulsive variations all reflect the prototype pattern's conscientiousness, discipline, and constricted cognitive style. The individual with a compulsive prototype personality is striving diligently to make the world function in a particular way, thereby rendering life and experiences safer and more controllable. The differences between the following personality styles are reflected in, among other factors, the individual's focus of attention and degree of optimism relative to the probability of creating a safe and controllable world.

The *conscientious compulsive* personality style is a subtle variant on the pure pattern. Individuals with this personality style display what Millon and Davis (2000) referred to as a "conforming dependency" (p. 176). Their decisions and behaviors are determined by what they believe others want. The sense of duty and loyalty expressed by these individuals is far greater than is justified by any benefit they receive from such loyalty. Because they struggle with fragile feelings of self-worth, they commit themselves to clear external standards that are self-defining and achievable. Through their loyalty and dedication, whether to an individual, a family, or an organization, individuals with a conscientious compulsive style expect to be respected, validated, and appreciated. As long as those in the environment are forthcoming with praise and validation, these individuals can function quite well. However, when their efforts are not recognized and appreciated, their sense of self-worth is in jeopardy, and they must do something to receive the validation they crave.

These individuals are vulnerable to being overwhelmed by their own internalized standards of performance. In the face of insurmountable internalized expectations, they may be plagued by relentless anxiety and self-contempt, recurrent somatic complaints, and periods of depression; the latter two reactions may provide the only opportunity for relief from their unrealistic standards and expectations. In addition, individuals with a conscientious compulsive style may embrace cultural standards that are associated with various negative consequences. For instance, in their quest to meet cultural standards of beauty and status, they may be more vulnerable to eating disorders.

For example, Teresa is a 38-year-old woman who has never married. She is a gifted violinist and teaches violin to children. She views her violin students as her surrogate children. She is an only child and feels considerable pressure to please and care for her parents. She never married because she could not find a suitor that she thought her parents would like; she has stopped trying. Teresa also feels a tremendous sense of obligation to take care of herself physically. She has always watched her weight and diet and has exercised regularly to the point of excess. She has recently cut back, however, because her aging parents have required more attention and because of a series of minor injuries. Subsequently, she has also cut back her food intake. Over the last few months she has lost approximately 20 pounds from her initial weight of 130 lbs. She is presenting for treatment at this time at the insistence of her mother.

The *bedeviled compulsive* personality style includes features of the negativistic style. Although individuals with other variations of the compulsive personality style may wish to give up their compulsive adherence to external rules and standards, persons with the bedeviled compulsive style of personality struggle with these feelings. On one hand, such individuals depend on the validation of others, which can come only from adherence to and satisfaction of imposed standards; on the other hand, they resent the power of validation that others hold over them. These individuals exist in a state of unavoidable conflict. The result of this conflict is subtle opposition to external constraints and expectations of the type observed in the negativistic personality, such as procrastination, indecisiveness, and hesitation.

Likewise, the ambivalence individuals with a bedeviled compulsive style feel may be expressed through various displays of moodiness, including grumpiness, cynicism, and general discontentment (Millon & Davis, 2000). The conflict these individuals feel can be quite distressing and can lead to a variety of emotional reactions and interpersonal difficulties. The conflict experienced contributes to feelings of anxiety, somatic symptoms, and depressive withdrawals. In addition, the thinking of these individuals may appear at times to be delusional, and behaviors are often enacted impulsively as a means of retaliation or situational control. For instance, Simon feels a need to win the praise and validation of his boss by working long hours, but he also resents his boss's expectation that he will work those long hours. Subsequently, the pace and quality of his work have declined, leading to reprimands by the boss, which have led to greater resentment and discontentment with the job and to periods of conflict between the two. As a result, Simon knows it is only a matter of time before he gets fired, which compels him to work harder.

The *parsimonious compulsive* personality style represents a combination of the compulsive and the schizoid styles. Unlike with other compulsive styles, individuals with the parsimonious compulsive prototype personality are not particularly concerned with satisfying others or living up to introjected values. Instead, these individuals are more concerned with protecting themselves from loss. What is theirs is theirs, and they wish to protect their possessions from the greediness of others. Although they are focused on others, as are the other variations of the pure compulsive style, the focus is on the threat represented by others to what is theirs. To these individuals, self-worth, self-satisfaction, and contentment are defined by what they own, and others are perceived as threats to those possessions. They are stingy, tight-fisted, and miserly. Vulnerable to a hoarding dimension of the obsessive–compulsive disorder, these individuals are well characterized by Ebenezer Scrooge of Dickens's A *Christmas Carol.*

The *bureaucratic compulsive* personality style combines features of the narcissistic personality style with the compulsive style. Individuals with a bureaucratic compulsive style define themselves and their worth by their adherence to rules and expectations. Whatever the organization they have identified with, they become the model member. They know what is expected, and they do it without fail and without complaint. They wear their conformity to expectation as a badge of worth and superiority. Beyond the organizational identity, these individuals often struggle with feelings of low worth and inadequacy, but on the job their sense of self and purpose is clearly defined. In their description of this compulsive style, Millon and Davis (2000) suggested that it can range from normal and functional adaptiveness in which persons with a bureaucratic compulsive style, although perhaps overcommitted to the job, function well at work, to use of their commitment to the organization's standards to terrorize and belittle others whom they perceive as less committed and thus less worthy.

At the mild level, this style is not necessarily problematic. As it becomes more extreme, these individuals are prone to serious interpersonal problems and a host of associated clinical conditions. For instance, Saul worked as an account manager at a national distribution office for a major retailer. He was highly conscientious in managing the accounts assigned to him. Because of his conscientiousness, he was made head of an account department and supervised the activities of several lower-level account managers. After an initial period of success, problems began to emerge as employees started complaining of his intrusive and "dictatorial" management style. Saul simply thought he was doing what needed to be done. When he was demoted back to the status of junior account manager, he became overwhelmed by debilitating somatic complaints that kept him out of work.

The *puritanical compulsive* personality style includes some characteristics of the paranoid style. For individuals with a puritanical compulsive prototype personality, there is a critical cause that must be pursued, and it is their job to see to it that others follow as well. For some, their commitment displays a personal attempt to avoid activities to which they are drawn but also repulsed. For instance, a person compelled to use pornography may campaign against it as a means of stamping it out and thereby being free of its appeal. Similarly, an adult who is sexually attracted to children may commit to a strict religious organization and practice abstinence in an attempt to control sexual impulses. In both cases, these individuals commit to the practice or organization with such fervor that they often lose perspective of their own motivations and the differences in their experiences and attitudes and those of others. Their beliefs regarding how others should behave may be so strong as to compel behaviors enacted to force compliance in others.

The compulsive style may be most often found among those with strong religious convictions. Millon (1999) described how these individuals feel that it is not enough to evangelize and encourage what they see as appropriate behaviors; it is also their responsibility to see to it that others comply. They may accomplish this through preaching, missionary work, or other appropriate acts or by threats of eternal damnation, confrontation, and various extreme acts. By creating a perceived sense of superiority over others through their greater adherence to the proper mode of conduct and belief, they are able to compensate for deeper feelings of low self-esteem and inadequacy. Through their compulsive behavior and dominance over others, they are able to effectively avoid feelings of social alienation and inadequacy.

TREATMENT OF THE COMPULSIVE PROTOTYPE

The task in treating clients with the compulsive style of personality is helping them to abandon their rigid, compartmentalized, and overdisciplined orientation to life. Encouraging these individuals to challenge their assumptions can be quite challenging itself. Similar in many ways to individuals with a paranoid style, individuals with a compulsive style see considerable risk in abandoning their established orientation. To change their worldview is akin to abandoning any hope for secular and often eternal security. As a result of the rigidity of their ideals, individuals with a compulsive style present unique challenges in treatment.

Balancing the polarities for the individual with a compulsive orientation involves decreasing his or her concern with external constraints and increasing his or her internal and more subjective orientation to life challenges, including enhancing his or her ability to make personal decisions independent of external factors. A blind abandonment of external influences is unnecessary, but the individual must adopt more insightful and reflective processes related to personal decisions. In addition, he or she may require a decrease in the tendency to be interpersonally defamatory.

The Therapeutic Relationship

Because one of the defining characteristics of the individual with compulsive personality style is being judgmental, the therapist may be subject to the client's criticism. It is important to be as structured as possible to avoid inspiring distracting criticisms and a lack of confidence in therapy (Freeman, Pretzer, Fleming, & Simon, 1990). A clear treatment structure also is more manageable for the client, thus maximizing his or her investment in treatment. The therapist is in a position to model greater flexibility and personal and interpersonal tolerance having started from a more organized and structured beginning. Similarly, in the collaborative determination of therapeutic goals it is useful to have the client consider the outcome of successful therapy. For instance, the therapist might ask, "If we were success-ful, how would things be different for you?" By defining the treatment goals, the therapist has the benefit of being able to prompt the client to reflect on how issues relate to his or her stated goals. The therapist can speculate aloud (i.e., use the "Colombo technique") on how current hesitancies ex-pressed by the client relate to the therapeutic goals that the client defined. For example, the therapist may wonder aloud how waiting for certain events to occur (e.g., waiting for work conditions to change before taking a long-delayed vacation) may prevent the desired outcome from ever occurring.

To prevent premature termination of treatment, it is important that the therapist not let an antagonistic conflict develop, which can happen when the client's beliefs appear clearly irrational and ultimately maladaptive to the therapist. Similar to those with a paranoid orientation, it is often helpful to take a "go with it" approach in discussing topics with these clients. Thus, rather than being confrontational, the therapist can consider the client's assumptions, offering subtle reflection on his or her implications. Through the use of Socratic questioning, the therapist can allow any mal-adaptive or irrational ideas to reveal themselves to the client. This technique takes patience, but it is ultimately more effective than taking a direct approach and pointing out the irrationality of the client's beliefs, which is almost certain to prompt a defensive reaction. It is also helpful to frame therapy in terms of improving a difficult situation. For instance, the issue of right or wrong may be justifiably debatable as it relates to a recent work conflict. If debating and determining right from wrong are not therapeutically helpful, focusing more on what could make the situation better may loosen the client from the rigidly held position of self-righteousness.

It may also be helpful to the client to discuss the nature of the fear behind the compulsive ideas. Carrying out an argument to its ultimate conclusions can reveal to the client the irrationality of the rigid beliefs. Validating the client's concern, while at the same time allowing him or her to reflect on the absurdity or irrationality of the belief, can help loosen the rigid assumptions. As an example, a compulsive father was encouraged to think about what would happen if he were to loosen his controls over his son. He expressed his concerns about his son's failure to be productive and his continued dependency on his father. When asked what he thought the probability was of his son ending up in either of those situations, given the established course, he was able to reflect on the list of considerable accomplishments his son had made thus far and his affinity for the standard of living they had acquired and to which the son had become accustomed. Although the father continued to struggle to change his parenting philosophy, such insights were effective in getting him to consider his parenting approach from different perspectives and to experiment with alternate parenting techniques.

Cognitive Goals

The constricted cognitive style and conscientious self-view of individuals with a compulsive prototype personality contribute to the pathologic process in important ways. These clients' concern with what they think is "right" and blindness to alternative perspectives lead to anxious, angry, and depressed emotions, despite their generally solemn mood. The challenge is getting them to view events from alternative perspectives and to relax their conscientious and compartmentalized views.

It may be helpful for the client to create some psychological distance from the compulsive orientation. Through discussion of childhood origins, the client may come to understand that the rigidity of his or her approach to life was an effective means for procuring desirable outcomes at a critical time in life; for example, it may have provided protection in a threatening home environment. However, the client can come to realize that his or her current reliance on the same orientation appears to be associated with various types of distress. As an example, the compulsive father was able to see that through his own diligence and obedience as a child, he was able to win his parents' praise, the respect of teachers, and status among his peers. He was further able to understand that his childhood circumstance of being reared by a relatively poor but proud father was different than the circumstance in which his son was raised.

Through guided discovery (see Freeman et al., 1990), the therapist can help the client to examine the evidence corresponding to several of his or her assumptions and in this way foster alternative perspectives. Further, to loosen the client's pervasive rigidity, the therapist can prompt discussion of the alternative viewpoints in such a way that the client comes to see the advantage of considering alternative views. However, individuals with a compulsive style are resistant to suggestions that contradict their established frame of reference. Because the task of introducing these alternative points of view can be quite challenging, it is helpful if the therapist presents them within the context of appropriateness. For instance, a father with a compulsive orientation whose son was rebelling against his restrictive parenting style was very resistant to suggestions that his parenting philosophy was problematic. This father was a construction engineer, and when the therapist asked what he would do if his construction design failed, he suggested that he would go back to the drawing board. The therapist suggested that a similar strategy might be appropriate in considering his restrictions on his son, as it was clear that the technique had not led to the success he had hoped. It is not typically the case that a single, similar analogy would be summarily effective, however, and it is more often the case that the rigidity of the client will be a recurrent concern.

Cognitively, the self versus other conflict relates to the difficulty clients with a compulsive style have in making independent decisions relative to the reactions and judgments of others. Thus, successful treatment involves the development of greater independent decision making and a greater ability to react to and cope with the critical reactions or disappointing behaviors of others.

Individuals with a compulsive prototype personality want to do the right thing, and they turn to external sources for that determination. In addition, they think that others should adhere to their notion of what is the "right thing." As a result of having introjected specific standards and values, they do not often possess a very sophisticated internal mechanism for making qualitative judgments of right and wrong. Fortunately for these individuals, their ability to challenge rigid thinking is greater than that of individuals with the compulsive personality disorder, for whom such challenges are far more difficult.

To decrease the rigid compartmentalization of the compulsive pattern, therapist and client can work to decrease external projections. This work might involve a modified thought-stopping or thought-altering procedure (see Freeman et al., 1990). When potentially threatening situations present themselves, individuals with a compulsive orientation typically reflect on the implications for the self and act in ways to protect the self from negative consequences. The inability to make a clear determination of right and wrong or to create a black-and-white scenario can make the decision-making task exceedingly difficult for these individuals. As a result of the need to make the right choice, these clients are likely to make future projections in which they speculate on the implications of making the right or wrong choice; this tendency to project is a good treatment target. The therapist can lead the client through the steps of the decision, encouraging him or her to make a choice and to practice thought-altering procedures as a means of preventing the obsessional concerns regarding the implications of the choices. Thought-altering procedures might include a cued thought or image that draws attention away from the source of the obsession, or the client can develop a battery of self-statements oriented to decreasing obsessional concerns. Paradoxically, it may be helpful to have the client write down every conceivable outcome relative to the decision. In this way, the individual is able to develop some aversiveness to the obsessional process.

Behavioral Goals

Behaviorally, the great challenge for the individual with a compulsive style is abandonment of perfectionistic striving as related to both personal behaviors and the behaviors of others. This task cannot be accomplished unless and until the client has come to see the value of making such behavioral changes. Combining clearly defined cognitive techniques and affective management techniques with designed behavioral changes enhances the effectiveness of all three modalities. It is also important that the client make adjustments to his or her interpersonal style. The rigidity characterizing an individual with a compulsive prototype personality contributes to a very respectful and disciplined style of behavior. Although these are clearly valued qualities, the rigidity of his or her interpersonal demeanor is too great and contributes to various interpersonal difficulties.

For instance, Bill was a financial consultant presenting for treatment secondary to feelings of depression, which he described as "emptiness." He reported that he had been married for 32 years but that he and his wife had not had sexual intimacies for the past 10 years. He admitted to having sexual urges but not acting on them. He indicated that he had been a good provider and had also treated his wife with respect. He could not understand why she did not seem to be interested in sex or any significant intimacy, such as simply sitting and talking with Bill. When asked what he did to initiate conversations or other forms of intimacy, he could not articulate a strategy beyond simply asking her about her day and assuming that it would evolve further from there. Regarding their sexual intimacy, as well as he could recall he never really initiated sex, it just seemed to occur. For Bill, his compulsive style of personality contributed to a dearth of social and intimacy skills necessary to foster close or intimate interpersonal relations.

To help clients with a compulsive orientation alter their striving for perfection, in addition to cognitive procedures they can be instructed in a procedure in which they engage in an activity and intentionally fail to complete the task or intentionally perform the task at a level below their standards. Often this procedure involves actual engagement in activities they have avoided. It is, of course, important that they undertake this activity in areas in which failure and task incompletion will not have deleterious effects. As an example, a client with a compulsive style may challenge himself to go home on time, rather than waiting until a job is done, and then test the subsequent outcome. Specifically, did horrible things occur as the result of his having left work on time?

Affective Changes

Stemming from their concerns with doing things inappropriately, individuals with a compulsive personality style often struggle with feelings of anxiety. They are also prone to feelings of anger, which for many cannot be expressed because anger displays would constitute a lack of self-control. As a result, much of the anger and resentment felt by these individuals is felt as an agitated form of depression. The negative emotions they feel can be targets of obsession and may interfere with efforts to alter assumptions and behaviors. As a result, it is often necessary to help a client with a compulsive style derive some initial relief from aversive emotional states prior to introducing cognitive or behavioral change techniques. Short-term pharmacotherapy or relaxation training may be effective in this regard. When introducing pharmacotherapy, it is important that the individual's investment in therapy not be compromised by overemphasis or overreliance on a biochemical explanation for the affective distress.

CASE EXAMPLE

Glen is 32 years old, married, and the father of three children ranging in age from 2 to 13 years old. He is a graphics designer for a small printing company. He presents for treatment on his wife's recommendation. She feels that he is being overly harsh with her and the children. In addition, he appears to be increasingly unhappy with work and has been spending far less time with his hobbies, which include fishing and cooking. She is concerned about possible depression and the potential for an emotional eruption. She is also concerned that he is working too much. She is both concerned and resentful that he is not home very much and that when he is home, he is irritable.

Glen was not resistant to seeking therapy, but he viewed it as a means of quieting his wife and possibly getting her to make some needed changes herself. In discussion with the counselor, he described his increasing frustrations with his boss and coworkers and with his adolescent son who, by

Glen's description, "seems hell-bent on violating every rule I have for him." In addition, he is frustrated with his wife's overaccommodation of their son. He described a rather rigid set of standards that he had for his son, which were not consistent with his wife's "softer and more lenient" views. He reported that he takes great pride in his work and believes that he is good at what he does. Recently, he has attended a few workshops and conferences to learn new professional skills and has been excited to implement what he has learned, only to be prevented by the demands of his employer, who wants him to do several other projects unrelated to his new skills. He has found that his enthusiasm for work has deteriorated, and his attitude toward his boss has become antagonistic.

Glen presents with moderate evidence of a dysthymic condition and an adjustment disorder with mixed affective features. He does not meet criteria for a specific Axis II disorder, but his prototypal personality is most consistent with a compulsive style. Although attention could be directed at the dysthymic and phobic-type symptoms independently, doing so would not necessarily address the underlying personality dimensions contributing to the clinical condition. By attending to the personality attributes and the role of the clinical conditions in meeting the survival task, treatment can produce greater gains as reflected in greater resiliencies to future challenges that have been dealt with in ways that involve moderate depression and anxiety.

Glen is very conscientious and self-disciplined and expects others to adhere to his worldview. Life is very compartmentalized, and when events threaten his compartmentalization, he reacts with a subtle sulkiness, occasional verbal criticisms, and occasional bouts of anger. He struggles to understand situations from others' perspective. For instance, he does not appreciate the general good behavior of his son and strives to get his son to follow more closely his ideal. Further, he does not stop to consider his boss's perspective regarding why he is not able to implement his new skills.

For Glen, a major objective is to decrease his egocentrism and subsequently to increase his ability to see events from another's perspective. In a related way, it will be necessary to get Glen to abandon his compartmentalized rigidity. He is preoccupied with rules and tends toward perfectionism, and the therapist feels that by loosening his constraints and decreasing his compartmentalization, Glen will be able to modify his problematic attitudes concerning rules and perfection. Glen's view that there is a right way and a wrong way to do things and that his view is the right one will be challenged in treatment. To minimize Glen's resistance, the therapist emphasizes his desire for the best outcome for his son and his company.

The two salient issues currently of concern in Glen's life, his son and his work responsibilities, provide useful topics for a collaborative process of guided discovery. The task was to get Glen to consider the realized and potential outcomes of maintaining his rigid views and to increase his appreciation for others' perspective. Beginning with discussion of his son and the conflict he is having with his wife regarding their son, the therapist discussed with Glen his tendency to make arbitrary inferences related to his son's behavior. Through this process, Glen agreed that many of the assumptions that he made were unfounded. However, he was quick to point out that his son had indeed made some bad choices, thereby validating his concern. His generalized assumption that without his intervention and control his son would continue down a path of delinquency was challenged. Glen was able to identify the relationship between his assumptions and his level of anxiety and anger. When he felt that his son was violating his rules, he became angry and used his anger to drive his efforts to gain control over his son. He also recognized that when his wife would intervene on their son's behalf, he would feel anger followed by resignation and a period in which he would not speak to his son or his wife.

Information was considered suggesting that although his son was in fact testing some limits, he was also showing considerable restraints in other situations. Glen was invited to test his son's limits by providing him with some privileges he was not initially inclined to give. Glen was also invited to consider his son's desire for greater freedom and opportunity. In this regard, Glen was encouraged to think about how his son was viewing his efforts to curtail his activities, most specifically his angry reactions. Through role-play, Glen was assigned the task of taking the perspective of the son responding to an angry father. Glen was also encouraged to consider similar circumstances in his own life when others attempted to control him with their anger. Through these exercises, Glen was able to see the impact he was having on his son and subsequently on his wife. As well, he was able to see how his own arbitrary interpretations and his tendency to magnify his son's misbehaviors were contributing to his episodes of anger and resignation. Once he was able to assume the perspective of his son and wife, similar procedures were undertaken to help Glen consider the perspective of his boss.

CONCLUSION

The compulsive prototype personality style is characterized by a conscientious self-image. Individuals with this style view themselves as responsible for themselves, as well as for others. As a result, they become overly self-disciplined, constricted in their range of experiences, and overcontrolled in their expression of behaviors. Although being compulsive is in many ways favored in Western societies, it can also be quite handicapping. At the disordered level of pathology, these individuals are virtually incapacitated by their personality attributes. In their fear of doing a task wrong, they become so focused on the potential failure that the task is never completed. At the level of prototypal style of personality, the task is often completed and frequently completed well. However, in the service of task completion, individuals with a compulsive orientation are wracked with self-doubt and concern with failure and so sacrifice other sources of enjoyment that the overall quality of life may be seriously compromised.

A compulsive personality style leaves the person vulnerable to a host of anxiety-based clinical conditions. Worrying about details contributes to the experiences of general anxiety and to the increased vulnerability to an obsessive–compulsive condition, somatic distress, and the abuse of substances as a means of reducing anxiety. In addition, the fear of failure or loss of control may contribute to greater vulnerability to panic, manic displays, and, potentially, dissociative states. Finally, because he or she needs to do things well, if not perfectly, but has a low probability of success, the individual is also at risk of reactive depression following task failure or in the face of increasing probability of failure.

Treating clients with a compulsive personality style can be a challenging activity as the result of the rigidity and compartmentalization of their thinking. These individuals see themselves as doing things the right way and assume that others should think and behave in the same manner. Most typically, their view is rigid and highly disciplined, with limited or constricted expression of emotion. The task in treating clients with a compulsive personality style is to help them to be able to process information from novel perspectives. This effort is enhanced by helping the clients to see how their own efforts are actually contributing to a worsening problem.

13

THE DEPRESSIVE PROTOTYPE

Key phrase: Hopeless
Evolutionary focus: Safety, lay low

The polarity balances of the depressive style indicate a generalized preoccupation with painful events. Individuals with a depressive style do little to pursue positive and enhancing outcomes and are highly concerned with the potential dangers that exist in the world. However, they do not take much initiative to minimize threats or procure enhancing outcomes. Being generally passive in their accommodation, the avoidance of painful occurrences is a function of happenstance, as they perceive themselves as having little ability to control events. As the victims of unpleasant events, individuals with a depressive prototype personality have adopted a generally disengaged orientation in which the likelihood of unpleasant occurrences is minimized.

Unfortunately, individuals with a depressive orientation perceive themselves as unable to take advantage of the pleasurable opportunities in life, as so many others seem to do. Occasional joyful events are typically the result of chance rather than proactive efforts to create joy. Their self-versus other-orientation reflects a relative balance on both dimensions. In this sense, individuals with a depressive style attend to both themselves and others as sources of both pain and relief. Thus, the pain they encounter is a function of their own failures and of the unavailability and the unwillingness of others to rescue them from themselves. Similarly, the lack of joy in life is a function of their own failure to bring about joyful outcomes and the lack of validating others. The depressive polarity balance is illustrated in Figure 13.1.

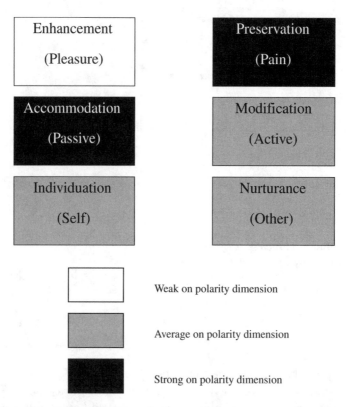

Enhancement (Pleasure)	Preservation (Pain)
Accommodation (Passive)	Modification (Active)
Individuation (Self)	Nurturance (Other)

Weak on polarity dimension

Average on polarity dimension

Strong on polarity dimension

Figure 13.1. Polarity balance of the depressive prototype. From *Personality-Guided Therapy* (p. 339), by T. Millon, 1999, New York: Guilford Press. Copyright 1999 by John Wiley & Sons, Inc. Reprinted with permission.

The depressive and avoidant styles are similar in terms of polarity balances; the difference is in the style of adaptation. Whereas the individual with an avoidant personality style takes active efforts to avoid painful encounters, someone with a depressive personality style is resigned to the occurrence of pain and does little to avoid recurrent pains and unpleasantness. Thus, in many ways the individual with a depressive personality style has taken on the role of social flotsam, easily ignored and easily discarded. Unlike an individual with a schizoid style, however, a person with a depressive style does care about deriving enhancement through social affiliations, and this desire contributes to his or her often considerable anguish.

The individual with a depressive style has essentially given up on the potential of positive, pleasurable, and enhancing life experiences and has committed to a life of enduring the pain and disappointment viewed as inevitable. Generally speaking, the individual puts forth some effort to avoid or cope with the inevitable pains, burdens, and disappointments in life and is most typically a passive–accommodating pawn in the social world. Such individuals maintain a relative balance on the self–other bipolarity, but they are generally rather cynical and otherwise pessimistic in their outlook on themselves and on others. Compared with the avoidant personality style, the depressive personality style is more hopeless and thus disengaged. Unlike an individual with a schizoid style, someone with a depressive style is not indifferent to social affiliations but, rather, is hopeless that rewarding affiliations can be fostered. Unlike one with a negativistic personality style, a person with a depressive style is, through a general hopelessness and retreat from life, less hostile and vengeful.

Throughout this volume, depression has been described as a retreat emotion, which implies its association with disengagement from hopeless situations. Consistent with Gilbert's (2000) refrain that depression is the emotion that allows one to retreat from a battle one is not going to win, the depressive prototype reflects a general rather than situational hopelessness and a retreat from many life-enhancing activities. Individuals with a depressive style attempt to live life by lying low, which describes their general efforts to avoid rocking the boat and soliciting painful social feedback.

PERSONALITY-GUIDED COGNITIVE–BEHAVIORAL CONCEPTUALIZATION

Not a great deal has been written about this proposed category of individuals with personality disorders, although a growing literature has evolved concerning this condition over the past several years. A great deal of this research has centered on whether the depressive personality disorder should or should not be included in the *Diagnostic and Statistical Manual of Mental Disorders* (4th ed., text revision; American Psychiatric Association, 2000; see also Millon & Davis, 1996a). Independent of that debate and regardless of the final conclusion, the depressive style is discussed in this volume as a separate and distinct personality prototype rendering the individual vulnerable to various clinical conditions. The attributes of the depressive prototype personality and their associated liabilities are summarized in Table 13.1.

According to Millon (1999), this passive–dependent personality is marked by a view of the self as *worthless*. Such individuals see themselves as having very few qualities of value, particularly related to interpersonal skills. In their history of interacting with others, those others have expressed contempt or ambivalence toward them (i.e., forsaken object relations). Subsequently, individuals with a depressed orientation are inclined to anticipate that current interactions will lead to similar rejections. As a means of protecting their fragile sense of self-integrity, they tend to remain disengaged, maintaining only a minimal degree of social participation. Their regulatory

TABLE 13.1

Structures and Functions of the Depressive Prototype
and Associated Liabilities

Personality domain	Liability
Self-image Worthless	View of the self as having little to offer others; consistently low self-esteem
Object representations Forsaken	Expectation, having been ignored or rejected by others, that others will forsake them
Morphological organization Depleted	General sense of hopelessness contributing to a disengaged, sluggish, and accommodating demeanor
Mood and temperament Melancholic	General melancholy reflecting their unhappy surrender and disengagement from the joys of life
Behavioral acts Disconsolate	Viewed by others as cheerless and likely to be avoided by them, reinforcing their worthless self-image and forsaken feelings
Interpersonal conduct Defenseless	View of themselves as having no interpersonal resources; overaccommodation and unassertiveness
Cognitive style Pessimistic	View of the world in discouraging terms
Regulatory mechanism Asceticism	Refusal to continue the pursuit of joy; acceptance of a meager, unimpassioned existence; goal of tolerating life rather than seeking joy

style is one of lying low and avoiding potentially painful social encounters. Millon described these individuals' social withdrawal and disengagement as *asceticism*. They are likely to see social interactions as burdens, although they might like to feel otherwise and to be able to find joy in social participation.

The mood state of individuals with a depressive prototype personality reflects general disengagement from the world. The term *melancholy* describes their unhappy withdrawal from the world of others. They engage in limited joyful behaviors and display a very limited range of interpersonal skills, which renders them ill prepared for the spontaneity required of casual social discourse. Not surprising, they tend to be quite pessimistic and manage their affective experience by avoiding most social discourse and active engagement with the world (Lyoo, Gunderson, & Phillips, 1998). Their morphological organization reflects their sense of being defeated by life. Described as *disconsolate*, they see themselves as having few resources, expect things to go badly, often experience a self-fulfillment of their pessimistic expectations, and accept the various interpersonal attacks (from social, familial, and occupational sources), which they view themselves as deserving. Millon (1999) described the interpersonal style of the depressive prototype personality as *defenseless*.

The core beliefs of those with the depressive style of personality reflect the view of the self as worthless, others as rejecting, and the future as more of the same. For instance, these individuals may believe, "I am worthless," "Others have it much better than me," "Things will always turn out poorly," and "No one cares about me." Their conditional beliefs are along the lines of "If I try to socialize, I will just blow it." Instrumentally, they maintain an attitude that "If I lay low, I will be safe" or "It's better if I just keep to myself." Although these attitudes are generally adaptive in keeping these individuals safe from immediate social failure, they do not have the benefit of social indifference seen in those with a schizoid personality style and are subsequently distressed by their social alienation.

PATHOLOGIC PROCESS OF THE DEPRESSIVE PATTERN

Those with a depressive style of personality encounter stress either when greater social engagement is required or when they reflect on their lack of life-fulfilling activities. For these individuals, it often does not take much in the way of external demand or stress to activate critical personality attributes. Their general orientation renders them susceptible to the negative influence even of common social discourse.

In these circumstances, the individual, as mediated by personality attributes, experiences negative emotional states associated with various clinical conditions. Perhaps most notable is the experience of anguished self-contempt, which can contribute to a host of associated clinical conditions, including anxiety, panic, somatic complaints, and suicidal ideations. Similar to the those with an avoidant style, individuals with a depressive style often see themselves as the source of their own distress and engage in various patterns of self-deprecation and self-blame, often enacted as a means of inciting the self into greater proactive activity. Lack of occupational and social resources often presents obstacles and frequently contributes to a depressive retreat from proactive efforts.

AXIS I VULNERABILITIES

Individuals with a depressive prototype personality carry a general sense of worthlessness and hopelessness that compels a retreat from many potentially validating experiences. Unfortunately, their avoidance of these enjoyable activities increases the probability that they will experience various clinical conditions associated with the depressive style. Although depression and dysthymia are obvious vulnerabilities, the hopeless and helpless attitudes characterizing this group of individuals contribute to additional clinical vulnerabilities, described in the sections that follow.

Depression and Dysthymia

The depressive personality style describes a general detachment from meaningful or intimate engagement with others. Quite often, there is an early history of interpersonal loss, negative parental perceptions, and hopeless perfectionism (Huprich, 2003a, 2003b). It has been argued that the depressive style of personality is merely an Axis I condition of dysthymia (Ryder, Bagby, & Schuller, 2002); however, mounting evidence suggests that the two conditions are unique (Huprich, 2000, 2001, 2003a, 2003b; Huprich, Sanford, & Smith, 2002; McDermut, Zimmerman, & Chelminski, 2003; Ryder, Bagby, & Dion, 2001). The differences appear to lie in the duration and intensity of the symptoms (Ryder et al., 2001). In some cases dysthymia may have developed later in life as the outcome of various life circumstances (Huprich, 2003a, 2003b), and the depressive-type symptoms of dysthymia may be more intensely felt (Ryder et al., 2001). Further, in many individuals with a dysthymic condition, a depressive style of personality is not evident (Ryder et al., 2001).

However, it may prove to be the case that those with a depressive personality are more inclined to both dysthymia and episodes of major depression as a function of their personality attributes. Indeed, it may be true that being depressive in personality style virtually guarantees that one will, at some point in time, meet criteria for dysthymia or depression; however, those who meet criteria for either condition are not necessarily certain to have a depressive style. For instance, an avoidant, depressive, compulsive, schizoid, or paranoid personality style may be identified in those who meet criteria for dysthymia. Whether the individual meets criteria for dysthymia or struggles with episodes of major depression, treatment of the underlying depressive attributes is necessary to promote clinically significant changes in the individual's vulnerability to depression.

Bipolar Disorder

Although not common, it is conceivable that an individual with a depressive style of personality could demonstrate periods of hypomania. This may be particularly likely among those with a restive or ill-humored style of depressive personality. Because these individuals are not indifferent to social opportunities and the enhancing outcomes associated with social affiliation, they do desire and may strive to derive validation through relationships with others or by way of professional accomplishment and advancement. Dissatisfied with their position in life and feeling some personal responsibility for their failure, these individuals often struggle with feelings of anguish and self-contempt. Although they might remain generally hopeless, they also remain vigilant to opportunities to escape their inferiority through engagement in some internally and externally validating accomplishment. When opportunity presents itself, individuals with a depressive orientation may pursue an anticipated outcome with tremendous enthusiasm and hope, displaying symptoms consistent with a manic episode. Unfortunately, these individuals often do not have the internal resolve to follow through when obstacles emerge. Rather than working through the problem or revising their intent, they are more inclined to return to self-disparaging internalizations and to retreat from their hopeful ambitions, becoming depressed in the process.

Somatoform Disorder

Gilbert (2000) suggested that depression is associated with a general retreat from life, an escape from an unwinnable situation. For those with a depressive personality, a general disengagement from life challenges is evident. These individuals view any engagement with the world as unenjoyable and unrewarding. Further, unlike individuals with the avoidant style, they have very little interest in or motivation for changing the situation. Most individuals with a depressive style desire that others rescue them from themselves and that others provide some sense of meaning and purpose in their otherwise unfulfilling life. In this regard, somatic complaints may be a common component in the pathologic process (Muratori et al., 1998). If the desire is to avoid engagement with an unrewarding world, somatic symptoms are adaptive, albeit unpleasant.

VARIATIONS ON THE TRADITIONAL DEPRESSIVE PERSONALITY

In each of the depressive variations, the general sense of detachment and hopelessness is revealed. What separates these variations is how the depressive features reveal themselves in styles of social engagement.

Those with the *restive depressive* personality style display features of the avoidant style (Millon & Davis, 2000). These individuals are anguished by their social alienation and negative emotional circumstance. Self-contempt is a common emotional experience because they blame themselves for their failure to foster meaningful and rewarding affiliations.

Unfortunately, because they are unable to reject and walk away from the source of their contempt, as they might when the source of the contempt is external, these individuals may be particularly vulnerable to suicidal ideation, attempts, and execution. Suicide is perceived as providing relief from this painful and hopeless circumstance. Similarly, because the anguished depression felt by these individuals is so distressing, they are also vulnerable to episodes of mania during which they strive to achieve goals associated with self-validation; however, when their efforts fail (which they typically do), the probability of suicidal ideations increases.

Individuals with a restive depressive orientation would like to find an intimate other who will help define their existence, but they feel certain that they are unworthy of another's investment or that they would ruin a relationship if they were to have one. Because of their depressogenic self-derogation, others who affiliate with these individuals often do abandon the relationship because of its depressing quality. The restive depressive personality contributes to dysthymia, episodic depression, anxiety, and other negative emotional states.

As an example, Mark is 30 years old and single. He works as a technical writer for a tool manufacturing company. He has dreams of being a famous novelist. In fact, over the past several years he has started to write several stories, only to lose his ambition when he became dissatisfied with some aspect of his writing. He has dated over the years but has not been able to secure a long-term relationship. He fantasizes about women that he knows and frequently uses these fantasies for masturbation, which he does with great frequency. He regularly compares himself with others whom he knows and sees himself only in negative and derogatory terms. He has been diagnosed with dysthymia and has been treated with antidepressant medications. Although these have been effective in reducing his suicidal ideations, they have not provided him with the liberation from his anguished feelings.

The *self-derogatory depressive* personality style reflects a combination of the depressive and dependent styles (Millon & Davis, 2000). For individuals with this style, the defining emotion may be guilt related to their perception of themselves as the source of their inability to foster and maintain interpersonal relationships. They are highly self-critical, self-blaming, and self-disparaging. Although others may find redeeming qualities in these individuals (e.g., their seriousness and honesty), these others often lose interest as a result of the depressed individual's self-loathing and constant need for reassurance. Needing others to validate them, these individuals often hope that others will provide them with some scrap of evidence that they are not as bad as they make themselves out to be. Often others will provide needed reassurance and thus enhancement, but the reinforcement of self-loathing often begets more self-loathing as a means of deriving the desperately desired validation. Eventually, those who reassure the individual get tired of the game and look to other affiliations for their own sense of social enjoyment. As a result, the individual is left with more justification for his or her guilt and self-loathing.

For example, Maria is a 23-year-old college junior who has struggled with periods of depression that have interfered with her ability to complete her college work in a timely manner. She has been hospitalized on two occasions for treatment of depression and an eating disorder. Throughout her life, Maria has been her own worst enemy. As a child in dance class, she viewed herself as inferior to the other girls and wanted to quit. In school, she viewed herself as too dumb and too ugly for anyone to want to associate with her. In high school, she began a pattern of binge eating and self-induced vomiting, which progressed to the point that she was hospitalized. Although the response prevention program ended her purging, it did not end her tendency to occasionally binge on various comfort foods. Currently she is 20 pounds overweight and sees this as another sign of her general failing as a human being. When in conversation with others, Maria has little to talk about other than her depression and eating disorder. She describes herself to others as fat and dumb.

The *voguish depressive* personality style includes features of the histrionic and narcissistic styles (Millon & Davis, 2000). To those with the voguish depressive style, unhappiness and negativism are a popular and stylish mode of social disengagement and social superiority. Depression is viewed and presented as self-glorifying and dignifying. Indeed, to these individuals, not to be depressed would be tantamount to being unaware of or insensitive to the injustices and desperate state of the world. Through their depression, these individuals are able to demonstrate their superiority over others, whom they view as too ignorant and naive to understand that there is no reason to not be depressed. Indeed, to be happy is to not pay attention and to be simple minded. Thus, their depression symbolizes the depth of their insightful awareness. Such individuals may be most often found among the avant-garde who see themselves as above commonality.

As might be expected, these individuals may not be particularly motivated to abandon their depression or to pursue therapy. For some, treatment serves to validate their disenchantment with the world. Others, however, may view the world as too hopeless to be worth wasting time on therapy. Individuals with a voguish depressive style may be susceptible to various substance abuse disorders through their participation in various counterculture activities. As an example, Daniel, who is 31 years old, is a writer, poet, and lyricist. He is from a medium-sized town in Virginia, but he moved to New York after college to pursue his ambition of being a playwright. He is deeply into existential philosophy and nihilism; his favorite philosophers are Albert Camus and Friedrich Nietzsche. He describes himself as depressed, and his writing is dark. He is an avid social critic and socializes with people who share his disdain for the direction of Western culture. He admits to suicidal ideations but says that he does not want to give society the satisfaction of his departure, yet.

The *ill-humored depressive* personality style is marked by attributes of the negativistic style. Individuals with an ill-humored depressive style are cynical and complain bitterly about the injustices of life and the self-centeredness of others to anyone who will listen. They are sour, distempered, cantankerous, and irritable. Being around these individuals can be rather depressing to others because their negativity creates an unpleasant environment. Other than people with similar depressive styles, most would probably prefer to avoid these individuals.

These individuals enjoy seeing others fail or face disaster. They seek the opportunity to complain to others and are invigorated by others' agreement with their dismal descriptions. When others attempt to put a more optimistic spin on their appraisals, they are quick to become defensive and argumentative, often resorting to verbal attacks of the person's character. They are self-pitying and often hypochondriacal. For example, Tim is 43 years old, married, and the father of two young children. His wife of 10 years is considering separation. When she married Tim, she was attracted by what she described as his insightfulness and idealism. Over the years, she has come to see his caustic cynicism. She reports that he complains about everything in life but does nothing to change his situation. She has become the only person available to him to complain to. He is negative about work, his coworkers, and his extended family and has begun to be hypercritical of the children. When his negativity started being directed at the children, she decided it was time for her to consider leaving. Their pursuit of therapy is their last attempt to rescue what they both see as a doomed relationship. To Tim, his wife's desire to leave the marriage is just one more indication of the failure of society and people, himself included.

The *morbid depressive* personality style includes masochistic prototype attributes. Individuals with this style are hopeless and helpless in their depression. They appear as dejected, gloomy, haggard, and intensely self-abnegating (Millon, 1999; Millon & Davis, 2000). These people find little reason to get excited about life and demonstrate little motivation for improving their own situation. They see themselves as helpless in dealing with life circumstances and have little hope that others will make their lives better. They are profoundly pessimistic. It is not uncommon for those with the morbid depressive style to struggle with episodes of major depression on top of a general dysthymic presentation. They will often neglect aspects of self-care, including hygiene, appearance, nutrition, and self-sustenance through employment. This style of the depressive prototype may be the most characterized by dysthymia. As an example, Beth is a generally pessimistic person. The glass is always half empty to her. She hates her job and finds little personal or social value in her work. She gives little attention to her appearance or to pursuing social or intimate relationships. She views herself as socially inept and intimately unappealing. She attempts to maintain a very low social profile to avoid a situation she feels unprepared to manage. As a result, she misses virtually all opportunities for enhancing life experiences, and this serves to reinforce her depressive orientation.

TREATMENT OF THE DEPRESSIVE PROTOTYPE

Individuals with a depressive orientation encounter stress when they are put in a position to reflect on their sense of social isolation. Thus, they are vulnerable to negative emotional states when social opportunities arise that prompt negative self-projections or when they reflect on their withdrawal and self-imposed isolation. One individual with a depressive prototype personality suggested that generally he felt alright, but his depressive symptoms would return when social opportunities arose. Unlike an individual with an avoidant style, this client did not necessarily want to participate in the social activity, yet unlike the individual with a schizoid style, he was not indifferent to the event. The social function served to activate schemas that highlighted his social inadequacy and "the emptiness of my life." Successful treatment of those with the depressive style requires a change in their orientation to interpersonal relationships and feelings of worthlessness. They see only the potential for failure in social interactions and therefore avoid them; the goal is to get them to see the potential for enhancement in social activities. Treatment of clients with the depressive style is similar to that of clients with the avoidant, dependent, and schizoid styles. As a result of the general social disengagement that has characterized a great proportion of their lives, these individuals are often lacking in basic social skills. Thus, it is necessary to attend to their basic social functioning and to teach any skills they lack. Unfortunately, these individuals often display a general lack of motivation given their depressive demeanor. As a result, it is often necessary, as it is with the individual with a schizoid orientation, to sell them on the value of therapy. However, unlike clients with a schizoid prototype personality, the greater experience of negative emotions felt by these clients provides a greater incentive for treatment.

The general pessimistic and withdrawn attitude and demeanor of the client with a depressive style gives extra importance to the therapeutic relationship. As he or she does in treating clients with a schizoid, dependent, or avoidant style, the therapist must serve as coach and therapist. Thus, it is necessary to keep the client motivated to prevent a withdrawal from treatment, which may be his or her typical response when faced with unpleasant circumstances. Preparing the client for treatment can help to minimize this risk by creating expectancies that may emerge in therapy. To the extent that lapses in motivation are anticipated, their impact can be minimized. It is also important to pace treatment in such a way that the client is challenged to do more but is not overwhelmed by the task of therapy. It is also important that the therapist be encouraging of client's progress but supportive of the difficulties he or she may have in meeting treatment goals. If the client believes that the therapist does not appreciate his or her feelings, the therapeutic relationship will be seriously undermined.

Cognitive Goals

To invest the client with a depressive orientation in the process of therapy, the therapist must first give attention to the pessimistic cognitive projections that often characterize these individuals. Until the client sees potential for greater enhancement, he or she is unlikely to commit to the task of therapy. Through collaboration with the therapist, the client can be encouraged to consider the emotional and practical disadvantages of social isolation and the benefits of greater social participation. Once the client's enthusiasm for greater social participation has increased, the therapist can introduce specific cognitive procedures to counter self-defeating statements. Direct cognitive techniques can be helpful to the client as rebuttals to ingrained cognitive distortions, most notably the automatic thoughts implemented to keep the individual safe from potential failures and disappointments.

To help clients distance the self from the depressive self-view, therapists many find it useful to discuss developmental patterns associated with the depressive style. Because individuals with a depressive prototype personality often struggle with feelings of low self-worth, it is useful to have them appreciate where or how their self-perceptions developed, thus understanding that their self-view is more a reaction to past events than a valid and inherent statement of their worth. These individuals often have had childhood experiences associated with loss, indifference and neglect, and perfectionism. Understanding early childhood origins of their orientation to life may help to create an objective reappraisal of their current orientation to life.

Behavioral Goals

It may be necessary to help the client identify sources of pleasure. Having withdrawn from pleasurable activities, he or she may not have developed hobbies or activities that bring him or her joy. As a result, exploration of potential sources of pleasure may need to be pursued. Once identified, the client may need encouragement to see to it that the task is pursued. Equipping the individual with adaptive cognitions as he or she pursues these activities will increase the probability of treatment success. In many cases, it is helpful to introduce antidepressant medications to elevate the baseline mood state. In some cases, long-term antidepressant medication may help to reduce the likelihood of a return to depressive features.

Once the client has come to counter negative and pessimistic automatic thoughts, specific attention can be given to countering self-defeating or insufficient social skills. As the person begins to have greater social success and feels more comfortable in social situations, the necessity for a depressive retreat should lessen. However, adaptive cognitions must accompany the changes in behavioral expression. The scheduling of positive activities coupled with the introduction of practiced positive self-statements can serve to elevate the client's mood state and counter pessimistic projections.

Affective Changes

Metaemotional processes may be particularly helpful with clients with a depressive orientation. By understanding that their feelings of anxiety and depression serve to compel their withdrawal behaviors, these clients are in the best position to identify and counter those feelings with more adaptive cognitive rebuttals and socially invested behaviors. If they can understand that the emotions serve to prompt a social withdrawal, they can then understand these emotions as part of the overall orchestration, as opposed to a valid assessment of the current state of affairs.

CASE EXAMPLE

Judith is a 43-year-old purchasing agent for a county school district. She is married and has a 15-year-old daughter, Anne. Her husband is an industrial technology teacher at one of the county high schools. Her initial contact with the therapist was to discuss her increasing conflict with her daughter, whom she described as becoming increasingly belligerent and oppositional. She indicated that she and her husband had adopted a laissez-faire attitude toward their daughter, and she now realized they had been overaccommodating. The conflicts they have with Anne relate primarily to their efforts to limit her freedom and spending; Anne would respond to these efforts with an emotional crisis that would ultimately lead the parents to give in to some aspects of her requests. Judith indicated that she was concerned about Anne's future, about the effects of this conflict on her relationship with her husband, and about the stress, which was making her own life miserable. Although attention to her daughter's behavior was a critical dimension of treatment, it was also important to consider Judith's depressive personality style, which appeared to have contributed to the current difficulties she faced and her husband's general lack of investment in the task of childrearing.

Over the years, Judith had found it much easier to give in to her daughter's emotionally mediated demands because she was afraid that her daughter would come to hate her if she had been more firm. Through discussion with Judith, it was clear that she had developed what she referred to as a "lay low" orientation to life, which reflects the common ascetic regulatory mechanism (Millon, 1999; Millon & Davis, 2000) of the depressive style. She had never seen herself as possessing the skills necessary to make friends. She had grown up in a very conservative and socially isolated family and had never had the opportunity for much peer interaction. She did have a few friends through the church she attended and enjoyed interacting with them, but she tended to feel like the other girls were best friends and that she was just an occasional addition to the group. Her mother was very strict and prone to being critical and harsh, whereas her father, a farmer, was usually not around but was encouraging and supportive when present. She developed a tendency to get her work done and then hide to avoid her mother. As an adolescent, she vowed that she would not be so critical with her children, and now she had a daughter with no limits and little respect. She viewed her daughter's current behavior as evidence of her inherent failures.

Judith has struggled for years with recurrent bouts of depression but has been able to maintain her basic home and work responsibilities throughout. Although she is quiet and generally uninvolved at work, she has never taken a sick day because of depression. In addition to bouts of mild depression, Judith has recurrent gastrointestinal problems. Although these are generally tolerable, they have interfered with intimacy with her husband for years and have on occasion resulted in her need to take time off work.

Judith clearly meets criteria for dysthymia with periods of double depression (i.e., major depression superimposed on dysthymia). In addition, her gastrointestinal symptoms appear to suggest somatic problems. Although she does not meet criteria for a depressive personality disorder, her Millon Clinical Multiaxial Inventory (Millon, 1997) elevations do suggest a depressive style. She also demonstrated relatively high scores on the dependent prototype, suggesting a self-derogatory depressive style. Although it would be useful to Judith to specifically address the issues related to her daughter's misbehaviors and her lack of intimacy with her husband, her depressive personality orientation would very likely interfere with her ability to make the necessary changes. Thus, attention to the personality attributes underlying the depressive style, within the context of adjusting her parental skills and potentially improving her marital relationship, was in order.

Judith viewed herself as being less able than others. Although her self-view is not one of abject worthlessness, as might be seen to those with a severe depressive personality disorder, it is most similar to the depressive style. Her self-doubts are reflected in her core beliefs. She feels that she is not as good a mother, wife, or employee as she should be. To be better in these roles, Judith believes she should do things that she is not doing, but she cannot find the inner resolve to alter her behaviors. She has a history of forsaken relationships with others—primarily her parents—and has developed a general feeling of incompetence and submissiveness. When things go wrong, she typically assumes that it is because she has failed in some capacity.

The primary goal is to alter Judith's negative self-image and her pessimistic cognitive style and to decrease her need for constant reassurance from others. Because of her basic beliefs about her inadequacy, she needs her daughter to be perfectly behaved, her husband to be constantly reassuring, and her employer to be constantly validating, all of which are unlikely outcomes. For Judith, successful treatment will involve altering biased conclusions and helping her to develop the skills necessary to function at a level that she would judge more positively. In a sense, Judith will need to attempt to increase her performance, particularly as it relates to her parenting skills, while at the same time reducing her unrealistic standards for herself and others.

During initial phases of treatment, Judith worked with the therapist in a collaborative effort to evaluate the evidence relative to her global assumptions about the self. Clearly, Judith displayed several strengths but also some liabilities related to her interpersonal functioning. Her need to do things perfectly, coupled with her view of herself as somewhat worthless, contributed to her "lay low" orientation reflected in the depressive style. Judith monitored her ongoing activities, recording the nature of the events, her thoughts and feelings, and her actions and their consequences. Quickly, her tendency to avoid confrontation and to disparage herself became evident. Using the monitoring data for discussion, Judith was asked about alternative reactions given the events she described. She displayed considerable difficulty in generating alternative reactions. During her course of treatment, she continued to record her experiences and brought her completed forms in for discussion. In addition, attention to specific parenting and interpersonal skills were introduced. Judith also worked to catch herself attempting to retreat from difficult situations by identifying the anxiety she would feel and the sense of frustration she would encounter when faced with situations she felt ill prepared to manage.

Through this activity, Judith was able to see and judge herself differently relative to the nature of her interpersonal skills. Because her relationship with her daughter was particularly salient in her life, this was the primary focus of treatment attention. As she began to have relative success in negotiating compromises with her daughter and was able to better tolerate her daughter's inevitable adolescent frustrations without taking it personally, attention was focused on aspects of her relationship with her husband and coworkers. Although Judith did not ever develop a strongly outgoing demeanor, she was able to abandon her general lack of engagement with others and to derive increased pleasure from her interactions. As she came to see herself as capable in social situations, and as she decreased her tendency to accept responsibility for others' moods and actions, she was able to see herself as other than worthless and was alternatively able to view herself more positively. As this schema-based belief changed, so too did her melancholic mood and pessimistic attitude.

CONCLUSION

Individuals with a depressive prototype personality are marked by a view of the self as worthless and others as unlikely to accept them or to provide them with the sense of personal validation they are unable to derive themselves. Social interactions are therefore perceived as threatening and are engaged in only with reluctance. They maintain a general melancholy mood state, underscoring their general disengagement from joyful activities. They are generally pessimistic and often develop a general demeanor of disengagement. Their depressive personality predisposes them to a general dysthymic condition, which may be coupled with episodes of major depression that emerge at times when they interpret the self as being particularly isolated and the future as particularly hopeless.

Treatment of clients with the depressive style presents unique challenges. These individuals are often resistant clients because therapy requires them to consider personal attributes closely, and they are already inclined to judge themselves in negative terms. Also, therapy may require them to engage in activities they feel ill prepared to manage. It is possible that engagement in therapy could lead to a worsening of depressive symptoms, which could serve to allow a retreat from the task of therapy. Successful treatment must be pursued at a pace that challenges clients without prompting a depressive retreat. It is important, as well, that therapists provide support and encouragement while clients develop the courage and willingness to challenge core beliefs and behavioral patterns.

14

THE NEGATIVISTIC PROTOTYPE

Key phrase: Contrary
Evolutionary focus: On my own terms

Individuals with a negativistic prototype personality are not particularly compelled toward pleasurable outcomes; they are more inclined to defend against potential pain and displeasure. They are more active than passive, and their activity is reflected primarily in their defensive attitudes and behaviors. Although not outwardly hostile and aggressive, they do act to protect and defend self-integrity from perceived affronts, albeit in an often indirect capacity. They struggle in their self- versus other-orientation. Although more oriented to the individuals' own pleasures and displeasures, these outcomes are perceived as very much tied to the activities of other people. Thus, there is a degree of conflict on the self versus other dimension. They hope that others will act to make their lives pleasant and fulfilling, yet they expect those hopes to go unsatisfied and perhaps even to be dashed by the critical and self-serving actions of others. Perhaps not surprising, the negativistic personality has been associated with the narcissistic personality style (Fossati et al., 2000). Individuals with a negativistic orientation want others to act a particular way toward them and even feel some sense of entitlement. Unlike individuals with a narcissistic orientation, however, they do not necessarily expect to be fulfilled by the activities of others, which is a prime source of their cynicism and irritability. The polarity balance of the negativistic prototype is illustrated in Figure 14.1.

275

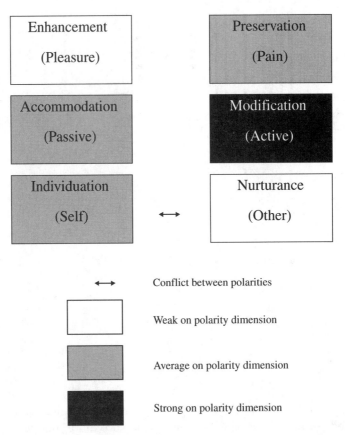

Figure 14.1. Polarity balance of the negativistic prototype. From *Personality-Guided Therapy* (p. 560), by T. Millon, 1999, New York: Guilford Press. Copyright 1999 by John Wiley & Sons, Inc. Reprinted with permission.

PERSONALITY-GUIDED COGNITIVE–BEHAVIORAL CONCEPTUALIZATION

Individuals with a negativistic personality maintain a *discontented* self-image. They are unhappy with life, yet not necessarily as hopeless as those with a depressive prototype personality. Their interpersonal histories are scattered with some relationships that have been promising, if not pleasant and rewarding, and others that were quite painful and disappointing. The implication is that they have a clear sense of how they would like relationships to go, but they remain pessimistic that they ever will. As a result, they tend to vacillate in their feelings for and about others, hoping for validation and expecting disappointment.

Their general discontentment is complemented by an *irritable* mood. Others might describe individuals with a negativistic style as acerbic, grumpy, and disgruntled. Indeed, their irritability reflects more cause than consequence of their discontentment. They feel unfairly treated or that they have gotten an unfair shake in life, and their irritability helps to ensure that they will continue to be exposed to the unpleasantries of life and interpersonal affiliation. They are resentful of the things they feel obligated to do, often feeling that the demands and expectations are unfair or unreasonable. They may be resentful about not having the things they want but that others possess.

In interpersonal interactions, they often act *contrary*. Mosak (1968, 1971) described such individuals as "aginners." For these individuals, it matters not what the issue is; they are "agin" (i.e., against) it. Some have referred to such individuals as "contrarians" to describe their negative and uncooperative attitudes and behaviors. These individuals tend to look for the negative in situations and are generally able to find it. Furthermore, they tend to be skeptical of positive motives and outcomes. Millon and Davis (2000) described the regulatory attitudes of these individuals using the term *displacement*, which represents their tendency to focus on external objects and events as the source of positive and negative outcomes. Thus, when something positive occurs, individuals with a negativistic prototype personality may attribute it to situational luck or some other random event. When negative events occur, they might be viewed as the unavoidable or inevitable outcome of dumb luck or the appropriate "balance of the universe." Their expectation that things will turn out badly reflects their *skeptical* cognitive style. Although they may hope for the positive, they are rather doubtful. Millon (1999) discussed the contribution of this skeptical style to their ambivalence. Even when they have determined a course of action, they doubt their own conclusion and find themselves inactive as a function of their own critical style and uncertainty. The personality functions and structures of the negativistic personality are summarized in Table 14.1.

From a cognitive–behavioral perspective (Beck et al., 1990), individuals with a negativistic style view themselves as capable yet subject to the "encroachment" of others. Others are viewed as demanding, interfering, intrusive, and dominating and in other ways as sources of unpleasantness; however, they are also perceived as sources of validation, support, and approval. Thus, although these individuals want approval and validation, they expect rejection or criticism and maintain a defensive shell to protect against the intrusion of others and against their disappointment with others. Their caustic demeanor represents their bolstered disposition to defend against their expected attack or disappointment. The beliefs held by these individuals are that they need others for a fulfilling and enjoyable life but that they will likely be disappointed in some way by those others. Thus, there is a dependency to this personality style coupled with a pessimistic outlook. Instrumentally, they act to maintain a sense of independence but

TABLE 14.1
Structures and Functions of the Negativistic Prototype
and Associated Liabilities

Personality domain	Liability
Self-image Discontented	View of self as misunderstood, luckless, unappreciated, jinxed, and demeaned by others; embitterment, disgruntlement, and disillusionment with life
Object representations Vacillating	Contradictory feelings and conflicting inclinations regarding relationships; drive to subtly degrade the achievements and pleasures of others
Morphological organization Divergent	Coping and defensive maneuvers directed toward incompatible goals, leaving conflicts unresolved
Mood and temperament Irritable	Frequent touchy, temperamental, and peevish moods, followed by sullen and moody withdrawal; petulance, impatience, and ready annoyance
Behavioral acts Resentful	Resistance against fulfilling expectations of others through procrastination, inefficiency, and obstinance; gratification by undermining and demoralizing others
Interpersonal conduct Contrary	Assumption of conflicting roles between acquiescence and hostility; envy and intolerance of others
Cognitive style Skeptical	Cynical, doubting, and untrusting style; disbelieving approach to positive events; pessimism about the future; tendency to whine and grumble about others' good fortune
Regulatory mechanism Displacement	Precipitous discharge of negative emotions mediated by unconscious processes; passive venting of disapproval by acting inept or perplexed

may define this simply as going against, either actively or passively, what is expected of them or what is simply common to the group.

As an example, Reny, a 25-year-old office worker, exhibits many of the features of the negativistic style. She has a history of employment problems since quitting college 6 years ago. She struggles frequently with periods of depression but is most typically cynical and sullen. She complains frequently about the behaviors and intentions of others and quickly gets a reputation wherever she works as grouchy and argumentative.

PATHOLOGIC PROCESS OF THE NEGATIVISTIC PATTERN

Individuals with a negativistic prototype personality are distressed by any of a large number of circumstances. They are threatened by their "loss of approval and abridgement of autonomy" (Beck, Freeman, & Associates, 1990, p. 46). They are distressed by the accomplishments of others, which might imply their inadequacy, and they are distressed by their own accomplishments, which are too fleeting and inconsistent. They look for the negative in situations, and they typically find it. As a result, they are vulnerable to a host of clinical conditions stemming from their defensive and caustic demeanor. It they do well, they look for evidence of things going badly. If others do well, they see it as evidence of their inadequacy or lack of luck. The one thing they might find enjoyable is the misfortune or relative suffering of others. Although not necessarily to the point of the individuals with a sadistic style, except perhaps in the case of those with the abrasive negativistic style, these individuals find the suffering of others to be gratifying in a personally reassuring sense. They see themselves as suffering and feel a sense of reassurance when others suffer as well. Indeed, this may motivate behaviors implemented to produce some degree of suffering in others. In a sense, they want to make sure that everyone is sharing in their misery.

Individuals with a negativistic orientation desire a rewarding and fulfilling life, but as the result of unfortunate circumstances they expect that fulfillment to perpetually elude them. However, rather than doing something proactive and adaptive to improve their lot in life, they complain, which is associated with a host of negative emotional and interpersonal experiences. In a sense, these persons would rather complain than actually do something to improve their circumstances.

AXIS I VULNERABILITIES

As a function of their negative and caustic demeanor, individuals with a negativistic prototype personality are vulnerable to a host of clinical conditions. In some cases, the clinical condition is a direct consequence of the negativistic style, such as the state of anxious irritation that comes with the negative and pessimistic outlook on life. In addition, a clinical condition may serve as a means of avoiding unpleasant obligations and activities and as a passive means of interpersonal control and retaliation. In any of these cases, the clinical outcomes reflect the orchestration by these individuals to avoid unpleasantness.

Depression

Being cynical and plagued by chronic feelings of irritability, individuals with a negativistic style are prone to periods of depression. Indeed, episodes of depression may provide for these people a retreat from their own caustic demeanor. Maintaining some hope that life will provide the fulfillment they desire without being willing to take proactive initiative, these individuals are in a state of near-constant frustration and disappointment. The advantage of depression is that rather than being anguished by unfulfilled hopes and desires, they stop caring. Unfortunately, the depression is itself unpleasant and may be one more reason to be resentful and pessimistic. Given their interpersonal orientation, these individuals may rely on their depression as a means to manage and punish others. When an individual with a negativistic style who is depressed is asked how he or she is doing, he or she will say, "Horribly!" and then imply that it is the fault of the person who asked.

As described by Beck et al. (1990), an individual with a negativistic orientation seeks the path of least resistance and is highly resistant to external demands and obligations. For this individual, who may be genuinely hopeless and depressed about a clear obligation, depression may provide the opportunity for a justifiable retreat that he or she desires. Although this may indeed be a feigned or exaggerated condition, it is important to note that the felt obligation to do something that one does not want to do can be "depressing." That the failure to meet an obligation inconveniences another may in some ways be gratifying to the individual, or simply inconsequential.

Dysthymia

Although there are no specific empirical studies looking at dysthymia and negativity, a chronic, low-grade detachment may best characterize the caustic disgruntlement of the negativistic personality. Reflected in feelings of negativity, hopelessness, and low self-esteem, the dysthymic diagnosis may reflect the individual's general pessimism and resentfulness. Dysthymia may be most typically observed in those with the discontented negativistic variant of the style.

Generalized Anxiety Disorder

Because they are constantly on guard against the intrusion and demands of others, it is useful for these individuals to remain hypervigilant. Likewise, they expect that no matter how good things are at any moment in time, circumstances will ultimately turn out badly, an orientation that contributes to feelings of anxiety—described by some as "waiting for the other shoe to drop." However, their anxiety may be observed more in the form of irritability because anxiety may display a weak, inferior vulnerability, whereas irritability may imply a sense of haughty superiority. Irritability also may serve to help keep unwanted demands at bay. These individuals rely on emotions, such as hostility and irritability, to defend against the unpleasant demands and inevitabilities of life in a social world.

Somatoform Disorder

The constant anxiety and agitation characterizing the person with a negativistic style may contribute to the experience of somatic complaints. Indeed, feeling constantly agitated and disgruntled can affects one's physical state. In addition, somatic distress can provide convenient benefits to the negativistic individual. For instance, he or she may be able to retain some degree of control over a situation by complaining of stomach irritation. In such a case, the gastrointestinal distress may be entirely feigned or may emerge with the threat of loss of control or obligation that is noxious to the individual (see Noyes et al., 2001). In some situations, the somatic distress, genuine or not, may also provide a convenient means of passive–aggression. For instance, one may be able to retaliate for a perceived wrong by forcing another to do extra work because of one's distressed physical condition.

Alcohol Abuse

The negativistic style may be associated with patterns of alcohol abuse (Kanost, 1997). With their devil-may-care attitude, individuals with a negativistic prototype personality may be little concerned with the implications of chronic or excessive alcohol use. Indeed, the chronic feelings of disgruntlement and irritability may be used as an excuse for drinking. Further, the distress they may experience in their interactions with others may simply motivate more drinking. Given the chronic feelings of irritability these individuals experience, the benefit of alcohol may be felt in its depressant effect; that the negativistic personality is also associated with marijuana use is consistent with this notion (Greenfield & O'Leary, 1999).

Anger and Aggression

The irritability, resentment, and contrary attitudes of the individual with a negativistic orientation may also contribute to displays of anger and aggressiveness. Perhaps diagnosed with an intermittent explosive disorder, he or she may rely on anger and irritability as a means of dealing with external expectations and for reaping some degree of revenge for perceived wrongs. Although the target of the aggressiveness may or may not be the source of the individual's anger, the general discontentment renders all guilty and perhaps deserving of retaliation.

VARIATIONS ON THE TRADITIONAL
NEGATIVISTIC PERSONALITY

Four variations of the negativistic prototype are described in Millon's personology model (Millon, 1999; Millon & Davis, 2000). Common to each variation is the discontented, irritable, and contrary disposition typical of the negativistic prototype. How they differ is reflected in their style of interpersonal engagement and reactive tendencies when events are unsatisfying.

Those with the *vacillating negativistic* personality incorporate aspects of the borderline prototype. For these individuals, emotional variability corresponding to rapidly changing cognitive appraisals is common. Whereas at one moment they may appear calm and collected, full of confidence and pride, with a subtle alteration in circumstance their affective reactions can change rapidly in correspondence with their capricious cognitive appraisals. For these individuals, life is often more threatening and uncontrollable than it is for others, and they have come to manage situations with greater expression of affect. Those with the vacillating style may be particularly prone to recurrent interpersonal conflicts and to episodes of intensified anger, resentment, and reactive depression.

As an example, Steven is a 36-year-old librarian at a small college. He is generally pretty easygoing and helpful to those who come to the library asking for assistance. He often gives library tours and conducts research resource workshops for various professors and their students. However, the professors are often reluctant to approach Steven because they never know what kind of a mood he might be in at the time they approach him. He may be in a very pleasant and helpful mood, or he may be in a mood that can best be described as surly. In fact, there have been times that he has been downright rude and even argumentative. Recently, a couple of students and professors have complained, and Steven has been reprimanded by the head of the library.

The *abrasive negativistic* personality style includes features of the sadistic prototype. Individuals with this style tend to be more contentious, intransigent, fractious, and quarrelsome than do those with other variations on the negativistic style. They are frequently irritable, contradictory, and acrimonious. Others may be inclined to keep their caustic demeanor to themselves, but those with the abrasive style are not reluctant to display their discontent quite openly and aggressively. They may complain bitterly to anyone who will listen and no matter what the circumstance. Similar to persons with the sadistic style, these individuals may find some satisfaction in knowing that they have created some degree of discomfort in others. For instance, these people may find some joy in driving particularly slowly, knowing that they are frustrating other drivers. The passive–aggressive style that is common to those with a negativistic personality may be somewhat less passive for those with this variation of the negativistic prototype.

As an example, Martin is a 28-year-old computer software consultant. He came to the attention of the mental health worker following a conflict that he had with a coworker. Martin has always been viewed as a hothead, and people tended to keep their interactions with him to a minimum. When they did have to interact with Martin, he would answer their questions or fulfill the obligation in whatever way necessary, but he was always a bit acerbic in attitude and frequently made negative comments about someone. When things did not go his way, which occurred frequently, he would slam down a hand or throw something. The episode that led to his being referred for counseling involved his failure to complete a task that his boss had repeatedly asked him to complete, then yelling obscenities when reprimanded for not getting the job done.

The *discontented negativistic* personality style includes aspects of the depressive prototype. Individuals with this style are dispositionally pessimistic. They grumble, complain, and act petty and cranky and are inclined to being embittered, fretful, and moody. They can find something to complain about regardless of the activity. Few things or activities provide any sense of satisfaction. Unfortunately, people find these individuals depressing to be around and often avoid them, thereby giving them more to complain about. Unlike those with a more typical form of negativistic personality, these individuals may be more hopeless than others and may demonstrate a dysthymic condition as well as episodes of depression.

Kara has been treated pharmacologically for recurrent episodes of depression for the past 15 years, but she has never gotten much relief. At times she has even considered suicide. She works in a coffee shop, having failed to get a job after finishing college with a degree in art history. Kara complains about her job, her boss, her customers, her tips, and, mostly, about the lack of fulfillment in her life. She smokes too much and does not take very good care of her health. She has friends, but they are similarly disgruntled, and their time together is generally spent talking about the horrid state of the world.

Those with the *circuitous negativistic* personality style display features of the dependent personality. Their sense of inadequacy contributes to their being less direct with complaints and oppositional behaviors. It may be the circuitous variation that is most passive in the expression of oppositional and aggressive behaviors. For instance, they may be most inclined to procrastination, inefficiency, and forgetfulness in situations in which others are depending on them for some specific outcome. The negative features of this prototype may contribute to the expression of feigned conditions or to the overaccentuation of genuine symptoms.

Jorge is 44 years old and is currently in his second marriage. His wife initiated marital counseling as a final effort before contacting an attorney and starting divorce proceedings. Her complaints about Jorge are that he has not maintained steady employment during their 23-year marriage, does not help around the house, does not follow through on his commitments to her or to anyone else, and has little good to say about anyone. She indicated that she felt he would rather walk over a mess than go to the trouble of picking it up, and then he would complain about the messiness of the house. She indicated that she has tried to be patient and supportive of his various difficulties, including some health problems and bad luck with bosses, but she feels that her patience is running out. Jorge indicates that he wants to work out their difficulties, but he feels that she should not blame him for the bad economy and his run of bad luck.

TREATMENT OF THE NEGATIVISTIC PROTOTYPE

One of the great challenges in working with clients with a negativistic orientation is keeping them motivated for change. Their negative and caustic demeanor is a constant source of resistance and frustration. One of the critical therapeutic goals is a change in their discontented self-image. To improve their life satisfaction, they must make several changes. They must modify the automatic thoughts contributing to negative affective experience, and they must change interpersonal behaviors that contribute to problematic interpersonal relationships. Indeed, treating clients with the negativistic personality can be quite challenging. Because these individuals are resistant to external demands, they will not likely do well in therapy that is too directive or in which the therapist appears to be coercing changes. Further, they may remain guarded in therapy, fearful that the therapist is going to try to get the upper hand. In addition, they may not value the process of therapy and may be ingenuinely compliant simply as a means of tolerating what they perceive as unwarranted intrusion by the therapist and whomever it was that urged them into therapy.

As suggested by Beck et al. (1990), it is important when working with clients with a negativistic style that they be given enough control over the nature and course of therapy that they do not feel controlled or coerced. It is also important that these clients appreciate the direction and benefit of therapy. If therapeutic goals are not made clear, the efforts of the therapist may well be judged as coercive. It is likewise important that the clients understand the course of treatment to minimize the risk of therapeutic resistance. These clients will have to occasionally face challenges that they have heretofore avoided, often by way of various clinical conditions that emerge as a function of the negativistic attributes. Treatment will have to be paced at a tolerable level, and the clients will have to anticipate challenges and see the advantages of meeting therapeutic tasks.

Several factors are of concern in treating this population of clients. Although it is important that their discontented self-image be altered to lessen their resentful and irritable demeanor, such changes may be unlikely in the absence of effective social skills, and there may be little motivation to improve social function as long as they maintain a negative and embittered attitude toward the external world. Subsequently, it may be most important to alter first their negative attitudes toward others, then to focus attention on the development of adaptive skills useful for fostering positive interpersonal relationships. This effort may require specific attention to their irritable mood through pharmacological intervention, relaxation training, or a meta-emotional process. Once they begin to experience greater satisfaction from interpersonal relationships, specific attention can be given to the discontented self-image.

Cognitive Goals

Through the process of guided discovery, the therapist and client can consider the nature of the client's interactions with others. The objective in this initial effort is to help the client develop a more patient, tolerant, and compassionate attitude toward others. This objective can best be accomplished by helping the client to consider the motives of others and to find a commonality with others. Through guided discovery, the therapist can have the client describe various interpersonal interactions that have been distressing in some way to the client. Using these situations, therapist and client can speculate on the motives of those involved, considering the possibility that each individual was attempting to draw from the interaction some degree of pleasure or enhancement, or at least to minimize its unpleasantness. In most situations, the client will come to recognize his or her commonality with others.

The individual with a negativistic style may express various forms of cynicism and pessimism in discussions with the therapist. Rather than countering these responses, the therapist might simply confirm the client's observation that at times people seem to act in their own interest, with little concern for others. That the individual with a negativistic prototype personality comes to see him- or herself as being as guilty as anyone else in this regard may hasten the therapeutic process. However, pointing it out to the client may elicit a hurtful or defensive response. It is perhaps better, then, to let the client see this connection him- or herself. Similar responses may be offered relative to comments often made by individuals with a negativistic orientation concerning such issues as selfishness; fairness and unfairness; and others' personal, social, and cultural maladies.

A cost–benefit analysis may be useful in helping the client consider the advantages of various interpersonal strategies. By considering how the others in the scenarios the client describes acted and the subsequent outcomes, the client may come to see the futility of the negative demeanor. Consideration of others' actions and related outcomes may make this topic less threatening to the client. Indeed, the opportunity to discuss the negative, self-serving attributes of others is quite consistent with the individual's general orientation to the world of other people. The therapist must be careful not to let this deteriorate into a nonproductive gripe session and should be attentive to the opportunity to have the client consider his or her own behaviors and the response of others to those expressed behaviors. By considering the thoughts and feelings experienced in situations, the therapist can help the client to develop a greater awareness and understanding of the relationship between thoughts, feelings, and actions. It may be useful at this stage in the process to introduce role-play scenarios in which the client is encouraged to consider the situation from different perspectives. Ultimately, it may be useful to use similar role-play situations as a means of promoting more prosocial behaviors.

By having the client consider recent and common social interactions, attitudes toward the self and others can be explored and reconsidered. It may be useful at this juncture to introduce a monitoring assignment in which the client considers ongoing interactions and his or her automatic thoughts and resultant reactions to common engagements. Similarly, the client can monitor ongoing thoughts and feelings associated with nonsocial events, noting most specifically automatic thoughts and resultant emotional and behavioral reactions. These forms can then be discussed in session as a means of helping the client to understand the role of automatic thoughts and core cognitive assumptions in the experience of unpleasant affect and counterproductive behaviors.

It may be useful at this point to administer the Early Maladaptive Schema inventory (Young, Klosko, & Weishaar, 2003). To the extent that the client's maladaptive schemas correspond to the data collected on the monitoring forms, the impact of the core beliefs can be reinforced in the client's appreciation. Further, the inventory results may reveal other core distortions that were not identified in the monitoring procedure and that may be useful to identify and highlight in therapy.

Behavioral Goals

Once the client has developed an understanding of how thoughts contribute to affective distress and counterproductive reactions and how this process plays out within a social context, the client is prepared to begin fostering more satisfying interpersonal relationships and confronting counterproductive cognitions. At this point, it is particularly useful to help the client foster more rewarding interpersonal engagements by teaching more adaptive social skills. This teaching can be accomplished in two stages. First, using common scenarios described by the client, role-play situations can be created in which the client takes the role of him- or herself and of others in the interaction. Through this process, the therapist can coach the client in ways to react, paying close attention to the automatic thoughts and activated core beliefs and his or her relationships with the affective and behavioral responses. Second, as the skill expressed in role-plays increases, the client can be encouraged to focus on specific targets in his or her daily interactions with others. Although it is very reasonable that this has occurred throughout therapy, at this stage the specific focus will enhance the connection between core beliefs and both pleasant and unpleasant interpersonal engagements. It may be beneficial to role-play the specific interaction before making an out-of-session assignment. The goal is for the client to derive greater pleasure and enhancement through more patient and tolerant behaviors. To embellish and solidify the cognitive and behavioral changes in the client, the therapist may find it both useful and necessary to consider more specifically the role of affect.

Affective Changes

Despite the beneficial cognitive changes exhibited by the client and the expression of more adaptive social skills, conditioned anxiety and irritability may impede the successful outcome of therapy. In the case of extreme anxiety or other emotion, pharmacotherapy may be useful and even necessary. However, it is important that the client be dissuaded from concluding that his or her condition is purely medical and hopeless without medication. If medication is initiated, the client can be prepared to reconsider the use of medication again later to determine whether it is still necessary. In less extreme cases, or when the client is resistant to the use of medication, the therapist might consider various forms of relaxation training, including progressive muscle relaxation or systematic desensitization in the case of a conditioned emotional reaction. Finally, it may be useful to introduce the metaemotional technique of using emotional reactions as a stimulus for identifying activated core beliefs and considering alternative behavioral reactions necessary to foster more rewarding interpersonal engagements (Rasmussen, 2003b). Through this process, the task is to help the client understand and control emotional reactions that compromise life quality and that compel negative and caustic behaviors that contribute to unrewarding interactions with the world.

CASE EXAMPLE

Doris is 38 years old and is currently unemployed. She is divorced and the mother of two teenage children who presently live with their father. Doris has a history of treatment for depression and was recently diagnosed with and treated for bipolar II disorder. She was working until a month ago, when she quit her job to "get away from my jerk boss." It was the episode surrounding her work conflict that prompted the attention to a bipolar condition. Her employment history is characterized by periodic job changes.

Doris has a long history of interpersonal conflicts. Although she has often been able to find others who shared her contempt and disdain for people and situations, most typically her negative attitude either came to include those others or became tiring to them. In either event, most friendships have been rather short lived. Her children opted to live with their father, whom they described as "easier to get along with." Although Doris comes close to meeting the proposed criteria for a negativistic personality, her negativism is more stylistic than disordered.

The primary goal in helping Doris was to decrease her negative and caustic attitude toward others and thereby render her a more appealing social partner. One of the greatest challenges in treating Doris was keeping her motivated for change. Indeed, she viewed successful therapy as simply acquiescing to the "simple-minded" and "superficial" state of the world. As a result, it was useful to initially validate her frustrations with the state of events rather than challenging them. Acknowledgment that there are clearly problems in the world and that people are often very much inclined to act in self-serving ways allowed Doris the opportunity to express frustrations and concerns without eliciting a defensive and therapy-ending response. However, it was important that the therapist not reinforce the cynicism, focusing instead on validating the frustrations. For instance, the following exchange describes a nonthreatening reaction to her frustrations:

> *Doris:* Everyone I meet is so demanding and self-centered. All anyone cares about is himself, and to hell with everyone else. For example, my ex-husband buys himself a new car while I'm driving an old clunker! Then he goes off on a

week trip to the Caribbean. Meanwhile, I'm sitting at home and driving a junk heap!

Therapist: It does seem that people do frequently put themselves first and fail to think of the other people in their lives. I know it can be very frustrating.

Although the therapist could have challenged Doris, pointing out that she and her husband were now divorced and that he was paying the agreed-on alimony and could do what he chose with the rest of his money, such a response would likely have alienated Doris from therapy. By validating the frustrations and real potential for self-serving motives in others, the therapist was best able to foster a therapeutic union, thereby setting the stage for later therapeutic work.

As therapy progressed with Doris, focusing initially on the emerging therapeutic relationship, the therapist began to increasingly speculate on how other people were reacting to Doris (using the Colombo strategy). By getting Doris to begin thinking about her own contribution to interpersonal conflicts, opportunities emerged for the discussion of social skills and relationship building. As Doris became more comfortable with therapy and with the task of challenging personal assumptions, she was able to discuss with the therapist her hopes and expectations for others, thereby revealing specific core and intermediate beliefs that contributed to her aversive affective experiences. Using the process of guided discovery, Doris and the therapist were able to discuss the probability of interpersonal interactions going as she hoped and the likelihood of her own interpersonal style serving to improve or worsen the situation.

Once Doris accepted that the world is indeed often frustrating and disappointing but that there are things that one can do to maximize the probability of positive interactions and experiences, therapy progressed rapidly. Using her relationship with her children and ex-husband as points of focus, the therapist helped Doris to develop a repertoire of interpersonal strategies useful for interactions with these individuals. Role-play scenarios were helpful throughout the process. In addition, Doris developed a series of cognitive reminders for herself to repeat when she began feeling frustrated or resentful of others. For instance, she reminded herself that "although it would be nice if people would consider my feelings first, they have other things more important to them to deal with."

Throughout the process of treatment, the therapist attended to the nature of the therapeutic relationship and Doris's investment in therapy. By emphasizing a cost–benefit approach and helping Doris to recognize her faulty expectations, the therapist helped her to understand and accept her own contribution to interpersonal conflicts. Doris was then able to make subtle changes in her style of interpersonal interaction that increased her ultimate resistance to the negative emotional reactions associated with the negativistic style.

CONCLUSION

Individuals with a negativistic style maintain a discontented self-image and a negative and caustic attitude toward the world, which contribute to a general irritability and resentful and contrary behaviors. These individuals often feel that they have gotten an unfair deal in life and view others as both the source of their frustration and the source of their validation. At a disordered level, the negativistic personality is so blatantly negative that nearly every aspect of life is tainted by the negative attitude. They find little joy in life and battle feelings of hostility and aggravation and hopeless despair. At the personality style level, the negativistic prototype struggles to find joy and with feelings of resentment and frustration, but such individuals are able to find enough satisfaction and contentment that they are not overwhelmed by their frustrations and aggravations. Their negative attitude often contributes, however, to recurrent conflicts with others and to feelings of discontentment.

Associated with the negativistic personality are vulnerabilities to several clinical conditions. For instance, a negativistic demeanor contributes to chronic feelings of irritability, anxious agitation, somatic complaints, and episodes of depression. Treatment of clients with the negativistic personality can be a challenging undertaking. The irritable and disgruntled attitude that they bring to session often undermines the strength of the therapeutic relationship and potential benefit of therapy.

Once the client commits to the therapeutic process, the task of therapy is to help the client adjust his or her attitude about and toward others. These goals can often be accomplished by helping the client appreciate his or her commonality with others. Similarly, through a cost–benefit assessment, the client can consider alternative ways of viewing and interacting with others, specifically the value of fostering cooperative relationships with others. Through guided discovery, role-play, and out-of-session assignments, the client can be directed toward more fulfilling interpersonal relationships.

15

THE SADISTIC AND MASOCHISTIC PROTOTYPES

The sadistic and masochistic prototypes constitute characterological patterns that are not currently recognized as distinct categories in the *Diagnostic and Statistical Manual of Mental Disorders*, (4th ed., text revision; *DSM–IV–TR*; American Psychiatric Association, 2000). Nonetheless, these patterns are recognized as distinct prototypes in the personologic model and are discussed in this chapter relative to the integrative model. Although there is a considerable literature discussing the nature of these conditions and the controversy over their inclusion in the *DSM–IV–TR*, that literature is not reviewed in this volume.

THE SADISTIC PROTOTYPE

Key phrase: Dominate or be dominated
Evolutionary focus: Power and control

The sadistic prototype personality style maintains an active–controlling orientation (Millon & Davis, 2000; see Figure 15.1). Individuals with a sadistic style are unique in that pleasure is attained through pain, and joyful encounters are sources of relative distress that must be undermined, reflected in the reversal pattern on the pain–pleasure polarity. These

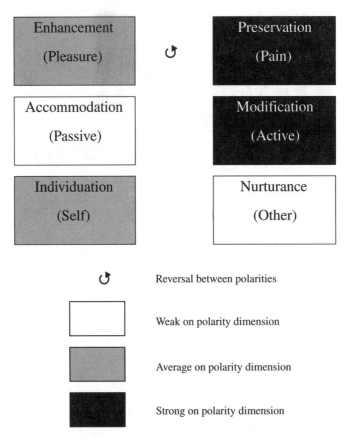

Figure 15.1. Polarity balance of the sadistic prototype. From *Personality-Guided Therapy* (p. 497), by T. Millon, 1999, New York: Guilford Press. Copyright 1999 by John Wiley & Sons, Inc. Reprinted with permission.

individuals are active and often aggressive and are concerned with the welfare neither of others nor, in many ways, of themselves. Their focus is to maintain power and control, even at an ultimate cost to their own welfare. The individual with a sadistic prototype personality has a reputation of being mean, malevolent, aggressive, and domineering. Often combined with various forms of paraphilia and sociopathy, these individuals derive a degree of pleasure from the suffering of others and strive to maintain dominance over those with whom they affiliate. In severe form, this drive to dominate may include acts of physical, sexual, or verbal domination and cruelty (see Holt, Meloy, & Strack, 1999). In less severe form, it includes teasing, criticism, or taunting that is expressed with the specific intent of embarrassing or humiliating other people.

The individual with a sadistic style undermines instances of communal pleasures; he or she finds no pleasure in others' joy, other than as an opportunity for personal enhancement through ruining the experience for others. Thus, the individual might revel in the opportunity to poke insults at another for characteristics displayed during uninhibited reverie. As an example, one individual derived pleasure by telling a woman he was interacting with that she "cackled" when she laughed, as if she were "having a seizure." A person with a sadistic makeup may find some degree of pleasure in another's failure and may even act in a way to ensure that failure. He or she can be bitterly competitive and revel in the joy not just of winning, but of making another lose. The winner who taunts his defeated opponent and proclaims his or her opponent's inferiority may reflect a sadistic orientation.

Although individuals with a sadistic style of personality strive for power and domination, it may be just as important to avoid being dominated or controlled. To these individuals, not being the one in control is paramount to being controlled. Thus, they perceive events in terms of opportunity for status through domination of others but are also highly aware of the potential for their own domination by others. Fear of losing can compel their competitiveness as much as the desire to win. An important characteristic of the sadistic prototype is the relative indifference to the welfare or feelings of others similar to the reproductive focus of the antisocial personality; the difference is that the individual with an antisocial style is typically more concerned with self-enhancement independent of the welfare of others, whereas for a person with a sadistic style it is the domination and exploitation of others that is gratifying. Combined features of the antisocial and the sadistic prototype personality (e.g., the person with a malevolent antisocial style) may be most associated with the predatory and violent criminal sociopath (see Hare, Cooke, & Hart, 1999).

Personality-Guided Cognitive–Behavioral Conceptualization

The sadistic orientation can be understood through consideration of an individual's self-view, view of others, and future projections (i.e., the cognitive triad). Individuals with a sadistic style view the self as under constant threat. They believe they should be in charge, a view that is reflected in their dogmatism, and they feel threatened when others take on a position of superiority. They perceive others as the source of threat and expect them to react with ill intent or resistance. Because individuals with a sadistic prototype personality believe they should be in charge, they are also attentive to opportunities to enhance themselves through domination over others. It is not surprising that others find these individuals abrasive and unpleasant. The reaction of others to such individuals no doubt reinforces their view that others are antagonistic, disobedient, and in need of a controlling influence (a pernicious view of others). Accordingly, Millon

TABLE 15.1

Structures and Functions of the Sadistic Prototype and Associated
Liabilities

Personality domain	Liability
Self-image Combative	View of life as a battle for domination
Object representations Pernicious	View of others as dangerous, hostile, threatening
Morphological organization Eruptive	Quick, aggressive reactions to possible danger
Mood and temperament Hostile	Hostile affect reflecting a ready willingness to aggress
Behavioral acts Precipitate	Impulsive, quick reactions oriented to defending against threat or jumping on opportunity
Interpersonal conduct Abrasive	Defensive, caustic demeanor that others find threatening and unpleasant.
Cognitive style Dogmatic	Narrow view of how the world should function; little insightfulness or empathy
Regulatory mechanism Isolation	Tendency to narrow and limit interactions to those that are nonthreatening or manageable

(1999) described the self-image of those with the sadistic prototype personality as *combative*.

This view creates a basic orientation to the world in which events are
sources of threat or opportunity for domination. Subsequently, the orienting
schema of the individual with a sadistic style is based on the quick assessment
of threat or opportunity and on the rapid activation of reactions necessary
to defend against threat or resistance or to take on a dominant role. With
this orientation, a rapid, eruptive, and abrasive demeanor characterized by
hostility and aggression serves the very useful purposes of defending self-
integrity and taking quick advantage of an enhancing opportunity. Indeed,
the relationship between these two outcomes is closely connected. Ever
attentive to resistance and the disobedience of others, the individual is
essentially under a constant state of threat. However, moments of domination that follow behaviors enacted to squelch resistance are felt quite
positively. Millon (1999) used the term *pernicious* to describe the object-
representation of these individuals, *abrasive* to describe their interpersonal
conduct, and *hostile* to describe their mood and temperament.

These personality attributes (see Table 15.1) illuminate how the individual processes information. Given the sadistic style, the individual's orien-

tation to the world is based on active efforts to protect the self from aversive circumstances. To the individual, the world is replete with threat from hostile entities, and it is necessary to protect the self from constant and recurrent threats, which typically come from others who are viewed as threatening (i.e., pernicious) to his or her *dogmatic* beliefs.

Regarding the individual's information-processing strategies, the orienting schema is based on alertness to threat. Subsequently, an individual with a sadistic personality style is hypersensitive to signs of threat and is very quick to respond defensively and aggressively. The nature of the various schemas activated reflects this sensitivity. This quick tendency is reflected in the individual's general orientation, described in a cognitive model by the orienting schema (Beck, 1996). Automatic thoughts reflect quick appraisals of opposition and resistance. With this quick appraisal, a more consolidated schema is activated relative to the perceived demands of the appraised situation. Included in this schema are specific core beliefs and intermediate beliefs, which contribute to specific mode reactions. The more the individual's schemas reflect the sadistic theme, the greater the probability that the individual will meet full *DSM–IV–TR* criteria for a sadistic personality disorder. However, the individual and others may feel the impact of the sadistic theme well before diagnostic criteria are met.

Pathologic Process of the Sadistic Pattern

Individuals with the sadistic personality style interpret information relative to their status among others. They react with hostile and eruptive expression implemented to establish a sense of superiority and domination over others. Although this reaction can occur in a very blatant context and result in serious violence, it may also emerge in more subtle form through passive–aggressive behaviors or subtle insult and criticism. For instance, an individual with a sadistic orientation may derive pleasure by holding up traffic while driving in his or her car. Another individual may derive pleasure by delivering clever insults to another.

Although many situations do not activate a combative posture, other situations may be marked by extreme reactivity. For instance, a college student with sadistic personality attributes had no problems in courses in which the teacher spoke with authority; however, he was known to be antagonistic in courses with female professors and with male professors who tended to be soft-spoken or hesitant. In those classes he was aggressive and confrontational in his questions; in courses with self-confident male professors, he was less aggressive and more respectful. Such individuals encounter stress when they feel that their status is being threatened or compromised. In these situations, their tendency is to become proactive and assert a position of power and authority over others. However, when they feel that their subordinate status is appropriate, they are more willing to act with respectful deference.

Not surprising, perhaps, those with a sadistic orientation are often described as possessing impulse problems associated with anger management. Although they may retreat into a depression in hopeless situations, more typically they will react with some degree of aggressiveness to establish themselves in the social hierarchy.

Axis I Vulnerabilities

Individuals with a sadistic personality style are vulnerable to a host of clinical conditions associated with the sadistic makeup. Most notably, perhaps, these conditions are associated with impulsive behaviors, such as intermittent explosive disorder. For these clients, the display of explosive and controlled anger is an effective means of eliciting compliance from others. If others worry that they might do something to elicit the explosive ire of the individual with a sadistic style, they may quickly adopt a submissive and accommodating posture relative to the individual's demands and expectations. Such a strategy is used with great effectiveness in the military, particularly among drill sergeants who are highly invested in eliciting the concerted compliance of the new recruits, who learn quickly that immediate compliance is in their best interest. A similar effect can be had on family members, employees, and others.

Those with a sadistic personality prototype may also be vulnerable to periods of anxiety and depression. Similar in many ways to the suffering expressed by the masochistic personality (described later in this chap.) as a means of managing relations, the individual with a sadistic prototype personality adds a threatening and menacing dimension that is not characteristic of the individual with a masochistic orientation. Rather than winning the investment of others through his or her own suffering, as an individual with a masochistic style would, the individual with a sadistic style elicits the compliance and control of others through the display of various physical or psychological symptoms. The individual may also be vulnerable to periods of paranoia, delusional disorder, and potentially to periods of psychosis, all of which emerge in the face of perceived threats to one's status in a social hierarchy.

Variations on the Traditional Sadistic Personality

Four subtypes of the sadistic prototype have been described (Millon, 1999; Millon & Davis, 2000). As is the case with other varieties of the primary personality prototypes, the subtypes of the sadistic prototype share basic attributes but have subtle differences in how the sadistic disposition is formed and how the individual interacts in interpersonal relationships.

The *explosive sadistic* personality style represents a subtle variation on the pure form. Individuals with this style, as the name implies, are prone to explosive fits that occur when they feel threatened or violated. As an example, the controlling father who demands obedience in his children may explode in a fit of rage when one or more of his children show signs of oppositional behavior. Such individuals have learned that through their explosive rages, they are able to derive a high degree of compliance in others. That they have learned this does not require a conscious manipulation, simply a sense of entitled compliance and a history of having been effective in compelling compliance through hostility. They may often feel entitled to the compliance, they may feel that they have been unjustly treated by another, or they may simply derive some degree of pleasure from the exaggerated expression of anger or rage. Whatever the motivation, individuals with an explosive sadistic style maintain interpersonal behaviors that others find highly unpleasant. Unless others are forced by some circumstance to remain in affiliation with these individuals, most will seek distance from them.

The *tyrannical sadistic* personality style combines features of the negativistic and paranoid patterns. Individuals with a tyrannical sadistic orientation derive greater pleasure from their domination of others than do those with the other sadistic patterns. Although oriented to protecting a fragile sense of self-integrity, they are motivated more by the pleasures they derive from brutalizing others. As an example, a tyrannical boyfriend derives a degree of pleasure from the domination of his girlfriend that is expressed by both subtle and blatant criticisms and put-downs. In other cases, these individuals may use some common cause as a means of dominating others. For instance, a football coach may rely on the pretense of "making winners" as an opportunity to express unnecessary harshness.

The *enforcing sadistic* personality style includes features of the compulsive pattern. Individuals with this sadistic style view themselves as the protectors of the cause. They maintain a sense of how things should be and strive diligently to see to it that others comply. In some circumstances this can be very adaptive. For instance, the military drill sergeant would likely not do as well in shaping soldiers if he were not somewhat sadistic in his approach. Many individuals would not experience their degree of business success if it were not for their prototypically sadistic personality. Indeed, when the cause is of concern, those with an enforcing sadistic personality may be particularly well suited. When the psychological well-being of an individual is of concern, time spent with individuals with an enforcing sadistic style may be less beneficial.

The *spineless sadistic* personality style is characterized by avoidant features. Individuals with this style feel particularly insecure and socially vulnerable and compensate with cruelty and insult. As Millon and Davis (2000) suggested, these individuals are on the outlook for scapegoats whom they can dominate as a means of creating an appearance of superiority. Feeling picked on by others, these individuals may turn their attention and wrath on weaker others as a means of compensation for the disparagements they received from others. For these individuals, clinical conditions may emerge following the retaliatory or disciplinary consequences of their abrasive behaviors.

Treatment of the Sadistic Prototype

The treatment goal with clients with a sadistic prototype personality is to decrease active efforts to defend against threats and to increase concern for the feelings and welfare of others. What should be understood in this model is that the information-processing and reactive styles described in this discussion reflect personality attributes.

Implied in these descriptions are core beliefs, intermediate beliefs, and mode reactions. Individuals with a sadistic style, reflecting a combative self-view and a view of others as pernicious, expect the world to provide constant threat of domination. These individuals are primed to attend to issues of domination and control and operate toward a central goal such as "I will not be controlled" and under an assumption that if one is not in control, then one is at risk of being controlled. Rules might include "Others should do as I say and should not order me around." These goals, assumptions, and rules compel rapid (eruptive morphological organization), aggressive (hostile mood and temperament) reactions characterized by impulsive anger and defensiveness (expressive and interpersonal behaviors) enacted to force others to adhere to the person's narrow views regarding how others should behave and perform. To maximize success, individuals with a sadistic style may constrain their world (isolation) to minimize threats to domination. This constrained world may be limited to domination over family members or coworkers, or it may extend into political realms.

For the individual with a sadistic orientation, depression takes on a different meaning than it would for a person with another personality style. Although the depression may reflect a simple clinical reaction secondary to biochemical abnormality, it more often serves the purpose of controlling others. Although this could be done intentionally, it does not require intentionality to be effective. If depression is understood in adaptive terms, as described by Gilbert (2000), it removes the person from a battle he or she cannot win. If efforts at domination fail, the individual with a sadistic prototype personality may effectively avoid being dominated by depression. Likewise, through guilt induced in others, the individual may be able to elicit compliance. Thus, depression may not be the individual's problem, per se, but rather a personality-guided (i.e., personality-mediated) solution to a threatening situation.

Of course, the clinician should not assume this to be the case in all depressed individuals with a sadistic style of personality. However, the astute clinician will look for the adaptiveness of the symptoms before making any treatment decision that might serve to perpetuate the pathology. For instance, concluding that the depression is solely a medical condition reinforces its use as an adaptive solution.

It is generally unlikely that an individual with a sadistic style would come to treatment of his or her own accord; treatment is sought as the result of involvement with another person who is presenting with aversive symptoms, probably associated in some way with the individual's sadistic pattern. Upon assessment, it may be determined that the individual is experiencing a mild to moderate depressive episode; more typically, however, an individual with a sadistic style is likely to be diagnosed with an impulse disorder. The task is to understand the depression relative to the individual's orientation (i.e., sadistic) to situational demands. The clinician might already assume that the individual's view is being challenged by the fact that he or she is in therapy. Even if the individual is there under the pretense of another individual's problem, the fact that that other person is seeking change suggests that the worldview of the individual with a sadistic pattern is being threatened.

Successful treatment of clients with a sadistic orientation is challenged by the fact that even in the absence of a specific personality disorder, and even in the face of clear clinical conditions, they may not want to admit to their own contribution to problems. Although there may be exceptions, most individuals do not readily admit to having sadistic qualities, despite the obvious expression of mean and often passive–aggressive behaviors.

When individuals with a sadistic orientation appear in a therapy office, it is typically for reasons other than their own distress; most often, it is because of someone else's distress. Consequently, investing these clients in their own improvement can be a difficult task. Similar to treating someone with the paranoid orientation, it is useful for the therapist to avoid any direct confrontation of the client's dogmatic beliefs and, rather, to provide the client with opportunities to reflect on how his or her actions are being perceived by others. Allowing the client opportunity to discuss frustrations with others often provides the chance to introduce reflection on how others might be seeing the circumstance. As the client comes to better appreciate another's perspective, the therapist can begin to address more directly the maladaptive aspects of the client's dogmatic beliefs. Once the client begins to appreciate his or her own dogmatism, discussion can turn to more adaptive ways to derive feeling of status and importance that are not burdened by the reactive resentments of those in the client's world.

It is important to note that efforts to minimize the client's desire for status among others are likely to contribute to treatment resistance. Instead, the therapist is wise to assist the individual in finding more adaptive, prosocial means for deriving enhancement. In a related sense, it is necessary to help the client to cope with feelings of threat. Using specific emotional reactions as cues, the client can consider his or her attitudes toward others and consider both the legitimacy of any perceived threat and alternatives for coping with the situation that do not include a disruptive display of hostilities. As the client comes to gain greater confidence in his or her ability to derive status among others through more prosocial behaviors, his or her need for domination through pernicious acts will decrease.

To alter the pathologic processes of clients with the sadistic personality style, it is necessary to alter the manner in which they interpret information and the ways in which they act to derive feelings of enhancement and protection. These individuals are quick to perceive threats to their sense of status and control and react to those perceived threats with eruptive and hostile displays of behavior that others find highly abrasive. Similar in many ways to those with the paranoid personality, these individuals are quick to perceive threats and to react in a dominating way, independent of any concern for the feelings or well-being of the other individuals, which frequently leads to resentment by the other people.

Behaviorally, it is necessary to modify the combative and abrasive interpersonal style of clients with a sadistic orientation. Because they have maintained a combative self-image and pernicious view of others, they are highly prone to hostile and eruptive emotional reactions. Even when they have derived a greater sense of interpersonal concern and sympathy and have begun to display greater prosocial behaviors, their reactive tendencies may persist. It may be helpful to implement various affective monitoring procedures to help the client with a sadistic style control affective reactions. Metacognitive approaches may also be helpful by informing the client of the intent of his or her affect, most notably anger, to control a situation. With greater awareness of his or her own emotional intentions, the client should be better able to control his or her affective reactions.

Conclusion: The Sadistic Prototype

Individuals with a sadistic prototype personality maintain a combative self-image and an abrasive interpersonal style. They believe that they should be in control in interpersonal affairs, and they feel threatened in situations where they are not in charge. When they are in a position of status or authority, they may be inclined to abuse their position. For instance, the coach with a sadistic style may be excessively aggressive with the players on the team. A boss with a similar orientation may rely on threat and intimidation to control employees. In disordered form, the abrasive behaviors of the individual may be abusive and dangerous. In stylistic form, the sadistic attributes may contribute to rudeness and overaggressiveness that is short of hostility.

Although in many cases the sadistic prototype personality may contribute to some degree of leadership success, it may more often contribute to problems in interpersonal relationships. In fact, it may most typically be the case that individuals with a sadistic style come to the attention of mental health professionals not because of their own distress but, rather, as the result of distress they have contributed to in others or of frustrations they have with others. For instance, the father with a sadistic personality may bring his oppositional son to therapy in hopes of regaining control over that son.

Treatment of the individual with a sadistic prototype personality is challenging because of the control that the individual sees him- or herself having to relinquish in therapy. As a result, it is important that the therapeutic relationship not be antagonistic and that the client's desire for status and authority not be too blatantly challenged. In fact, the client's desire for status may prove to be the catalyst for change. Helping the individual to derive legitimate authority by way of more sensitive and prosocial behaviors may serve to redirect the sadistic orientation in ways that are conducive to the client and beneficial to those in association with the client.

THE MASOCHISTIC PROTOTYPE

Key phrase: Rescue me
Evolutionary focus: Protection first

Individuals with a masochistic prototype personality are strongly motivated to avoid and eliminate a broad range of unpleasant and painful experiences. A defining feature of the masochistic style, however, is suffering. For these individuals, a relative degree of pleasure is derived by way of their suffering, thus explaining the reversal on the pleasure–pain polarity (Millon, 1999). They are not inactive or passive but are inclined toward more passive adaptation associated with the masochistic impairments. They are not highly aware of their own motives and impulses and tend to be deferential to others, on whom they depend for support and reassurance. The polarity balance of the masochistic prototype is illustrated in Figure 15.2.

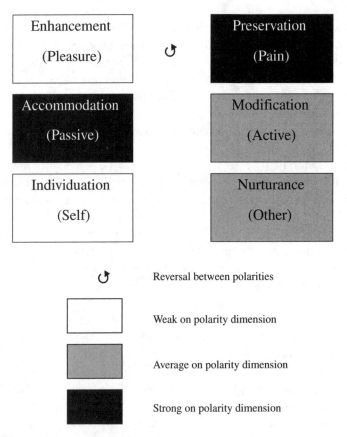

Enhancement (Pleasure)	↻	Preservation (Pain)
Accommodation (Passive)		Modification (Active)
Individuation (Self)		Nurturance (Other)

↻ Reversal between polarities

☐ Weak on polarity dimension

▨ Average on polarity dimension

■ Strong on polarity dimension

Figure 15.2. Polarity balance of the masochistic prototype. From *Personality-Guided Therapy* (p. 589), by T. Millon, 1999, New York: Guilford Press. Copyright 1999 by John Wiley & Sons, Inc. Reprinted with permission.

Personality-Guided Cognitive–Behavioral Conceptualization

The masochistic style represents a passive–accommodating personality (Millon, 1999) in which the individual disparages and subserves the self to secure the commitment and protection of others. Whereas the individual with a sadistic style strives for domination, the individual with a masochistic style strives for rescue, which requires that one be in need of rescue. Similar in many ways to those with dependent, depressive, and negativistic personalities, individuals with a masochistic style differ in that rather than seeing themselves as inept, worthless, or discontented, they see themselves as *undeserving* of special or even fair and appropriate treatment from others. They lack confidence (*diffident* cognitive style) in their ability to meet life challenges and defer (interpersonal conduct) to others to provide protection and validation. Thus, to win and maintain affiliations and intimacies, rather than being submissive and accommodating, defenseless, or antagonistic, they create crises and desperations that enlist others in their suffering.

Why he or she views him- or herself as undeserving is unique to the individual. One may perceive the self as needing punishment for past wrongs, whereas another may feel undeserving because of past privileges. Whatever the motivation for the individual, the self-criticism and self-disparagement that are common serve as a stylistic means (i.e., modus vivendi) for securing protective and validating connections with others. Furthermore, although the individual with a dependent orientation acquiesces to the desires of others, he or she is not necessarily self-disparaging. To this individual, as long as others are valuing his or her dependency, he or she can function reasonably well. It is when the dependent relationship is threatened that the individual suffers. For the individual with a masochistic orientation, the relationship with others is based in very large part on his or her suffering; thus, suffering is more typical. Also unlike the individual with a dependent style, the person with a masochistic style does not view the self as having any redeeming value that would appeal to others. Such a view stems from the individual's history of relationships in which his or her abilities and connections with others were discredited. Thus, the individual has learned to put him- or herself in positions where he or she needed to be rescued. Dreikurs described a pattern of behavior he called the "display of inadequacy" (see Dreikurs & Soltz, 1964). From this display, which may be exaggerated (*exaggerated* regulatory mechanism), the individual is able to derive relief from unpleasant and undesirable activities and is able to solicit the reassurance, assistance, and nurturance of others. Unfortunately for such individuals, the nature of their relationship with others is defined by their suffering, and they do not develop adaptive skills necessary for meeting critical life challenges. It is not surprising that Millon (1999) described the typical mood of the individual with a masochistic style as *dysphoric*.

Like the other personality prototypes, a masochistic prototype describes a pattern of behavior that has some benefit to the individual. Problems occur when those attributes become too specific and too extreme. For instance, selflessness and a willingness to sacrifice personal benefits and comforts for a greater good are socially noble and revered qualities. When taken to an extreme, however, selfless sacrifice to secure the validation and investment of others is detrimental. Those with the masochistic personality style create their own suffering and do little to improve their circumstance in positive ways.

Similar to the sadistic prototype, the masochist style of personality displays a reversal on the pleasure–pain polarity. Individuals with a masochistic orientation derive a sense of pleasure from their own experience of misery and react to pleasurable events as if they were threats to their status with others. When things are going well, these individuals may fear the loss of relationships and thus are compelled to minimize the pleasure to maintain the investment of others in their suffering. For those with the masochistic style rather than personality disorder, masochism may be defined by less extreme displays of suffering or by less frequent reliance on such methods. For these individuals, the experience of pleasure does not necessarily compel an undercutting of the positive experience, but such behaviors may define the typical response during times of stress or when relationships are threatened or compromised by other circumstances.

Over the years individuals with a masochistic prototype personality have come to define themselves through their relationships with others and have secured and maintained relationships through their suffering. In a sense, they have come to believe that were they not suffering, others would not be interested in or likely to invest in them. Thus, it is important that they suffer. Subsequently, they are at times very active in promoting their own suffering or, alternatively, passive as a means of receiving pain. They are highly focused on the availability, intentions, and actions of others, which is necessary to maintain the investment of those others in their suffering.

In extreme form, the individual with a masochistic style places the self in compromising positions that threaten psychological integrity and physical health and safety. For instance, the individual may put him- or herself in extreme financial crisis and potentially a health crisis by repeatedly quitting jobs to fulfill another's wants. In another extreme case, an individual may antagonize another to promote a violent confrontation to reduce tension and to promote the calm that follows the tension and conflict. Although this is a very adaptive strategy on one hand, in more ultimate or optimal terms it is very dangerous and not without potential alternatives.

In less extreme form, the masochistic style may be exemplified in what may appear initially as selfless acts of kindness. For instance, the individual who donates large sums of money to a worthwhile charity may appear noble on the surface, but that nobility is tainted when the financial crisis he or she has created leads to needy clinginess on intimate others. Similarly, one may make sacrifices to assist another and then rely on the consequences of one's sacrifice to enlist the support of the person the individual assisted. In this classic case of martyrdom, one maintains the pleasure of affiliation and validation by creating one's own suffering.

The self-image of these clients is that they are undeserving of reasonable treatment by others. Their view is that others are stronger and more capable and thus are sources of protection and nurturance; however, they are also not immediately available or naturally inclined to provide care and protection. Thus, it is necessary that they keep others invested and engaged. The personality attributes of the masochistic prototype and the liabilities of individuals with this style are summarized in Table 15.2.

TABLE 15.2
Structures and Functions of the Masochistic Prototype
and Associated Liabilities

Personality domain	Liability
Self-image Undeserving	View of the self as deserving of shame and debasement; attentional focus on own worst qualities and minimization of positive attributes
Object representations Discredited	Past history of failed relationships; tendency to look at the worst aspects of past relationships and to maintain expectations of future failures brought about by personal shortcomings
Morphological organization Inverted	Inversion of pleasure and pain; belief that to be accepted or loved, one must suffer; tendency to undermine positive experiences and put the self in a compromising or debased position
Mood and temperament Dysphoric	Disposition to feel anguish and torment; dysphoric mood that "serves to glorify their ultimate state of misery, providing proof of the fundamental nobility of their suffering" (Millon, 1999, p. 596)
Behavioral acts Abstinent	Absence of pleasure seeking; maintenance of the self in a position of sacrifice and suffering
Interpersonal conduct Deferential	Deference to the will of others in order to secure their commitment, support, and protection; use of personal suffering as a means of interpersonal connection
Cognitive style Diffident	Pessimism and self-effacement; interpretation of events relative to the negative impact on the self and relative to one's own failing and incapacities
Regulatory mechanism Exaggerated	Exaggeration of personal failures and shortcomings as a means of enlisting the support and protection of others

Pathologic Process of the Masochistic Pattern

To individuals with a masochistic prototype personality, information is interpreted relative to its validation of their own disparate circumstance. Stress may be most typically encountered when a relationship is threatened. However, because relationship threats are often constant, the need for minor and major crisis situations is ever present. Because these individuals define themselves relative to their relationships and depend on stress as a means of securing affiliations, stress is a ubiquitous experience manifested in near-unlimited varieties. Indeed, it is through their stressful disparagement that they secure, maintain, and separate from relationships. For these individuals, anything that signifies suffering may be manifested as a clinical condition.

The masochistic personality is uniquely associated with such conditions as somatization, factitious disorder, anxiety, depression, eating disorders, and potentially malingering (see Elliot, 1987). Indeed, where to draw the line between genuine psychological disorder, factitious disorder, and malingering can be quite difficult, particularly with this group of clients.

Axis I Vulnerabilities

Those with a masochistic personality style are vulnerable to a host of clinical conditions. Indeed, given their reliance on personal suffering, there are few limits on what might occur to demonstrate their suffering. For those with a masochistic personality style, there may be no rules or patterns. Their objective, given their lack of self-confidence, is to keep others invested, yet on the basis of past failures, they do not see themselves as able to maintain that investment in positive, active, and independent fashion. Rather, they maintain the investment of others through their suffering, which may take on numerous forms.

In an early description of individuals with the masochistic style of personality, Elliot (1987) discussed their common presentation of somatic complaints, factitious symptoms, eating disorders, substance abuse, and other conditions. More recently, masochism was linked with the controversial medical condition known as fibromyalgia (Mcallister, 2000). To be sure, an ambiguous medical condition that cannot be treated with specific certainty would prove extremely adaptive to one oriented to keeping others invested through one's own suffering. Elsewhere, Gendrault (2000) connected masochistic tendencies with chronic pain symptoms. Given the uncertainty of their relationships with others, it is not surprising to find that those with a masochistic personality struggle with anxiety that is actively expressed or suffer from depression. However, in the face of depression, they may be less inclined to retreat into a depressed period of withdrawal, being more inclined to express the anguish of depression as a means of managing their relationship with others. Eating disorders may also provide a unique means for being so incapacitated by symptoms that the individuals are unable to meet basic life responsibilities and must then turn to others for assistance.

With individuals with a masochistic orientation, the potential for malingering is high. However, recourse to general somatic suffering, factitious disorder, or malingering may be incidental to the superordinate masochistic makeup. Indeed, attention to the masochistic features may minimize the need to differentiate between the various conditions, at least beyond the need to respond to the immediacy of the symptoms, most notably in the case of a factitious condition.

Variations on the Traditional Masochistic Personality

Millon and Davis (2000; Millon, 1999) described four variations on the masochistic prototype demonstrating unique differences in the ways that the masochistic style is represented.

The *self-undoing masochistic* personality style includes qualities of the dependent personality. As Millon and Davis (2000) described, individuals with this style experience "victory through defeat." In the face of impending victory, they may undermine themselves to ensure defeat. Success may create for these individuals external expectations and contingencies that they do not feel prepared to face or that they simply do not want to face. For instance, through the display of competence in financial matters, the individual with a self-undoing masochistic personality may be expected to be more responsible for personal resources, such as staying within a specific budget or balancing his or her own checkbook. Through displayed incompetence in financial affairs, the individual can enjoy the benefits of inadequacy. However, he or she cannot simply claim to be inadequate but must convince others of that inadequacy, which typically requires failure and crisis.

The *possessive masochistic* personality style includes features of the negativistic pattern. Through their constant arrangement of negative outcomes, individuals with this style are able to retain, up to a point, the commitment of others. Their quest is to retain through manipulative efforts the obligation of others to protect or provide for them. They become efficient in putting themselves in a mistreated role that they can then exploit for their benefit. For instance, a possessive spouse may, through accusation of impropriety of a mate, put that mate in the position of needing to prove his or her devotion. Using his or her own suffering, which may or may not be genuine, the individual is able to leverage some degree of control in a relationship.

The *oppressed masochistic* personality style includes features of the depressive personality. Individuals with this style create their own misery and use it to induce guilt and sympathy in those who might then provide care and protection. This may best represent the theme of martyrdom. They wallow in their own misfortunes and use them as a means of soliciting support and assistance from others. Through their behaviors, they are able to very effectively avoid unwanted responsibilities and—at least until the other wearies of their behavior—are able to control the behaviors and expectations of others. Somatic complaints may be particularly common among this group of clients.

The *virtuous masochistic* personality style demonstrates evidence of histrionic features. Individuals with this masochistic style proudly advertise their selflessness and sacrifice and expect admiration and validation through their sacrifices. Without the advertisement, their behaviors may border on saintliness and could potentially be overlooked. Because their intent is to secure the commitment and validation of others through their sacrifice, they must ensure that others are aware of their sacrifice and suffering. With the histrionic advertisement, the virtue of their acts is lost in self-serving benefit.

Treatment of the Masochistic Prototype

Altering the pathologic process of the masochistic style requires close attention to the individual's lack of confidence and inability to function without the strength and support of a stronger other. Often these individuals are more capable than they think, yet they do not express their abilities as a function of their learned tendency to defer to others or simply as a function of their desire to not engage in any activity they find unpleasant or threatening. It is helpful with these clients to have them consider the alternatives to remaining in a defenseless and helpless position. It is often quickly apparent that their dependency on others exposes them to the exploitation and unreliable mercy of others.

Unfortunately, this client population has various somatic-type complaints that either are real in a medical sense or feel real enough to the client that they must be accommodated. As a result, clients with a masochistic prototype personality may be very hesitant to take on activities that may be associated with a real or perceived exaggeration of their symptoms. As an example, a client with the diagnosis of fibromyalgia was very hesitant to take on new and independent activities for fear of the fatigue that might occur afterwards. The therapist noted that her daily shopping trips did not seem to affect her symptoms. She responded that she had figured out how to pace herself in her shopping to avoid worsening of her symptoms. The therapist further suggested that she might curtail some of her shopping to do these other activities, thereby maintaining a similar pace and amount of activity. It is interesting to note that the therapeutic value the client felt she received from her shopping was not something that she wanted to sacrifice. When asked if she would rather continue suffering from her fibromyalgia or give up the extent of her shopping, she recanted and offered to curtail her shopping some.

It is important that individuals with a masochistic orientation experience relatively quick success in therapy to see the advantage of treatment. If therapy appears too strenuous or otherwise unpleasant, they may be quick to abandon any gains in therapy to retreat to the relative comforts of incapacitation brought about by somatic symptoms or other complaints.

Fortunately, the therapeutic relationship can be a powerful tool in maintaining these clients' commitment to treatment. Perceiving the therapist as a caring, compassionate, and encouraging individual will provide motivation to these clients to remain in therapy. Indeed, if the therapist appears to be indifferent, insensitive, or disbelieving of their symptoms, they will not likely remain in therapy or will set out to prove to the therapist their dismal state of existence.

Cognitively, it is important that clients with a masochistic personality style challenge their own sense of incompetence and the undeservingness that compels their pessimistic projections and interpersonal deference. Without committing them to any significant behavioral changes, the therapist can consider their assets and liabilities with the intent of determining, as far as physical limitation may allow, ways to minimize the impact of perceived liabilities. Similar to treatment of those with the dependent personality, it is important not to challenge too soon their interpersonal dependencies but, rather, to allow them to remain in the safety and comfort of those dependencies while treatment evolves.

Through monitoring assignments, the clients can record ongoing activities and their reactions to events. Most notably, they can be encouraged to consider their own reactions in light of the tendency many of these individuals have to overexaggerate the severity of the threat and the severity of their own affective reactions. It is useful to have them record the intensity of their initial reaction and then to later reconsider the circumstance and their reaction from a more objective perspective. Through in-session discussion, these clients can reconsider their reaction and gradually become more objective and less reactionary given situational events. Their morphological organization style, described by Millon (1999) as *inverted,* results in the tendency for these clients to put themselves in an inferior position and to emphasize risks and personal shortcomings. Through monitoring and subsequent discussion, these clients should be able to reduce their tendency to focus on the negative and to think more positively about their ability to bring about a positive outcome.

Behaviorally, it is necessary for clients with a masochistic style to take a more proactive stance to bringing about positive, enhancing outcomes. To begin, they can consider activities that they have recently or in the past enjoyed. Given the nature of the masochistic style, they will likely come up with numerous reasons for why they cannot engage in a pleasurable activity; therefore, it is necessary to provide incentives and to introduce activities at a very gradual pace, striking a balance between therapeutic pressure and support.

Individuals with a masochistic prototype personality may benefit from a metaemotional focus in which the adaptive role of anxiety and depression are described. By understanding that their anxiety represents concern with potential threats and their depression a desire to retreat from an activity, when these emotions occur, which is inevitable, they will be better prepared to counter the tendencies compelled by these emotions and be in a position to challenge the cognitions behind the feelings.

Conclusion: The Masochistic Prototype

Individuals with a masochistic orientation are characterized by an undeserving self-image, are deferential to others, and rely on personal failing and incapacities as a means of enlisting stronger others. Because they view themselves in undeserving terms, they do not believe that others would be invested in them for any reason other than their need. As a result, these individuals are particularly vulnerable to a variety of physical and psychological symptoms that serve to keep others invested and provide escape from activities they feel unprepared or unwilling to manage. These individuals are particularly vulnerable to somatic conditions and are perhaps more likely to display symptoms of a factitious condition than are those with other personality prototypes. Indeed, the benefits of medical impairment are particularly strong for this population of individuals. In addition, their helpless and undeserving sense of self and tendency toward exaggeration contribute to their experience of anxiety, helplessness, and depression.

Clients with the masochistic personality are often reluctant to commit to the task of therapy. To be sure, treatment can be tremendously threatening to these individuals because it requires engagement in activities for which they feel poorly suited. Treatment requires patience and reassurance in helping these clients to develop a greater sense of self-reliance and self-confidence. Careful attention to self-defeating assumptions through guided discovery and the teaching of adaptive skills necessary for efficient functioning are critical with this population.

APPENDIX A:
THE MILLON CLINICAL
MULTIAXIAL INVENTORY

The Millon Clinical Multiaxial Inventory (MCMI) was initially constructed in the early 1970s as an outgrowth of the influential 1969 publication *Modern Psychopathology* (Millon, 1969). The intent was to construct an inventory that would complement the theoretical and practical constructs presented in the 1969 publication. After 7 years of work, relying on criterion keying test construction methodology, the first MCMI was published in 1977 (Millon, 1977). Reflecting refinements in the test and changes in the *Diagnostic and Statistical Manual of Mental Disorders* (3rd ed., rev.; DSM–III–R; American Psychiatric Association, 1987), specifically the inclusion of the self-defeating and sadistic personality disorders, the test was expanded and published as the MCMI–II in 1987 (Millon, 1987a). Further refinements were made, along with adjustments to accommodate the *DSM–IV* (American Psychiatric Association, 1994), and the MCMI–III, the most current version, was published in 1994 (Millon, Millon, & Davis, 1994). The history, theory, and validation of the MCMI were summarized by Millon and Millon (1997).

The MCMI–III was developed to aid clinicians in their assessment and conceptualization of patients. Tied to the *DSM–IV,* the MCMI–III provides data that allow consideration of presently accepted standards of diagnosis while being specifically consistent with the personology model described by Millon and his associates, which is summarized in chapter 2 of the current volume. Data obtained from the MCMI–III provide indexes of administration validity (modifying indexes); indexes of personality prototype patterns, separated into clinical personality patterns and severe personality pathology (i.e., schizotypal, borderline, and paranoid patterns), and indexes of clinical syndromes and severe syndromes (i.e., thought disorder, major depression, and delusional disorder).

The advantage of the MCMI–III relates primarily to the theoretical grounding of the inventory in the personology model. The inventory allows clinicians to hypothesize about a client's personality domains and to conceptualize the identified Axis I conditions relative to Axis II patterns. In this way, the clinical conditions can be conceptualized as part of the individual's overall orchestration of thoughts, feelings, and behaviors relative to existential demands and not simply as random or unrelated clinical outcomes. As a result, the clinician is able to introduce treatment strategies that are not only best suited to the needs of the individual client, but also reflective of established patterns of diagnosis (see Retzlaff, 1997).

The Millon Personality Diagnostic Checklist (MPDC), published in 1987 (Millon, 1987b), and the Millon Index of Personality Styles (MIPS), published in 1994 (Millon, 1990; Millon, Weiss, Millon, & Davis, 1994), provide further elaboration on the evolutionary theme of the personology model.

The MPDC, initially constructed to assist in the development of the MCMI (Tringone, 1997), provides client assessment in five of the eight domains described in the personology model: expressive acts, interpersonal conduct, cognitive style, self-image, and mood or temperament (Millon, 1999). This inventory is useful as a rapid measure of personality attributes that the clinician can use in conceptualization and treatment planning.

The MIPS, the newest of the Millon instruments (see Weiss, 1997), provides data relative to the client's position on each of the imperative polarities (Millon et al., 1994). This inventory can be used to assess a client's motivating aims (i.e., pleasure vs. pain, active vs. passive, self vs. others), cognitive style, and style of interpersonal behaviors. Conceptually, this inventory allows the clinician to assess the client's degree of distinction on the relative polarities and bipolarities and thereby the relative degree of change necessary for the establishment of polarity balance. In addition, the MIPS provides indexes of the client's style of perceiving and interpreting information and style of interpersonal engagement. The usefulness of this information is reflected in its potential to help clinicians fine-tune treatment, take advantage of personal assets, and avoid the pitfalls of personality-mediated liabilities.

APPENDIX B: FORMAT FOR CASE CONCEPTUALIZATION AND TREATMENT PLAN

The following format for doing a personality-guided cognitive–behavioral conceptualization and treatment plan is adapted from Persons, Davidson, and Tompkins's (2001) model for cognitive–behavioral therapy with patients with depression. Headings are bolded and followed by a brief description of the information covered in that section. Appendix C provides an example of the use of the format with a specific client.

Personality-Guided Cognitive–Behavioral Case Conceptualization and Treatment Plan

Client's name: **Date:**

Date of birth: **Age:**

Identifying information:

Relevant personal and demographic information, including education, employment, family status, and living arrangements

Presenting problem:

Brief description of the problem as the client perceives it; may include a list of current problems experienced by the client

Axis I consideration:

Description of clinician's Axis I impressions

   Assessment measures:

   Examples of measures to assess Axis I conditions:

   Beck Depression Inventory–II (Beck, Steer, & Brown, 1996)

   State–Trait Anxiety (Spielberger, 1983)

Axis II consideration:

Description of clinician's Axis II impressions

Assessment measures:

Examples of measures to assess personality factors:

MCMI–III

MPDC

MIPS

Clinical level of pathology:

Nature of the condition (i.e., simple clinical reaction, complex clinical syndrome, personality disorder)

Schemas:

Assessment measures:

Early Maladaptive Schema Questionnaire (Young, Klosko, & Weishaar, 2003)

Core beliefs:

Self:

Others:

World:

Future:

Precipitating factors:

Factors contributing to the onset of the current episode; typically include factors that would be recorded on Axis IV of the *DSM* system

Activating situations:

Immediate activating events; current factors that contribute to an aversive reaction

Developmental considerations:

Childhood experience relevant to the clinical outcome

Diagnosis:

Axis I:

Axis II:

Axis III:

Axis IV:

Axis V:

Working summary:

Flexible, conceptual summary useful to guiding treatment decisions

Treatment plan:

Goals:

Objectives of treatment relative to imperative balances

Modality:

Intervention method (e.g., behavioral, cognitive)

Interventions:

Specific treatment strategies for addressing mode components

Relevant assets and liabilities (not mentioned in problem list):

Assets:

Factors contributing to resiliency and positive coping; may include social supports, skills, resources, financial resources

Liabilities:

Factors currently exacerbating the condition or potentially contributing to a worsening situation; may include medical conditions that would be recorded on Axis III of the *DSM* multiaxial system; such factors as limited intellectual, financial, or social resources; and personal characteristics such as hyperloquaciousness, attention deficit, or other attributes thought to be noteworthy

Adjunctive therapies:

Other strategies useful to enhancing the treatment outcomes; may include pharmacotherapy, family therapy, occupational therapy

Outcome tracking measures:

Specific methods for assessing treatment effectiveness

APPENDIX C:
SAMPLE CLIENT CASE
CONCEPTUALIZATION
AND TREATMENT PLAN

Personality-Guided Cognitive–Behavioral Case
Conceptualization and Treatment Plan

Client's Name: Mark Dotson   **Date:** December 29, 2004

Date of birth: 07/24/1959   **Age:** 44

Identifying information:

This 44-year-old man is married and the father of two children, a son age 20 and a daughter age 16. He has been married for 22 years. He lives with his wife and children. He is a college graduate and is currently employed as a sales manager for an international corporation.

Presenting problems:

1. Depression (BDI[a] = 20). Loneliness and isolation. He reports feelings of emptiness and discontent with life. Depressive symptoms have not compromised his capacity to meet his family or employment responsibilities.
2. Poor relationship with wife. Wife is described as self-centered and obsessed with her parents. There is no physical or emotional intimacy in the relationship. He is certain that his wife will not change. He is not willing to consider divorce seriously because of the financial constraints.
3. His daughter has a significant disability associated with a childhood automobile accident.
4. His son recently produced a child out of wedlock and is refusing responsibility.
5. He has been involved in an extensive extramarital relationship. She ended the physical aspect of the relationship because of the

317

negative emotions it elicited in him and the resentment those emotions engendered in her.

6. His relationship with his mother and stepfather is a source of frustration.

Axis I consideration:

Dysthymia and Generalized anxiety disorder

Axis II consideration:

MCMI–III assessment:

Depressive personality disorder

Schizoid personality disorder with self-defeating and avoidant personality traits

MIPS assessment:

Motivating aims:

Preserving

Accommodating

Individuating

Cognitive style:

Introversing

Feeling orientation

Interpersonal behaviors:

Retiring

Conforming

Yielding

Complaining

Clinical level of pathology:

Personality disorder with Axis I conditions

Schemas:

EMS[b]: Emotional deprivation, defectiveness, self-sacrifice, emotional inhibition

Core beliefs:

> **Self:** "I do not receive the love I need." "I am inferior."
>
> **Others:** "Others demand too much and give too little."
>
> **World:** "The world is not OK."
>
> **Future:** "The future could be better, if people would change."

Precipitating factors:

> Chronic condition with no specific precipitating factor; wife's active indifference and unresponsiveness perpetuate condition; ongoing relationship is unpredictable

Activating situations:

> Perceived indifference by others from whom he desires more; demands from close others without reciprocation

Developmental considerations:

> Only child born to young mother and older father; father left soon after his birth as the result of mother's infidelity; mother self-centered and demanding; mother married cold ("mean and psychotic") and distant stepfather; emotionally neglected in childhood; lack of effectual adult role models; absence of socializing peer relationships

Diagnosis:

> **Axis I:** Dysthymia (300.40)
> Generalized anxiety disorder (300.02)
>
> **Axis II:** Depressive personality disorder (301.90)
> Schizoid personality disorder (301.20) with self-defeating and avoidant personality traits
>
> **Axis III:** No diagnosis. No significant medical history.
>
> **Axis IV:** Problem related to social environment.
> Marital dissatisfaction. Family problems. Loneliness.
>
> **Axis V:** 55

Working summary:

> This client struggles with chronic feelings of loneliness and isolation. He is dependent on others for emotional validation, but in his

environment such validation is not forthcoming. As the result of his early childhood experiences, he is not well skilled in interpersonal give and take. He is not likely to know when his feelings are in fact being validated, as he relies on his emotional cues for evidence of satisfaction, but he is continually feeling underappreciated. He vacillates between self-blame and externalizing the source of his problems. He has an extensive history of extending himself and his resources to others in the hopes of gaining reciprocation. This strategy works well in his employment, as he is able to elicit validation through comments and positive evaluation, yet the strategy fails in his intimate relationships because the people he relies on for validation are not forthcoming—certainly not to a level that would assure him of their love and commitment. He restrains his emotional expression and relies on his assessment of objective means for eliciting intimacy. He equates emotional expressiveness with weakness.

Treatment plan:

Goals:

1. Decrease pain avoidance.
2. Confront wife and act on personal desires independent of her reactions.
3. Increase pleasurable activities.
4. Find partner for desired activities.
5. Increase active adaptation. Take more personal initiative.
6. Increase sense of worth and efficacy.
7. Promote optimistic outlook.
8. Increase intimate relationships with close others.
9. Increase social affiliations.
10. Decrease emotional investment and self-sacrifice in nonreciprocating relationships.
11. Resolve ambivalence toward girlfriend and wife.
12. Increase encouragement of children's independence.

Mode: Personality-guided cognitive–behavioral intervention

Frequency: Weekly

Interventions:

1. Assessment of self-statement
2. Cognitive intervention aimed at decreasing negative self-statements

3. Assessment of daily activities
4. Techniques to increase positive activities
5. Assistance in resolving marital ambivalence

Adjunctive therapies:

Pharmacological intervention for treatment of depression and anxiety

Relevant assets and liabilities:

Assets:

Stable employment and salary

High motivation for treatment

Liabilities:

Financial factors associated with marital relationship

Real nature of son's and daughter's situation

Compulsive nature, causing hesitation and overanalysis

Tracking measures:

Weekly BDI[a]

Weekly STAI–Trait[c]

---

[a] Beck Depression Inventory–II (Beck, Steer, & Brown, 1996)
[b] Early Maladaptive Schema Questionnaire (Young, Klosko, & Weishaar, 2003).
[c] State–Trait Anxiety (Spielberger, 1983)

REFERENCES

Adler, A. (1956). *The individual psychology of Alfred Adler* (H. L. Ansbacher & R. R. Ansbacher, Eds.). New York: Basic Books.

Adler, A. (1979). *What life should mean to you.* London: Unwin Books. (Original work published 1932)

Akhavan, S. (2001). Comorbidity of hopelessness depression with borderline and dependent personality disorders: Inferential, coping, and anger expression styles as vulnerability factors [Abstract]. *Dissertation Abstracts International: Section B: The Sciences & Engineering, 61,* 6694.

Akiskal, H. S., Azorin, J. M., & Hantouche, E. G. (2003). Proposed multidimensional structure of mania: Beyond the euphoric–dysphoric dichotomy. *Journal of Affective Disorders, 73,* 7–18.

American Psychiatric Association. (1987). *Diagnostic and statistical manual of mental disorders* (3rd ed., rev.). Washington, DC: Author.

American Psychiatric Association. (1994). *Diagnostic and statistical manual of mental disorders* (4th ed.). Washington, DC: Author.

American Psychiatric Association. (2000). *Diagnostic and statistical manual of mental disorders* (4th ed., text rev.). Washington, DC: Author.

Anderluh, M. B., Tchanturia, K., Rabe-Hesketh, S., & Treasure, J. (2003). Childhood obsessive–compulsive personality traits in adult women with eating disorders: Defining a broader eating disorder phenotype. *American Journal of Psychiatry, 160,* 242–247.

Arlow, J. A. (1953). Masturbation and symptom formation. *Journal of the American Psychoanalytic Association, 1,* 45–58.

Arsenio, W. F., & Lemerise, E. A. (2001). Varieties of childhood bullying: Values, emotion processes, and social competence. *Social Development, 10,* 59–73.

Baker, C. A., & Morrison, A. P. (1998). Cognitive processes in auditory hallucinations: Attributional biases and metacognition. *Psychological Medicine, 28,* 1199–1208.

Barlow, D. H. (2000). Unraveling the mysteries of anxiety and its disorders from the perspective of emotion therapy. *American Psychologist, 55*(1), 1247–1263.

Beck, A. T. (1963). Thinking and depression. *Archives of General Psychiatry, 9,* 324–333.

Beck, A. T. (1967). *Depression: Clinical, experimental, and theoretical aspects.* New York: Harper & Row.

Beck, A. T. (1973). *The diagnosis and management of depression.* Philadelphia: University of Pennsylvania Press.

Beck, A. T. (1976). *Cognitive therapy and the emotional disorders.* New York: International Universities Press.

Beck, A. T. (1996). Beyond belief: A theory of modes, personality, and psychopathology. In P. M. Salkovskis (Ed.), *Frontiers of cognitive therapy* (pp. 1–25). New York: Guilford Press.

Beck, A. T., & Emery, G. (with Greenberg, R. L.). (1985). *Anxiety disorders and phobias: A cognitive perspective.* New York: Basic Books.

Beck, A. T., Freeman, A., & Associates. (1990). *Cognitive therapy of personality disorders.* New York: Guilford Press.

Beck, A. T., Newman, C. F., & Liese, B. S. (1993). *Cognitive therapy of substance abuse.* New York: Guilford Press.

Beck, A. T., Rush, J., Shaw, B., & Emery, G. (1979). *Cognitive therapy of depression.* New York: Guilford Press.

Beck, A. T., Steer, R. A., & Brown, G. K. (1996). Beck Depression Inventory— II manual. San Antonio, TX: The Psychological Corporation.

Beck, A. T., & Weishaar, M. E. (2000). Cognitive therapy. In R. J. Corsini & D. Wedding (Eds.), *Current psychotherapies* (6th ed., pp. 241–272). Itasca, IL: F. E. Peacock.

Bermanzohn, P. C., Arlow, P. B., Albert, C., & Siris, S. G. (1999). Relationship of panic attacks to paranoia. *American Journal of Psychiatry, 156,* 1469.

Bernstein, A. (2001). Problems in treating paranoia: A case illustration. *Modern Psychoanalysis, 26,* 237–247.

Blackburn, R., & Lee-Evans, J. M. (1985). Reactions of primary and secondary psychopaths to anger-evoking situations. *British Journal of Clinical Psychology, 24,* 93–100.

Bodner, E., & Mikulincer, M. (1998). Learned helplessness and the occurrence of depressive-like and paranoid-like responses: The role of attentional focus. *Journal of Personality & Social Psychology, 74,* 1010–1023.

Bohus, M., Limberger, M., Ebner, U., Glocker, F. X., Schwarz, M., & Lieb, K. (2000). Pain perception during self-reported distress and calmness in patients with borderline personality disorder and self-mutilating behavior. *Psychiatry Research, 95,* 251–260.

Bornstein, R. F. (1995). Comorbidity of dependent personality disorder and other psychological disorders: An integrative review. *Journal of Personality Disorders, 9,* 286–303.

Bothwell, R., & Scott, J. (1997). The influence of cognitive variables on recovery in depressed inpatients. *Journal of Affective Disorders, 43,* 207–212.

Brooks, R. B., Baltazar, P. L., McDowell, D. E., Munjack, D. J., & Bruns, J. R. (1991). Personality disorders co-occurring with panic disorder with agoraphobia. *Journal of Personality Disorders, 5,* 328–336.

Brown, G. W. (2000). Emotion and clinical depression: An environmental view. In M. Lewis & J. M. Haviland-Jones (Eds.), *Handbook of Emotions* (2nd ed., pp. 75–90). New York: Guilford Press.

Brown, E. J., Heimberg, R. G., & Juster, H. R. (1995). Social phobia subtype and avoidant personality disorder: Effect on severity of social phobia, impairment, and outcome of cognitive behavioral treatment. *Behavior Therapy, 26,* 467–486.

Candel, I., Merckelbach, H., & Kuijpers, M. (2003). Dissociative experiences are related to commissions in emotional memory. *Behaviour Research & Therapy, 41,* 719–725.

Carpiniello, B., Lai, G., Pariante, C. M., Carta, M. G., & Rudas, N. (1997). Symptoms, standards of living and subjective quality of life: A comparative study of schizophrenic and depressed out-patients. *Acta Psychiatrica Scandinavica, 96,* 235–241.

Chiesa, M. (1996). Paranoid transference as resistance to progress. *Psychoanalytic Psychotherapy, 10,* 221–231.

Cicchetti, D., & Cohen, D. J. (1995). Perspectives on developmental psychopathology. In D. Cicchetti & D. J. Cohen (Eds.), *Developmental psychopathology: Vol. 1. Theory and methods* (pp. 3–20). New York: Wiley.

Coon, D. W. (1994). Cognitive–behavioral interventions with avoidant personality: A single case study. *Journal of Cognitive Psychotherapy, 8,* 243–253.

Cosmides, L., & Tooby, J. (1995). From evolution to adaptations to behavior: Toward an integrated evolutionary psychology. In R. Wong (Ed.), *Biological perspectives on motivated activities* (pp. 11–74). Norwood, NJ: Ablex.

Cosmides, L., & Tooby, J. (2000). Evolutionary psychology and the emotions. In M. Lewis & J. M. Haviland-Jones (Eds.), *Handbook of emotions* (2nd ed., pp. 91–115). New York: Guilford Press.

Dreikurs, R., & Soltz, V. (1964). *Children: The challenge.* New York: Duell, Sloan, & Pearce.

Dumont, F., & Lecomte, C. (1987). Inferential processes in clinical work: Inquiry into logical errors that affect diagnostic judgments. *Professional Psychology: Research & Practice, 18,* 433–438.

Durbin, D. L., Darling, N., Steinberg, L., & Brown, B. (1993). Parenting style and peer group membership among European-American adolescents. *Journal of Research on Adolescence, 3,* 87–100.

Dyck, I. R., Phillips, K. A., Warshaw, M. G., Dolan, R. T., Shea, M. T., Stout, R., et al. (2001). Patterns of personality pathology in patients with generalized anxiety disorder, panic disorder with and without agoraphobia, and social phobia. *Journal of Personality Disorders, 15,* 60–71.

Ellason, J. W., Ross, C. A., & Fuchs, D. L. (1995). Assessment of dissociative identity disorder with the Millon Clinical Multiaxial Inventory—II. *Psychological Reports, 76,* 895–905.

Ellason, J. W., Ross, C. A., & Fuchs, D. L. (1996). Lifetime Axis I and II comorbidity and childhood trauma history in dissociative identity disorder. *Psychiatry: Interpersonal & Biological Processes, 59,* 255–266.

Elliot, R. L. (1987). The masochistic patient in consultation–liaison psychiatry. *General Hospital Psychiatry, 9,* 241–250.

Ellis, A. (1973). *Humanistic psychotherapy: The rational–emotive approach*. New York: McGraw-Hill.

Ellis, A. (1988). *How to stubbornly refuse to make yourself miserable about anything— Yes, anything!* Secaucus, NJ: Lyle Stuart.

Follette, V. M., Ruzek, J. I., & Abueg, F. R. (2001). *Cognitive–behavioral therapies for trauma*. New York: Guilford Press.

Fossati, A., Maffei, C., Bagnato, M., Donati, D., Donini, M., Fiorilli, M., et al. (2000). A psychometric study of DSM–IV passive–aggressive (negativistic) personality disorder criteria. *Journal of Personality Disorders, 41,* 72–83.

Freeman, A., Pretzer, J., Fleming, B., & Simon, K. (1990). *Clinical applications of cognitive therapy*. New York: Plenum Press.

Freeman, A., & Urschel, J. (1997). Individual psychology and cognitive–behavioral therapy: A cognitive therapy perspective. *Journal of Cognitive Psychotherapy, 11,* 165–180.

Frosch, J. P. (1983). *Personality disorders*. Washington, DC: American Psychiatric Association.

Gallagher, N. G., South, S. C., & Oltmanns, T. F. (2003). Attentional coping style obsessive–compulsive personality disorder: A test of the intolerance of uncertainty hypothesis. *Personality & Individual Differences, 34,* 41–57.

Garyfallos, G., Adamopoulou, A., Karastergiou, A., Voikli, M., Ikonomidis, N., Donias, S., et al. (1999). Somatoform disorders: Comorbidity with other DSM–III–R psychiatric diagnoses in Greece. *Comprehensive Psychiatry, 40,* 299–307.

Gendrault, P. K. (2000). Chronic pain and masochism in adults: A correlational study. *Dissertation Abstracts International: Section B: The Sciences & Engineering, 61*(1-B), 575.

Gilbert, P. (2000). Social mentalities: Internal "social" conflict and the role of inner warmth and compassion in cognitive therapy. In P. Gilbert & K. G. Bailey (Eds.), *Genes on the couch: Explorations in evolutionary psychotherapy* (pp. 71–92). Philadelphia: Brunner-Routledge.

Gilbert, P. (2001). *Overcoming depression: A step-by-step approach to gaining control over depression* (2nd ed.). New York: Oxford University Press.

Gilbert, P. (2002a). Evolution theory and cognitive therapy. *Journal of Cognitive Psychotherapy, 16,* 259–262.

Gilbert, P. (2002b). Evolutionary approaches to psychopathology and cognitive therapy. *Journal of Cognitive Psychotherapy, 16,* 263–294.

Gilbert, P., & Allan, S. (1998). The role of defeat and entrapment (arrested flight) in depression: An exploration of an evolutionary view. *Psychological Medicine, 25*(3), 585–598.

Gilbert, P., & Bailey, K. G. (2000). *Genes on the couch: Explorations in evolutionary psychotherapy*. Philadelphia: Brunner-Routledge.

Gilligan, C. (1982a). *In a different voice: Psychological theory and women's development*. Cambridge, MA: Harvard University Press.

Gilligan, C. (1982b). New maps of development: New visions of maturity. *American Journal of Orthopsychiatry, 52*, 199–212.

Gottman, J. (2001). Meta-emotion, children's emotional intelligence, and buffering children from marital conflict. In C. D. Ryff & B. H. Singer (Eds.), *Emotion, social relationships, and health* (pp. 23–40). London: Oxford University Press.

Greenfield, S. F., & O'Leary, G. (1999). Sex differences in marijuana use in the United States. *Harvard Review of Psychiatry, 6*, 297–303.

Gurwitt, A. R. (1995). Aspects of prospective fatherhood. In J. L. Shapiro & M. J. Diamond (Eds.), *Becoming a father: Contemporary, social, developmental, and clinical perspectives* (pp. 294–315). New York: Springer.

Haliburn, J. (2000). Reasons for adolescent suicide attempts. *Journal of the American Academy of Child & Adolescent Psychiatry, 39*, 13–14.

Hamberger, L. K., Lohr, J. M., & Gottlieb, M. (2000). Predictors of treatment dropout from a spouse abuse abatement program. *Behavior Modification, 24*, 528–552.

Hare, R. D., Cooke, D. J., & Hart, S. D. (1999). Psychopathology and sadistic personality disorder. In T. Millon & P. H. Blaney (Eds.), *Oxford textbook of psychopathology* (pp. 555–584). London: Oxford University Press.

Haynes, S. N. (1986). A behavioral model of paranoid behaviors. *Behavior Therapy, 17*, 266–287.

Herpertz-Dahlmann, B., Mueller, B., Herpertz, S., Heussen, N., Hebebrand, J., & Remschmidt, H. (2001). Prospective 10-year follow-up in adolescent anorexia nervosa: Course, outcome, psychiatric comorbidity, and psychosocial adaptation. *Journal of Child Psychology & Psychiatry & Allied Disciplines, 42*, 603–612.

Heuser, I. (1998). The hypothalamic–pituitary–adrenal system in depression. *Pharmacopsychiatry, 31*(1), 3–10.

Hofmann, S. G., Newman, M. G., Ehlers, A., & Roth, W. T. (1995). Psychophysiological differences between subgroups of social phobia. *Journal of Abnormal Psychology, 104*, 224–231.

Holle, C., Heimberg, R. G., Sweet, R. A., & Holt, C. S. (1995). Alcohol and caffeine use by social phobics: An initial inquiry into drinking patterns and behavior. *Behaviour Research & Therapy, 33*, 561–566.

Holt, S. E., Meloy, J. R., & Strack, S. (1999). Sadism and psychopathology in violent and sexually violent offenders. *Journal of the American Academy of Psychology & the Law, 27*(1), 23–32.

Huprich, S. K. (2000). Describing depressive personality analogues and dysthymics on the NEO-Personality Inventory—Revised. *Journal of Clinical Psychology, 56*, 1521–1534.

Huprich, S. K. (2001). The overlap of depressive personality disorder and dysthymia, reconsidered. *Harvard Review of Psychiatry, 9*, 158–168.

Huprich, S. K. (2003a). Depressive personality and its relationship to depressed mood, interpersonal loss, negative parental perceptions, and perfectionism. *Journal of Nervous & Mental Disease, 191*, 73–79.

Huprich, S. K. (2003b). Evaluating facet-level predictions and construct validity of depressive personality disorder. *Journal of Personality Disorders, 17,* 219–232.

Huprich, S. K., Sanford, K., & Smith, M. (2002). Psychometric evaluation of the Depressive Personality Disorder Inventory. *Journal of Personality Disorders, 16,* 255–269.

Iketani, T., Kiriike, N., & Stein, M. B. (2002). Relationship between perfectionism and agoraphobia in patients with panic disorder. *Cognitive Behaviour Therapy, 31,* 119–128.

Jaffe, S. R., & Lansing, S. (Producers), & Lyne, A. (Director). (1987). *Fatal Attraction* [Motion picture]. United States: Paramount Pictures.

Johnson, J. K., Tuulio-Henriksson, A., & Pirkola, T. (2003). Do schizotypal symptoms mediate the relationship between genetic risk for schizophrenia and impaired neuropsychological performance in co-twins of schizophrenic patients? *Biological Psychiatry, 54,* 1200–1204.

Kanost, R. E. (1997). An investigation of the relationship between personality disorders and substance use among adolescents in the community [Abstract]. *Dissertation Abstracts International: Section B: The Sciences & Engineering, 58,* 3318.

Kellerman, H. (1990). Emotion and the organization of primary process. In R. Plutchik & H. Kellerman (Eds.), *Emotion, psychopathology, and psychotherapy: Theory, research, and experience* (Vol. 5, pp. 89–113). New York: Academic Press.

Kemperman, I., Russ, M. J., & Shearin, E. (1997). Self-injurious behavior and mood regulation in borderline patients. *Journal of Personality Disorders, 11*(2), 146–157.

Kimble, M. O. (2000). The case of Howard. *Cognitive & Behavioral Practice, 7,* 118–122.

Kinderman, P., & Bentall, R. P. (1996). Self-discrepancies and persecutory delusions: Evidence for a model of paranoid ideation. *Journal of Abnormal Psychology, 105,* 106–113.

Kinderman, P., & Bentall, R. P. (1997). Causal attributions in paranoia and depression: Internal, personal, and situational attributions for negative events. *Journal of Abnormal Psychology, 106,* 341–345.

Kingden, D. G., & Turkington, D. (2002). *Cognitive–behavioral therapy of schizophrenia.* New York: Guilford Press.

Koerner, B. (2002, July/August). Disorder made to order. *Mother Jones,* p. 58.

Kutchins, H., & Kirk, S. A. (1997). *Making us crazy.* New York: Free Press.

Lewin, K. (1946). Behavior and development as a function of the total situation. In L. Carmichael (Ed.), *Manual of child psychology* (pp. 791–844). New York: Wiley.

Lilienfeld, S. O. (1992). The association between antisocial personality and somatization disorders: A review and integration of theoretical models. *Clinical Psychology Review, 12,* 641–662.

Lilienfeld, S. O. (2001). Anxiety sensitivity: Relations to psychopathology, *DSM–IV* personality disorder features, and personality traits. *Journal of Anxiety Disorders*, *55*, 367–393.

Linehan, M. M. (1987). Dialectical behavioral therapy: A cognitive behavioral approach to parasuicide. *Journal of Personality Disorders*, *1*, 328–333.

Linehan, M. M. (1993a). *Cognitive–behavioral treatment for the borderline personality disorder*. New York: Guilford Press.

Linehan, M. M. (1993b). *Skills training manual for treating borderline personality disorder*. New York: Guilford Press.

Linehan, M. M., Cochran, B. N., & Kehrer, C. A. (2001). Dialectical behavior therapy for borderline personality disorder. In D. H. Barlow (Ed.), *Clinical handbook of psychological disorder: A step-by-step treatment manual* (pp. 470–522). New York: Guilford Press.

Loas, G., Perdereau, F., Verrier, A., Guelfi, J., Halfon, O., Lang, F., et al. (2002). Comorbidity of dependent personality disorder and separation anxiety disorder in addictive disorders and in healthy subjects. *Psychopathology*, *35*, 249–253.

Loranger, A. W. (1996). Dependent personality disorder: Age, sex, and Axis I comorbidity. *Journal of Nervous & Mental Disease*, *184*, 17–21.

Lyoo, I. K., Gunderson, J. G., & Phillips, K. A. (1998). Personality dimensions associated with depressive personality disorder. *Journal of Personality Disorders*, *12*, 46–55.

Mahoney, M. J. (1991). *Human change processes: The scientific foundations of psychotherapy*. New York: Basic Books.

Mahoney, M. J. (1995). *Cognitive and constructive psychotherapies: Theory, research, and practice*. New York: Springer.

Manicavasagar, V., Silove, D., & Curtis, J. (1997). Separation anxiety in adulthood: A phenomenological investigation. *Comprehensive Psychiatry*, *38*, 274–282.

Maslow, A. H. (1970). Holistic emphasis. *Journal of Individual Psychology*, *26*, 39.

Maxmen, J. S., & Ward, N. G. (1995). *Essential psychopathology and its treatment* (2nd ed., rev.). New York: W. W. Norton.

Mcallister, M. J. (2000). The unvanquished: Prevalence of moral masochistic personality characteristics in persons with fibromyalgia [Abstract]. *Dissertation Abstracts International: Section B: The Sciences & Engineering*, *61*(1-B), 540.

McDermut, W., Zimmerman, M., & Chelminski, I. (2003). The construct validity of depressive personality disorder. *Journal of Abnormal Psychology*, *112*, 49–60.

McGinn, L. K., & Young, J. E. (1996). Schema-focused therapy. In P. M. Salkovskis (Ed.), *Frontiers of cognitive therapy* (pp. 182–207). New York: Guilford Press.

Medewar, C. (1997). The antidepressant web: Marketing depression and making medicines work. *International Journal of Risk and Safety in Medicine*, *10*, 75–126.

Meichenbaum, D. (1977). Dr. Ellis, please stand up. *Counseling Psychologist*, *7*, 43–44.

Meichenbaum, D., & Cameron, R. (1974). The clinical potential of modifying what clients say to themselves. *Psychotherapy: Theory, Research & Practice, 11*, 103–117.

Mellor, C. S. (1988). Depersonalization and self-perception. *British Journal of Psychiatry, 153*(2), 15–19.

Meyer, B., & Carver, C. S. (2000). Negative childhood accounts, sensitivity and pessimism: A study of avoidant personality disorder features in college students. *Journal of Personality Disorders, 14*, 233–248.

Millon, T. (1969). *Modern psychopathology: A biosocial approach to maladaptive learning and functioning.* Philadelphia: W. B. Saunders.

Millon, T. (1977). *Millon Clinical Multiaxial Inventory manual.* Minneapolis, MN: National Computer Systems.

Millon, T. (1987a). *Millon Clinical Multiaxial Inventory—II: Manual for the MCMI–II.* Minneapolis, MN: National Computer Systems.

Millon, T. (1987b). On the nature of taxonomy in psychopathology. In C. Last & M. Herson (Eds.), *Issues in diagnostic research* (pp. 3–85). New York: Plenum Press.

Millon, T. (1990). *Toward a new personology: An evolutionary model.* New York: Wiley.

Millon, T. (1991a). Classification in psychopathology: Rationale, alternatives, and standards. *Journal of Abnormal Psychology, 100*, 245–261.

Millon, T. (1991b). Normality: What may we learn from evolutionary theory? In D. Offer & M. Sabshin (Eds.), *The diversity of normal behavior: Further contributions to normatology* (pp. 356–404). New York: Basic Books.

Millon, T. (1992). Millon Clinical Multiaxial Inventory: I and II. *Journal of Counseling & Development, 70*, 421–426.

Millon, T. (1996). *Personality and psychopathology: Building a clinical science.* New York: Wiley-Interscience.

Millon, T. (1997). *The Millon inventories: Clinical and personality assessment.* New York: Guilford Press.

Millon, T. (1999). *Personality-guided therapy.* New York: Wiley.

Millon, T., & Davis, R. D. (1996a). Developmental pathogenesis. In T. Millon & P. H. Blaney (Eds.), *Oxford textbook of psychopathology* (pp. 29–48). New York: Oxford University Press.

Millon, T., & Davis, R. D. (1996b). An evolutionary theory of personality disorders. In J. Clarkin & M. Lenzenweger (Eds.), *Major theories of personality disorder* (pp. 221–346). New York: Guilford Press.

Millon, T., & Davis, R. D. (2000). *Personality disorders in modern life.* New York: Wiley.

Millon, T., & Kotik-Harper, D. (1995). The relationship of depression to disorders of personality. In E. E. Beckham & W. R. Leber (Eds.), *Handbook of depression* (2nd ed., pp. 107–146). New York: Guilford Press.

Millon, T., & Millon, C. (1997). The MCMI: History, theory, & validation. In T. Millon (Ed.), *The Millon inventories: Clinical and personality assessment* (pp. 23–40). New York: Guilford Press.

Millon, T., Millon, C., & Davis, R. D. (1994). *Millon Clinical Multiaxial Inventory—III*. Minneapolis, MN: National Computer Systems.

Millon, T., Weiss, L. G., Millon, C., & Davis, R. D. (1994). *The Millon Index of Personality Styles manual*. San Antonio, TX: Psychological Corporation.

Mitchell, M. (1936). *Gone with the wind*. New York: Macmillan.

Mischel, W. (1981). Current issues and challenges in personality. In L. T. Benjamin, Jr. (Ed.), *The G. Stanley Hall lecture series* (Vol. 1, pp. 85–99). Washington, DC: American Psychological Association.

Mosak, H. H. (1968). The interrelatedness of the neuroses through central themes. *Journal of Individual Psychology, 24,* 67–70.

Mosak, H. H. (1971). Lifestyle. In A. Nikelly (Ed.), *Techniques for behavior change* (pp. 77–81). Springfield, IL: Charles C Thomas.

Muratori, F., Luccherino, L., Siri, R., Tancredi, R., Maestro, S., Bruni, G., et al. (1998). Depressive personality and symptomatology in latency age: Continuity or discontinuity of clinical expressivity. *Giornale di Neuropsichiatria dell'Eta Evolutiva, 18,* 87–109.

Needleman, L. D. (1999). *Cognitive case conceptualization: A guidebook for practitioners*. Mahwah, NJ: Erlbaum.

Nesse, R. M. (1990). Evolutionary explanations of emotions. *Human Nature, 1,* 261–289.

Nesse, R. M. (1999). Proximate and evolutionary studies of anxiety, stress and depression: Synergy at the interface. *Neuroscience & Biobehavioral Reviews, 23,* 895–903.

Nesse, R. M. (2001). Motivation and melancholy: A Darwinian perspective. In J. A. French, D. Ledger, & A. C. Kamil (Eds.), *Evolutionary psychology and motivation* (Vol. 47, Nebraska Symposium on Motivation, pp. 179–203). Lincoln, NE: University of Nebraska Press.

Nesse, R. M., & Williams, G. C. (1994). *Why we get sick: The new science of Darwinian medicine*. New York: Times Books.

Nestadt, G., Addington, A., Samuels, J., Liang, K., Bienvenu, J. O., Riddle, M., et al. (2003). The identification of OCD-related subgroups based on comorbidity. *Biological Psychiatry, 53,* 914–920.

Noyes, R., Jr., Langbehn, D. R., Happel, R. L., Stout, L. R., Muller, B. A., & Longley, S. L. (2001). Personality dysfunction among somatizing patients. *Psychosomatics: Journal of Consultation Liaison Psychiatry, 42,* 320–329.

Noyes, R., Reich, J. H., Suelzer, M., & Christiansen, J. (1991). Personality traits associated with panic disorder: Change associated with treatment. *Comprehensive Psychiatry, 32,* 283–294.

Öhman, A. (2000). Fear and anxiety: Evolutionary, cognitive, and clinical perspectives. In M. Lewis & J. M. Haviland-Jones (Eds.), *The handbook of emotions* (2nd ed., pp. 573–593). New York: Guilford Press.

Osler, W. (1932). *Aequanimitas, with other addresses to medical students, nurses and practitioners of medicine.* Philadelphia: Blakiston's Son & Co.

Overholser, J. C. (1996). The dependent personality and interpersonal problems. *Journal of Nervous & Mental Disease, 184,* 8–16.

Overholser, J. C., Stockmeier, C., Dilley, G., & Freiheit, S. (2002). Personality disorders in suicide attempters and completers: Preliminary findings. *Archives of Suicide Research, 6*(2), 123–133.

Parke, R. D. (1996). *Fatherhood.* Cambridge, MA: Harvard University Press.

Paykel, E. S. (1994a). Epidemiology of refractory depression. In W. A. Nolen, J. Zohar, S. P. Roose, & J. D. Amsterdam (Eds.), *Refractory depression: Current strategies and future directions* (pp. 3–17). New York: Wiley.

Paykel, E. S. (1994b). Historical overview of outcome of depression. *British Journal of Psychiatry, 165,* 6–8.

Persons, J. B., Davidson, J., & Tompkins, M. A. (2001). *Essential components of cognitive–behavior therapy for depression.* Washington, DC: American Psychological Association.

Perugi, G., & Akiskal, H. S. (2002). The soft bipolar spectrum redefined: Focus on the cyclothymic, anxious–sensitive, impulse–dyscontrol, and binge-eating connection in bipolar II and related conditions. *Psychiatric Clinics of North America, 25,* 713–737.

Perugi, G., Toni, C., Benedetti, A., Simonetti, B., Simoncini, M., Torti, C., et al. (1998). Delineating a putative phobic–anxious temperament in 126 panic–agoraphobic patients: Toward a rapprochement of European and US views. *Journal of Affective Disorders, 47,* 11–23.

Perugi, G., Toni, C., Travierso, M. C., & Akiskal, H. S. (2003). The role of cyclothymia in atypical depression: Toward a data-based reconceptualization of the borderline–bipolar II connection. *Journal of Affective Disorders, 73,* 87–98.

Picot, A. K., & Lilenfeld, L. R. (2003). The relationship among binge severity, personality psychopathology, and body mass index. *International Journal of Eating Disorders, 34,* 98–107.

Plutchik, R. (1980). *Emotion: A psychoevolutionary synthesis.* New York: Harper & Row.

Plutchik, R. (1984). Emotions: A general psychoevolutionary theory. In K. R. Scherer & P. Ekman (Eds.), *Approaches to emotion* (pp. 197–219). Hillsdale, NJ: Erlbaum.

Plutchik, R. (2000). *Emotions in the practice of psychotherapy: Clinical implications of affect theories.* Washington, DC: American Psychological Association.

Plutchik, R. (2003). *Emotions and life: Perspectives from psychology, biology, and evolution.* Washington, DC: American Psychological Association.

Price, J. S. (1972). The dominance hierarchy and the evolution of mental illness. *Lancet, 7502*, 243–246.

Rasmussen, P. R. (2002). Resistance: The fear behind it and tactics for reducing it. *Journal of Individual Psychology, 58*, 148–159.

Rasmussen, P. R. (2003a). The adaptive purpose of emotional expression: A lifestyle elaboration. *Journal of Individual Psychology, 59*, 388–409.

Rasmussen, P. R. (2003b). Emotional reorientation: A clinical strategy. *Journal of Individual Psychology, 59*, 345–359.

Rasmussen, P. R., McAnulty, R. D., & Mangum, J. (2001). The purpose of sexual deviancy: Clinical implications and adjunctive treatment strategies. *Journal of Individual Psychology, 57*, 173–181.

Rastam, M., Gillberg, C., & Wentz, E. (2003). Outcome of teenage-onset anorexia nervosa in a Swedish community-based sample. *European Child & Adolescent Psychiatry, 12*, 178–190.

Reich, J., & Braginsky, Y. (1994). Paranoid personality traits in a panic disorder population: A pilot study. *Comprehensive Psychiatry, 35*, 260–264.

Renshaw, K. D., Chambless, D. L., & Steketee, G. (2003). Perceived criticism predicts severity of anxiety symptoms after behavioral treatment in patients with obsessive–compulsive disorder and panic disorder with agoraphobia. *Journal of Clinical Psychology, 59*, 411–421.

Retzlaff, P. (1997). The MCMI as a treatment planning tool. In T. Millon (Ed.), *The Millon inventories: Clinical and personality assessment* (pp. 217–244). New York: Guilford Press.

Rosenfeld, H. (1947). Analysis of a schizophrenic state with depersonalization. *Journal of Psycho-Analysis, 28*, 130–139.

Rosenthal, M., Stelian, J., & Wagner, J. (1999). Diogenes syndrome and hoarding in the elderly: Case reports. *Israel Journal of Psychiatry & Related Sciences, 36*(1), 29–34.

Rossi, A., Marinangeli, M. G., Butti, G., Scinto, A., Di Cicco, L., Kalyvoka, A., et al. (2001). Personality disorders in bipolar and depressive disorders. *Journal of Affective Disorders, 65*, 3–8.

Rotter, J. B. (1966). Generalized expectancies for internal versus external control of reinforcement. *Psychological Monographs, 80*, 1–28.

Rushton, J. P. (1985). Differential K theory: The Sociobiology of individual and group differences. *Personality and Individual Differences, 6*, 441–452.

Ruth, W. J. (1992). Irrational thinking in humans: An evolutionary proposal for Ellis's genetic postulate. *Journal of Rational–Emotive & Cognitive Behavior Therapy, 10*, 3–20.

Ryder, A. G., Bagby, R. M., & Dion, K. L. (2001). Chronic, low-grade depression in a nonclinical sample: Depressive personality or dysthymia? *Journal of Personality Disorders, 15*, 84–93.

Ryder, A. G., Bagby, R. M., & Schuller, D. R. (2002). The overlap of depressive personality disorder and dysthymia: A categorical problem with a dimensional solution. *Harvard Review of Psychiatry, 10,* 337–352.

Saugstad, L. F. (2000). Suicide and resilience: The role of mental illness, psychotropic medication and abuse. *International Medical Journal, 7,* 169–179.

Schulte, H. M., Hall, M. J., & Crosby, R. (1994). Violence in patients with narcissistic personality pathology: Observations of a clinical series. *American Journal of Psychotherapy, 48,* 610–623.

Scott, J. (1988). Chronic depression. *British Journal of Psychiatry, 153,* 287–297.

Sharp, C., Smith, J. V., & Cole, A. (2002). Cinematherapy: Metaphorically promoting therapeutic change. *Counseling Psychology Quarterly, 15,* 269–276.

Shearer, S. L. (1994). Dissociative phenomena in women with borderline personality disorder. *American Journal of Psychiatry, 151,* 1324–1328.

Shulman, B. H. (1985). Cognitive therapy and the individual psychology of Alfred Adler. In M. J. Mahoney & A. Freeman (Eds.), *Cognition and psychotherapy* (pp. 243–258). New York: Plenum Press.

Shulman, B. H., & Watts, R. W. (1997). Adlerian and constructivist psychotherapies: An Adlerian perspective. *Journal of Cognitive Psychotherapy, 11,* 181–194.

Siever, L. J. (1992). Schizophrenia spectrum personality disorders. *American Psychiatric Press Review of Psychiatry, 11,* 25–42.

Skinstad, A. H., & Swain, A. (2001). Comorbidity in a clinical sample of substance abusers. *American Journal of Drug & Alcohol Abuse, 27,* 45–64.

Skodol, A. E., Gallaher, P. E., & Oldham, J. M. (1996). Excessive dependency and depression: Is the relationship specific? *Journal of Nervous & Mental Disease, 184,* 165–171.

Sloman, L., Price, J., Gilbert, P., & Gardner, R. (1994). Adaptive function of depression: Psychotherapeutic implications. *American Journal of Psychotherapy, 48,* 401–416.

Sperry, L. (1997). Adlerian psychotherapy and cognitive therapy: An Adlerian perspective. *Journal of Cognitive Psychotherapy, 11,* 157–164.

Spielberger, C. D. (1983). *Manual for the State–Trait Anxiety Inventory.* Palo Alto, CA: Consulting Psychologists.

Steiner, H., Carrion, V., Plattner, B., & Koopman, C. (2003). Dissociative symptoms in posttraumatic stress disorder: Diagnosis and treatment. *Child & Adolescent Psychiatric Clinics of North America, 12,* 231–249.

Suzuki, K., Muramatsu, T., Takeda, A., & Shirakura, K. (2002). Co-occurrence of obsessive–compulsive personality traits in young and middle-aged Japanese alcohol-dependent men. *Alcoholism: Clinical & Experimental Research, 26,* 1223–1227.

Thase, M. E. (1994). The roles of psychosocial factors and psychotherapy in refractory depression: Missing pieces in the puzzle of treatment resistance? In W. E. Nolen & J. Zohar (Eds.), *Refractory depression: Current strategies and future directions* (pp. 83–95). New York: Wiley.

Tienari, P., Wynne, L. C., & Laksy, K. (2003). Genetic boundaries of the schizophrenic spectrum: Evidence for the Finnish Adoptive Family Study of Schizophrenia. *American Journal of Psychiatry, 160,* 1587–1594.

Tillfors, M., Furmark, T., Ekselius, L., & Fredrikson, M. (2001). Social phobia and avoidant personality disorder as related to parental history of social anxiety: A general population study. *Behaviour Research & Therapy, 39,* 289–298.

Toole, J. K. (1980). *A confederacy of dunces.* Baton Rouge: Louisiana State University Press.

Tringone, R. F. (1997). The MPDC: Composition and clinical applications. In T. Millon (Ed.), *The Millon inventories: Clinical and personality assessment* (pp. 449–474). New York: Guilford Press.

Turley, B., Bates, G. W., Edwards, J., & Jackson, H. J. (1992). MCMI–II personality disorders in recent-onset bipolar disorders. *Journal of Clinical Psychology, 48,* 320–329.

Tzelepis, A., Schubiner, H., & Warbasse, L. H., III. (1995). Differential diagnosis and psychiatric comorbidity patterns in adult attention deficit disorder. In K. G. Nadeau (Ed.), *A comprehensive guide to attention deficit disorder in adults: Research, diagnosis, and treatment* (pp. 35–57). Bristol, PA: Brunner/Mazel.

Uecok, A., Karaveli, D., Kundakci, T., & Yazici, O. (1998). Comorbidity of personality disorders with bipolar mood disorders. *Comprehensive Psychiatry, 39,* 72–74.

Unterberg, M. P. (2003). Personality: Personalities, personal style, and trouble getting along. In J. P. Kahn & A. M. Langlieb (Eds.), *Mental health and productivity in the workplace: A handbook for organizations and clinicians* (pp. 458–480). San Francisco: Jossey-Bass.

Van den Bergh, O., Stegen, K., & Van de Woestijne, K. P. (1997). Learning to have psychosomatic complaints: Conditioning of respiratory behavior and somatic complaints in psychosomatic patients. *Psychosomatic Medicine, 59,* 13–23.

Vollrath, M., Togersen, S., & Alnaes, R. (1998). Neuroticism, coping and change in MCMI–II clinical syndromes: Test of a mediator model. *Scandinavian Journal of Psychology, 39,* 15–24.

von Knorring, L., von Knorring, A., Smigan, L., Lindberg, U., & Edholm, M. (1987). Personality traits in subtypes of alcoholics. *Journal of Studies on Alcohol, 48,* 523–527.

Vostanis, P., & Dean, C. (1992). Self-neglect in adult life. *British Journal of Psychiatry, 161,* 265–267.

Watkins, C. E. (1997). An Adlerian reaction in the spirit of social interest. *Journal of Cognitive Psychotherapy, 11,* 211–214.

Watts, R. E., & Critelli, J. W. (1997). Roots of contemporary cognitive theories in the individual psychology of Alfred Adler. *Journal of Cognitive Psychotherapy, 11,* 147–156.

Wedding, D., & Niemiec, R. M. (2003). The clinical use of films in psychotherapy. *Journal of Clinical Psychology, 59,* 207–215.

Weiss, L. G. (1997). The MIPS: Gauging the dimensions of normality. In T. Millon (Ed.), *The Millon inventories: Clinical and personality assessment* (pp. 498–522). New York: Guilford Press.

Westen, D., & Gabbard, G. O. (1999). Psychoanalytic approaches to personality. In L. A. Pervin & O. P. John (Eds.), *Handbook of personality: Theory and research* (2nd ed., pp. 57–101). New York: Guilford Press.

Wewetzer, C., Jans, T., Mueller, B., Neudoerfl, A., Buecherl, U., Remschmidt, H., et al. (2001). Long-term outcome and prognosis of obsessive–compulsive disorder with onset in childhood or adolescence. *European Child & Adolescent Psychiatry, 10,* 37–46.

Whitters, A., Troughton, E., Cadoret, R. J., & Widmer, R. B. (1984). Evidence for clinical heterogeneity in antisocial alcoholics. *Comprehensive Psychiatry, 25,* 158–164.

Widiger, T. A., & Anderson, K. G. (2003). Personality and depression in women. *Journal of Affective Disorders, 74,* 59–66.

Wildgoose, A., Clarke, S., & Waller, G. (2001). Treating personality fragmentation and dissociation in borderline personality disorder: A pilot study of the impact of cognitive analytic therapy. *British Journal of Medical Psychology, 74,* 47–55.

Wolfradt, U., & Watzke, S. (1999). Deliberate out-of-body experiences, depersonalization, schizotypal traits, and thinking styles. *Journal of the American Society for Psychical Research, 93,* 249–257.

Young, J. E. (1994). *Cognitive therapy for personality disorders: A schema-focused approach* (rev. ed.). Sarasota, FL: Professional Resource Press.

Young, J. E. (1999). *Cognitive therapy for personality disorders: A schema-focused approach* (3rd ed.). Sarasota, FL: Professional Resource Press.

Young, J. E., Klosko, J. S., & Weishaar, M. E. (2003). *Schema therapy: A practitioner's guide.* New York: Guilford Press.

Young, J. E., & Lindemann, M. D. (1992). An integrative schema-focused model for personality disorders. *Journal of Cognitive Psychotherapy, 6,* 11–23.

Zaretsky, A. E., Fava, M., Davidson, K. G., & Pava, J. A. (1997). Are dependency and self-criticism risk factors for major depressive disorder? *Canadian Journal of Psychiatry, 42,* 291–297.

Zidanik, M. (2002). Suppression of aggression in regard of some personality disorders. *Horizons of Psychology, 11,* 109–118.

Zimmerman, M., & Mattia, J. I. (1999). Axis I diagnostic comorbidity and borderline personality disorder. *Comprehensive Psychiatry, 40,* 245–252.

AUTHOR INDEX

Abueg, F. R., 3
Adler, A., 5, 20
Akhavan, S., 223
Akiskal, H. S., 57, 128, 224
Albert, C., 55
Allan, S., 129
Alnaes, R., 128
American Psychiatric Association, 6, 31,
    54, 76, 132, 169, 236, 261, 291,
    311
Anderluh, M. B., 245
Anderson, K. G., 223
Arlow, J. A., 194
Arlow, P. B., 55
Arsenio, W. F., 56
Azorin, J. M., 57

Bagby, R. M., 264
Bailey, K. G., 20, 115
Baker, C. A., 68, 98
Baltazar, P. L., 197
Barlow, D. H., 187
Bates, G. W., 156
Beck, A. T., 3, 5, 19, 28, 30, *32*, *34*, 53,
    75, *76*, 80, 82, 85, 112, *123*, 125,
    132, 169, 171, 172, *180*, 194,
    216, *218*, *239*, 277, 279, 280,
    284, 295
Bentall, R. P., 53, 56
Bermanzohn, P. C., 55
Bernstein, A., 62
Blackburn, R., 107
Bodner, E., 56
Bohus, M., 128
Bornstein, R. F., 219, 221
Bothwell, R., 20
Braginsky, Y., 55
Brooks, R. B., 197
Brown, B., 15
Brown, E. J., 197
Brown, G. K., 321
Brown, G. W., 8
Bruns, J. R., 197

Cadoret, R. J., 106
Cameron, R., 139
Candel, I., 154
Carpiniello, B., 16
Carrion, V., 154
Carta, M. G., 16
Carver, C. S., 193
Chambless, D. L., 242
Chelminski, I., 264
Chiesa, M., 62
Christiansen, J., 197
Cicchetti, D., 193
Clarke, S., 127
Cochran, B. N., 127
Cohen, D. J., 193
Cole, A., 85
Cooke, D. J., 293
Coon, D. W., 207
Cosmides, L., 20
Critelli, J. W., 5
Crosby, R., 176
Curtis, J., 220

Darling, N., 15
Davidson, J., 208, 313
Davidson, K. G., 223
Davis, R. D., 5, 7, 12, 17, *21*, 34, 51, 57,
    59, 91, 108, 111, 130, 131, *155*,
    156, *157*, 193, 200, 201, 224,
    225, 226, *246*, 247, 248, 261,
    265, 266, 267, 268, 272, 277,
    282, 291, 296, 298, 307, 311, 312
Dean, C., 78
Dilley, G., 96
Dion, D. R., 264
Dreikurs, R., 303
Dumont, F., 33
Durbin, D. L., 15
Dyck, I. R., 220, 241, 242

Edholm, M., 106
Edwards, J., 156

337

Ehlers, A., 197
Ekselius, R. A., 197
Ellason, J. W., 198
Elliot, R. L., 306
Ellis, A., 19
Emery, G., 3, 125

Fava, M., 223
Fleming, B., 61, 83, 97, 132, 149, 227, 250
Fleming, J., 28
Follette, V. M., 3
Fossati, A., 275
Frederiks, C. S., 197
Freeman, A., 3, 5, 28, 53, 61, 67, 69, 75, 76, 83, 97, 112, 114, *123*, 132, 140, 141, 149, 159, 160, 169, 181, 182, 194, 207, 212, 216, 227, *239*, 250, 251, 252, 279
Freiheit, S., 96
Frosch, J. P., 112
Fuchs, D. L., 198
Furmark, R. G., 197

Gabbard, G. O., 35
Gallagher, N. G., 241
Gallaher, P. E., 219
Garyfallos, G., 221
Gendrault, P. K., 306
Gilbert, P., 8, 20, 28, 38, 42, 115, *128*, 129, 193, 199, 223, 244, 261, 265, 298
Gillberg, C., 245
Gilligan, C., 17
Gottlieb, M., 62
Gottman, J., 206
Greenfield, S. F., 281
Gunderson, J. G., 262
Gurwitt, A. R., 17

Haliburn, J., 242
Hall, M. J., 176
Hamberger, L. K., 62
Hantouche, E. G., 57
Hare, R. D., 293
Hart, S. D., 293
Haynes, S. N., 65
Heimberg, R. G., 197

Herpertz-Dahlmann, B., 245
Heuser, I., 36
Hofmann, S. G., 197
Holle, C., 197
Holt, C. S., 197
Holt, S. E., 292
Huprich, S. K., 264

Iketani, T., 242

Jackson, H. J., 156
Jaffe, S. R., 131
Johnson, J. K., 95
Juster, H. R., 197

Kanost, R. E., 281
Karaveli, D., 130
Kehrer, C. A., 127
Kellerman, H., 57
Kemperman, I., 125
Kimble, M. O., 55
Kinderman, P., 53, 56
Kingden, D. G., 3
Kiriike, N., 242
Kirk, S. A., 6
Klosko, J. S., 66, 286
Koerner, B., 6
Koopman, C., 154
Kotik-Harper, D., 56, 57
Kuijpers, M., 154
Kundakci, T., 130
Kutchins, H., 6

Lai, G., 16
Laksy, K., 95
Lansing, S., 131
Lecomte, C., 33
Lee-Evans, J. M., 107
Lemerise, E. A., 56
Lewin, K., 31
Liese, B. S., 3
Lilenfeld, L. R., 245
Lilienfeld, S. O., 107, 219
Lindberg, U., 106
Lindemann, M. D., 207
Linehan, M. M., 127, 132, 133, *134*, 145
Loas, G., 220

Lohr, J. M., 62
Loranger, A. W., 223
Lyne, A., 131
Lyoo, I. K., 262

Macallister, M. J., 306
Mahoney, M. J., 19
Mangum, J., 209
Manicavasagar, V., 220
Maslow, A. H., 15
Mattia, J. I., 127, 129
Mattia, T., 128, 129
Maxmen, J. S., 169
McAnulty, R. D., 209
McDermut, W., 264
McDowell, D. E., 197
McGinn, L. K., 23
Medewar, C., 6
Meichenbaum, D., 115, 139
Mellor, C. S., 80
Meloy, J. R., 292
Merckelbach, H., 154
Meyer, B., 193
Mikulincer, M., 56
Millon, C., 34, 311, 312
Millon, T., 5, 7, 12, 15, 17, 19, *21*, 25,
        27, 34, 36, 44, 45, *49*, 50, 51, 55,
        56, 57, 59, 60, 74, 76, 79, 90, 91,
        94, 102, 108, *110*, 111, 112, 122,
        123, 128, 130, 131, 148, 150,
        151, 152, *155*, 156, *157*, 163,
        168, 169, 177, *178*, 187, 192,
        193, *196*, 199, 200, 201, 211,
        216, 224, 225, 226, 232, 236,
        237, *241*, 242, 245, *246*, 247,
        248, 249, 260, 261, 263, 265,
        266, 267, 268, 272, 276, 277,
        291, 292, 293, 294, 296, 298,
        301, 302, 303, 307, 309, 311, 312
Mitchell, M., 154
Morrison, A. P., 68, 98
Mosak, H. H., 277
Munjack, D. J., 197
Muramatsu, T., 245
Muratori, F., 265

Needleman, L. D., 25, 27, *29, 30*
Nesse, R. M., 8, *20, 128*, 196, 223
Nestadt, G., 243

Newman, C. F., 3
Newman, M. G., 197
Niemiec, R. M., 85
Noyes, R., 197, 281

Öhman, A., 8, 54, 196, 197, 219, 241
Oldham, J. M., 219
O'Leary, G., 281
Oltmanns, T. F., 241
Osler, Sir W., 7
Overholser, J. C., 96, 223

Pariante, C. M., 16
Parke, R. D., 17
Pava, J. A., 223
Paykel, E. S., 20
Persons, J. B., 208, 313
Perugi, G., 128, 224
Phillips, K. A., 262
Picot, A. K., 245
Pirkola, T., 95
Plattner, B., 154
Plutchik, R., 20, 34, 196, 223
Pretzer, J., 28, 61, 83, 97, 132, 149, 227,
        250
Price, J., 199
Price, J. S., 8

Rabe-Hesketh, S., 245
Rasmussen, P. R., 21, 134, 142, 206, 209,
        288
Rastam, M., 245
Reich, J. H., 55, 197
Renshaw, K. D., 242
Retzlaff, P., 311
Rosenfeld, H., 80
Rosenthal, M., 78
Ross, C. A., 198
Rossi, A., 199, 200
Roth, W. T., 197
Rotter, J. B., 18
Rudas, N., 16
Rush, J., 3, 125
Rushton, J. P., 17
Russ, M. J., 125
Ruth, W. J., 19
Ruzek,. I., 3
Ryder, A. G., 264

Sanford, K., 264
Saugstad, L. F., 16
Schubiner, H., 197
Schuller, D. R., 264
Schulte, H. M., 176
Scott, J., 20
Sharp, C., 85
Shaw, B., 3, 125
Shearer, S. L., 125
Shearin, E., 125
Shiakura, K., 245
Shulman, B. H., 5
Siever, L. J., 81
Silove, D., 220
Simon, K., 28, 61, 83, 97, 132, 149, 227, 250
Siris, S. G., 55
Skinstad, A. H., 107, 200
Skodol, A. E., 219, 222
Sloman, L., 199
Smigan, L., 106
Smith, J. V., 85
Smith, M., 264
Soltz, V., 303
South, S. C., 241
Sperry, L., 5
Steer, R. A., 321
Stegen, K., 174
Stein, M. B., 242
Steinberg, L., 15
Steiner, H., 154
Steketee, G., 242
Stelian, J., 78
Stockmeier, C., 96
Strack, S., 292
Suelzer, M., 197
Suzuki, K., 245
Swain, A., 107, 200
Sweet, R. A., 197

Takeda, A., 245
Tchanturia, K., 245
Thase, M. E., 20
Tienari, P., 95
Tillford, C., 197
Togersen, S., 128
Tompkins, M. A., 208, 313
Toni, C., 224
Tooby, J., 20
Toole, J. K., 174

Travierso, M. C., 224
Treasure, S. J., 245
Tringone, R. F., 34, 45, 312
Troughton, E., 106
Turkington, D., 3
Turley, B., 156
Tuulio-Henriksson, A., 95
Tzelepis, A., 197

Uecok, A., 130
Unterberg, M. P., 241
Urschel, J., 5

Van den Bergh, O., 174
Van de Woestijne, K. P., 174
Vollrath, M., 128
von Knorring, A., 106
von Knorring, L., 106
Vostanis, P., 78

Wagner, J., 78
Waller, G., 127
Warbasse, L. H., III, 197
Ward, N. G., 169
Watkins, C. E., 5
Watts, R. W., 5
Watzke, S., 91, 95
Wedding, D., 85
Weishaar, M. E., 3, 19, 66, 286
Weiss, L. G., 34, 312
Wentz, E., 245
Westen, D., 35
Wewetzer, C., 197
Whitters, A., 106
Widiger, T. A., 223
Widmer, R. B., 106
Wildgoose, A., 127
Williams, G. C., 8, 20, *128*, 196
Wolfradt, U. S., 91, 95
Wynne, L. C., 95

Yazici, O., 130
Young, J. E., 23, 66, 132, 207, 286

Zaretsky, A. E., 223
Zidanik, M., 223
Zimmerman, M., 127, 128, 129, 264

SUBJECT INDEX

Abrasive negativistic personality style, 282–283
  sadistic features in, 282–283
Accommodating dependent personality style
  histrionic features in, 226
Acting "as if"
  in antisocial prototype treatment, 115
Active–independent orientation, 17
Adaptation imperative
  active orientation, 16
  description of, 14–15
  passive orientation, 15–16
Adaptive functioning
  balance and, 18–19
  in clinical conditions, 20
Adler, A., 5, 20
Affective processes
  personality attributes and, 36, 37
Affective system
  cognitive system and, 35
Affectless schizoid personality style
  compulsive features in, 81
  indifference of, 81
Aggression
  in negativistic prototype, 281–282
Agitated depression
  in borderline prototype, 129
  in compulsive prototype, 244
  in dependent prototype, 223, 224
Agoraphobia
  in avoidant prototype, 197
  in compulsive prototype, 242
Alcohol abuse
  in negativistic prototype, 281
Alcohol dependency
  as self-medication, 244–245
Alternative statements
  for avoidant prototype, 212
Amorous narcissistic personality style
  histrionic features in, 178
Anger
  in compulsive prototype, 254

in narcissistic prototype, 175
in negativistic prototype, 281
in paranoid prototype, 54, 56
Anger, impulsive
  antisocial prototype case, 119–120
Anorexia
  in borderline prototype, case example, 142
  in compulsive prototype, 245
Anticipation of consequences
  for antisocial prototype, 114
  for narcissistic prototype, 184
Antidepressant medication
  for depressive prototype, 271
Antisocial prototype
  aggressiveness of, 102
  anxiety and, 106, 119
  autonomy and self-advocacy in, 103–104
  Axis I vulnerabilities of, 106–108
  behavioral style of, 104
  beliefs of, 104
  bipolar condition and, 107
  callousness of, 104
  case example, 118–120
  cognitive style of, 104–105
  covetous, 108–109, 118–120
  criminality *versus* impulsivity debate and, 112
  dissociation and, 107–108
  malevolent, 110
  nomadic, 109–110
  pathologic process of, 105
  personality attributes and liabilities of, 103
  personality-guided cognitive–behavioral conceptualization of, 103–105
  polarity balance of, 101, 102
  reputation-defending, 111–112
  risk-taking, 110–111
  somatic complaints and, 107
  substance-related syndromes and, 106

Antisocial prototype, *continued*
    treatment of
        goals in, 114
        strategies in, 114–118
        therapeutic relationship in,
            112–114
    variations on, 108–112
Anxiety
    in avoidant prototype, 196–197
    in borderline prototype, 127
    in compulsive prototype, 254
    in depressive prototype, 271
    in masochistic prototype, 310
    in narcissistic prototype, 173, 176,
        182–183, 189
    in obsessive–compulsive prototype,
        240
    in paranoid prototype, 54
    in sadistic personality type, 296
    in schizotypal prototype, 91, 93
Appeasing histrionic personality style, 157
Arbitrary reference
    in paranoid prototype, 67
Asceticism
    of depressive prototype, 262, 272
Automatic thoughts. *See also under*
        specific prototype
    beliefs and, 28
    emotional reactions and, 29–30
    implicit rules and, 28
    survival bipolarity and, 28–29
Avoidant prototype
    anxiety disorders and, 196–197
    Axis I vulnerabilities of, 196–200
    beliefs of, 194
    case example, 210–212
    conflicted, 202
    delusional and psychotic disorders
        and, 200
    dissociative disorders and, 198
    fantasy as regulatory mechanism in,
        193–194, 195, 209
    hypersensitive, 203–204
    mood disorders, 199–200, 211
    mood state of, 193, 195
    morphological organization of, 193,
        195
    obsessive–compulsive disorder and,
        197–198
    panic disorder and agoraphobia and,
        197, 211

pathologic process of, 194–195
personality attributes and liabilities
    of, 194, 195, 211
personality-guided cognitive–
    behavioral conceptualization of,
    192–194
phobic, 202–203
polarity balance of, 191–192
self-destructive, 201–202
self-focus of, 191
self-image of, alienated, 192
social phobia and, 197, 211
somatoform disorder and, 198–199
substance abuse and impulse
    disorders and, 200
treatment of
    arranging, 205–206
    cognitive assessment in, 207–
        208
    cognitive goals of, 205
    emotion-based, 208–210
    social skills in, 206
    therapeutic relationship in, 204
variations on, 200–204
Avoidant style
    in depressive personality, 265

Beck, A. T., *32, 34, 123, 180, 218*
Bedeviled obsessive–compulsive personal-
    ity style, 247
Behavioral system, 36, 38
    expressive behaviors and, 38, 39
    interpersonal style and, 38, 39
Belief(s)
    core, 23–25
    intermediate, 25, 27–28
    personality structures and functions
        in, 47
Binge eating disorder
    in compulsive prototype, 245
Bipolar disorder
    in antisocial prototype, 107
    in borderline prototype, 129–130
    in compulsive prototype, 244
    in dependent prototype, 223–224
    in depressive prototype, 264–265
    in histrionic prototype, 156, 162,
        165
    in paranoid prototype, 56
    in schizoid personality, 79–80

Bipolar II
    in avoidant prototype, 199–200,
        202
Borderline prototype
    anxiety and, 127
    autonomy *versus* dependence in, 123
    Axis I vulnerabilities of, 127–130
    beliefs of, 123
    bipolar disorder and, 129–130
    case example of, with anorexia, 142
    dichotomous thinking of, 125
    discouraged, 130–131
    dissociation and, 127–128
    dysthymia and, 128–129
    example, 124–125
    fear of rejection and abandonment
        in, 123, 125
    impulsive, 131
    major depression and, 129
    pathologic process of, 126
    personality attributes and liabilities
        of, 123, 124
    personality-guided cognitive–
        behavioral conceptualization of,
        122–126
    petulant, 131–132
    polarity balance of, 121–122
    self-destructive, 132
    self-injurious behavior of, 125, 126
    somatoform conditions and, 128
    treatment of, 132–142
        absolute thinking in, 140–141
        cognitive processes in, 135–136
        dichotomous thinking in, 134,
            136–139, 140
        emotional control strategies in,
            141–142
        goal of, 132
        inpatient, 132
        relationship skills in, 134–135,
            142–145
        self-instructional techniques in,
            139–140
        suicidality and, 133
        therapeutic relationship in,
            132–133
    vacillation of, 121–122, 123
    variations on, 130–132
Bureaucratic obsessive–compulsive person-
        ality style, narcissistic features in,
        248

Callousness
    of antisocial prototype, 104
Challenging absolutes
    in antisocial prototype treatment,
        118
Chronic pain symptoms
    in masochistic prototype, 306
Circuitous negativistic personality style,
        283–284
    dependent personality features in,
        283–284
Clinical conditions
    adaptive value of, 7–8
    biochemical processes in, 6
Cognitive behavioral model, 3–4
    complex, 4
    simple, 3
Cognitive biases and distortions
    in avoidant prototype, 207
Cognitive monitoring
    for avoidant prototype, 208
Cognitive shift, 30
Cognitive styles, 34, 35
Cognitive system, 34
    affective system and, 34–35
Cognitive triad, 23, 25, 26
Colombo technique
    for narcissistic prototype, 182
    for negativistic prototype, 289
Compensatory narcissistic personality
        style
    negativistic and avoidant features in,
        178
    pretentiousness of, 178–179
Compulsive prototype
    anxiety in, 240
    Axis I vulnerabilities of, 241–246
    bedeviled, 247
    beliefs of, 239–240
    bipolar disorder in, 244
    bureaucratic, 248
    case example, 254–256
    characterization of, 235–237
    cognitive style of, 240
    conscientious, 246–247
    depression in, major, 244
    dissociative disorder in, 242
    dysthymia in, 243–244
    eating disorders in, 245
    example of, 237–238
    generalized anxiety in, 241–242

Compulsive prototype, *continued*
   obsessive–compulsive disorder in,
      243
   parsimonious, 248
   pathologic process of, 240–241
   personality attributes and liabilities
      of, 239
   personality-guided cognitive–
      behavioral conceptualization of,
      238–240
   phobic disorder in, 242
   polarity balance of, 237
   puritanical, 248–249
   schizophrenia in, disorganized and
      catatonic, 245–246
   somatoform disorder in, 242–243
   substance-related syndromes in,
      244–245
   treatment of, 249–250
      affective changes in, 254
      behavioral goals in, 253–254
      cognitive goals in, 251–253
      fear in, 251
      goals of, 250
      therapeutic relationship in,
        250–251
   variations on, 246–249
   view of others, 238–239
Conditional assumptions, 25, 27
Conflicted avoidant personality style, 202
Conscientious compulsive personality
    style, 246–247
Conscious control system, 38
Core beliefs
   changes in through treatment, 45
   equivalence to self-image and object
      representations, 25
   influence of stage of development
      on, 24–25
   pathologic process and, 40, 41, 42
Cost–benefit analysis
   for antisocial prototype, 117
   for negativistic prototype, 286, 289
Covetous antisocial personality style,
    108–109, 118–120
Cued awareness
   for antisocial prototype, 114–115

Davis R. D., *21, 155, 156, 157, 246*
Delusional disorder

   in avoidant prototype, 200
   in sadistic personality type, 296
Delusional thoughts
   in paranoid prototype, 68
Dependency
   conforming type, in conscientious
      compulsive personality, 246
Dependent prototype
   accommodating, 226
   agitated depression in, 223, 224
   anxiety in, 219–220
   Axis I vulnerabilities, 219–224
   behaviorally incompetent, 217, 219
   beliefs of, 218
   case example of, college dropout,
      231–233
   characterization of, 215
   compulsive prototype and, 222–223
   disquieted, 225
   dissociation in, 220–221
   example of, 215–216
   hypomanic episodes in, 223
   immature, 224–225
   immaturity of, 217, 218
   ineffectual, 225–226
   pathologic process of, 219
   personality attributes and liabilities
      of, 216–217, 232
   personality-guided cognitive–
      behavioral conceptualization of,
      216–218
   phobia in, 220
   polarity balances of, 215, 217
   self as inept, 216, 219, 224
   selfless, 226
   somatic complaints in, 221–222
   submissiveness of, 216, 217, 219
   treatment of
      behavioral goals in, 230
      client goal in, 227
      cognitive goals in, 229–230
      encouragement of adult skills and
        self-initiative, 231
      self-focus in, 229
      therapeutic relationship in,
        228–229
      therapist goal in, 228, 233
   variations on, 224–226
Depersonalization
   in schizotypal prototype, 95
   schizoid personality and, 80

Depersonalized schizoid personality type disengagement in, 81–82
Depression. *See also* Agitated depression; Major depression
  adaptive, in masochistic prototype, 310
  episodic
    in paranoid prototype, 54
  in avoidant prototype, 199, 209
  in depressive prototype, 264
  in histrionic prototype, 155
  in narcissistic prototype, 174–175, 176–177
  in negativistic prototype, 280
  in paranoid prototype, 56–57
  in sadistic prototype, 296, 298, 299
  in schizoid prototype, 79, 81
  in schizotypal prototype, 94, 95, 96
Depressive prototype
  asceticism of, 262, 272
  attributes and liabilities of, 261, 262
  Axis I vulnerabilities in, 263–269
  beliefs in, 263
  beliefs of, 263
  case example of, purchasing agent, 272–274
  characterization of, 259–261
  comparison with avoidant personality, 260, 261
  depression and dysthymia in, 264
  hypomanic periods in, 264–265
  ill-humored, 268
  interpersonal style of defenselessness, 263
  melancholy mood in, 262
  morbid, 268–269
  pathologic process of, 263
  personality-guided cognitive– behavioral conceptualization of, 261–263
  polarity balances of, 259, 260
  restive, 265–266
  self-derogatory, 266–267
  somatic complaints in, 265, 272
  treatment of, 269–270
    affective changes in, 271
    behavioral goals in, 270–271
    cognitive goals in, 270
    discussion of developmental patterns in, 270

  variations on, 265–269
  voguish, 267–268
Deviance
  of antisocial prototype, 104–105
Dialectical behavior therapy
  in borderline personality disorder, 134, 145
Dichotomous thinking
  in borderline prototype, 125, 130, 134, 136–139, 140
  in obsessive–compulsive prototype, 238
  in paranoid prototype, 67–68
Discontented negativistic personality style, 283
Discouraged borderline personality style, 130–131
Disingenuous histrionic personality style, 157–158
Disquieted dependent personality style, 225
  avoidant features in, 225
Dissociative disorder
  definition of, 154
  in antisocial prototype, 107–108
  in avoidant prototype, 198
  in borderline prototype, 127–128
  in compulsive prototype, 242
  in dependent prototype, 220–221
  in histrionic prototype, 154
Dysthymia
  in avoidant prototype, 199, 211
  in borderline prototype, 128–129
  in compulsive prototype, 243–244, 255
  in depressive prototype, 264
  in histrionic prototype, 155–156
  in narcissistic prototype, 174
  in negativistic prototype, 280
  in schizoid personality, 79

Early Maladaptive Schema inventory, 23, 24
  for negativistic prototype, 286
Eating disorders
  in compulsive prototype, 245
  in masochistic prototype, 306
Eccentric behavior
  in schizotypal prototype, 91–93, 94

Elitist narcissistic personality style, 176–177
Emotional experience
adaptive value of, 5
Empathy
narcissistic prototype and, 183–185
Empathy training
for antisocial prototype, 115–116
Enforcing sadistic personality type, 297
Evolutionary imperatives
adaptation, 14–16
cognitive–behavioral model and, 5
cognitive–behavioral perspective
and, 20–21
existence, 13–14
function of, 12
human nature and, 12
in personality theory, 12
personality prototypes and, 19
reproduction–replication, 16–21
survival, 21
Existence imperative
bipolarity in, 14
goals of, 13
individual differences in, 13–14
Explosive disorder, intermittent
in sadistic personality type, 296
Explosive sadistic personality type, 297
Expressive behaviors, interpersonal style
and, 38, 39

Fanatical paranoid personality style
narcissistic features in, 59–60
Fantasy as regulatory mechanism
in avoidant prototype, 193–194,
195, 209
Fear of rejection or abandonment
in dependent prototype, 218, 219
Fibromyalgia
in masochistic prototype, 306
Freeman, A., 123, 129, 180
Function, 21–22, 23
Future-view, 23, 25

Generalized anxiety disorder
in antisocial prototype, 106
in avoidant prototype, 196–197, 212
in compulsive prototype, 241–242
in dependent prototype, 219–220

in histrionic prototype, 153
in negativistic prototype, 280–281
in paranoid prototype, 54–55, 60
in schizoid personality, 77–78
in schizotypal prototype, 94
Gilbert, P., 128
Goals
central, 27
Graduated exposure techniques
for phobic avoidant personality, 203
Graduated task assignments
for antisocial prototype, 117–118
Grandiosity
in narcissistic prototype, 185–186
Guided discovery
for avoidant prototype, 212
for borderline prototype, 140
for compulsive prototype, 252
for dependent prototype, 228–229
for histrionic prototype, 160. 164
for narcissistic prototype, 183–184
for negativistic prototype, 285–286,
289

Harm to self and others
potential for, in narcissistic
prototype, 176
Histrionic prototype
anxiety in, 153
appeasing, 157, 163
attention seeking in, 148–149, 150–
151, 161, 163
Axis I vulnerabilities of, 153–156
behavioral style of, 152
beliefs of, 150–151, 150–152
bipolar disorder and, 156, 162, 165
cognitive style of, 152
dependency of, 149, 161, 162, 163
depression in, 155
disingenuous, 157–158
dissociative states in, 154
dysthmyia in, 155–156
example of, 147–148
fickleness of mood and temperament
in, 152
infantile, 157
interpersonal relationships of, 152,
160–161
obsessive–compulsive disorder in,
154

other-orientation of, 149
pain avoidance in, 148
pathologic process of, 152–153, 163
personality-guided cognitive–
    behavioral conceptualization of,
    150–152
phobias in, 153–154
polarity balance of, 147, 148
somatization in, 155
symptoms of, 149–150
tempestuous, 158
theatrical, 156–157
treatment of
    affective changes in, 161–162
    behavioral goals in, 161
    cognitive goals in, 160–161
    therapeutic relationship in,
        158–160
    variations on, 156–158
    vivacious, 157
Hopelessness
    of depressive prototype, 261
Hostility
    in narcissistic prototype, 175
Hypersensitive avoidant personality style,
    203–204
Hypersensitivity
    in narcissistic prototype, 185–186
Hypomania
    in dependent prototype, 223
    in depressive prototype, 264–265
    in histrionic prototype, 156
    in schizoid prototype, 79–80

Ill-humored depressive personality style
    negativistic style and, 268
Immature dependent personality style,
    224–225
Implicit rules
    automatic thoughts and, 28
Impulse disorders
    in avoidant prototype, 200
Impulsive borderline personality style,
    131
Impulsiveness
    of antisocial prototype, 104
Ineffectual dependent personality style,
    225–226, 232
Infantile histrionic personality style,
    157

Information processing
    cognitive system and cognitive styles
        in, 34, 35
Initiative
    in dependent prototype, 229, 233
Insipid schizotypal personality style
    depression in, 95, 96
    detachment in, 95
Institutional care
    of disquieted dependent individual,
        225
Insular paranoid personality style, avoid-
        ant and schizoid characteristics
        in, 58
Integrated model
    benefits of, 5–6
    description of, 11–12
    evolutionary imperatives in, 12–21
    objective in, 7
    personality in, 21–45
    personality, stress, clinical condition
        in, 7, 8, 9
    treatment implications of, 45–46
Integrity, sense of, 18
Intermediate beliefs
    central goals, 27
    conditional assumptions, 25, 27
    implicit rules, 28
    morphological organization, 27–28
Irresponsibility, interpersonal
    of antisocial prototype, 104

Labeling distortions
    in antisocial prototype treatment, 118
Languid schizoid personality style
    depressive personality features in, 81
Linehan, M. M., 134

Major depression
    in avoidant prototype, 199
    in borderline prototype, 129
    in compulsive prototype, 244
    in dependent prototype, 223
Malevolent antisocial personality style,
    110
Malignant paranoid personality style
    sadistic attributes in, 58
Malingering, potential for
    in masochistic prototype, 306–307

Mania
    in restive depressive personality,
        266
Manic episodes. *See also* Hypomania
    in paranoid prototype, 57
Masochistic prototype
    "display of inadequacy" in, 303
    Axis I vulnerabilities of, 306–307
    dysphoria of, 303
    pathologic process of, 304–306,
        305–306
    personality attributes and liabilities
        of, 305
    personality-guided cognitive–
        behavioral conceptualization of,
        302–305
    polarity balance of, 302, 303
    self-concept, undeserving, 302–303,
        304
    suffering in, 301, 303, 304
    treatment of, 309–310
        behavioral goal in, 309
        cognitive goal in, 309
        metaemotional focus in, 310
        resistance in, 308–309
    variations on, 307–308
Mental health
    adaptive functioning and, 19–20
Metaemotional techniques
    for avoidant prototype, 209
    for masochistic prototype, 310
    for negativistic prototype, 287–288
Millon, T., *21, 49, 110, 155, 156, 157,
        178, 196, 236, 241, 246*
Modes
    definition of, 32
    personality and, 33–34
    personality structures and functions
        in, 47
Monitoring assignments
    for negativistic prototype, 286
Mood disorders
    in avoidant prototype, 199–200
Morbid depressive personality style,
        268–269
    masochistic prototype attributes in,
        268
Morphological organization, 27–28
    central goals and, 27–28
    personologic concept of, 31–32
Motivational system, 38

Narcissistic prototype
    amorous, 178
    anxiety disorders and, 172–173
    Axis I vulnerabilities of, 172–176
    beliefs of, 171–172, 188
    bipolar disorder in, 175–176
    case example, academic performance
        failure, 186–188
    characterization of, 167–169
    compensatory, 178–179
    depression in, 174–175, 476–477
    dysthymia in, 174
    elitist, 175, 176–177
    passive–independent orientation of,
        168
    pathologic process of, 172
    personality attributes and liabilities
        of, 170–171
    personality-guided cognitive–
        behavioral conceptualization of,
        169–172
    polarity balance of, 167, 168
    self-admiration of, 170–171
    self-focus of, 168–169
    somatoform disorder and, 173–174
    treatment of, 179–186
        challenges of, 180–181
        changes in, 179–180
        decreasing grandiosity and hyper-
            sensitivity in, 185–186
        focus on presenting problem,
            181–182
        fostering empathy in, 183–185
        therapeutic relationship in, 181
    unprincipled, 177–178
    variations on, 176–179
Needleman, L. D., *29, 30*
Negativistic prototype
    abrasive, 282–283
    alcohol abuse in, 281
    anger and aggression in, 281–282
    anxiety in, 280–281
    Axis I vulnerabilities of, 279–282
    case example of, 287–290
    characterization of, 275
    circuitous, 283–284
    cognitive style of, 277
    cognitive–behavioral perspective on,
        277–278
    depression in, 280
    discontented, 283

displacement in, 277
dysthymia in, 280
example of, 278
interpersonal interactions of,
    contrary, 277, 278
narcissistic prototype and, 275
pathologic process of, 279
personality attributes and liabilities
    of, 278
personality-guided cognitive–
    behavioral conceptualization of,
    276–278
polarity balance of, 276
self-image of, discontented, 276
somatic complaints in, 281
treatment of
    affective changes in, 287
    behavioral goals in, 287
    cognitive goals in, 285–286
    goals in, 284
    vacillating, 282
    variations on, 282–284
Nesse, R. M., 20, 128
Nomadic antisocial personality style,
    109–110

Obdurate paranoid personality style
    paranoid and compulsive
        characteristics in, 58–59
Object representations, 28
Obsessive–compulsive disorder
    in avoidant prototype, 197–198,
        209
    in dependent prototype, 222–223
    in histrionic prototype, 154
Obsessive–compulsive disorder
    in compulsive prototype, 243
    in paranoid prototype, 55–56, 61
    in schizoid personality, 78
Oppressed masochistic personality style,
    307
Orienting schema
    function of, 30
    influence on, 30–31

Panic disorder
    in avoidant prototype, 197
    in compulsive prototype, 242
    in histrionic prototype, 153–153

in obsessive–compulsive prototype,
    242
in paranoid prototype, 55
Panic reaction
    in narcissistic prototype, 182–183,
        187–188, 197
Paranoid prototype
    anger in, 54, 56
    anxiety in, 54–55
    automatic thoughts in, 53
    Axis I vulnerabilities in, 54–57
    bipolar pattern in, 57
    case example: marital conflict, 60–61
    childhood experiences and, 65–66
    core beliefs of, 53
    defensive posture in, 53
    depression in, 56–57
    developmental factors in, 65–66
    fanatical, 59–60
    insular, 58
    irascibility of mood and, 53
    malignant, 58
    manic episodes in, 57
    obdurate, 58–59
    obsessive–compulsive disorder and,
        55–56, 60
    other-focus in, 51
    panic reaction and, 55
    pathologic process of, 54
    personality attributes and liabilities
        of, 51, 52
    polarity balance of, 49, 50
    psychotic thinking and episodes in,
        57
    querulous, 59
    self-focus in, 50–51
    self-image of inviolability in, 51–53
    suspicious cognitive style in, 53
    treatment of, 61–70
        automatic thoughts distortion
            and, 67–68
        balancing imperative polarities
            in, 62–63
        behavioral goals in, 69–70
        cognitive goals in, 64–66
        feedback techniques in, 69
        focus of, 63–64
        paranoia as strategy in, 66–69
        therapeutic relationship in,
            61–62
    variants of, 57–60

Paranoid schizophrenia
    in paranoid prototype, 57
Parsimonious obsessive–compulsive
        personality style, schizoid style
        in, 247
Passive–dependent orientation, 17
Passive–accommodating personality
    of masochistic prototype, 302
Passive–aggressive
    of negativistic personality, 283
Pathologic process
    activation of, 44
    aspects of personality in personality
        prototypes and, 43
    definition of, 40
    identification of, 46
    in challenged self-view of college
        student, 40, 42
    in self view of verbal abuse victim,
        43
    personality and, 40, 41
Pathology, 7
Personality
    attributes of, 21–22
    automatic thoughts and, 28–30
    definitions of, 21
    in integrative model, 11
    intermediate beliefs and, 25, 27–28
    Millon model of, 44–45
    modes and mode activation and,
        32–40
    orienting schemas and, 30–31
    pathologic process and, 40–44
    personology and schemas and,
        31–32
    relationships with schemas, situa-
        tional demands, and survival
        imperative, 32
    schemas and, 47
        core beliefs and, 22–25
    structures and functions of, 21–22
    survival imperative and, 21
Personality attributes
    affective processes and, 36, 37
    in integrated model, 7, 8, 9
    role of in pathologic processes, 44
Personality disorder, 43
Personality-guided cognitive–behavioral
        model
    relationships in, 32, 33
Personologic model, 5

Personology
    and schemas, 31–32
Pessimism
    of depressive prototype, 262
Petulant borderline personality style,
        131–132
Pharmacotherapy
    for avoidant prototype, 209
    for compulsive prototype, 254
    for depressive prototype, 271
    for negativistic prototype, 287
    in phobic avoidant prototype, 203
Phobia
    in avoidant prototype, 197
    in dependent prototype, 220
    in histrionic prototype, 153–154
    in narcissistic prototype, 173
Phobic avoidant personality style,
        202–203
Physiological system
    demarcation from psychological
        processes, 36
Possessive masochistic personality style,
        307
Priming
    schema and, 30
Psychological collapse
    disorganized schizophrenia in,
        245–246
    dissociative disorder as, 242
Psychotic episodes. *See also* Schizophrenia
    in sadistic personality type, 296
Puritanical obsessive–compulsive personal-
        ity style, paranoid features in,
        248–249

Querulous paranoid personality style
    negativistic features in, 59

Relaxation therapy
    for avoidant prototype, 209
    for compulsive prototype, 254
    for negativistic prototype, 287
Remote schizoid personality type
    avoidant features in, 82
Reproduction–replication imperative,
        16–21
    adaptive balance in, 18–19
    in species regeneration, 16–17

other-orientation in, 17
reinforcement in, 17–18
self- *versus* other-orientation and
survivability in, 17
self-orientation in, 16–17
survival task in, 18
Responsibility
in dependent prototype, 233
Restive depressive personality style,
265–266
Risk-taking antisocial personality style,
110–111
Role-play
for narcissistic prototype, 184
for negativistic prototype, 287,
289
for obsessive–compulsive prototype,
256
Rules, implicit, 28

Sadistic orientation, 299–300
Sadistic prototype
abrasiveness of, 294, 300
Axis I vulnerabilities of, 296
characterization of, 291–292
enforcing, 297
explosive, 297
focus on control and power,
282–283
hostility of, 294
impulse problems in, 296
information processing strategies of,
295
leadership success and, 301
pathologic process of, 295–296
personality-guided cognitive–
behavioral conceptualization of,
293–295
polarity balance of, 292
self-image of, combative, 294, 300
spineless, 298
treatment of, 298–300
tyrannical, 297
variations on, 296–298
Schema(s)
core beliefs in, 23–25
definition of, 22
maladaptive, 23, 24, 286
modes and mode activation and,
32–40

orienting, 30–31
personology and, 31–32
structure and function of, 22–23
Schizoid prototype, 73–87
affectless, 81
anxiety in, 77–78, 86–87
apathetic mood in, 67
Axis I vulnerabilities of, 77–80
case example: exploitation of laboratory employee by coworkers,
84–87
cognitive style of, 76
core beliefs of, 75–76
depersonalization in, 80
depersonalized, 81–82
depression in, 79
indifference of, interpersonal, 76, 77
intermediate beliefs of, 76
languid, 81
manic or hypomanic reaction in,
79–80
obsessional concerns in, 78
pathologic process of, 76–77
personality attributes of, 74–75
personality-guided cognitive–
behavioral conceptualization of,
74–76
polarity balance of, 73, 74
remote, 82
self-image of, complacent, 75
somatic symptoms in, 78
treatment of, 82–83
variations on, 80–82
Schizophrenia
in avoidant prototype, 200
in compulsive prototype
catatonic, 246
disorganized, 245–246
in schizotypal prototype, 95
paranoid, 57
Schizotypal prototype
affective nature of, 93
anxiety in, 94
Axis I vulnerabilities of, 94–95
beliefs of, 91
cognitive style of, 93
college dropout example of, 89–90
depersonalization in, 95
depression in, 94
eccentricity of, 91–93
insipid, 95–96

Schizotypal prototype, *continued*
    pathologic process of, 93–94
    personality attributes and liabilities
        of, 92
    personality-guided cognitive–
        behavioral conceptualization of,
        91–93
    polarity balance of, 89, 90
    schizophrenia and, disorganized, 95
    secretiveness of, 93
    self-estrangement of, 91
    timorous, 96
    treatment of, 96–99
        cognitive strategies in, 98
        interpersonal adjustments in,
            96–97
        social skills training in, 98–99
    variations on, 95–96
Secretiveness
    in schizotypal prototype, 93, 94
Selective abstraction
    in paranoid prototype, 67
Self-derogatory depressive personality
    style
        characterization of, 266–267
        dependent features in, 266
        example of, eating disorder and,
            267
Self-destructive avoidant personality
    style, 201–202
Self-destructive borderline personality
    style, 132
Self-estrangement, of schizotypal personal-
    ity style, 91
Self-injurious behavior
    of borderline prototype, 125, 126
Self-instructional training
    in antisocial prototype treatment,
        115
Self-monitoring
    for histrionic prototype, 162
Self-statement monitoring, for avoidant
    prototype, 208
Self-undoing masochistic personality
    style, 307
Self-view, 23, 25, 26
Self–other conflict
    in compulsive prototype, 252,
        256
Selfless dependent personality style
    masochistic features in, 226

Social phobia
    in avoidant prototype, 197
    in narcissistic prototype, 173
Social skills
    in avoidant prototype, 206
    in depressive prototype, 269, 271
    in narcissistic prototype, 188–189
    in schizotypal prototype, 98–99
Social skills training
    for antisocial prototype, 117
    for negativistic prototype, 287, 289
Somatoform disorder
    in antisocial prototype, 107
    in avoidant prototype, 198–199
    in borderline prototype, 128
    in compulsive prototype, 242–243
    in dependent prototype, 221–222
    in depressive prototype, 265, 272
    in histrionic prototype, 155
    in narcissistic prototype, 173–174
    in negativistic prototype, 281
    in schizoid personality, 78
Spineless sadistic personality type, 297
Structure, 21–22
Substance abuse
    in avoidant prototype, 200
    in voguish depressive personality,
        267
Substance-related syndromes
    in antisocial prototype, 106
    in compulsive prototype, 244–245
Suicidality
    in avoidant prototype, 201
    in borderline prototype, 125, 133
    in narcissistic prototype, 175
    in obsessive–compulsive prototype,
        242
    in restive depressive personality, 266
Symptoms, in integrated model, 20–21

Tempestuous histrionic personality style,
    158
Theatrical histrionic personality style,
    156–157
Therapy
    cognitive behavioral perspective on,
        45
Therapy, task of, 45
Thought-altering procedures
    for compulsive prototype, 253

Thought-stopping
    for compulsive prototype, 252–253
Timorous schizoptypal personality style
    avoidant and negativistic features
       of, 96
Treatment
    identification of pathologic process
       and personality attributes in, 46
    orientation to imperatives and, 46
    task of therapy in, 45–46
Triggering, schema and, 30
Tyrannical sadistic personality type, 297

Unprincipled narcissistic personality
    style, exploitation by, 177

Vacillating negativistic personality style
    borderline prototype aspects in, 282
    interpersonal conflicts in, 282

Victim role
    in dependent prototype, 226
Videotaped role-play
    for narcissistic prototype, 184
Virtuous masochistic personality style,
    308
Vivacious histrionic personality style,
    157
Voguish depressive personality style
    histrionic and narcissistic features
       in, 267–268
    substance use disorders in, 267

Williams, G. C., 20
World-view, 23, 25

Young, J. E., 66

ABOUT THE AUTHOR

Paul R. Rasmussen, PhD, is an associate professor of psychology at Furman University in Greenville, South Carolina. He holds a PhD in clinical psychology from the University of Georgia, a masters in experimental psychology from Florida Atlantic University, and an undergraduate degree in psychology from Southern Utah University. He teaches courses in psychopathology, psychopathic personality, and counseling and psychotherapy. He lectures regularly to lay and professional audiences on topics in mental health and clinical intervention. He is a clinical strategies and contributing review editor for *The Journal of Individual Psychology* and has numerous publications on topics related to personality and psychopathology, stress, attention-deficit/hyperactivity disorder, the adaptive nature of affective reactions, and clinical intervention and case-conceptualization strategies. He maintains a private practice for families and individuals.